"With impressive detail, Steven High probes the challenges of the social democratic left in power through a reexamination of the Ontario New Democratic government of the early 1990s. High argues that understanding the failure of the NDP government requires attending to the 'industrial crisis' that saw the party's base of support in labour decimated and disorganized by free trade and plant closures. Anyone seeking to understand the origins of the myriad crises facing the Canadian labour movement and the electoral Left today must read *The Left in Power.*"

ADAM D. K. KING, assistant professor, Labour Studies, University of Manitoba

"The 1980s saw the growth of neoliberal globalization. At the same time the NDP was transitioning from left nationalism to progressive competitiveness to deal with the new world order. Their surprise 1990 election came as the province struggled with the worst economic downturn since the Second World War. Looking for solutions, the party abandoned its old social democracy ideals. The result was a split in the party and the labour movement. One of Canada's preeminent oral historians, Steven High, has collected the voices of those inside the Ontario NDP government and the labour movement. With them he examines the Left in power."

KEN CLAVETTE, lifelong Ottawa-based trade unionist

"Drawing on extensive oral history interviews with key actors, Steven High's *The Left in Power* is a thoughtful and detailed account of how Bob Rae's NDP government and organized labour in Ontario responded to the challenges of deindustrialization, neoliberalism, and the recession of the early 1990s. Not every reader will agree with High's prescriptions for what the Rae government should have done in these years, but they will surely come away enlightened about why they made the decisions that they did."
MATTHEW HAYDAY, professor, Department of History, University of Guelph

"Steven High's insightful study of the Rae government's response to industrial restructuring will no doubt reopen old wounds for the social democratic left in Canada, but more importantly, *The Left in Power* offers critical historical lessons for those seeking to reestablish a working-class politics rooted in economic justice."
LARRY SAVAGE, professor, Department of Labour Studies, Brock University

"*The Left in Power* is a well-researched and insightful account of one of the most controversial provincial governments in recent Canadian history. This book is informative for the next generation of social democrats as they think about the legacy of the NDP in power."
DAVID MCGRANE, professor, Department of Political Studies, University of Saskatchewan; author of *New NDP: Moderation, Modernization, and Political Marketing*

"How does a social democratic government respond to industrial crisis? What is lost when the politics of partnership and pragmatism supersede the politics of class? And for Bob Rae and the Ontario NDP, how did it all go so spectacularly wrong? In *The Left in Power*, Steven High provides insightful answers to these questions and many more. Essential reading for anyone interested in bringing about a very different version of the Left in power, the book is certain to become a touchstone text for students of left politics, labour, and neoliberalism—in Canada and around the world."
EDWARD DUNSWORTH, assistant professor, Department of History, McGill University; coauthor of *Harvesting Freedom: The Life of a Migrant Worker in Canada*

"Steven High's thorough and balanced account of the Rae government in Ontario provides an invaluable contribution to understanding the province's politics and political economy in a period of globalization and a world-wide ideological shift to neoliberalism. For the NDP (and social democracy generally), these developments intensified earlier trends towards the abandonment of class and political economy analysis, which, in turn, contributed to the government's inability to meet the challenges. Its experimentation with new doctrines of communitarianism and competitiveness, and rupture with its traditional working-class base, led ultimately to its failure and neoliberalization."
STEPHEN MCBRIDE, professor, Department of Political Science, McMaster University

THE LEFT IN POWER

BOB RAE'S NDP
AND THE WORKING CLASS

STEVEN HIGH

Between the Lines
Toronto

The Left in Power: Bob Rae's NDP and the Working Class
© 2025 Steven High

First published in 2025 by
Between the Lines
401 Richmond Street West, Studio 281
Toronto, Ontario · M5V 3A8 · Canada
1-800-718-7201 · www.btlbooks.com

All rights reserved. No part of this publication may be photocopied, reproduced, stored in a retrieval system, or transmitted in any form or by any means, electronic, mechanical, recording, or otherwise, without the written permission of Between the Lines, or (for copying in Canada only) Access Copyright, 69 Yonge Street, Suite 1100, Toronto, ON M5E 1K3.

Every reasonable effort has been made to identify copyright holders. Between the Lines would be pleased to have any errors or omissions brought to its attention.

Library and Archives Canada Cataloguing in Publication
Title: The Left in power : Bob Rae's NDP and the working class / Steven High.
Names: High, Steven C., author
Description: Includes bibliographical references and index.
Identifiers: Canadiana (print) 20240498054 | Canadiana (ebook) 20240500075 | ISBN 9781771136679 (softcover) | ISBN 9781771136686 (EPUB)
Subjects: LCSH: New Democratic Party of Ontario. | LCSH: Rae, Bob. | CSH: Ontario—Politics and government—1990-1995. | CSH: Ontario—Economic conditions—1991-
Classification: LCC FC3077.2 .H54 2025 | DDC 971.3/04—dc23

Cover and text design by DEEVE

Printed in Canada

We acknowledge for their financial support of our publishing activities: the Government of Canada; the Canada Council for the Arts; and the Government of Ontario through the Ontario Arts Council, the Ontario Book Publishers Tax Credit program, and Ontario Creates.

CONTENTS

Preface / xiii
Introduction / 1

1
Fighting Plant Shutdowns / 25

2
The Hamilton Challenge / 51

3
Competing in the New Global Economy / 77

4
An Agenda for People / 113

5
Bob Mackenzie's Labourism / 157

6
Worker Ownership and Labour-Led Venture Capital / 193

7
Northern Exceptionalism / 225

8
From Downsview to Davos / 259

9
Corporatism's Moment / 289

10
New Left Communitarianism / 335

Conclusion
The Seductive Mist of Pragmatism / 357

Notes / 377
Index / 447

PREFACE

> Our plans miscarry because they have no aim. When a man does not know what harbor he is making for, no wind is the right wind.
>
> —Seneca (4 BC–65 AD)[1]

Seneca's prophetic words of wisdom were the first thing that the fifty-five participants read at the weekend retreat of the Ontario New Democratic Party (NDP), upon opening their delegate kits in May 1989. In advance of the next election, the party had brought together members of the NDP's elected caucus, the Provincial Executive, and the leadership of the Ontario Federation of Labour (OFL) to brainstorm about the party's election plans. The soon-to-be Premier of Ontario, Bob Rae, and many future cabinet members were there, as were a who's who of Ontario's trade union movement along with key NDP staff advisors. As leader of the third party in the Ontario Legislative Assembly, representing the riding of York South, Rae opened the weekend with a speech on the challenges facing the party.

On the retreat's first day, participants divided into breakout groups to consider the party's goals and strategies. On the second day, the conversation shifted to tactics. Some of the electoral strategies discussed included targeting "working people, social activists and middle-income groups" and establishing the party's "economic competence." One breakout group earnestly thought that achieving a majority government in the next election was a realistic goal, which caused considerable mirth. Everyone else aimed lower. In my own handwritten notes from the retreat—I was there as the youth representative on the Provincial Executive (and thus surely the most inconsequential person in attendance)—I emphasized the need for "meaningful policy debate" and "long term planning." Like almost everyone else, I frankly did not expect to see the NDP win power anytime soon, and few outside the party considered it possible either. The NDP's shocking 6 September 1990 victory would be the first time that the social democratic party governed Canada's most populous province, home to much of the country's industrial heartland.

No one, not least the party itself, was prepared for the NDP's unexpected ascendence to power. The next five years were chaotic and proved to be deeply disillusioning for many party members. The province was plunging into the worst economic crisis since the 1930s, forcing the government to scramble and govern on the fly. Three hundred thousand manufacturing jobs were lost in the province between 1989 and 1992, while a series of small but corrosive scandals further destabilized the government. Like a punch-drunk boxer, the government staggered from one blow to the next, never truly finding its political footing. One by one, cherished party policies were discarded, such as public auto insurance (with its considerable symbolic value to many party members) as well as opposition to casinos and Sunday shopping. When the party's Provincial Council voted to reaffirm several of these long-standing policies, Bob Rae responded that he was now the Premier of all Ontarians and not just of the NDP membership. By the time Rae decided to forcibly open public-sector collective agreements and impose negotiated austerity in 1993 under the guise of a new "social contract," the government's relationship with organized labour was effectively shattered. By then, the Rae government had shifted from fighting the recession to fighting the deficit. Thousands of long-time party members quit, quietly or otherwise, over these five years. Even the Ontario Federation of Labour could no longer stomach the erstwhile party of labour. Not surprisingly, the NDP lost the 1995 election in a landslide. But beneath this well-worn story of "giving away a miracle"[2] is another, perhaps more interesting one, as an avowedly social democratic party grappled with the industrial crisis. This other story is the focus of the book.

I come to this history not simply out of interest, but as someone who lived through those years, and who, a lifetime ago, was active in the Ontario NDP. Born into a working-class family in

Thunder Bay, located on the isolated north shore of Lake Superior, I grew up thinking of myself as a democratic socialist. Ours was a union household. My political activation came as a teenager in the early 1980s over US foreign policy in Central America and Prime Minister Pierre Trudeau's decision to allow US cruise missile testing over Canada. The Cold War was still very much present in our lives. At age sixteen, I joined the NDP in time for the 1984 federal election that saw Brian Mulroney's Tories sweep into power. One of my fondest memories of that election was participating in my first "plant gate" during a shift change at the now closed paper mill in Red Rock, an hour's drive east of the city, with Ernie Epp, our federal candidate, and a pair of old-time provincial NDP politicians, Jim Foulds and Jack Stokes, who regaled me with stories from the early days of the socialist Co-operative Commonwealth Federation (CCF; the predecessor of the NDP). It was heady stuff.

Two years later, I travelled to Toronto for the conference of the party's youth section; it had only just been reconstituted after being disbanded in the early 1970s during the purge of the left-wing Waffle movement, which argued against the party "waffling" to the political centre.[3] I was elected to represent the youth of my region on the Provincial Council, which meant flying down to Toronto two or three times a year. My world opened up. I sat on the Provincial Executive from 1988 to 1990, serving as president of the Ontario New Democratic Youth. We campaigned on the usual student issues, such as tuition fees, but what stands out in my mind was our work on the minimum wage. The NDP favoured raising the province's minimum wage so that it represented 60 percent of the average industrial wage. However, Ontario was one of five provinces across the country that had a discriminatory two-tier minimum wage where workers under eighteen could be paid 85 cents less per hour than the regular minimum wage.[4] At the time, that meant that the hourly minimum wage for workers under eighteen years of age was just $4.15. This issue was highly personal for me; a few years earlier, I had been hired by my hometown library as a student "page." A week or two into the job, two of us were called into the head librarian's office and told that they had made an administrative error and would need to pay us the lower rate, as we were only seventeen. Over the next year, we had little choice but to work for substantially less than the other students hired to do the same work. I got a big pay raise on my eighteenth birthday, but the work remained the same.

The NDP Youth decided to focus on the two-tier minimum wage issue over 1989 and 1990, arguing that this was a clear-cut case of age discrimination that contravened Article 15 of the 1982 Charter of Rights and Freedoms. As I wrote at the time, "If the two-tiered system was based upon any other category [of difference], it would not be tolerated."[5] Our fact sheet "Minimum Wage— Maximum Discrimination" made the case that it was "unfair to value one person's labour less than another's simply on the basis of age. This leads to unfair hiring and firing practices by employers of students."[6] To that end, we organized regional press conferences, inviting representatives of organized labour, anti-poverty groups, and students to share the stage with us. Future Ontario Minister of Finance Floyd Laughren participated in the event at the Steelworkers Hall in Sudbury. We also conducted "school gates" at high schools across the province, passing out leaflets, circulating petitions, and even conducting a series of short sit-ins at the offices of Liberal cabinet ministers.[7]

Meanwhile, organized labour put us in touch with a prominent Toronto labour lawyer, Steven Barrett, who took up our charter challenge. *Sarah Brophy and Jason Baines, Plaintiffs v. Attorney General of Ontario* was submitted to the Supreme Court of Ontario in April 1990; Sarah and Jason were members of the NDP Youth. The first hearing had been scheduled for 22 June, but our legal team convinced us to delay proceeding in order to wait for a ruling of the Supreme Court of Canada on another age discrimination case, the McKinney case, relating to mandatory retirement.[8] With the NDP's unexpected victory that September, however, it seemed strange to bring our own government to court, and so a deal was struck to withdraw our case in exchange for a promise to phase out the age differential over two installments. But the NDP government caved to the business lobby after the first step. The Ontario under-eighteen minimum wage has remained in place ever since, growing to a differential of one dollar in the mid-2020s.

Notwithstanding what I've written so far, I am no insider to the story that this book tells. A couple months before the Ontario NDP victory, I was elected president of the national party's youth wing and I spent the next two years organizing youth from Newfoundland to northern British Columbia, steering clear of Ontario. I therefore watched from afar the slow-motion train wreck that was the Rae government. For me, the final straw came in late 1993—a year or so after I shifted gears from politics to grad school. I had been teaching basic math to refugee kids in a church basement in Thunder Bay when I was directed to teach a cutesy song for them to sing to a visiting government minister and the media. If that wasn't enough, the NDP cabinet minister's advance team told us to find more Black children for the photo op, as if the mainly Indigenous children from Central America were not racialized enough for our anti-racism grant. It was strongly suggested that renewal of our funding depended on this. It still makes me angry thirty years later. When I got home, I ripped up my NDP membership card and never looked back . . . until now.

What follows is thus no political memoir. In deciding to disclose some of my own experiences, I do so to be transparent about my political positioning and to dispel any notion of having an insider's perspective to the NDP years in power from 1990 to 1995. To some degree, being so transparent about my own political history runs counter to my training as a historian. We tend to prefer to maintain a measure of professional separation. This aspect of my life is not something I share often. But with time comes distance. I am far enough removed today from the emotional rollercoaster of those heady and heartbreaking years that I feel quite prepared to revisit them *as a historian*, so as to see what can be learned about how one social democratic party responded to the industrial crisis.

Methodologically, newly opened archival records and oral history interviews form the basis of what follows. I am thankful to those NDP politicians and policy advisors who donated their records to public archives or agreed to be interviewed. Only three cabinet members—Richard Allen, himself a historian, and responsible for the government's worker retraining efforts, Finance Minister Floyd Laughren, and Premier Bob Rae—donated their records to public archives. I also learned a great deal from the records, held at the University of Toronto, of David Wolfe, a key economic policy advisor in the Cabinet Office. As thirty years have now elapsed, I was also able to access a large number of government files, but most remain closed to researchers. Some government records were made available on condition that I anonymized any personal information. The records of the Ontario NDP held by Queen's University proved essential, as did trade union records found at a variety of public archives. Thanks to Jim Foulds, the Thunder Bay Museum had considerable information about the employee buyout at Provincial Paper, where he served as an independent member of its board of directors. The Université de Hearst also had material on the worker buyout of the paper mill in Kapuskasing. The archivists were universally outstanding.

The book features the photographs taken by the *Toronto Star* of unfolding political events, as well as those of Toronto's Peter MacCallum, who documented the city's vanishing manufacturing industries throughout the 1980s and 1990s. Rather than industrial ruins, however, his photographs feature people still at work—reminding me of the work of Milton Rogovin in Buffalo and others. Each chapter ends with one of MacCallum's personal portraits taken at the National Rubber Company plant over 1993–94, a reminder of the real lives on the line when we talk about labour and economic policy.

My archival research led me to identify the Ontario NDP's economic and labour market brain trust, almost all of whom generously agreed to be interviewed. This remarkable group straddled the labour movement, the party, the civil service, and academia. I would like to thank John O'Grady, David Wolfe, Riel Miller, Peter Warrian, Ken Delaney, and Hugh Mackenzie for agreeing to talk to me. This all-male group stood at the centre of decision-making on economic and labour policy. Three others, Neil Bradford, Tim Armstrong and Sue Colley, agreed to informal conversations that helped provide further context. I also interviewed top advisors in the Premier's Office, such as Ross McClellan as well as the Deputy Secretary of the Cabinet Office, Michael Mendelson, and one person who preferred to remain anonymous. Civil servant turned academic Bryan Evans, who worked in the Employments Standards and Workplace Conditions Unit of the Ministry of Labour, was also a great help, as was Alan Ernst, who worked closely with the ministry as the Queen's Park staffer for the parliamentary assistant (PA) for labour. Sam Gindin from the Canadian Auto Workers (CAW) likewise offered critical perspectives.

Four key NDP politicians also agreed to be interviewed: Bob Rae, Floyd Laughren, Frances Lankin, and Bud Wildman. Shelley Martel was unfortunately unavailable. I greatly enjoyed each of these conversations and appreciated the politicians' willingness to speak reflectively about these years. Their commitment to public service was, and is, impressive and did not end with the defeat of the Ontario NDP government in 1995. At the time that I interviewed them, Bob Rae was Canada's ambassador to the United Nations and Frances Lankin was a Canadian senator. After his retirement from active politics, Bud Wildman continued to serve his community of Sault Ste. Marie as chair of the board of governors of Algoma University, helping to establish it as an independent post-secondary institution; and Floyd Laughren still serves on the board of Sudbury's regional hospital. No matter how one judges the NDP government, there is no doubting their commitment to serving the wider community. I also interviewed Jim Foulds, deputy Ontario NDP leader during the 1980s from my hometown, who served on the board of Provincial Paper after the employee buyout. The little things stand out. After I finished interviewing Bud Wildman, the former Minister of Natural Resources (MNR) as well as the cabinet minister responsible for Indigenous issues, I sent him a thank-you email and an electronic copy of a recent article I'd published on the closure of Quebec's Schefferville mine in the early 1980s by Brian Mulroney, when he led the US-based Iron Ore Company of Canada. I thought he would enjoy reading it, as we had discussed the ways that industrialism gets bound up in colonialism. First thing the next morning, he wrote me back with some comments on the piece.

One of the great surprises in my research is the degree to which the party defied government pressure, holding the NDP government to account for the breach of party policy or its failure to consult. It is a reminder that the NDP was, in fact, more democratic than other parties. Ed Dale and Jill Marzetti generously connected me to people to interview. Huge thanks to everyone who agreed to talk to me. All but three of the interviewees also agreed to provide feedback on the draft manuscript. It was a big ask, but their comments helped me correct small factual errors and flag aspects I may have missed or misunderstood. We may or may not agree on my historical interpretation, but I am very grateful for their input. I have worked hard to strike a fair balance in the pages that follow. While I conducted all the oral history interviews myself, the transcriptions were completed thanks to a team of transcribers coordinated by Amanda De Witt and Sophia Richter.

None of this research would have been possible without funding from the Social Sciences and Humanities Research Council, which awarded a seven-year partnership grant for Deindustrialization & the Politics of Our Time that brings together research centres, trade unions, and industrial museums across Western Europe and North America. This book benefited enormously from our ongoing conversation and helped me situate the history of the Ontario NDP government within a wider international perspective. There are connections to be made between what happened in Canada and what occurred in other countries. I especially want to thank Stefan Berger from the Ruhr University–Bochum, who served as the other co-leader of our Industrial Closure initiative, and Marion Fontaine from Sciences Po in Paris, who served as the other co-leader of the Race, Populism and the Left initiative, of which this monograph is part. Dimitry Anastakis and Fred Burrill also provided feedback on parts of this manuscript.

As the father of a severely disabled daughter, I don't have the same mobility as I used to for out-of-town archival research. While I did considerable archival research myself, the DePOT project enabled me to employ a group of outstanding graduate students to conduct research in Hamilton (Shelby McPhee, Tim Liebregt, Philip Roth, Isadora Galwey), Detroit (Tom Macmillan), Thunder Bay (Temitope Moses Ojo), and Toronto (Nick Fast). I also had the support of DePOT staff, especially Lauren Laframboise and Gabrielle McLaren, who provided essential administrative support, and from the Centre for Oral History and Digital Storytelling, where DePOT is based. As always, I have learned a great deal from past and present graduate students under my supervision.

I would be remiss in not taking this once-in-a-lifetime opportunity to thank old friends from my NDP Youth days. They include Andrew McNeill, Christine Lorée, Alan Hall, Rob Dobrucki, Andrew Lauer, Rob Cottingham, Kathy Baylis, David Wright, Chris Frontin, Maureen Hall, Lori Lucier, Alec McIsaac, Tara Haddrell, Jean Lazure, Greg Duggan, Marc Molgat, Rick Pollard, Craig Saunders, Pierre Ducasse, Corey Oxelgren, Edith Garneau, Tim Gallagher, Glenn Fraser, Paul Whiteley, Steve Hemphill, Carolyn Cade, Scott Piatkowski, Lindsay McKay, Brian Kyle, Jason Baines, Jocelyn Tellier, and so many others. Also, the NDP-adjacent Duane Schippers.

Finally, I want to thank Amanda Crocker from Between the Lines for agreeing to publish this book, Tilman Lewis, who copy-edited the manuscript, and most of all my partner, Barbara Lorenzkowski, and our children, Sebastian and Leanna. My political activism owes much to my mother, Carolyn (Graham) High, who when I was growing up shared not only her own activist stories with me, but also those of her grandparents who were involved in early social struggles in British Columbia. Stories of police beatings and bricks being thrown through house windows linger in family memory. I am proud to be her son. This book is dedicated to her.

INTRODUCTION

> Our task as a party is not to say change can't happen or shouldn't happen. The critical challenge for us is to take the insecurity and inequality out of change. We cannot any longer argue that any person has a property [right] in an individual job—the craft vision of the trade union movement a century ago—or even in an individual company. What we should be arguing is that we must create a society where change does not mean dramatic income loss, it does not mean loss of self-esteem, it does not mean the dark hole of poverty and helplessness that social and industrial change has come to mean to millions of workers since the Industrial Revolution. That means, more clearly than ever that we can't be on the defensive. The vision of democratic socialism cannot be that we shall defend every bureaucracy, every large institution, every bulwark of the status quo, against the attacks of the populist right. That is a recipe for defeat; it is also an admission of intellectual bankruptcy.
>
> —Bob Rae, Leader of Ontario's New Democratic Party, 10 January 1990[1]

Bob Rae's landmark "What We Owe Each Other" speech is impressively erudite. A former Rhodes Scholar, Rae set out an expansive vision for social democracy in the immediate post Cold War era. The Berlin Wall had fallen only months beforehand; everywhere, capitalism seemed triumphant. Rae cheered the collapse of the communist dictatorships of Eastern Europe, reminding his listeners of their brutality and corruption. But he refused to "interpret those astonishing events as a vindication of capitalism or a repudiation of anything I would call democratic socialism." Yet it was clear that the old certainties about economic growth were gone. The postwar era of unionized prosperity in North America, which Rae felt "flowed from the New Deal and the sense of social solidarity of the home front in World War II," had been shattered by the oil crisis of the early 1970s and the "rise of competing industrial states in Europe and Asia." Facilitated by new information technologies and containerization, trade liberalization had radically restructured the international division of labour, intensifying global competition. The new Free Trade Agreement with the United States, and the re-election of the federal Tories in 1988, were game changers in his mind. Just as Margaret Thatcher and Ronald Reagan had fundamentally recast the politics of the United Kingdom and the United States, respectively, so too had Canadian Prime Minister Brian Mulroney. There was no going back. New times required new ideas.

Despite the confusion and deep malaise on the left internationally, and while the neoliberal right and its Washington Consensus seemed to have all the political momentum, Bob Rae still believed that social democracy had much to offer the world. He was openly critical of the poisoned chalice of scientific Marxism, but he was also critical of the intellectual legacies and patrician attitudes of the British Fabians, the subject of his Oxford thesis. The technocratic responses of recent leaders of the US Democratic Party likewise came under fire: "[President Jimmy] Carter paralysed by the complex ambiguities of office, [Walter] Mondale immersed in discussions of import substitution, and [Michael] Dukakis trying to convince everyone that he was really more competent in a technical sense than the other guy." Rae's was a values-based appeal grounded in community and shared humanity. A kinder, fairer social democratic future was on offer, and the warm embrace of community infused his language.

Having come of age during the 1960s, Bob Rae was clearly influenced by the generational outlook of the New Left with its investments in participatory democracy, decentralization, and community empowerment as well as its deep ambivalence towards the centralized state.[2] Herbert Marcuse, an early New Left thinker, also spoke of its strong libertarian and anti-authoritarian streak.[3] There were, of course, different currents within the New Left, ranging from post-materialist politics to anti-capitalism. For my purpose here, I draw a sharp distinction between the communitarian impulse of the New Left and left-nationalists who sought to use the power of the state to build democratic socialism in Canada. As we will see, left-nationalism had an enormous impact on the Ontario NDP and the trade union movement, leading the party to emphasize public ownership and the state regulation of the market during the 1970s and early 1980s. Only the state, they regularly asserted, could serve as a counterbalance to US-based multinational corporations.

While Bob Rae was cool to left-nationalism, he saw a far greater role for trade unions in the economy. In his speech, he thus told listeners that "one hundred and fifty years of social struggle have given governments and workers some rights around the edges of the economic system." Rae then made the case for extending the democratic principle to the economy. By this, he did "not simply mean nationalizing every large firm in sight," but rather opting for fundamental changes to labour and corporate law or employment standards. He wanted to see workers on corporate boards of directors and for them to become an "equal partner" in economic decision-making. He thought the vast capital held in union pension plans could be harnessed for the interests of workers in the years ahead. There would be resistance, to be sure, but it could be overcome: "If Lech Walesa can do it to the Communist bureaucracy, we ought to be able to do it here to Conrad Black." For many on the Canadian left, Black personified the destructive greed of unrestrained capitalism during these years.[4]

Bob Rae's landmark speech was a clear-eyed rejection of the status quo and an eloquent call for the left to rise above a defence of the welfare state. Social democrats, he believed, needed to shape the direction of economic change, channelling it rather than resisting it outright, and work hard to ensure that the negative social consequences of industrial restructuring are shared more fairly. Today, we would call this a just transition. Differing class interests were recognized in the speech, but were transcended through a process of bipartite social bargaining between business and labour. This was no straightforward call to surrender to the logics of neoliberalism, though its yearning for consensus might very well have led there. These ideas would animate and guide the NDP's five years in power from 1990 to 1995, even though there was no hint of the emerging "progressive competitiveness" agenda in its election platform.

To the contrary, in 1990 the NDP ran on its traditional redistributive politics, emphasizing worker protection as well as social and environmental justice. Much like the set list of an aging rock 'n' roll band, the NDP relied on the well-worn lyrics of the old favourites found in its policy book. Canadian social democratic thinking on the economy during the post-1945 boom years was reformist, emphasizing the redistribution of growth rather than something more fundamental, but the Ontario NDP's economic and labour policies became more radical during the 1970s thanks to left-nationalism's ability to politicize economic issues. During the recession of the early 1980s, for example, workers literally wrapped themselves in Canadian flags and sang O Canada as they occupied their closing plants to demand a fairer deal. At the same time, with a minority Tory government, the Ontario NDP caucus used its influence to hold departing companies accountable by compelling them to justify their decisions to a select committee of the Ontario legislature and even forced them to open their financial records under threat of a Speaker's warrant (the equivalent of a subpoena). A decade later, such democratic interference in management "rights" was almost unthinkable.

The signing of the Canada–United States Free Trade Agreement in 1987 and the crushing defeat of economic nationalism in the federal election the following year represented a political and economic watershed in recent Canadian history. The fight against free trade had mobilized the trade union movement to an unprecedented degree and forged a broad-based coalition under the banner of the Pro-Canada Network. However, trade nationalism was vulnerable to charges of protectionism. Understanding this risk, the Canadian Auto Workers had "tried to change the nature of the policy debate from the current one of free trade vs protectionism, to one of whether multinational corporations—be they American, Japanese or whatever—should be free to locate and move jobs as they please."⁵ Unfortunately, this effort to reframe the debate around investment rather than trade failed to take hold. Protectionists became to the new global order what the Luddites had been to the Industrial Revolution: objects of ridicule and scorn.⁶

If political defeat stung, what angered the trade union movement most was the decision of Ed Broadbent's federal NDP, riding high in the polls going into the 1988 election, to play down the free trade issue, allowing the weakened Liberals to capture the issue and the Tories to win another majority.⁷ It was as though the NDP had decided not to show up at the field of battle. The free trade election of 1988 rocked the federal NDP to its very foundations. Bob White, president of the Canadian Auto Workers and a vice-president of the federal party, was livid. He drafted an angry seven-page letter to the federal NDP executive, as he "watched

Effigies of Uncle Sam and Prime Minister Brian Mulroney are held aloft as over 1,000 people—many of them from an Ontario Federation of Labour conference—protest free trade outside the first ministers' meeting in Toronto, 26 November 1987. Photo by Ken Faught / *Toronto Star* via Getty Images.

the disintegration of what should have been the New Democratic Party's finest hour."[8] For White, the election strategy and electoral result were nothing short of disastrous and warranted a full debate within the party. The executive of the Canadian Labour Congress met two days after the 21 November election "and their level of anger, frustration and concern about the campaign, was the most emotional [he had] ever seen." Somehow, the NDP, the party of labour, did not grasp the central importance of free trade for working-class Canadians. White reminded the party leadership that for the past three years the labour movement had mobilized on this issue across the country:

> While a lot of our concern was expressed about jobs, even more dealt with social programs, environment, regional assistance, energy, privatization, deregulation, etc, in other words, not a narrow self-interest approach. We helped to form and participated actively in broad based coalitions made up of many diverse organizations, some of which share our political point of view, others were liberals and others were farther left than the NDP. All had one thing in common; to raise public awareness of the dangers to Canada of the free trade deal.

With business organizations lining up on the other side of the debate, why, then, didn't the party of working people understand what was at stake? In answering his own question, White declared: "We didn't fail by accident—but rather, we failed by design." Indeed, "if ever there is an issue the social democratic movement in Canada should oppose with total emotion and strength, it is this deal." But the NDP's skittishness on economic issues didn't come from nowhere. The signs were already there three years earlier when the federal NDP policy review backed away from the state as an instrument of redistribution, highlighting instead the ambiguous promise of community economic development (CED). At the time, the federal NDP's research director, James Laxer, went even further, calling on the party to turn away from the politics of class entirely and to focus instead on new middle-class constituencies.⁹ This is precisely what the federal NDP tried to do, with disastrous results.

The Left in Power originates in my interest in the apparent failure of centre-left parties to respond effectively to the industrial crisis, or their outright ideological betrayal of working-class communities, opening up a political opportunity for the rise of right-wing populism in some countries. Deindustrialization and union decline during the 1980s and 1990s threw social democratic and other progressive parties across Western Europe and North America into disarray. Many of these parties had, to borrow the words of the British Labour Party's Ernest Bevin, grown "out of the bowels of the trade union movement."¹⁰ Yet almost everywhere, social democratic and other progressive parties now turned their backs on the weakened trade union movement. Sociologist Frances Fox Piven, for example, noted in 1998 that "labor parties in most countries [were] deserting the field, acknowledging the necessity of adapting to international markets and of austerity policies capital has demanded."¹¹ A new generation of highly educated centre-left leaders sought to reimagine social democracy for a new era.¹² The "Third Way" politics of Bill Clinton's "New Democrats" in the US, Tony Blair's "New Labour" in the UK, and Gerhard Schröder's "Neue Mitte" in Germany is, of course, familiar to many of us.¹³ Even the Swedish Social Democrats, long the social democratic full-employment "model," now embraced some neoliberal assumptions about labour force flexibility and global competition.¹⁴

Central to Third Way discourse was the recognition that the new global economy was here to stay. There was, in the view of these politicians, no point pretending otherwise. Tony Blair famously told the British Labour Party, gathered at its 2005 conference, that debating globalization "was like debating whether autumn should follow summer."¹⁵ The challenge, as they saw it, was to forge a progressive competitive strategy based on skills training and labour force flexibility that would enable wealthy countries to specialize in high-skill and high-value manufacturing, leaving more routinized labour-intensive industries to low-wage countries. Deindustrialization was to be managed, even facilitated, rather than resisted. Social partnership and stakeholder collaboration were considered essential for ensuring a country's competitive position. Shamefully, however, Third Way social democrats emphasized the moral dimension of poverty rather than its structural causes.[16] Welfare reforms, taking the form of restricted eligibility and reduced duration and payment levels, combined with new active labour market policies to push people back into low-wage jobs. Better to be the working poor than dependent on the state; at least this was the underlying logic of the moralizing "culture of poverty" theory—a corrosive idea that essentially blamed the poor for being poor. Supply-side corporatism, a key feature of the progressive competitiveness agenda, promised a "gentler, more humane mode of integration into the world economy."[17] It left very little room, however, for the old redistributive class politics.[18]

The US Democratic Party is a case in point. A younger generation of modernizing New Democrats were elected to Congress, state houses, and governor's mansions during the late 1970s and early 1980s. For many, Colorado senator Gary Hart's unsuccessful run for the Democratic Party's presidential nomination in 1984 signalled their arrival on the national political stage. By then, a growing number of state governors—such as Michael Dukakis (Massachusetts), James Blanchard (Michigan), and Bill Clinton (Arkansas)—were already emphasizing consensus building and partnership with business, as well as individual social responsibility and equality in opportunity rather than outcome. Unwilling to regulate plant closings or interfere with market forces (unless it was a bailout of a corporation too big to fail), these New Democrats, many of whom belonged to the Democratic Leadership Council (DLC) formed in 1985, turned to community economic development as a way to help distressed working-class communities pick up the economic and social pieces.[19] These states were the laboratories where a new politics first emerged.

After serving as the president of the national governors' association, Bill Clinton was elected US President in 1992, the first

Democrat in the White House since Jimmy Carter. Clinton championed free trade with Mexico (triggering further plant closures), deregulation of the financial sector (eventually, with disastrous results in 2009), and welfare reform (hurting poor families), and fought the deficit rather than unemployment or poverty. At the 1996 AFL-CIO (American Federation of Labor and Congress of Industrial Organizations) union convention, Vice President Al Gore even "refused to commit himself to the statement put forth that 'unions are good for workers.'"[20] Clinton and Gore were among a new generation of highly educated Democratic Party leaders from affluent suburban districts, once dubbed "Atari Democrats" (after an early video-game maker), who made it a badge of honour to reject the old redistributive politics of the New Deal.[21]

The writings of Robert Reich, Bill Clinton's Secretary of Labour, offer a good example of this mode of thinking. Clinton and Reich became good friends when they were at Oxford University together as Rhodes Scholars. Reich opened his bestselling 1991 book, *The Work of Nations*, by saying:

> We are living through a transformation that will rearrange the politics and economics of the coming century. There will be no national products or technologies, no national corporations, no national industries. There will no longer be national economies, at least as we have come to understand that concept. All that will remain rooted within national borders are people who comprise a nation. Each nation's primary assets will be its citizens' skills and insights.[22]

Reich went on to present the labour force in bifurcated terms as either new economy "symbolic analysts," who are creative problem solvers, or old economy "routine producers," who are "governed by standard procedures and codified rules."[23] Traditional industries employing the latter were doomed to disappear, as production moved offshore to lower-wage countries. Skills training was therefore essential to future prosperity. As Reich later explained in an oral history interview, the book had a very simple, but important, thesis: "In a global economy, in a rapidly globalizing economy, the only assets a nation has that are truly national, that are not footloose, are its people and the infrastructure linking its people together. So that investments, public investments in education and infrastructure is critical in terms of attracting global capital to create high wage jobs."[24] However, historian Christopher Lasch has rightly criticized Reich's fawning over the Ivy League–trained creative class and the "cosmopolitanism of the favored few," arguing instead that upper-middle-class liberals failed to grasp "the importance of class differences."[25] Their belief that we live in a meritocracy prevented them from recognizing structural inequality. Thomas Frank, another sharp-witted American critic, writing two decades later, concurred, writing: "Despite [Reich's] acknowledgement of rising inequality, he seemed rather satisfied with the way things were unfolding. *The Work of Nations* appeared to be a critique, but it was in fact a long valentine to society's winners."[26]

These post-industrial ideas circulated across the anglosphere, inspiring a growing number of modernizing social democrats and centrist progressives. In a 2010 oral history interview, former British Prime Minister Tony Blair noted that he closely followed the "whole concept of the New Democrats" throughout this period.[27] The American approach chimed with his own, as "there was a rather good confluence in the imitation and also our own belief in the right way for progressives to approach modern policy." Blair admired how the rising generation of New Democrats in the Democratic Leadership Council occupied the "centre" of American politics. As he explained it, it was not simply a political strategy, but an "intellectual concept as well, which was in a new world, close of the twentieth century, where we'd kind of gone over the major ideological battles of the twentieth century. It was time to find a third way, if you like, between laissez-faire markets and an overbearing state." Blair appreciated Clinton's soaring rhetoric of offering Americans a hand up and not a handout. The two men met for the first time after Blair became leader of the Labour Party in 1994. According to Blair, "There was an immediate intellectual, political bonding. Obviously, he'd read about what we'd done and so on, and the changes I was making in the Labour Party."

The rise and fall of political orders is one way to understand this moment in history. For American historian Gary Gerstle, political orders "connote a constellation of ideologies, policies, and constituencies" that bend political opponents to their will. Gerstle has suggested that the New Deal Order, which emerged in North America during the 1930s and 1940s, and which welcomed a period of unionized prosperity, had fractured by the 1970s and 1980s under the combined pressure of high inflation and high unemployment. In its place emerged a new neoliberal order that "prizes free trade and free movement of capital, goods, and people. It celebrates deregulation as an economic good that results when governments no longer interfere with the operation of the market."[28] The origins of neoliberal thinking are usually associated with the Mont Pèlerin Society, which formed in Switzerland in the early post-war period, or the later work of University of Chicago economist Milton Friedman.[29] European neoliberals were key architects of postwar trade liberalization under the General Agreement on Tariffs and Trade (GATT), which integrated national economies and insulated the emerging global economy from democratic accountability or interference. The Kennedy (1963–67) and Tokyo (1973–79) rounds of trade liberalization brought down world trade barriers significantly, prompting the radical restructuring of the international division of labour that eviscerated many higher-wage working-class communities in North America and Western Europe. During the 1980s and 1990s, the International Monetary Fund and World Bank also required countries elsewhere to open up to global trade and investment.[30] Hence, the shock therapy imposed on Eastern Europe after the fall of communism saw mass privatizations and liquidations of industries that had deadly results.[31]

To some degree, the emancipatory language of neoliberalism dovetailed with the anti-statism of much of the New Left. Communitarianism, with its emphasis of collective bonds and shared values, offered middle-class social democrats and other progressives an alternative to the old Marxian language of class struggle. According to philosopher Fredric Jameson, community is a "pious" word that is "congenial to the right as well as to the left."[32] As such, it attempts to forge a "third language" that transcends old left-right political divisions and an ideological pathway somewhere between the welfare state and the free market. The language of shared values wherein structural divides were submerged now took centre stage. Communitarians "regret the collapse of social trust"[33] and look forward "to a social order in which politics has given way to administration."[34] However, the abandonment of class analysis, which underpinned the old redistributive politics, ultimately led to the kind of neoliberal politics that we now associate with the Third Way.

To what extent, then, did the Ontario New Democratic Party's five years in power between 1990 and 1995 reflect this wider ideological transition? Was it an early manifestation of neoliberal Third Way economic thinking or was it something different? Much of the book grapples with these two overlapping questions. Blair, Clinton, and Reich were clearly drawing from, and contributing to, the same pool of ideas as Bob Rae. Rae shared the same middle-class sensibility and international outlook as the others. During his Oxford years, he came to know Ira Magaziner, a future Clinton advisor and management consultant with the Boston Consulting Group, who co-authored *Managing America's Business* in 1982 with Reich. As a member of Parliament in the federal NDP caucus, Rae recalls how he "talked with Ed [Broadbent] a lot about how social democratic parties around the world are going through a deep process of change and discussion and internal debate about how to move forward, and a lot of the old formulas are not relevant."[35] Then, as Ontario NDP leader, his principal secretary for several years was Robin Sears, who worked in Europe previously for Socialist International, the international body representing social democratic parties. Sears then hired Riel Miller to bolster the party's economic research capacity, as Miller worked previously for the Organisation for Economic Co-operation and Development (OECD) in Paris. Rae was therefore used to thinking in terms of a wider social democratic project.

To self-identify as a party "modernizer" in the late 1980s, as Rae did, was to enter into a wider transnational conversation about social democracy and the pursuit of power in a new global economy.[36] Rae would have been well aware of the efforts of Neil Kinnock to modernize the British Labour Party, purging the radical left, and initiating a far-reaching policy review from 1987 to 1989 that led the party to abandon the language of class in favour of citizenship.[37] The Labour Party also recognized the advantages of the free market, promising not to nationalize any industries if elected. These changes offered Rae a model long before Tony Blair adopted the Third Way slogan as his own. That said, the Rae government accorded organized labour a more central, indeed expanded, role on economic issues than was the case under Clinton, Blair, or Schröder. Thus, when I suggested to Bob Rae in an oral history interview that his government seemed to occupy a transitional moment distinct from what would later become known as Third Way social democracy, the idea resonated with him.[38]

Founded in 1961, the New Democratic Party brought together the remnants of the Co-operative Commonwealth Federation, an older socialist party born during the Great Depression, with its greatest strength in the western provinces, and the Canadian Labour Congress.[39] Modelled on the British Labour Party, the NDP had a formal link with organized labour whereby trade unionists were represented at all levels of the party. Union locals could vote to formally affiliate, paying dues to the party, and in return send delegates to party conventions. The alliance with organized labour was strongest in Ontario, where 200,000 of the 275,000 unionists affiliated with the party in 1992 lived and worked (see table of Organizations Affiliated to the NDP). The Ontario NDP was therefore the closest Canada had, since the 1920s, to a true labour party. This status was reinforced by the fact that the provincial party's areas of historic strength were the highly unionized industrial cities of Windsor and Hamilton, the east and west end ridings of Toronto, which in those days were still mostly working class, and northern Ontario. The Ontario NDP, like the union movement

Organizations Affiliated to the New Democratic Party (31 December 1992)		
Province	Affiliated Locals (#)	Affiliated Membership
British Columbia	64	37,868
Alberta	38	7,810
Saskatchewan	44	13,472
Manitoba	39	12,254
Ontario	503	200,827
Quebec	24	2,714
New Brunswick	5	319
Nova Scotia	9	804
Prince Edward Island	1	195
Newfoundland	7	375
Total	734	276,638

Accession 2003-027. Box 5/8. Ontario New Democratic Party Fonds. Queen's University Archives.

itself, provided working people with the opportunity to widen their horizons and have a say in their own destiny.

The centrality of the labour movement within the Ontario NDP was such that I believe it useful to consider the party's stance on economic and labour issues to be a continuation of a longer working-class tradition of radical labourism. Calling labourism the "neglected child of the Canadian left," historian Craig Heron locates this ideological stream in the independent labour parties that emerged in different parts of Canada during the late nineteenth and early twentieth centuries.[40] These small parties were very much led by, and anchored in, the working class, infusing their politics with a distinct class sensibility. Ten Independent Labour Party members of the provincial parliament (MPPs) even joined the United Farmers of Ontario as a junior governing partner from 1919 to 1923—though their record in power has generally been dismissed as halting and lacklustre. If Heron believed that labourism died with the birth of the Co-operative Commonwealth

Federation, historian James Naylor shows us otherwise.[41] The tenacity of labourism ensured that it lived on and was, I suggest, reinvigorated with the CCF's merger with the Canadian Labour Congress, especially in Ontario, and the end of the postwar boom. As we will see in the next chapter, Heron's overall assessment of early labourism could just as easily apply to the Ontario NDP during the 1970s and early 1980s: While they might not have been "fundamentally at odds with capitalism, they were certainly opposed to the version of it which was reshaping Canadian society. This was not a revolutionary challenge, but a resistance movement."[42]

The NDP was a house with many rooms, to borrow a good analogy from Naylor, and labourism occupied the biggest room, just not the front room. Its elected leaders were rarely of working-class origin. A son of a prominent Canadian diplomat, Bob Rae grew up as a world citizen—giving him a strong international outlook. Left-nationalism was not something that came naturally to him. Originally a Liberal, Rae joined the British Labour Party while in the UK. When Rae returned to Toronto and became a lawyer, a chance encounter with Peter Warrian, a former president of the Canadian Union of Students during its most influential and radical phase, who had since gone on to work for the United Steelworkers of America (USWA), led Rae to be hired by the union. What becomes clear from the interviews is just how small the world of social democratic labour and economic policy making was in Ontario, and the ways that this cohort bridged the party and union movement. Many had known each other since their student days at the University of Toronto. Warrian had been part of a wave of student activists hired into the trade union movement as researchers, educators, and legislative directors. As he told me, "That happened in Europe, that happened in the United States, but I think it was more impactful in Canada. Partly because Canada's a smaller place." It might have been thirty people in total, but they had real impact. The Steelworkers connection proved helpful in Bob Rae's meteoric rise within the NDP, first in the federal caucus, and then, after 1982, as Ontario NDP leader. Rae had just turned forty-two years of age when he was elected Ontario Premier in September 1990.

The NDP leadership had no idea they would win until late in the campaign and, even then, did not initially believe it. On 25 August, just twelve days before election day, the party pollster "delivered a bombshell: not only was the NDP campaign doing extremely well, he advised that the strategists should start thinking about an NDP minority, or possibly even a majority, government."[43] As NDP advisors Chuck Rachlis and David Wolfe later recalled, "the reaction was telling. After a moment's stunned silence, the group broke into guffaws. 'What's the matter, haven't you been paid yet?' asked the caucus research director. The meeting moved on." Wolfe also said that a few days before the election, three or four of Bob Rae's "closest advisors sat down with a copy of the Government of Ontario phone book and started going through the list of positions for the Premier's Office and trying to guess with each other what each of the titles meant and what the person in that position actually did, what their job was."[44] Riel Miller, another senior advisor, who worked closely with Finance Minister Floyd Laughren, shook his head in disbelief at how unprepared the party was for governing: "They were not ready. I mean not even vaguely ready. It was a massive shock."

It was a government like no other. The new Minister of Labour, Bob Mackenzie, who'd represented the riding of Hamilton East since 1975, had left school after grade seven to work in a paper mill before joining the merchant marine. He says that was where he became a convert to democratic socialism. Next door, David Christopherson, another new cabinet minister, had left school in grade nine to work at a local factory. Both men got their real education in the union movement. They were not alone. Fully 40 percent of the NDP caucus were trade unionists.[45] Believe it or not, there were only five lawyers in a caucus of seventy-four. It was also a feminist government. Forty percent of the new cabinet were women, including Marion Boyd, who previously ran a women's shelter, and Frances Lankin, who had been a prison guard, one of the first women to work in a male prison in Ontario. These two women emerged as powerhouses within cabinet.

For Ontario's political, business, and media elites, however, the collective profile of the new government was unnatural, even laughable. As a result, soon after the election, media pundits and opposition members took to calling the ragtag NDP caucus the "Clampetts" from the *Beverly Hillbillies*, a popular American sitcom from the 1960s about a poor extended family of uneducated dim-wits who strike it rich and move into a mansion in California, where much hilarity ensues. Applied to the NDP, it was, of course, an aspersion dripping with class condescension. Recognizing this in his June 1991 speech to the party's Provincial Council meeting, held in the auto town of Windsor, Bob Rae lashed out at the elitism of those who were making the analogy: "What they're really saying is that workers, teachers, ordinary people, can't govern themselves. . . . That's the anti-democratic insinuation in that joke."[46] It is the same ugly classism that is regularly directed against the trade union movement itself.

To be fair, nothing had prepared the Ontario NDP for coming to power so unexpectedly. And the timing didn't help. The province was entering the worst economic crisis since the Great Depression, forcing the government to deal with a tidal wave of plant closures that resulted in hundreds of thousands of job losses.[47] Welfare rolls doubled. For the first time since the 1930s, provincial tax revenues actually decreased in real terms. When I interviewed members of cabinet, including Rae, as well as senior economic and labour policy advisors, they all said they were "firefighting" most of the time, trying to douse the economic wildfires breaking out across the province. A series of small scandals and costly missteps, mostly the result of inexperience, didn't help. Crisis management was the order of the day, especially in the first year or two. Yet Bob Rae told another researcher that his government was "sometimes accused" of not knowing what it was doing. He strongly disagreed: "We actually did know what we were doing, it's just that we were doing a lot. Because in addition to the firefighting, if you like, and the restructuring that we had to do, we were also trying to figure out how do we turn this around in a major way."[48]

Rae could point to a long list of government achievements. New pro-union labour reforms were pushed through (including an anti-scab law), pay equity expanded, employment equity initiated, massive new investments made in daycare, more cooperative housing supported, and the minimum wage hiked. Workers' wages were also protected when their employers went bankrupt. The Rae government even facilitated worker buyouts of a string of closing mills in northern Ontario as well as other strategic investments—saving a number of single-industry communities from economic disaster. Toronto's De Havilland, a leading global manufacturer of turboprop passenger planes and the largest industrial employer in the city, was also saved by the NDP government after it took a minority ownership stake. The government even tried to introduce Swedish-style corporatism in polarized Ontario, creating the Ontario Training and Adjustment Board. By ceding decisions to an arm's-length corporatist body run by the key stakeholders (in this case labour, management, trainers, and equity groups), the government hoped to forge consensus and avoid more bureaucracy. A new Industrial Policy Framework likewise encouraged employers and unions to cooperate in the development of sectoral strategies. The overall goal was to manage the economic transformation underway for the common good and to share the pain more equitably.

But we must distinguish the government's initial push in the first year or two from what followed. The turning point came during the summer of 1991 after Ontario Treasurer Floyd Laughren declared war on the recession, rather than the deficit, investing hundreds of millions of dollars into public works to put people back to work. However, the resulting $9.7 billion deficit sparked a ferocious political backlash and a downgrading of Ontario's credit rating by the New York bond agencies. Ontario became the world's largest non-sovereign borrower. With its polling numbers plunging downwards from a honeymoon high of 60 percent, but its electoral base solidly behind the government's initial direction, the Rae government suddenly reversed course and prioritized deficit reduction instead. One by one, cherished party policies were discarded. Even public auto insurance, which had been a central promise in multiple elections and had considerable symbolic value for party members, was abandoned.

The 1993 decision to forcibly open public-sector collective agreements and impose negotiated austerity, under the guise of a new "social contract," effectively shattered the government's relationship with the labour movement and nearly did the same with the party itself, prompting mass resignations and union disaffiliations. In fact, the party's membership collapsed from 31,791 members in 1992 to 14,674 in early 1994.[49] Many of those leaving were long-time supporters, the kind of people who donated time as well as money. The party also saw a large number of affiliated union locals formally cut their ties or go into arrears, a form of quiet quitting. Some chose to direct their dues exclusively to the federal party. As a result, the party in power in Ontario was thrown into financial crisis, forcing staff at its provincial office to take extended unpaid leaves to avoid layoffs.

We can see the blast pattern left by the government's refusal to abide by party policy across dozens of as-yet-unprocessed boxes in the Ontario NDP (ONDP) Fonds held by Queen's University. Meeting minutes, resolutions, membership lists, and other material traces record the divergence between government and party. One person spoke movingly of the hundreds of letters of protest that flooded into the party's provincial office, some with their torn-up membership cards inside. The party, to its credit, did not simply defer to the government and instead defiantly passed resolutions reaffirming party policy as well as a strong government accountability resolution that insisted that the party determined policy; the job of the caucus was to determine the timing of implementation. Julie Davis, president of the provincial party and vice-president of the Ontario Federation of Labour, told a union convention: "We have a government in Ontario that seems to have lost sight to some NDP priorities in its preoccupation with the deficit and debt."[50] She even told the media that the "government is not the party, this party stands for workers. If there is going to be a fight, it will be with Bob Rae and not with the public service coalition."[51] I can't think of another example, internationally, where a social democratic party so publicly defied its own government. To understand the divergence in thinking, we need to recognize the economic and political pressure that the Rae government was under, as well as the wider ideological pivot of social democratic parties towards a new progressive neoliberalism. It begins with the cautionary tale of the French Socialists. Elected in 1981 after decades in the political wilderness, the Socialists under President François Mitterrand, in coalition with the French Communist Party, embarked on an ambitious program of nationalization of key industries and financial institutions as well as the further expansion of the welfare state, with the view of relaunching the country's economy in a time of global crisis. This defiant economic nationalist strategy, however, led to a spike in inflation and a balance of trade deficit that convinced Mitterrand to suddenly reverse direction in one of history's great political U-turns. A new prime minister was named in 1983 to impose financial discipline and austerity.[52] The message was clear to social democrats everywhere: resistance is futile. There is little doubt that the Mitterrand U-turn loomed large in the minds of Rae's inner circle, stoking fears of the disciplinary power of the international money markets. "In order to avoid the mistakes of some previous socialist administrations dealing with recessions, like Mitterrand in 1982," counselled Riel Miller, soon after the NDP election victory, "this government must pursue a carefully balanced package of positive adjustment policies aimed at building a coalition of labour, business and community interests for change."[53]

In one form or another, the progressive competitive model that we saw emerge in Ontario was adopted by social democratic and progressive parties across the OECD.[54] Indeed, this book suggests that the pivot towards Third Way progressive neoliberalism was already visible in the mid-1980s, rather than the mid-1990s as commonly assumed, and that the Ontario NDP ended its brief tenure as very much a Third Way social democratic government. This ideological pivot was undertaken mostly in the name of political and economic pragmatism. Bob Rae saw himself as the "ultimate pragmatist," returning to this idea again and again during our interview as well as in his published memoirs. Pragmatism is clearly central to his political identity. Thus, with the defeat of the opponents of free trade in the 1988 federal election, his view was one of acceptance: "Once it's over, it's over. That election was lost, the decision was made; you couldn't go on fighting it." You had to accept political and economic reality if you were to get things done. But the funny thing about pragmatism, the perception of reality has as much to do with dominant ideologies as with anything else. Writing about Thatcherism in the 1980s, Stuart Hall once explained:

> Ruling or dominant conceptions of the world do not directly prescribe the mental content of the illusions that supposedly fill the heads of the dominant classes. But the circle of dominant ideas does accumulate the symbolic power to map or classify the world for others. ... It becomes the horizon of the taken-for-granted: what the world is and how it works, for all practical purposes.[55]

A crucial part of politics is therefore the struggle to define economic reality.[56] The Ontario Federation of Labour understood this fact when it declared in the mid-1980s that the "debate over economic policy is in reality, a debate over economic and political power."[57] The challenge, then as now, is to capture the public's imagination "about what is and is not economic 'reality,' about what the market can and cannot deliver."

Just as the NDP was grappling with the significance of free trade and trade liberalization, so too was organized labour. In fact, Ontario's trade union movement was bitterly divided over the corporatist impulse towards labour-management partnership. On the one hand, the Canadian Auto Workers, which separated from the US-based United Auto Workers in 1984 over their divergent responses to the industrial crisis, adopted a defiant no concessions policy and challenged what they called the false promise of partnership in industrial restructuring. In its 1989 Statement on the Reorganization of Work, the CAW declared that as a union it needed to "look behind the surface of 'partnership' and ask ourselves what it really means and what the results will be."[58] Though it could be pragmatic, the union called for resistance, not accommodation, to industrial restructuring. On the other hand, the United Steelworkers of America in Ontario embraced labour-management partnership and co-determination in its far-reaching 1991 policy document Empowering Workers in the Global Economy. At the outset, it declared that the "structural changes in Canada and in the global economy have changed fundamentally the context in which we frame our priorities and our strategies."[59] This new economic reality required new creative strategies from the trade union movement. The Steelworkers sought to extend the role of trade unions in the economy via labour-management partnerships over training and adjustment, worker ownership, labour venture capital funds, and extended bargaining rights over a host of longer-term labour issues. Not surprisingly, as these were mostly his own government's priorities, Rae hailed the Steelworkers' political leadership and "maturity": a not-so-subtle dig at the auto workers' union.[60]

Overall, the set of ideas that found voice in Rae's landmark January 1990 speech, and to some degree that of the Steelworkers' 1991 discussion document, shared key characteristics with later Third Way thinking. Without question, Rae and his inner circle were changed by the experience of governing during neoliberal times. With the radical restructuring of Ontario's manufacturing sector, competitiveness became the central lens through which politicians of all stripes viewed the economy. Politically, at least, the "new global economy" now wielded a power all its own. Moreover, free trade and the GATT placed new limits on what governments could do in response to industrial restructuring. As Rae explained, "From a simple point of view, it means that there are limits on what governments can do. We are not as free as we might like to be to make the kinds of decisions that we would like to make, or in another time would have liked to have been able to make."[61] The fear of countervailing duties or a de facto "capital strike" loomed large during these years, shaping the legislative agenda. If Rae had not entered government in 1990 as a Third Way thinker, he certainly left it as one five years later. However, as we will see, his government's ideological pivot was uneven, contested, and partial—and was ultimately rejected by the party itself.

The Left in Power speaks to the inherent tension between the far-reaching aspirations of the left and the real-world limits of political power in a liberal democracy under global capitalism, and within this the dramatic shift of class power during these years. Bob Rae understood this tension in the linear terms of political maturity. He thus began his 1996 memoirs, appropriately entitled *From Protest to Power*, not with the thrill of election night nor the euphoria of the swearing-in ceremony, as one would have expected him to do, but with the government's retreat from deficit financing and its eventual embrace of negotiated austerity. *From Protest to Power*, like most political autobiographies, is a sustained self-justification, even an "I told you so" or a "you wish you had me as your premier now," given the slash-and-burn brand of right-wing conservatism that followed after the NDP's defeat. Rereading it, I am struck today by how angry and bitter Bob Rae was *at his own party*. It could not be more different in tone, or substance, from his 1990 speech. In its place was a much more defensive posture that was frequently expressed by measuring people on the basis of their perceived "loyalty" to him. Rae clearly felt under siege, though it is his critics within the NDP, rather than his political opponents in the legislature or the wild imaginings of the business sector, that receive the full force of his sharp wit. Internal party critics are thus regularly dismissed as "ideologues," "nervous nellies," or "the usual gang of would-be proletarian anarchists."[62] In his mind, these were the people who preferred the virtuous certainties of oppositional protest to the hard realities of power. Yet, as Mel Watkins reminds us in his review of *From Protest to Power*, "the irony here is that when a government of the left wholly abandons protest, it loses its power."[63] Protest and power are therefore best understood as complementary and not competing. I am in fundamental agreement with Watkins on this point.

The years in government proved profoundly divisive and disillusioning for almost everyone in Ontario's left, including those in government. There was a sadness across the interviews, and hurt too, even after three decades. Some in government felt shunned or disowned by the party they had dedicated their lives to. Others felt betrayed by a government that squandered this once-in-a-lifetime opportunity to effect real change. Peter Warrian, the Rae government's chief economist, recently wrote that with the election of the Rae government, the "vision of the Holy City crumbled, and activists were left not with the fruits of victory but with the taste of ashes. The experience shakes you to your inner core."[64] It left much of his generation exhausted: "It was the worst feeling in the world. . . . This was a collective defeat and eclipse of a shared ethical and social horizon." The New Democratic Party has spent the last thirty years trying to put this crushing defeat behind it, but these years in power still seem to have the power to haunt Canadian social democrats. Rae's defection to the federal Liberals in 2006 prompted the NDP caucus at Queen's Park to take his portrait down from their meeting room.[65] When I raised this in my interview with Rae, he quietly replied, "I became an unperson, like George Orwell," referencing Orwell's classic dystopian novel of a totalitarian future in *1984*.[66]

Rather than treat the Rae government as a bad memory, or pretend it didn't happen, today's NDP needs to come to terms with this experience. There is much to learn from these five difficult years in power. Only in understanding better what happened and why will it be able to move on. Where did the Rae government go wrong and where did it do things right? Ontario also offers a window into a wider transnational story, as social democrats grappled with the existential economic and political challenge of neoliberal globalization. By shining a critical light on this transitional moment, my hope is that *The Left in Power* will contribute to renewed reflection on how the political left can, and must, respond to industrial restructuring and economic transitions more generally. It is my contention that economic issues are essential to governing from the left.

1
FIGHTING PLANT SHUTDOWNS

> Reading the Committee testimony and discussion, one gets the distinct impression that the Committee is looking for a villain—a villain who can be forced to pay the price of his own malfeasance. Members must ask themselves, which corporation is responsible for high interest rates? Whose fault is foreign-ownership? Who is forcing structural change on the Ontario economy? Who is responsible for the saturation of the Ontario market by imports? Whose fault is poor management of a business and how do you force the individual to pay? This business of assigning fault for layoffs and shut-downs is a fruitless exercise.
> —CANADIAN FEDERATION OF INDEPENDENT BUSINESS, Brief to the Ontario Select Committee on Plant Shutdowns and Employee Adjustment, 1981[1]

Industrial closures during the 1970s and early 1980s were often met with a cacophony of voices, some trade union, others simply local, urgently calling for state intervention to save their mine, mill, or factory. Mostly, in Ontario as elsewhere, these panicked calls for action were met with soothing words and a collective shrug of the shoulders: there was nothing that could be done. A pervasive sense of inevitability, bolstered by the ideology of the free market, effectively immobilized communities, unions, and governments. There were moments, however, like the one that produced the Ontario Select Committee on Plant Shutdowns and Employee Adjustment in 1980–81, when the political winds shifted and fundamental questions could be asked. Why are industrial workplaces being closed? Did they need to close? Who decided that they should be closed? It was in these moments of heightened public awareness and concern when assigning fault provided the basis for political action. Bob White, the Canadian director of the United Auto Workers (later Canadian Auto Workers, after the Canadians broke away), who subsequently became one of the country's most celebrated labour leaders, was remarkably candid in his own testimony to the select committee, telling provincial politicians that his union's primary mission was to stop factories from closing. Compulsory advance notification of mass layoffs not only helped workers adjust to job loss but also helped union efforts to reverse management's decision to shut down. Likewise, mandatory severance pay offered more than a "monetary cushion" to those displaced: it was also "a disincentive—a cost—to closing the facility."[2] He noted that existing legislation failed to "address the most critical question: *did the plant have to close in the first place?*" White then made the case that working people acquired "certain rights" over their job after "doing a job day-in and day-out, year after year" that necessitated the checking of "unilateral corporate power over that job." For White, as for other Canadian trade unionists, it was about making corporations socially accountable.

That the select committee was entertaining such radical ideas frightened the right-wing Canadian Federation of Independent Business (CFIB). "The impulse for further employee protections originates with the concept of a so-called proprietary right to a job," it observed. "Because of the seriousness of this new concept" the federation addressed it "in some detail."[3] The CFIB conceded that long service created "certain obligations" from the employer, but said this did not justify the erosion of managerial rights. The plant closing problem, such as it was, was explained away as a few bad corporate apples. Ultimately, the CFIB reasoned that workers' job security was best secured by economic growth driven by entrepreneurship and the free market. That the business lobby was so obviously on the political defensive in 1980–81 is remarkable, given that the CFIB's neoliberal vision for Canada would triumph just a few years later with the signing of the 1987 Free Trade Agreement with the United States. The next major industrial crisis in Ontario, however, would result in the election of the first social democratic government in the province's history. Bob Mackenzie, one of the three outspoken NDP members of the select committee, became Minister of Labour, and Shelley Martel, the daughter of another, became the Minister of Northern Development and Mines. It was a long road to the first NDP government in Ontario. This chapter explores the politics of plant closures up to the early 1980s.

THE RISE OF LEFT-NATIONALISM IN ONTARIO

The political struggle over capital flight in Ontario has its roots in the early 1950s when the Ford Motor Company decided to move its assembly operations from Windsor to Oakville, 333 kilometres to the east. Windsor had earned a reputation as a militant union town after the ninety-nine-day strike in late 1945 of Ford Windsor that, famously, included a three-day automotive blockade of the strike-bound plant. Many auto parts plants left the city over the next decade.[4] Capital flight from the city was cast in one of two ways: as either anti-union "runaway shops," when employers moved to rural Ontario in search of lower wages and non-union workers, or as "plant movements," when they shifted production to the more populous Toronto area.

Labour historians often criticize the "postwar compromise" in labour-management relations where unions (in theory at least) won recognition and the closed shop in exchange for agreeing not to strike during a contract and respecting management rights. As

The Runaway Shop.
Fred Wright.
United Electrical Workers.
University of Pittsburgh.
UE 13.1.135.

a result, "unions were drawn into the existing capitalist structures with the lure of material prosperity."[5] There is considerable truth to this critique. Collective bargaining proved incapable of dealing with the plant closing problem, as management rights were explicitly recognized in many existing agreements and supported by labour law. "It is long past time that the Canadian labor movement challenged the 'management right' to tear communities apart and move willy-nilly to greener fields in pursuit of profit," concluded the Canadian UAW in September 1959. District director George Burt believed that the union movement and Canadians in general had become "too docile" in the face of corporate dictates. "For too long," said Burt, "we, the public and our government have stood aside while company after company blithely dumped workers and communities for who they had no further use. This crime against society has gone on in the name of free enterprise." Clearly building up rhetorical steam, Burt went on to say: "Just as the robber barons of another generation moved into various parts of the country and stripped them of timber, coal or minerals, so do present day companies exploit the available industrial sites, the water supply, the manpower, etc, and move along when it suits their purpose without let or hindrance from society."[6] That these defiant words were spoken in the middle of the long postwar boom, not in the depths of the recessionary 1980s, is significant.

For Ontario trade unionists, Europe offered a solution to the unfolding problem. There, governments had legislated protections for workers and hard-hit regions. Before Margaret Thatcher, even Great Britain was exemplary in this regard; Canadian trade unionists cited British efforts to direct the location of new plants to areas of higher unemployment and their power to reject permission when companies sought to locate in areas of labour shortage. Hence, public scrutiny of corporate (dis)investment decisions was urgently needed, placing "restraint upon its freedom to arbitrarily re-locate its operations and to turn its parent communities into blighted and distressed areas."[7] But union protests largely failed to sway politicians from the governing Tories or Liberals.

The laissez-faire approach of the United States loomed large in the Ontario debate about possible restrictions to managerial prerogatives. In 1971, for example, the Ontario Federation of Labour published a book on plant shutdowns that concluded that "there is a growing realization that industry can no longer, with impunity, make unilateral decisions that throw hundreds of workers on the industrial scrap heap, and destroy whole communities."[8] After being sent a copy, Ontario Treasurer Darcy McKeough, a Tory, wrote back to say he was opposed to the study's major recommendations, rebutting the OFL's argument in a four-page letter. While the Progressive Conservative government shared the union movement's concern about job security, it did not agree with the proposal that "government should undertake an extensive investigation when shutdowns are planned. Regardless of ultimate cause, permanent lay-offs are almost invariably associated with unprofitable operations."[9] Accordingly, further investigation was unlikely to uncover anything new. And if outside intervention was pursued, he reasoned, it would effectively freeze capital and labour in areas that could be more productively deployed elsewhere. It would take another wave of plant closures to sweep through rural areas and small towns, as well as larger unionized towns or cities, for concern over plant closings to become more generalized and thus cross party lines. Only then was it truly seen as a province-wide issue that urgently demanded political attention, if not action.

Things only began to change politically in the early 1970s when the long boom came to a crashing end and factories began to close in large numbers. The period also saw growing national anxiety about the future of Canada as an independent country. Fundamental questions were being asked about the Americanization of Canadian culture and economy. A radical new critique of US multinational corporations and their subsidiaries and branch plants operating in Canada had already emerged, evidenced in a series of influential federal government reports that called for the regulation of foreign direct investment to ensure its net benefits to Canada.[10] Canadians were especially concerned by a perceived shift in economic decision-making outside of the country and, in the words of the 1972 Herb Gray report, a "Canadian industrial structure which largely reflects the growth priorities of foreign corporations."[11] The spectre of the American branch plant loomed large during these early post-boom years.

Underpinning the left-nationalist critique of underdevelopment was the staples theory developed by economic historian Harold Innis, a liberal nationalist who chaired the Department of Political Economy at the University of Toronto. Over the course of his career, which spanned much of the first half of the twentieth century, Innis wrote a series of expansive books on staples production and showed how staples exports like fur and fish set the pace for economic growth.[12] His essential insight was that commodity booms exposed Canada to "structural imbalances" and a destructive boom-to-bust cycle.[13] It was a history of arrested development and cyclonic growth. Economist Mel Watkins, who took a few classes with Innis during his undergraduate studies, translated Innis's staples theory to a new generation in an influential 1963 article, "A Staple Theory of Economic Development."[14] Watkins investigated the relationship between resource extraction and the manufacturing industries.[15] The article was so influential that Jim Stanford, Canada's most prominent labour movement economist, organized a series of lectures to mark its fiftieth anniversary. Stanford noted that Watkins's original article "laid the intellectual foundation for so many subsequent theoretical and policy interventions during the tumultuous 1960s and 1970s."[16]

Both the Liberals and the NDP grappled with the issue of foreign direct investment during these years. In 1967, Watkins was appointed by the federal cabinet in Ottawa to lead the Task Force on Foreign Ownership and the Structure of Canadian Industry. The resulting Watkins Report recommended that Canada set up a development corporation to encourage Canadian ownership of the economy and to regulate foreign takeovers of Canadian companies. While the Liberal government initially rejected these steps, the actions of US President Richard Nixon altered the political calculation and led to the creation of the Canada Development Corporation and Foreign Investment Review Agency in the early

1970s. By then, however, Watkins had turned away from the Liberal Party and towards socialism.

In the 1960s, the federal NDP was also wrestling with the significance of foreign direct investment and Canada's branch-plant economy. The party approached Kari Levitt, a faculty member in McGill University's Department of Political Science—and daughter of renowned political economist Karl Polanyi[17]—to write a series of background papers on the problem, culminating in an oral presentation to the NDP's Federal Council in 1966.[18] A specialist on economic development in the Caribbean, Levitt explained the economic consequences of US economic domination using a combination of Innis's staples theory and the dependency theory then emerging out of Latin America. Dependency theory, she reasoned, offered Canadians a framework for understanding domestic class relations as well as the wider international division of labour within a chain of exploitive relations between the economic centre and periphery. One Latin American theorist defined dependency as "a situation in which the economy of certain countries is conditioned by the development and expansion of another economy to which the former is subjected."[19] Asymmetrical relationships between core and peripheral countries resulted.

Initially, Levitt set out her thinking on these matters in an article published in *New World Quarterly*, a journal of Caribbean commentary.[20] Watkins later noted that photocopies of this hard-to-get article circulated underground on campuses across Canada.[21] Levitt then expanded her analysis into *Silent Surrender: The Multinational Corporation in Canada*, published in 1970, which offered a far-reaching analysis of "Canada's slide into a position of economic, political and cultural dependence on the United States."[22] Labelling this the "new mercantilism," Levitt provocatively argued that the multinational corporation was a "modern re-incarnation of the chartered companies of the mercantile era that pre-dated industrial capitalism." Her book took "the campuses by storm"[23] and resonated as far as the Caribbean, given its critical examination of US multinational corporations.[24] Soon after, R. T. Naylor offered a historical framework for a new mercantilist understanding of Canada's past. In this formulation, industrial capitalism had been prevented, or at least delayed, from taking root in Canada because the country's mercantile and financial elite were wedded to staples exports.[25]

The Liberal Party's initial refusal to act on the policy recommendations of the Watkins Report, combined with his growing radicalization, led Mel Watkins to help write the left-nationalist Waffle Manifesto of September 1969 and campaign for James Laxer as a radical young candidate for NDP federal leader. Both were defeated due to the fierce opposition of the major US-based international unions that were a force within the party. The Waffle Manifesto called for an "independent socialist Canada" in order to combat the "major threat of Canadian survival today," namely "American control of the Canadian economy." Canada's political independence required that "these bonds must be cut," and the only way to effect this change was for capitalism to "be replaced by socialism, by national planning of investment and by the public ownership of the means of production in the interests of the Canadian people as a whole." After these confrontations, the Waffle's relationship with the international unions continued to deteriorate. Forty years later, Watkins recalled that the Waffle was "too weak to win and too strong to be tolerated, [so] the Waffle was, in effect, turfed out of the party. It struggled on, like a dead man walking, and by 1974 was no more."[26]

Before the Waffle died, however, the plant closing issue burst into the open. The closure of British multinational Dunlop Tire's industrial rubber division on Toronto's downtown Queen Street East in 1970, displacing 597 workers, sparked considerable public outrage and a new round of appeals for legislation that would force departing companies to open their financial books and justify their decisions. This time, however, the issue gained some political traction with the NDP and student activists who saw in Dunlop the manifestation of all that was wrong with Canada's dependent relationship on foreign capital. The timing of the Dunlop announcement was important, as was its central location, but it was the defiance of the local union that "made Dunlop a symbol.

They didn't accept that a corporation should be able unilaterally to close a plant on short notice and without public justification."[27] Nor did the City of Toronto, which called on the province to introduce said legislation.[28] Dunlop, according to Mel Watkins, was "not exactly your corner buggy whip manufacturer driven to the wall by the competitive struggle," but operated 120 plants across five continents and had more than 100,000 employees. At the time, it was the world's forty-second-largest corporation, with sales of $1 billion.[29] Not usually a fan of state intervention, even the Toronto *Globe and Mail* conceded that "it is in the interests of both government and companies like Dunlop to come forward with all the information that has led to the closing, if indeed the closing is inevitable. Otherwise, they invite legislation compelling them to do so."[30]

The sense of injustice after Dunlop was so great that one Tory MP even praised communist Yugoslavia as a "country where consultation, discussion and decision making have a very particular and unique meaning. In my view, what the Yugoslavs are doing has relevance to us." The comparison, he added, makes our system look "almost feudal."[31] But the Progressive Conservative government of Ontario proved unwilling to go beyond legislating mandatory advance notice in the name of facilitating worker adjustment. Jim Renwick, the New Democratic Party MPP for Riverdale, where Dunlop was located, found it "difficult to conceive of a more pathetic response to the efforts of the NDP and the labour movement and the people of Ontario to ensure fair job security at Dunlop and elsewhere."[32] That may be true, but only a couple other jurisdictions in North America had gone even this far.

Clearly, the Ontario NDP wanted to go further. It formed a Branch Plant Task Force to undertake research into the underlying issues. Among the task force's many recommendations was the establishment of a Take-over Review Board, which would "examine proposals for [corporate] take-overs by foreign interests and which would work out methods of preventing the loss of Canadian control or lay down terms which will protect Canadian interests. No take-over could occur without permit."[33] Similar legislation existed in France and Japan, so why not here? Just such a measure was adopted by the federal government, under pressure from the NDP, a couple years later. The task force also suggested that outright public ownership remained an option, citing the 1967 nationalization of the Dominion Steel and Coal Corporation's integrated steel mill in Sydney, Nova Scotia. But task force members cautioned that "it was more feasible and attractive as an instrument of overall economic strategy, on the 'commanding heights', than as a separate make-work gamble in a dead-end canyon."[34]

In the Ontario legislature, NDP MPP Stephen Lewis submitted a bill that would have prevented other Ontario firms from "doing a Dunlop." It failed, as almost all private member's bills do in Canada, but Dunlop proved to many people that stronger measures were needed. As the *Toronto Star* editorialized, "tragedies of this kind must be expected as long as we have our present branch-plant economy."[35] Later that year, when Lewis successfully ran for the Ontario NDP leadership, he proposed a ten-point "labour charter" that included the "termination of the managerial rights clauses" in collective agreements in order to enable the collective bargaining of technological change, layoffs, pricing policies, and "all other economic and social relationships that derive from the labor-management relationship." Lewis believed in full financial disclosure and the creation of a government agency that would examine the economic justification of proposed industrial closures.[36] In the face of such demands, the conservative *Globe and Mail* pushed back: "What would he have the government do if it disagreed with plans to shut down? Seize bank accounts? Lock everyone in the plant and string barbed wire around it?"[37]

A defining moment came in August 1971 when US President Richard Nixon decided to overturn the global monetary system of fixed exchange rates, encourage US multinationals to repatriate manufacturing jobs, and temporarily place a 10 percent surcharge on all imported goods.[38] The so-called Nixon shock threatened the Canadian economy, as it received no special treatment, despite the fact that 85 percent of Canada's exports went to the United States. A federal government assessment of Nixon's surcharge on

Canadian industry found that 158 companies operating in the country would be forced out of business.[39] Another 72 companies, employing 14,000 Canadians, reported that the surcharge could force them to relocate all or part of their businesses to the United States. One senior Toronto banker called the surcharge a "nuclear warfare type of tax" that threatened Canadian prosperity.[40] These measures caused many Canadians to make a political connection between US economic domination and the wave of factory closures devastating industrial Ontario.

It was at this critical juncture that Canadian left-nationalists in the Waffle developed the deindustrialization thesis to explain industrial decline. It emerged during a series of twelve lectures held in the auditorium at the Ontario Institute for the Study of Education (OISE) in Toronto. David Wolfe, who later became a key economic policy advisor during the NDP government, attended all twelve, and recalls the excitement in the auditorium: "It was packed for every one of those lectures."[41] The single best articulation of the emerging nationalist critique of plant closings can be found in Robert Laxer's 1973 edited volume *(Canada) Ltd: The Political Economy of Dependency*, which argued that US corporations under pressure from Nixon were shifting manufacturing jobs back home. To halt the hollowing out of Canadian manufacturing would require "a basic change in relations of social power. This idea, much more than public ownership, requires a revolution in people's thinking."[42] In James Laxer's contribution, he wrote that the protectionist policies imposed by Nixon meant "deindustrialization, even in terms of this already truncated manufacturing sector." In this formulation of its meaning, deindustrialization thus referred "to the special distorting effects of US ownership of Canadian manufacturing" and was "the price workers pay for Canada's dependent status in the American empire."[43] Strong measures needed to be taken to counter this destructive process. For the Waffle, the political prescription included public ownership and state planning within an independent socialist Canada.

The Waffle may have dissolved, but its left-nationalist ideas still found fertile ground within Canada's trade union movement and the New Democratic Party. A number of Canadian districts of US-based international unions broke away during the years that followed, forming their own national unions. These included the powerful unions representing Canadian paper workers and auto workers. The Science Council of Canada, an arm's-length advisory body for the federal government, also helped to popularize the deindustrialization concept by publishing a series of controversial reports. In *The Weakest Link* (1978) and *Forging the Links* (1979), it argued that the limited (and declining) technological capability of Canada's branch-plant economy put the country at a competitive disadvantage and risked the "deindustrialization of Canada." Only an industrial policy could protect Canada's "technological sovereignty."[44] Right-wing economists pushed back, arguing that the state should not interfere with the free market.[45] Thereafter, the spectre of deindustrialization was invoked repeatedly in Canada's Parliament as the opposition parties hammered away at the Liberal government. It sounded like a "slogan," one journalist wrote, but deindustrialization was justified as "a short form for the serious structural problems in the economy."[46]

Economic nationalism thus provided the political lens through which a growing number of Canadians, especially those on the left, interpreted structural changes to the economy. It also served to radicalize the NDP's economic policies. In *Industrial Sunset: The Making of North America's Rust Belt* (2003), I spoke of this brand of economic nationalism as a form of investment nationalism, as it focused on corporate ownership and decision-making rather than on foreign trade. Corporations were thus held accountable for the decisions they made rather than blaming their foreign competitors for rising imports. One can therefore see how this brand of economic nationalism provided a ready conceptual framework, and rhetorical weapon, for those most concerned by factory closures.

The mid-1970s had seen considerable political tension between organized labour, which prioritized the fight against unemployment, and the federal government, which, along with the Bank of Canada, prioritized the fight against inflation. Wage controls, which seriously compromised collective bargaining in Canada, were greatly resented. Social democrats and the labour movement argued for an industrial strategy for Canada and with it, full financial disclosure from corporations. Indeed, the Canadian Labour Congress (CLC) argued in 1978:

> If Canada is no longer competitive in some areas of manufacturing it is not because of high wages—it is because the corporations have refused to invest in modern plants and machinery with which workers in Canada can meet foreign competition. It is because corporations have chosen to invest profits made in Canada in low wage countries where profits are bigger. Workers and unions in Canada have been systemically excluded by management on issues such as corporate investment policy and productivity.[47]

For the CLC, it was the "cracks and weaknesses" in the economic system, and the continued foreign domination, that were pushing Canada into economic crisis. Multinationals stood "astride national boundaries transferring capital and investment wherever they find the highest rate of return, regardless of the social chaos they produced; what plants will be shut down; and what plants will survive." Indeed, trade liberalization under GATT was "determining which industries will 'go to the wall' and which will survive and grow." A new policy direction was needed to achieve full employment, starting with social and economic planning.

Numerous trade union delegations crossed the Atlantic to find out more about worker participation in economic decision-making and the ways that labour-management corporatism functioned. As part of one such investigative mission, L. H. Lorrain, national president of the Canadian Paperworkers Union (CPU), travelled in 1977 to Sweden and West Germany, where he found "an almost unbelievable degree of commitment to social harmony or, in the language of Sweden and West Germany, commitment to the social partnership, which has evolved through the last three decades."[48] If a company wanted to shut a plant in Sweden, it had to negotiate with the union. German Works Councils, for their part, were able to see the financial books of the company. Hence, "if a mill or plant shutdown is proposed by management, or if there is a substantial reduction in employment, the works council is entitled to what is referred to as a social plan, to provide security for those who are to be laid off." For Canadian trade unionists, the emerging ethos of industrial democracy had everything to do with the struggle to "protect one's job against unilateral lay-offs and shutdowns."[49] Europe thus offered an alternative point of reference for Canadian trade unionists to the savage capitalism on offer south of the border in the United States.

During these critical years, the Ontario Federation of Labour adopted a series of landmark policy statements on the unfolding industrial crisis. The first of these, on developing an industrial development strategy for full employment, adopted at its 1978 convention, expressed the "growing unease and despair" about the economy as "halting industrialization" had been replaced "by a steady de-industrialization."[50] Federal and provincial governments were simply "limping from crisis to crisis, wallowing in indecision, and trying to bluff it through." The time for "conventional tinkering" was over and nothing less than a "major overhaul and restructuring of our system, a complete redirection of our economic policies" was required. For the OFL, the core problem was that Canada had a "branch plant economy," where fully two-thirds of the one hundred largest manufacturing companies were foreign owned. Due to historically high tariffs, foreign companies had located branch plants in Ontario to serve the domestic market. Canada's manufacturing sector was therefore highly vulnerable to trade liberalization and the "unrestricted capital movements" of multinational corporations. Only the repatriation of the Canadian economy could resolve the problem. While not a "panacea for all the problems of foreign ownership," the OFL favoured bringing "under social ownership certain key resource industries." Building on some of these ideas, at its 1979 convention the OFL adopted a second statement on Economic Nationalism and Foreign

Ownership, which took direct aim at the foreign multinational corporation. It warned that foreign multinational corporations were taking up an increasing proportion of the world's output of manufactured goods. As a result, they "ship capital and investment to where they could get the highest return, regardless of the economic and social chaos they leave in their wake."[51] What was urgently needed were some "ground rules for industry" so that a company wishing to close a factory was "compelled by law to show cause for its decision."

At the same time, the Ontario NDP undertook its own comprehensive review of its economic policy. The Task Force on Manufacturing placed considerable emphasis on state planning, regulation, and public ownership to counter the domination of foreign-owned multinational corporations, which were blamed for underdevelopment and capital flight.[52] The task force went so far as to suggest that "obsolescence of our industries" was "built into the structure of the economy." It then spoke of the value of "public economic levers" such as state planning, including a "reassertion of the Canadian genius for public enterprise." The memory of the essential role played by Canada's Crown corporations during World War II remained very much alive, serving to legitimate state intervention in the economy: that had been "a time of memorable public inventiveness and confidence, and those companies thoroughly out-performed private industry during that crucial period."[53]

Yet the draft report did not go far enough for the Sudbury-area Nickel Belt riding association of Floyd Laughren, Ontario's future Treasurer. For starters, it understated the importance of the resource sector in a provincial industrial strategy: "What is essential is that our primary resources be used as a lever for development and this demands that our resource industries be brought under full public ownership."[54] Backward and forward linkages are "the stuff on which an industrial strategy grows." Indeed, "only major corrective surgery in the form of a determined assault on the bastions of corporate power can begin to turn the corner on economic underdevelopment and high inflation."[55] The riding wanted to see the entire resource sector nationalized: "Either big business owns government or government owns big business. Public ownership is essential if we are to break the monopoly of power presently held by foreign and domestic corporations and build a socialist society based on popular control." The final resolution from the task force, adopted by the NDP's Provincial Council in April 1980, recognized the "fundamental conflict between private and public interests." Accordingly, the party proposed a manufacturing strategy "based upon expanding public enterprise, stimulating domestic industries, and drawing the private sector within the sphere of public economic and social planning."[56] Import replacement would be its primary aim and the proposed industrial policy would build on natural linkages to the province's natural resources. Indeed, departing multinational corporations would be compelled to sell their shuttered factories to Canadian buyers at an arbitrated price.

While Canadian economic nationalism legitimated calls for the regulation of plant closings, the existence of such legislation in Europe proved essential in countering those who suggested that this could not be done in a free market system. The "European model" of regulating plant closings involved substantial worker adjustment measures alongside mandatory disclosure, consultation, and state authorization of industrial closures. In truth, European laws varied considerably from one country to another and they were strengthened over the course of the 1960s and 1970s. Only a few countries, however, went so far as to require government authorization of plant closing decisions, with most opting for compulsory negotiations with unions and works councils. West Germany's Works Constitution Act of 1972, for example, strengthened worker protection by requiring mandatory consultation with works councils before layoffs or closures. Job losses therefore had to be socially justified.[57] Indeed, the principle of job security had been largely accepted across much of Western Europe. As early as 1963, the International Labour Organization (ILO) had recommended that employment termination should not occur "unless there is a valid reason for such termination."[58]

NATIONALIST RESISTANCE TO PLANT SHUTDOWNS

Ontario's economic situation continued to deteriorate in the early 1980s. Twenty-five thousand Ontario workers were laid off in the first nine months of 1980.[59] Chrysler, one of the Big Three automakers, teetered on oblivion. Only a massive government bailout saved it. The "relentless daily pounding" of dismal economic news in 1980 drove "deeper the public's conviction that the economy is in a profound and morose crisis," prompting *Time* magazine to ask on its April 1980 cover: "Is Capitalism Working?"[60] Its own answer was an emphatic yes, but not everyone agreed. That year's OFL policy statement on Shutdowns, Cutbacks and Layoffs painted a bleak economic picture:

> From day to day, week after week the de-industrialization of this province is taking place. It may be a shoe factory in Toronto, a farm equipment plant in Brantford, a newspaper in Ottawa, an auto-parts plant in Windsor, a furniture factory in Cambridge or an electrical plant in Hamilton which suddenly closes its doors or drastically reduces its work force. Thousands upon thousands of jobs have been lost, many never to be replaced as executives in distant corporate suites knock pins representing plants off the maps of their industrial empires like generals in war offices disposing of enemy locations.[61]

Employers needed to justify their plant closing decisions, and if those mills and factories were found to be viable, the union movement believed that the Ontario Development Corporation should take them over. To soften the blow further, displaced workers needed longer advance notice periods, mandatory severance pay, transfer rights to other company operations in the province, wage protection in cases of bankruptcy, and pension security.

Plant closings and layoffs were having a devastating impact on trade unions like the United Steelworkers of America. Unlike the United Auto Workers, which had amalgamated locals that cushioned the impact, the Steelworkers prided themselves in their numerous small stand-alone locals. More often than not, when the plant closed, so too did the union local. Yet merging locals proved to be "politically complicated," according to Hugh Mackenzie, the union's director of research in Canada during these difficult years. He and Leo Gerard, the director of District 6, covering Ontario, had a "running bit of black humour," as they had to negotiate a closure agreement at a major plant (employing more than five hundred workers) every month for two years.[62] It was time consuming: "I mean, we spent all of our time—literally all of our time—arguing severance and pension issues with plants that were closing." Mackenzie recalls that the union had a somewhat stronger hand to play in closures involving companies that had other factories organized by the union. He cites the Steel Company of Canada (Stelco) as an example, as it closed a string of finishing mills in the 1980s: "They basically had to make a deal with us because if they didn't, the guys at Lake Erie [a more modern integrated mill] would stay home and they wouldn't be making any steel at all. It was a pretty soul-destroying time to be involved in that." If they were lucky, they could negotiate preferential hiring rights. Mostly, however, it felt to him like they "were just fighting for scraps on the table." At the end of the day, it "really boils down to get as much as you possibly can . . . that's all you can do." Mackenzie and Gerard literally went "through it over and over and over and over again." Looking back forty years later, Mackenzie realizes that they were "just scrambling" to find "any kind of leverage" they could find.

Another perspective is offered in my interview with Ken Delaney, whose working life in the union movement has been dominated by the plant closing issue. He graduated with a degree in economics and business administration from the University of Windsor and went to work in the research department of the United Auto Workers across the river in Detroit. The UAW was "hiring people with some financial background to advise them on what to do when employers were in financial difficulty. And it was sort of a new thing for unions to do." It was the early 1980s and plants were closing in droves. His year in Solidarity House, however, coincided with the Canadian Auto Workers leaving the

US-based international union. He therefore didn't see a future for himself there, so he applied for a job and got it with the United Steelworkers back in Toronto. Of course, things were bad in Canada too, but the Steelworkers did what they could to protect jobs and people's pensions, even if that meant concession bargaining. To survive, many unions in Canada merged in the face of falling union membership. Delany was critical of this institutional response to the industrial crisis:

> I think it's more accurate to call union mergers acquisitions. Because what really happens is the senior management of the union gets taken care of and the members get delivered to the bigger union. I mean, pardon my cynicism, but I've been around a long time, and that's how the world works. If you want to call that a merger, go ahead and call it a merger, but that's what happens. And unions weren't that good at managing the decline. They weren't that good at shifting, like minimizing fixed costs, trying to have things more in a variable cost, structuring themselves in a way that enabled them to deal with that rise and fall of membership. They weren't. So, a lot of smaller unions just got themselves in financial trouble and they didn't have any choice ... Are workers better represented just because there was a merger or acquisition? No, I don't think so.

The trade union movement understood the early 1980s recession to be "at root, political." Monetarism and supply-side economics were contributing factors in what was seen as a "systematic attempt" to "redistribute wealth, income and power in Canada."[63] Interest rates needed to be lowered and the economy stimulated. At the time, David Wolfe wrote that the recent policy statements of the International Confederation of Free Trade Unions (ICFTU), International Metalworkers Federation (IMF), British Trades Union Congress (TUC), and Canadian Labour Congress all expressed a "consensus around a programme of public sector–led initiatives to get us out of the recession and back on a path of growth." Faced with the "accelerated process of restructuring of the world economy, a shift in the international division of labour," the CLC worried that newly industrialized countries could become "the bastions for an attack on the living standards and trade union rights of North American and European workers."[64] Unions had every reason to worry.

Public calls for government action mounted over the course of the first ten months of 1980. Each new plant closure in Ontario produced sympathetic headlines. A growing chorus of voices insisted that long-term employees deserved more than a generic notice on the factory bulletin board a few weeks before the decision took effect. Trade unionists continued to insist that plant closing decisions needed to be reviewed with full disclosure of financial records. Then Ontario workers began to respond to the closures of their factories by illegally occupying them. The list of occupied plants included Houdaille Bumper in Oshawa, Bendix Automotive in Windsor, Beach Foundry in Ottawa, and Tung-Sol in Bramalea, the last of these located in the Ontario Premier's own riding. The Ontario Federation of Labour mobilized support across the province. A growing number of municipalities agreed to endorse legislation that would require corporations to "justify to a public tribunal any proposed closing."[65] Both opposition parties, the NDP and Liberals, now favoured some form of justification law. In October 1980, the Ontario Federation of Labour organized a big protest rally at Queen's Park, placing dozens of coffins, each representing a closed factory, on the stairs of the legislative building.

Under considerable political pressure, the minority Tory government scrambled to contain the political fallout. It repeatedly rejected the idea of interfering with management rights, fearing that this kind of intervention would drive away needed investment.[66] To placate its critics, the Tory government announced the creation of a Select Committee on Plant Shutdowns and Employee Adjustment to study the problem and report back as soon as possible. From the very outset, then, the justification issue was at the heart of the committee's deliberations. The select committee's rigorous cross-examination of corporate executives and managers is the closest Canada ever came to a public tribunal over plant closures. The questioning was not friendly, given the political urgency of the moment, and corporations were subpoenaed if they refused to provide detailed financial information or to appear. Much of the questioning was focused on the underlying reasons for the closure and how the decision was reached. Corporate executives were also asked if they could live with stricter regulations, comparable to those prevailing in some Western European countries.

One by one, the representatives of the companies were asked their opinion about the possibility that Ontario might pass legislation to compel companies to justify their closure decisions before a public tribunal or administrative board. To a person, they were opposed to the idea. For Armstrong Cork's J. Jordin: "I know I do not have to remind this committee about the fact that Ontario as an investment community is obviously competing with other areas for that same investment dollar." Outboard Marine's Canadian president was more hard-line: "We must address ourselves to ensuring an environment which encourages industrial growth and investment in Canada.... The committee's primary concern must be how to encourage industry to invest in Canada. A favourable and less restrictive environment will provide that incentive. A punitive restrictive and controlled environment will serve only to discourage present and future investors." He suggested that those European countries that passed such legislation, especially Belgium, "have reached the point that industry just will not locate there because of the restrictive legislation."[67] That Ontario was competing against the anti-union right-to-work states in the US Sun Belt was reason enough not to do more.

By contrast, trade unionists spoke passionately in favour of the regulation of plant closing decisions. Day after day, they pointed to the more restrictive legislation found in Sweden, Germany, France, Belgium, Netherlands, and Great Britain. If those countries could do it, why not Canada? Charles Clark, co-director of the Amalgamated Clothing and Textile Workers Union (ACTWU), argued that the "laws of Ontario are simply not enough if we wish to have a stable economy and discourage companies from moving operations elsewhere." Therefore, "as long as a company is making a profit and not losing on its original investment, then surely there should be some compulsion to keep that company in business."[68] The representative from the International Association of Machinists (IAM) was even more adamant, observing: "One thing that stands out is how much further advanced they are in Europe in terms of public disclosure, advance information and the actual requirement to sit down with the workers' representatives." The IAM insisted, "We believe this total lack of accountability on the part of foreign corporations would be a disgrace to a banana republic."[69]

The two worst examples of corporate callousness examined by the select committee were Essex Wire, a subsidiary of United Technologies, which closed its plant in Dunnville, a tiny community on the Niagara Peninsula, and Bendix Automotive in Windsor. In the first instance, the committee had to resort to a Speaker's warrant to even get the company to appear before it.[70] Essex was a classic runaway plant, leaving Windsor for Dunnville in 1961, and was now moving production of automotive wire harnesses to St. Thomas (another small industrial town in southwestern Ontario) and the United States. The mostly female workforce in Dunnville received low wages and had no pension, but they were unionized. The UAW noted that the corporation was one of the toughest the union had ever dealt with.[71] Bob Mackenzie called this "the best example" he had "ever seen of colonialism, God-damned near slavery, in terms of how an international corporation deals with a company in this country." Even Tory members were swayed.

The select committee's exchanges with the executives and lawyers of United Technologies were among the most heated. The company explained it closed five North American plants in 1979 and another six in 1980, including the one in Dunnville. It wasn't personal: these decisions were made "regardless of whether the plant is in US or in Canada."[72] When the committee continued to push the issue, Bill Trachsel, the lawyer for United Technologies, complained: "If we went around and asked people which plants they wanted closed, we would still have 43." To this, Bob Mackenzie guffawed: "There is a little thing like a border." To which another company executive retorted: "There are people like yourselves in state governments throughout the United States who have exactly the same situation." This answer did not please anyone on the committee. Several elected members questioned the "morality" of the company's actions. To this, Martel acidly commented on the "attitude displayed in response to some of the questioning . . . put forward is as if you were dealing with the country bumpkins, we being the country bumpkins." Later, an obviously frustrated company official sputtered: "If you want to know why we shut a plant down, we are trying to tell you. If you listen to us we will tell you. We have nothing to hide. We are trying to tell you why we did something. We thought that is what you are here to hear."

These prickly conversations formed the basis of the Interim Report, which sketched out the issues of concern that were emerging from the hearings, including the committee's recommendation that the government immediately proceed with mandatory severance pay. It recognized that "the decision to close has been a company monopoly," then asked if there was a role for government in requiring the public justification of these decisions.[73] After the Christmas holidays, it heard from other "umbrella groups" such as business associations and unions. These presentations spanned the political spectrum from Bob White's presentation on behalf of the United Auto Workers to that of Canadian Federation of Independent Business. For its part, the Ontario Mining Association argued that industrial closures were "as inevitable as the future," so the government should stick to mitigating the social effects.[74] But before the select committee could issue its final report in February 1981, the Tories called an election, which they promptly won with a majority of seats. The committee was abruptly terminated and the radical idea of restricting plant closings was once again shelved. Outraged, the NDP members of the committee went ahead and published their own final report, entitled *Job Security: The Unwritten Report of the Select Committee on Plant Shutdowns and Employee Adjustment*, which challenged the idea that layoffs and plant closings were inevitable.[75]

CONCLUSION

During the 1970s and early 1980s, plant closings came to symbolize Canada's economic dependence on US-based multinational corporations, which was now blamed for deindustrializing Canada. The deindustrialization thesis thus offered a nationalist explanation for the industrial crisis, shining a critical light on the decision-making of US-based multinational corporations. What constituted an adequate return on investment was found to be relative to the expanding choices available to capital. With the formation of a select committee of the legislature, employers found themselves forced to participate and open up their books, on pain of subpoena. Ontario's select committee was ready to recommend compulsory financial disclosure and negotiation over plant closing decisions when the Tories called an election and dissolved the legislature.

In the years that followed, the OFL and the NDP continued to fight for tough new legislation.[76] Thus, when the 1985 election saw the end of forty-two years of Tory rule in Ontario, instead of propping up another minority Tory government, the Liberals and NDP reached an accord on a range of issues that David Peterson's Liberals committed to implementing in exchange for NDP support. Within the NDP caucus, Ross McClellan set up a process to negotiate the accord whereby the group came up with "a big list of priority issues" and then he whittled it down to thirty-two or thirty-three, bringing the list back to them. The Liberals accepted almost everything the NDP proposed. McClellan suggested, however, that much of the NDP executive was strongly opposed to the idea of an accord: "The Party went really nuts. The provincial secretary was running around with a button that said 'Bob Rae is a Liberal.' That was our provincial secretary."[77]

One of the issues agreed to was mandatory justification. Two years later, the Liberal government still hadn't delivered on this commitment. What happened instead is that Ontario's Standing Committee on Resource Development, chaired by Nickel Belt NDP MPP Floyd Laughren, issued a Report on Plant Closures and Community Adjustment in 1987. Committee members had reviewed the earlier recommendations of the select committee and held a new set of hearings. The old battle lines between labour and business remained firmly entrenched, but opinion on the committee itself was much more fractured than had been the case a few years earlier. Its final report noted: "Perhaps the issue which caused the most controversy during the Committee's deliberations was the question of whether an employer should be required to justify the closing of a plant before some kind of tribunal or public body."[78] A narrow majority found that a justification board would be "an unworkable concept and would be harmful to Ontario in the long run," favouring instead a process of consultation rather than authorization. Two minority reports disagreed. A group of dissenting Tories felt that even this middle ground went too far; whereas NDP MPPs Bob Mackenzie and Bud Wildman argued that the report did not go nearly far enough. Mackenzie and Wildman insisted that a public audit board should hold hearings and examine the financial records of companies closing plants:

> We believe that even where a closure or layoff is found to be justified, the employer must bear its share of the social costs. But where a closure is found to be unjustified, then the corporation must be made to pay more, including some appropriate measure of damages. In addition, we believe that the government has a role to play in trying to prevent the closure by examining all reasonable alternatives to the shutdown.[79]

My interview with Sam Gindin, the research director for the Canadian Auto Workers, reveals much about the political limits of resistance. The 1980s were a "stubborn period" for the union, as it initially refused to bend to the demands of employers for concessions and fought plant closures with every weapon available. The Canadian auto workers were protected to some extent by the Auto Pact (with its production guarantees), which taught the union that "you had to have rules [imposed] on companies, you didn't have to bribe them." While direct action won better legislation and improved severance packages, it still "wasn't an answer to the problems. You can take over plants, but you're taking over things that nobody wants." Taking over what capital shucks off was not a long-term strategy, Gindin concluded: it was more a protest. Even so, it was one that "kept the union healthy, people were fighting. And they knew somebody had their back, even if there wasn't a solution."[80] Eventually, even the CAW came to the conclusion that resistance wasn't enough: "And that was one of the real difficulties. What do you do?"[81] The NDP was grappling with the same question.

National Rubber Company, Toronto: Eugenia Tome at trimming station behind the multi-daylight press, 1994.
Photo by Peter MacCallum.

2

THE HAMILTON CHALLENGE

> Perhaps the principal dilemma of the New Democratic Party since its formation has been to devise economic policy that speaks at once to the fundamental weaknesses of the Canadian economy, the roots of injustice in capitalist economics, and the needs of local communities, and is at the same time publicly saleable.
> —RICHARD ALLEN, Ontario NDP Convention, 1988[1]

With the failure of the old Keynesian macro-economic mechanisms to control stagflation, the political and economic conditions were in place for the rise of the neoliberal order in the 1980s.[2] British Prime Minister Margaret Thatcher crushed the militant National Union of Mineworkers over 1984–85, remaking the United Kingdom in the process; and US President Ronald Reagan slashed the highest tax rate for the wealthiest from 70 percent to just 28 percent.[3] Gregory Inwood has called Canada's Royal Commission on Economic Union a "switch-point mechanism," as its August 1985 final report prompted a "historic change of direction for Canada," by recommending that Canada embrace free trade with the United States.[4] Brian Mulroney's federal Tories, first elected in 1984, promptly began negotiations with the United States, which culminated in the 1987 Free Trade Agreement.[5] Free trade quickly turned into a monumental political battle, but one the labour movement ultimately lost in 1988.

While the emerging neoliberal order increasingly bent Canadian politics towards its will, there was still political room for alternative futures in 1980s Ontario. Political scientists call this transitional period "post-Keynesianism," and in Ontario at least, it stretched from 1985, when forty-two years of Tory rule came to an abrupt end with the NDP-Liberal Accord that saw the Liberals govern with a minority of seats for two years, and through the Liberal (1987–90) and NDP (1990–95) majorities. Neoliberalism only fully triumphed with the return of a reborn hard-right Tory party led by Mike Harris in 1995 under the banner of the "Common Sense Revolution."[6] But its growing influence could be seen throughout this transitional period. Even so, this interregnum was a time of experimentation, as the Ontario Liberals and NDP attempted to forge an alternative growth strategy for the province. As we will see, communitarianism offered progressive politicians a consensual language and a philosophy seemingly fit for the times.

Thus, when Richard Allen, the MPP for Hamilton West, stood before six hundred delegates gathered at the 1988 Ontario NDP convention in my hometown of Thunder Bay to talk about a new approach to economic issues, he signalled to those present that it was time for the party to set aside left-nationalism in favour of communitarianism. Gone was the old emphasis on American branch plants and foreign ownership. Gone, too, were the policy prescriptions of state planning, regulation, and public ownership. Instead, Allen told delegates that ever since he was first elected in a by-election in 1982, he had been struck by "a general failure to bring provincial economic policy down out of the stratosphere." He urged the convention to anchor "economic abstractions" in local community. As he saw the problem:

> [It] was not that [the party's] concepts and policies were wrong, but that they were not developed or applied in a way that local communities could understand their relevance to their immediate problems—perhaps more to the point, policy was not seen to be generated out of their local experience, and we were not seen as a provincial party to be participating in the struggle to resolve local economic problems.[7]

The framing of economic problems as local, at a time of global economic integration and capital flight, reflected growing ambivalence towards top-down, state-centred approaches within some sections of the NDP. Many social democratic and progressive parties around the world were profoundly influenced by the post-materialist politics of the New Left, especially by the 1980s as the baby boom generation established themselves in politics.[8]

Communitarianism offered a more consensual approach to economic issues than the confrontational class politics of left-nationalism. Allen shared the story of the "Hamilton Challenge," a community-driven economic envisioning process that he had initiated along with the two other NDP MPPs from the city, Bob Mackenzie and Brian Charlton; Allen was its driving force. Similar consensus-building "challenges" had also been issued by the party in Windsor and Sudbury. In Hamilton, it took the form of fifteen consultative meetings between October 1984 and March 1985 that brought together small groups of stakeholders to talk about the future of the city. The first exploratory meeting, for example, involved major industrial employers such as Westinghouse, Stelco, and Dofasco. These small conversations culminated in a one-day community conference and a final report, entitled *Challenge to Hamilton*. According to Allen, what was needed was not only "a plan but a process" that could be applied elsewhere.

Formerly a historian at McMaster University, Allen had spent much of his career studying the history of the social gospel, which aimed to apply Christian ethics to the social problems of the day. He remained personally rooted in this reformist tradition.[9] Allen's communitarianism thus originated in a long history of middle-class Christian activism in Canada, which had a sizeable influence on the NDP and its predecessor, the CCF. Left-wing Methodist and United Church ministers, from the CCF's first federal leader, J. S. Woodsworth, to the NDP's first one, Tommy Douglas, had long spoken in moralistic terms about social inequality alongside the Marxian class analysis of labour socialism.[10] There was, therefore, a certain ideological confluence between this longer social tradition and the localism of a younger generation of secular baby boomers influenced by the communitarianism of much of the New Left. Canada's New Leftists "envisioned a decentralized society, operated largely by self-managed communities."[11] They therefore differed from left-nationalists, which is why I make a clear distinction between the two.

The purging of the Waffle faction from the Ontario NDP meant that the next generation of party leaders would be those who did not strongly embrace Canadian left-nationalism in the late 1960s and early 1970s. Bob Rae, elected Ontario NDP leader in 1982, was a case in point. The son of a diplomat, he was an internationalist at heart. In fact, at the time of our interview, he was Canada's ambassador to the United Nations—a job he was in many ways born for. After making a name for himself in federal politics, Rae set a new consensual tone in the provincial party. His 1983 speech on "Jobs, Justice and Recovery" in Hamilton thus called for "true partnership" on the economy. With the postwar compromise (such as it was) in tatters with the end of the long boom, Rae tapped into growing calls for a new social contract (something we will discuss in chapter 9) by drawing together labour and management into "new forms of cooperation in economic life."[12] Ontario must become "Atari planners as well as smokestack planners," he reasoned: it was "our challenge in Hamilton."

DEINDUSTRIALIZING HAMILTON

With its two giant integrated steel mills lining the harbourfront as well as its finishing mills and foundries, Hamilton was very much Canada's Steel City.[13] What is less well known is that it was also a major centre of secondary manufacturing and that many of these other plants employed mostly women. The city's economy started to erode in the 1960s with the growing problem of runaway shops. Labour-intensive sectors such as textiles and electrical products were the first to relocate to smaller towns in search of a cheaper, preferably non-union, workforce. Hamilton women, therefore, bore the brunt of early job losses. For example, soon after it received a regional development grant from the federal government in 1972 to open up a new factory in Amherst, Nova Scotia, Aerovox closed its recently unionized textile mill in Hamilton.[14] Westinghouse likewise closed its Hamilton switch and gear plant in 1980, displacing seven hundred workers, when it relocated the work to several plants in small-town Ontario.[15] In response, the left-wing United Electrical (UE) workers union filed an unfair labour practice complaint against the company, as it had failed to disclose the decision during collective bargaining and had thus bargained in bad faith. The UE won its case, but the company was allowed to proceed with the move.[16] The Tokyo round of the General Agreement on Tariffs and Trade concluded in 1979, reducing tariffs an additional 40 percent over the next eight years. This change, combined with the signing of the Free Trade Agreement with the United States in 1987, meant that labour-intensive sectors were under extreme competitive pressure to lower wages or go out of business.

Hamilton's male-dominated steel industry and iron foundries were also hit hard during the 1980s. According to Ken Delaney from the United Steelworkers, "because the steel industry went through ungodly technological change at the time, steel mills were modernizing and cutting literally more than 50 percent of their workforce and staying in business. And then other mills were closing on top of that." As a result, the Steel Company of Canada (Stelco) and Dofasco laid off large numbers of workers as the mills modernized. A two-day conference on the steel layoffs, held in March 1983 in the auditorium of the city's Steelworkers Centre, brought together trade unionists and left-nationalist intellectuals like Mel Watkins.[17] A panel on the Fight for Jobs in Hamilton featured United Steelworkers of America Local 1005's fightback campaign at Stelco. Other workshops focused on the day-to-day struggles of job loss. Soon thereafter, Stelco announced the closure of its Hamilton finishing mill, the Canada Works, displacing another 750 workers. The company made the closure announcement only after herding its employees onto buses without explanation and driving them to the Royal Botanical Gardens in Burlington, where they were unloaded, told the bad news, and driven back to the plant.[18] You can't make this up.

In its submission to the Royal Commission on the Economic Union and Development Prospects for Canada in October 1983, the Social Planning and Research Council of Hamilton and District noted that nearly ten thousand manufacturing jobs had been lost in just a year. Unemployment in the city had risen from 6.5 percent in 1981 to 11.8 percent in 1982, peaking at 15 percent. Those displaced from the Canada Works were therefore entering an unforgiving job market. For the local social planning council, the policy prescription for mass unemployment was a combination of a national guaranteed annual income, new investments in worker retraining, and the creation of a network of community development corporations along the lines of those found in the United States. Indeed, "the Hamilton area provides a graphic illustration of the potential benefits of a Community Development Corporation."[19]

The Hamilton and District Labour Council had a very different understanding of the unfolding industrial crisis and what to do about it. Its submission to the royal commission identified the problem as not so much unemployment itself, but its underlying causes. "With plants moving to the Third World Countries that ban fundamental Trade Union Rights," the labour council directed its wrath at the "global strategies of the TransNational Corporation, the international monopolies. Any examination of a future for Canada and our people must recognize the role the TransNationals have planned for our Country. This is at the root of de-industrialization, the destruction of secondary manufacturing."[20] Its condemnation extended to those political leaders who spoke in terms of "'sunrise' and 'sunset' industries," as they had already "abdicated our base of heavy industry and extraction to the elusive dream of 'high-tech' as the production base of the future." While the language of the submission was rough and idiosyncratic at times, the thrust of its political critique is a good example of the ways that investment nationalism was infused with class analysis in the labourism of the period. Indeed, the Hamilton and District Labour Council warned of the development of:

global industrial Feudal State, where those beyond the "pale" exist in semi-poverty and provide markets for the "high tech" produced commodities. For those essential to "high-tech" production there will be security and comfort under the patronage of the global royalty of the transnationals. We believe that the majority of Canadian will live beyond the pale of this new feudal system and that the trends which will shape the future are at work today.

The brief went on to speak of the need to resist multinational corporations or risk being reduced to the "techno-peasantry," those we would now call precarious or the left-behind. To that end, the labour council called for a Canadian Development Fund to "create" homegrown secondary manufacturing as well as public ownership. Foreign takeovers of Canadian firms needed to be stopped and companies closing plants should be penalized. "This nightmare is not inevitable," the labour council insisted, if the power of the state was used to turn the international tide against these corporations. In content and tone, these two submissions could not be more different, even though both briefs originated from progressive circles in the city.

Though the differences between the social planning and labour councils in nearby Toronto were not so stark, they are worth exploring further for what they tell us about the evolving economic thinking of those on Ontario's social democratic left. The Labour Council of Metropolitan Toronto used the opportunity of the royal commission to offer an alternative economic strategy. For labour, the central goal must be full employment and "the principle of democratic economic planning" at the local level.[21] Unlike its counterpart in Hamilton, Toronto's labour council recommended worker buyouts as a viable strategy of "preventing unnecessary plant closures," as well as an industrial land bank to ensure that manufacturing industries continued to have a place within the transforming city.[22] Like Hamilton, however, it faulted the "hypermobility of capital" for the deindustrialization of the city. "We do not accept the inevitability of the erosion of major industrial sectors of the Metro economy," it declared.[23]

Much like its Hamilton counterpart, the Social Planning Council of Metropolitan Toronto emphasized economic democracy and community economic development in its substantial policy brief, authored by a committee headed by David Wolfe, who became a senior economic advisor to the NDP government, and that included Chuck Rachlis, head of NDP Research at Queen's Park, who would subsequently work for Bob Rae in the Premier's Office. Their submission therefore offers some insight into the early thinking of key NDP policy advisors. "Canada has undergone and will continue to undergo enormous changes in the structure of its economy," it began: a new international division of labour was causing the "global reorganization of production on a massive scale."[24] So far, Canadian workers were paying a disproportionate price for the changes underway. In 1982, Canada's unemployment rate was 11 percent, whereas the OECD average was only 7.1 percent. In fact, Canada was ranked twentieth of twenty-four OECD countries, with only the UK, Belgium, Turkey, and Spain having higher rates of unemployment. However, the social planning council seemed more concerned, at times, with the "bureaucratic and inflexible state" than with departing capital, prompting a strong preference for local participatory approaches to economic development whenever possible. In these twin proposals we see early signs of a core tension, which I would attribute to divergent class interests among Ontario social democrats, that will run throughout this book.

Given the scale of industrial restructuring, and a weakened trade union movement, the Hamilton Challenge represented a sustained effort on the part of the NDP to bridge political and economic divides in Ontario's Steel City. The resulting report recommended a comprehensive community-based approach to economic renewal. Indeed, the three local NDP MPPs concluded that "community must be viewed as an economic whole."[25] Chief among their recommendations was the creation of a Community Development Investment Fund to assist worker buyouts of troubled factories, as well as a Community Economic Renewal Unit, enabling representatives from business, labour, local governments, and community groups to work collaboratively on economic planning. Not everyone, however, was impressed by the new emphasis. Talk of a single community interest risked submerging very real class divides. Thus, the Hamilton and District Labour Council's Full Employment Committee strongly objected to the Hamilton Challenge's recommendation in favour of worker cooperatives.[26] For the labour council, industrial restructuring must be resisted, not accommodated to. The response to the NDP's Hamilton Challenge was thus bifurcated between those who sought a cross-class consensus and those who believed that the class divide was real and growing.

THE TURN TOWARDS WORKER OWNERSHIP

On 1 January 1983, the Canadian Conference of Catholic Bishops released its "Ethical Reflections on the Economic Crisis," which spoke of the growing unfairness and "deepening moral disorder" of capitalism. The bishops went so far as to blame government policies for placing "the burden of the economic decline on the shoulders of workers, unemployed, and low income people."[27] It then cited worker ownership as a promising alternative economic model.[28] Not surprisingly, the bishops' statement sparked heated debate in Canada about the morality of capitalism and the role of today's church. By all accounts, the statement resonated within the NDP. Some members, such as theologian Gregory Baum, saw the bishops' statement as nothing less than a new articulation of social democracy: "It is important for the NDP to find a language that suggests alternative models of economic development and at the same time avoids a terminology that sounds like centralizing socialism, a form of organization that has produced totalitarianism."[29] Former Saskatchewan Premier Allan Blakeney agreed, suggesting that "if you want to hear people talking about progressive ideas and how to reshape society, don't bother going to a NDP or union meeting, go down to a Catholic parish meeting."[30]

Otherwise, Canadian proponents of worker ownership mostly looked to the United States for inspiration. Richard Allen, for example, closely followed the grassroots efforts to save steel mills from closing in what was becoming known as the US Rust Belt. His personal papers, housed at McMaster University, include press clippings from the Tri-State Conference on Steel, formed by a coalition of local unions, church groups, and community activists in 1979 to stop divestment from Pittsburgh, Pennsylvania, and Youngstown, Ohio. Among other things, it developed an alternative economic plan for the troubled region.[31] In 1984, the Allegheny Conference on Community Development released a blueprint for revitalizing the regional economy that emphasized the need to diversify out of "sunset" industries. The Monongahela Valley, which extends south from downtown Pittsburgh, also saw the emergence of the Denominational Ministry Strategy, formed in 1979 by radical Lutheran and Episcopal pastors, which committed itself to direct action. Most ambitiously, perhaps, the Steel Valley Authority, formed by nine steel towns in 1986, used its power of eminent domain to threaten to expropriate closing mills unless they were put up for sale or their workers given the option to evaluate the feasibility of worker ownership.[32]

There were two competing visions for worker ownership in North America. On the one hand, there was the democratic vision, grounded in the cooperative movement, where workers controlled the companies that they owned. On the other hand, there was the far more common but non-democratic version where workers' ownership shares were held in trust, thereby preventing them from actually controlling the companies they owned. American employee stock ownership plans (ESOPs) were mostly in the second category. ESOPs were the brainchild of Louis Kelso, an investment banker from San Francisco, who had been promoting the idea since the mid-1950s. One gains a sense of the man in his correspondence with UAW president Leonard Woodcock, after the two met in Detroit in 1973. Before that meeting, Woodcock was briefed about Kelso's "mumbo jumbo" and told that his ideas were often confusing and included the "noblest of sentiments" and "highly reactionary notions."[33] Kelso was nothing if not eccentric. In one letter, Kelso immodestly referred to his employee ownership scheme as "the only effective technique devised since the Homestead Acts for building capital ownership into employees without taking anything out of their paychecks, while assisting corporations to finance their growth and accomplish other conventional corporate objectives."[34] For Kelso, ESOPs promised nothing short of the rebirth of American capitalism. His lofty rhetoric resonated in Washington and his proposal enjoyed cross-party appeal.

The United States Congress approved generous tax credits for ESOPs as part of its pension reforms of 1974, giving employers good reason to sell a stake in their companies to employees. Thereafter, employee ownership took off in the US, expanding from 300 firms in 1974 to 7,000 by 1990.[35] Only rarely did this translate into real worker control, however. Instead, there was a litany of "notorious abuses" by employers who used ESOPs as a tax shelter, a source of financing, or simply as an effective method to extract massive wage and benefit concessions from their employees.[36] It was not unusual to see wages and benefits rolled back 20 or 30 percent in exchange for company shares. Occasionally, workers' pension plans were terminated in favour of a share in the company. This was a high-risk move, to say the least. Whereas a defined pension was a legal commitment by an employer to pay a regular benefit to employees, backed up to a certain extent by the state, there was no such guarantee under an ESOP. The fundamental problem with Kelso-inspired ESOPs was what happened in case of bankruptcy, plant closure, merger, or acquisition: workers could lose their jobs, their savings, and their retirement funds in one devastating blow.

Despite its problems, ESOPs offered trade unionists a financial and legal mechanism to potentially save their closing plants. As companies with Employee Stock Ownership Plans were much less likely to relocate their operations elsewhere, this geographic anchoring became an important selling point in the face of capital flight. Worker buyouts of closing plants, however, were just a small proportion of ESOPs. One estimate suggested that only 200 of the first 8,000 ESOPs fell into this category.[37] The risks involved in a worker buyout were considerable. Yet, in their zeal for employee or community ownership, community activists sometimes failed to recognize these pitfalls. Jeremy Brecher, for example, blamed the union for the failure of workers at Century Brass in Connecticut to gamble their savings to save it from shutting. Whereas the union had a "narrow definition of class struggle," he preferred "a broader orientation of local community versus capital."[38]

Brecher's framing of the struggle as one pitting capital against community owed much to the influential 1982 book *The Deindustrialization of America*, by radical economists Barry Bluestone and Bennett Harrison, which was originally commissioned by an alliance of US trade unions and advocacy groups fighting industrial closures. Given that the postwar economic hegemony of the United States was being heavily eroded, Bluestone and Harrison singled out capital flight as the main driver of industrial closures. Community abandonment was also emphasized, offering a moral argument against plant closings. As Bluestone came out of the same industrial policy circles as Ira Magaziner, he favoured labour-management partnership and worker ownership.[39] This variant of the deindustrialization thesis resonated on both sides of the Canada-US border by the mid-1980s, supplanting the earlier left-nationalist formulation.[40] It was thus Barry Bluestone, the son of UAW vice-president Irving Bluestone, himself an advocate of worker ownership, who delivered the keynote lecture at the left-wing Canadian Centre for Policy Alternatives' conference in Toronto on Fighting Deindustrialization in February 1983.[41]

Even so, there were few cases of worker buyouts in Canada before the 1990s. Unlike the US, the Canadian tax system did not offer much financial incentive for companies to sell their plants to their workforce or for workers to take the risk. The worker buyout in 1972 of the closed paper mill in Témiscaming in northwestern Quebec was, therefore, exceptional.[42] Thus, when the departing company tried to float its logs past the closed mill to another mill down the Ottawa River, the river was blockaded by fishing boats for five weeks, forcing the company to sell the mill to its employees, and Tembec was born. Several Quebec businessmen, notably Joe Mason, were integrally involved, as were the federal and provincial governments, which contributed loans and loan guarantees.[43] Tembec served as an inspiring example for others, especially after the National Film Board produced a documentary on the successful effort.[44]

When Outboard Marine, a US-based multinational, announced that it would close its Pioneer Chainsaw plant in Peterborough, Ontario, in 1977, it wasn't long before Tembec's Joe Mason came calling. Pioneer Chainsaw was an iconic Canadian consumer brand, so the announced closing made national headlines. The factory's six hundred workers proposed to buy out the company and there was strong public support, especially after a feasibility study concluded that it was a viable operation. Mason proposed an arrangement where he would control 51 percent of the new company for his own modest investment and workers would own 24 percent in exchange for a pay cut of one dollar per hour. On this basis, the plant was reopened and did well until the Swedish multinational corporation Electrolux entered the picture, offering to buy the shares at a premium. Mason was enthusiastic about the offer, but the United Steelworkers representative on the board opposed the sale, arguing: "Why sell out and go back into the same situation you were in before . . . once bitten by a multinational is enough."[45] The union continued to oppose the sale when it came before the Foreign Investment Review Agency (FIRA), which approved the transaction after Electrolux promised to keep the plant open for the next five years. The money on offer was too good to pass up and local union members agreed to sell one-third of their shares, eventually selling the rest to Electrolux. Like clockwork, five years later, Electrolux shut the Peterborough plant, confirming the limitations of minority employee ownership.

Despite these challenges, there was growing interest in worker ownership as a vehicle for achieving industrial democracy in Canada. The Ontario NDP endorsed worker cooperatives in 1980 and the party's organ, the *Ontario New Democrat*, ran a series of articles on the subject in the years that followed.[46] In November 1982, for example, Judith Forrestal asserted worker cooperatives were "practical alternatives to work place instability" and should be a component of the party's industrial strategy.[47] Thirty-four Canadians had recently toured worker cooperatives in Europe and a new periodical, *Worker Co-ops*, was being published. Then in June 1983, the Labour Council of Metropolitan Toronto produced a report entitled *A Time for Public Leadership*, which recommended worker buyouts to save industrial jobs. The United Steelworkers of America likewise embraced the concept. Elected in 1984, Lynn Williams, the first Canadian-born president of the international union, was a strong advocate of employee buyouts as a last resort to keep struggling steel mills open.[48]

Given all of the above, Richard Allen was enthusiastic about the transformative potential of worker ownership, so when opportunity arose, he threw himself into the effort to save a Hamilton factory from closing. Established in 1912, Canadian Porcelain was Canada's only maker of high-voltage electricity insulators, selling its porcelain to hydro commissions across Canada. However, in the early 1980s, the company struggled due to dumping by its foreign competitors. Lapp Industries in the US was one of the worst offenders. By the time that Canadian Porcelain won a ruling in its favour from the Canadian Import Tribunal in early January 1985 and new retaliatory tariffs were introduced, the company had been forced into bankruptcy.[49] Ninety-one members of the Aluminum, Brick and Glass Workers International Union were displaced as a result. It could have ended there, as it usually does, but Allen and Christians for a Cooperative Society initiated a community campaign to reopen the closed plant as a worker cooperative. In this, Allen found a strong ally in local union president Bill Thompson.

The first step in the campaign to save Canadian Porcelain was to raise funds for a full feasibility study. To that end, a trust fund was set up and several prominent businessmen in the city including the vice-president of operations for Westinghouse, as well as the Catholic bishop, agreed to sit as trustees.[50] The resulting financial appeal was distributed to thousands of households via 240 Hamilton-area church congregations. In making the group's pitch, Allen tapped into the long history of Christian cooperative activism:

New occasions teach new duties! The gospel brings new life in many ways—and resurrecting a viable plant and involving workers in new challenges is surely one. Whatever one thinks of the recent statements of the Canadian Bishops, their advocacy of workers' ownership stands in longstanding Catholic tradition, the most renowned of which are the fabulously successful Mondragon industries in northern Spain and the Maritime cooperatives founded by Moses Coady in Canada.

By any measure, the community campaign was a huge success. The Hamilton Chamber of Commerce endorsed the campaign, as did the Rotary Club, Kiwanis, and other groups hardly known for their pro-worker activism. Politicians from all three parties, including the federal Tory MP for the area, got on the local bandwagon, and donations flooded in.

The Canadian Porcelain campaign generated considerable media attention not only in Hamilton but across Canada. If successful, it would have been the third worker buyout (if we include a string of breweries in northern Ontario in 1979) of a major factory in English-speaking Canada. The editorial boards of the *Hamilton Spectator* and the *Toronto Star* endorsed the effort, as did other media outlets. Allen was in full organizing mode during the first half of 1985, when his constituency office became the de facto campaign headquarters. In his handwritten notes from the time, he scribbled that "everybody is calling everybody else about it."[51] Allen also urged Andy Brandt, Ontario's Tory Minister of Industry and Trade, to support the campaign. "Time is too short," he argued; "resources are slim, feasibility studies are difficult to arrange—and costly."[52] Many of the employees at Canadian Porcelain did not own their own homes, and so their only equity was their pension plan. "But who would advise that?" Allen asked. Brandt quickly came through, agreeing to match the money raised by the community for the feasibility study. Brandt told the media that the community's plan for a worker-owned Canadian Porcelain "was a model" that "could be transferred to other Ontario cities faced with plant closures and bankruptcies."⁵³ Things were moving forward quickly. "Already we are getting results, Canadian Porcelain has become a byword," reported the chairperson of Christians for a Cooperative Society.⁵⁴

The resulting feasibility study found that a worker-owned enterprise was, in fact, viable, thanks to the retaliatory tariffs in effect. Sufficient financing was then lined up to submit a $1.1 million bid. After it was turned down by the receivers, the group was preparing a higher second offer when it was informed that a $1.3 million bid from Lapp Industries had been swiftly accepted.⁵⁵ "They were cut off in mid negotiation," recalled Allen.⁵⁶ It left a bitter aftertaste in their mouths, not least because American-owned Lapp had been one of the reasons Canadian Porcelain went into bankruptcy in the first place. Canadian Porcelain workers naturally feared that Lapp would reduce the plant to a warehouse for products manufactured elsewhere once the temporary tariffs clocked out.

On 3 April 1985, Bob Rae and Richard Allen met with Canadian Porcelain workers; Rae told them that "companies should be required to justify plant shutdowns to a government tribunal and offer employees the chance to buy them out." He took the opportunity to propose a $30 million fund to promote and support worker buyouts and cooperatives. Rae then said it was "an idea whose time has come."⁵⁷ In the accompanying press release, the NDP declared that workers and the community had been well on their way to saving the plant until they were thwarted at the last minute: "Government should be playing a leadership role by helping people protect their own jobs. Our proposals will help potential buy-outs get started. The Employee and Community Ownership Fund will provide technical and financial support to workers and community groups to purchase and upgrade plants, and to establish new operations."⁵⁸

At this point, the fight shifted to Ottawa, as the sale had to be confirmed by the federal government under the Foreign Investment Review Act. Since coming to power in 1984, Brian Mulroney's Tories had not rejected any of the six hundred applications that came before it.⁵⁹ In fact, Canadian Porcelain would be the last case reviewed by the federal agency, as the federal Tories had declared Canada open for business. Under these circumstances, the Tories were unlikely to intervene.[60] Nevertheless, the *Hamilton Spectator* and the *Toronto Star* urged the federal Tories to block the sale, noting the broad community support for the workers' co-op.[61] The editors of the *Toronto Star* argued that the proposed cooperative was "the kind of imaginative response we need to the threat of plant closures and unnecessary foreign takeovers."[62] The Hamilton conference of the United Church of Canada said much the same.

In the end, the sale was approved after Lapp Industries promised in writing to maintain previous production levels and to invest another $3.4 million into plant modernization.[63] FIRA's decision sparked much media commentary and community reflection. As a journalist at the *Hamilton Spectator* observed: "Their community-backed struggle has created a wealth of lessons for the future. Their fight was a six-month education crash course—for the workers, for the ecumenical group which backed them, for politicians of all stripes, and for the community itself."[64] Despite the assurances, just as workers feared, Lapp Industries closed its newly acquired Hamilton plant in 1988, two and a half years after acquiring it, shutting it five days into a strike for higher pay. As the company employed fewer than fifty workers at the end, it was not even required to provide severance pay or form a joint labour-management adjustment committee to assist those who lost their jobs.[65] While the lessons learnt from the Canadian Porcelain fiasco were debated for years to come, it served to solidify NDP support for worker ownership as an integral part of its wider response to the industrial crisis.

COMMUNITY AND SECTORAL WORKER ADJUSTMENT

The failure of Canada's highly fragmented adjustment regime to effectively respond to the closing of Canadian Porcelain prompted Richard Allen to dive into the world of worker adjustment, training, and community economic development. In Canada, worker adjustment and training were a shared responsibility between the federal and provincial governments, though the feds historically took the lead with their unemployment insurance program and national network of employment centres. It also formed the Industrial Adjustment Services (IAS) in 1963 after six hundred asbestos miners in Thetford Mines, Quebec, were abruptly laid off and Quebec initiated its own system of placement committees.[66] The IAS oversaw the formation of joint labour-management adjustment committees in cases of mass layoff or plant closure. The committees were voluntary, however, and required both labour and management to agree to participate. Typically, these joint committees created a skills inventory of those displaced, offered job search workshops, and then contacted area employers to help place them into new jobs or retraining programs. Their ad hoc nature, and the consequent lack of experience of members, could limit their effectiveness, as did the fact that only half of mass terminations of fifty or more workers (the minimum threshold in Ontario for advance notice) formed such adjustment committees.[67]

Despite its limitations, the Canadian adjustment model was heralded as a success story in the United States in the mid-1980s. It was flexible, quick, inexpensive, and, most importantly, voluntary. American politicians also liked the fact that the IAS's entire complement of sixty professional staff, almost all located in regional offices, served as "advisors, consultants, catalysts, expediters, facilitators, and sources of information to employers, unions and workers in setting up joint labor-management approaches for worker dislocations due to technological and other industrial changes." There was no big bureaucracy and companies were not compelled to do anything they didn't want to. Impressed, the US secretary of labour, a Republican, appointed a task force to examine the issue:

> Of all the foreign endeavours studied, the quick response capability of the 25-year-old Canadian Industrial Adjustment Service (IAS) appeared to offer the highest degree of replicability for the United States. The Task Force recognized, however, that the Canadian approach is conducted in a different framework.[68]

The dangling caveat at the end is noteworthy, as the Canadian system of adjustment was tied to advance notice legislation in many provinces. Only a couple of US states had passed similar legislation, even though research had firmly established that the period between the closure announcement and the last shift was critically important for worker adjustment. After all, this was when displaced workers were still together and easily reachable. Once the plant closed, workers dispersed. To learn more, the US Secretary of Labour and the National Governors Association invited state governors to send representatives to an orientation session on the "Canadian approach" to adjustment. Due to the "remarkable interest from Governors," two workshops had to be given to accommodate thirty-five state delegations. Nine of these states were then selected to participate in field training in Canada. Actual pilot projects followed in six of these states under the direction of Arkansas Governor Bill Clinton, now chairman of the National Governors Association.[69]

While this was going on, back in Canada, new approaches to adjustment were emerging in cities like Hamilton. Formed in 1985, the Canadian Steel Trade and Employment Congress (CSTEC, or the Steel Congress), the first of many sectoral councils funded by the federal government, provided sectoral adjustment in support to displaced workers in that hard-hit sector. The federal government even gave displaced steelworkers access to extended unemployment insurance while they went back to school for retraining. As Peter Warrian explains it, his task at the Steel Congress as its director was to "take fourteen thousand people out of the steel industry and re-employ them at comparable wages, and we did." Between 1988 and 1994, the Steel Congress's fifty-nine local adjustment committees helped place displaced steelworkers into new jobs, and quickly established itself as an essential "adjustment mechanism" for Hamilton steelworkers.[70] It was, as Warrian says, "the poster child to the sector council thing at the federal level."[71] Researchers David Wolfe and D'Arcy Martin have since argued that the Steel Congress was able to transcend the traditional oppositional roles of management and labour by social bargaining that, they explained, involved "a method for reconciling diverse interests through a process that requires both consensual and adversarial styles of operation."[72] Social bargaining, at its best, represented the extension of collective bargaining processes to areas that, in North America at least, were the sole prerogative of management or the state.

The other inspiring example of worker adjustment in 1980s Hamilton was grounded in a community-based approach rather than a sectoral one. The Firestone Adjustment Program, headed by the former regional government chairperson, Anne Jones, was formed after Firestone announced in July 1987 that it would close its local tire factory in January 1989, displacing 1,200 rubber workers. This unusually long eighteen-month window of opportunity gave the community adjustment committee the time to place 95 percent of the workforce into new jobs.[73] Inspired by this example, the three Hamilton-area NDP MPPs issued a press release in December 1988, demanding a permanent labour adjustment centre in the hard-hit city. They argued that "it is time all Hamilton workers displaced by plant shutdowns, downsizing or reorganization get the same help in finding new jobs that Firestone workers got."[74] They called the current system a "discriminatory, two class approach," as workers in smaller plants got almost no extra support. The editors of the *Hamilton Spectator* endorsed the NDP's call for a community adjustment board, noting that the Firestone placement team "turned in a bang-up performance this year."[75] Indeed, they wrote, "there's sound logic in the New Democrats' reasoning that a job adjustment system should be set up in Hamilton for general job finding duties." The *Spectator* even equated the need for "a well-equipped team to cope with job crises" to the necessity of keeping "professional police and fire departments on hand to cope with life and property emergencies."

To develop just such a proposal, a broad-based community inquiry led by the president of the local community college studied the idea over the course of 1988 and early 1989.[76] In doing so, it confirmed that smaller workplaces, with fewer than fifty employees, were ill-served by Canada's existing adjustment system. These workplaces fell below the minimum legal threshold for advance notification. What's more, as these employers were not required to notify the provincial government of the closure, few, if any, were then approached by the IAS to form an adjustment committee. Nor were these displaced workers even eligible for severance pay. That said, there were also persistent adjustment problems at some of the bigger plants. Of seventeen reported plant closures in Hamilton between 1987 and 1989, only nine saw IAS joint committees formed, with another two contracting with a private agency to deliver basic job search workshops. How much an employer voluntarily contributed to worker adjustment therefore varied enormously. The community-based inquiry, which included NDP MPPs Richard Allen and Bob Mackenzie, found that displaced women were especially ill-served by the existing adjustment regime. After all, they were concentrated in smaller, non-union workplaces in industries that, with the reduction in tariff barriers, were subject to extreme competitive pressures. In its January 1989 final report, the group proposed the creation of a regional adjustment unit that could coordinate the community's response as well as those of senior levels of government.

Having received the report, the Hamilton regional government expressed its interest in the proposed idea, again citing Firestone as the "ideal model,"[77] but it remained concerned with possible duplication. The region proceeded to form its own working committee on employment adjustment, with Richard Allen as its chairperson, to identify gaps and shortfalls in adjustment services in the region and to propose a solution and an action plan. Starting in October 1989, Allen and the other members of the committee met to examine the issue.[78] Their July 1990 report reiterated the earlier recommendation, expressing particular concern for small closures that "go undetected and thus un-serviced."[79] As we will see in the next chapter, the Ontario Liberal government was drawing some of the same conclusions. But it was in Hamilton where we first see the corporatist and communitarian beginnings of what would become the Ontario Training and Adjustment Board (OTAB) under the Ontario NDP. The minister responsible, none other than Richard

Allen, sought to meld the two approaches into one comprehensive system of training and adjustment for the province. The Hamilton Challenge would become Ontario's.

CONCLUSION

The language of class, so central to left-nationalism and the NDP for a decade and a half, was quickly giving way in the mid-1980s to the more inclusive language of community and social partnership. Worker ownership especially appealed to New Leftists given their belief that industrial workplaces could be democratized through worker ownership, cooperatives, and worker participation on boards of directors. We see this transition in the Ontario NDP policy book, which gathers all of the resolutions proposed by NDP riding associations, affiliated unions, youth clubs, and the party's Provincial Council that made it to the floor of convention and were then adopted by a majority of delegates. In his book *Rae Days*, journalist Thomas Walkom dismissed the party's policy book as a "bewildering array of contradictory resolutions" and then insisted that the party had no clear economic vision.[80] What he failed to recognize, however, is that the Ontario NDP policy book is best understood as the accumulated policy ideas over the previous thirty years. Old ideas thus stood alongside newer ones: a kind of political palimpsest. The timing of the resolutions therefore mattered.

If we take a closer look at the 1988 policy book, we can see clear evidence of the shift inside the party towards community economic development, worker cooperatives, and social partnership.[81] Some thematic sections, like that for Corporate Ownership and Control, are the product of a single time period—in this case the 1970s. In soaring left-nationalist rhetoric, the party called for fundamental change:

> Ontario has become a branch plant society. Our economic, social, cultural and educational life is dominated by foreign corporations and American influences. The next stage could be political annexation if we do not take

steps to establish our independence. We do not advocate nationalism in a narrow parochial sense. We urge it to enable us to build a distinctive socialist society which can join with likeminded societies to produce a more humane world.

To counter the "erosion of Canadian sovereignty," an Ontario Development Corporation would be created and public ownership expanded. Foreign ownership would be strictly controlled. In 1973, the party reaffirmed an earlier 1969 resolution calling for the nationalization of resource-based industries, and in 1978, in response to massive layoffs in Sudbury, the party called for the immediate nationalization of the International Nickel Company (INCO).

The Technological Change section of the policy book, in turn, comprises a set of resolutions adopted at the 1984 party convention in Hamilton. These resolutions were the outcome of the Task Force on People and Technological Change, chaired by Michael Cassidy and Jim Foulds, which had travelled to industrial centres across the province.[82] It was a high-profile initiative. For example, the June 1984 cover of the party's newsletter featured a child gazing in excited wonderment at a computer with the headline: "Here comes the future. Will New Democrats be ready?" Oddly, the same issue included a piece from a self-described "futurist consultant" who presented readers with a post-industrial future where "new rules" made older blue-collar industries entirely redundant. As for the technological change resolutions themselves, the first, on The Future of Work, calls for the development of a comprehensive policy on technological change, and the second, on Training for a New Society, emphasizes the need to upgrade skills. The language of both resolutions mirrors that of the party's newsletter: a new technological age was dawning. Another resolution on Sharing Responsibility in the Workplace calls for joint labour-management committees on technological change, and yet another, on Economic Democracy, calls on the province to make working people "equal partners" in the economy and to encourage "cooperative, community-based enterprises and other new forms of joint ownership." The political impulse here is clear.

Finally, the substantial Industry section of the policy book includes resolutions spanning two decades. While it initially emphasizes the urgent need for state intervention, the resolutions adopted in the 1980s increasingly embrace communitarian ideas. For example, in 1988, the party adopted a Community-Based Economic Development resolution in response to the province's "major restructuring, resulting in de-industrialization and intensification of regional disparities and increased concentration of corporate power." Clearly influenced by the Hamilton Challenge, the resolution notes how party policy had hitherto only addressed these issues from above, but locally rooted initiatives are also needed. Community economic development thus emerged in response to social inequality, economic underdevelopment, and deindustrialization, first in the United States in the 1950s and 1960s and then in Canada in the 1980s and 1990s.

National Rubber Company: Rui Santos working on a sheet press, 1993. Photo by Peter MacCallum.

3
COMPETING IN THE NEW GLOBAL ECONOMY

> The economic world is changed now, and we are no longer as naturally fortunate as we once were. A country of over 25 million cannot live well on resources alone, even ones as rich as ours. We must increasingly compete by dint of our creativity, our productivity, and our skill in working together. Success in the high-growth industries of today and the emerging industries of tomorrow will require a set of economic skills we have not yet mastered.
>
> —ONTARIO PREMIER'S COUNCIL,
> *Competing in the New Global Economy*[1]

Liberal Premier David Peterson proudly informed the Ontario legislature in April 1988 that the first report of his Premier's Council on the Economy was a unique attempt to forge political consensus about the way ahead. "Setting aside private interests," he continued, the council had "dedicated close to 1,000 hours of research, discussion and debate to develop a common plan which will serve the interests of all Ontarians."[2] This was no easy task. New digital technologies were transforming how people worked and communicated, enabling manufacturers to more easily manage complex systems over great geographic distances. Containerization meanwhile reduced the cost of transporting goods over land and sea. Where things were made thus fundamentally changed by the late 1980s, as trade liberalization had progressed to the point where national economies were now largely integrated into the "new global economy." More than ever, manufacturers were free to locate their factories anywhere in the world, including in lower-wage countries in Asia and Latin America, resulting in the radical restructuring of the international division of labour.

If high-wage countries faced an uncertain future, Canada had the added challenge of being a branch-plant economy in a world increasingly without economic borders. Trade liberalization not only opened the door to cheap foreign imports, it also triggered far-reaching industrial restructuring, as multinational corporations no longer needed their old networks of branch plants to serve national markets. Better to concentrate production in fewer low-cost plants serving the global market or contract the work out to the cheapest bidder. Where these global factories and supply chains would be located was therefore in question. Competition for new capital investment generated the same kind of hyper-competitive atmosphere that had long pitted jurisdictions against each other within the United States, only now, competition for investment extended to the entire world. In this giant pressure cooker, concern over a jurisdiction's "business climate" placed new limits on state intervention in the economy, politically insulating capital from democratic interference, and drove down corporate tax rates. The political defeat of economic nationalism in the 1988 Canadian election, a veritable referendum on free trade with the United States, swept aside nationalist resistance to these changes.[3]

Extraordinary times demanded bold new strategies. The ruling Ontario Liberals established the Premier's Council in 1986 with a mandate to "steer Ontario into the forefront of economic leadership and technological innovation." Its two ground-breaking reports, *Competing in the New Global Economy* (1988) and *People and Skills in the New Global Economy* (1990), called for a new social partnership between labour and business as part of a wider progressive competitiveness strategy in response to globalization. The twenty-eight-member advisory body included Premier David Peterson, six Liberal Party cabinet ministers, as well as prominent business leaders and three senior trade union leaders: Leo Gerard, president of District 6 of the United Steelworkers of America;

Gord Wilson, president of the Ontario Federation of Labour; and Fred Pomeroy, president of the Communications and Electrical Workers of Canada (CEW). Their presence meant that the effort to build an economic policy consensus extended into the labour movement and, through it, to the opposition NDP. Several key economic policy advisors in the future NDP government also served as council researchers and consultants. One of these, David Wolfe, later observed that the Premier's Council "presented the most coherent vision of an industrial and technology strategy espoused by either of the two mainstream parties in Canada. It depicted effective international competition as the key to a high wage economic strategy and higher standards of living."[4] In this rapidly changing context, the Premier's Council sought to forge a third way between neoliberalism and welfare-state liberalism.

The two reports from the Premier's Council became intellectual reference points for Ontario politicians across the political spectrum, but social democrats were particularly swayed by the alternative economic vision on offer.[5] With communitarian and neocorporatist thinking already ascendant within the NDP, the progressive competitive strategy laid out in the two reports promised to fill the ideological void left by the crushing defeat of Keynesianism and left-nationalism. However unlikely, the Premier's Council, named by the Liberals and stacked with business leaders, infused efforts to "rethink," "renew," or "modernize" social democracy in Ontario in the late 1980s. A series of major conferences and workshops was held and the provincial NDP undertook an economic policy review. No fewer than three edited volumes exploring social democratic futures were published as a result. Yet there remained sharp debate, especially in the union movement. Duelling union statements on work reorganization attest to the divergent thinking about labour-management partnership, in particular. Taken together, this short period from 1986 to 1990 offers us essential insights into the economic thinking of Ontario social democrats on the eve of their unexpected electoral victory. For better or worse, the new politics, rather than the old, guided the Ontario NDP's policy making once in power.

Pier No. 6, Toronto Waterfront. File 3. Ellis Wiley Fonds 124. City of Toronto Archives.

THE PREMIER'S COUNCIL ON THE ECONOMY

The Premier's Council was founded on the corporatist idea that a successful economic strategy for Ontario was best formulated through a consensus-building process involving different stakeholders. The turn to corporatism reflected growing skepticism of top-down bureaucratic responses to societal problems. Far better to let stakeholders hammer out an agreement that they could live with. References to Swedish and West German corporatist models in turn bolstered the social democratic bona fides of labour-management partnership in the face of criticism from those trade unionists and democratic socialists who favoured resistance over accommodation to industrial restructuring. For them, social bargaining represented the extension of workplace collective bargaining into areas of traditional managerial or state prerogative. Organized labour's old dream of negotiating technological change, workplace reorganization, and plant closures suddenly seemed within reach.

The first report of the Premier's Council, *Competing in the New Global Economy*, offered a detailed analysis of the unfolding economic situation and the urgent challenge facing the province.

"We are now firmly ensconced in a new global economy in which our ability to compete will be increasingly called into question," it explained.[6] Rejecting the neoliberal race to the low-wage bottom, the Premier's Council concluded that the province could not compete with the newly industrialized countries of Asia and Latin America. Ontario's labour-intensive industries, such as clothing and textiles, were therefore doomed. Recognizing this hard reality, the Premier's Council recommended that the Ontario government redirect its financial support from declining "mature industries" to promising "high value-added" economic sectors as part of a wider high-growth strategy based on high tech. Economic winners, not losers, should be backed, as they were the future of the province.[7] With tariff barriers coming down, Canada needed to develop competitive export-oriented firms able to thrive on the global stage: the absence of Ontario-based multinationals was therefore a cause for concern. To make the post-industrial transition, major investments in skills training and labour adjustment were needed to ensure labour force flexibility. Worker ownership even had a place in the emerging progressive competitive strategy.[8]

While "the spread of new ideas is seldom easy to track with any precision," the Premier's Council's alternative vision appears to be a distillation of "new paradigm" thinking in the United States.[9] The 1980s was a decade of considerable experimentation, as a new generation of Democratic Party governors struggled to respond to the "profound and wrenching economic transition" to a new post-industrial economy.[10] Many of these experiments shared the same assumptions, language, and policy prescriptions as the Premier's Council. According to David Osborne, these efforts included public-private partnerships, community economic development, job training, venture capital funds, and welfare reform.[11] In his foreword to Osborne's 1990 book *Laboratories of Democracy*, Arkansas Governor Bill Clinton, then the head of the National Governors Association, emphasized that the baby boom generation of governors were "forced to take ground-breaking initiatives" and that they were largely "pragmatic responses to real problems" rather than ideologically driven ones.[12] The language of political pragmatism permeated the political discourse of modernizing centrist and social democratic politicians, at once substantially narrowing the policy options seemingly available to progressive politicians and justifying the radical break from redistributive politics in the name of moderation and realism. Despite assertions otherwise, pragmatism justified the socio-democratic accommodation to ascendant neoliberalism.

Founded in 1985, the US Democratic Leadership Council brought together a new generation of party modernizers who had turned away from the class politics of the New Deal.[13] Under the leadership of Bill Clinton, the DLC's March 1990 New Orleans Declaration emphasized opportunity, responsibility, and community.[14] "We believe the promise of America is equal opportunity, not equal outcomes," it grandly declared.[15] American "New Democrats" preferred a decentralized community-based vision to the welfare state, which was now negatively associated with welfare dependency and a culture of poverty. According to Osborne, "the task is to develop new community-based approaches to social and economic problems. The 'evils' that need to be avoided today are bureaucratic and inflexible programs that (by and large inadequately) compensate victims instead of solving problems."[16] Ideas flowed easily between a new generation of young, well-educated, and affluent politicians across the United States and into Canada.

Let's briefly take a closer look at the work of the young New Democrat governors of Michigan and Massachusetts in the years immediately prior to the Premier's Council. Michigan Governor James Blanchard set up the Commission on Jobs and Economic Development, naming Chrysler's Lee Iacocca and the UAW's Doug Fraser as co-chairs, and hired management consultants to help write *The Path to Prosperity* report (1988), which "argued that Michigan's future rested upon technological innovation" and called for a "coordinated human investment strategy" to "train those left behind." The similarities with Ontario's process of consensus building are striking, as are its conclusions. Governor Blanchard proudly declared that his Rust Belt state had become "in part an incubator" for these management consultant models, adding that Michigan had three choices: get poor, get out, or get smart.[17]

A similar story unfolded in Massachusetts. Today best known as a failed presidential candidate in the 1988 election, as governor, Michael Dukakis was widely known for revalorizing deindustrialized areas by bringing them back into the "growth process" by building a state-wide community economic development network.[18] This emerging "third sector" was viewed as a counterpoint to the large state bureaucracies created by welfare-state liberalism. Dukakis also introduced workfare for unemployed men and created training and transition pathways for those on welfare to re-enter the workforce. The Massachusetts model quickly spread across the US and influenced the policy discussion in Canada.

Dukakis had promised the labour movement in 1982 that he would pass mandatory advance notice legislation for plant closures if elected governor. Once safely in power, however, he instead formed a thirty-eight-member multipartite commission to find a political compromise that resulted in a watered-down "social compact" of voluntary standards of good corporate behaviour.[19] Predictably, these guidelines made no discernible difference for working people. As we will see, the very same compromise was later resorted to by the Ontario Premier's Council in its second report to break an impasse between labour and management representatives over the issue of regulating plant closings. In a key insight, Osborne concludes that the emphasis on finding agreement in these multipartite processes usually meant that the harder questions had to be taken off the policy-making table first and that, ultimately, consensual processes led to watered-down solutions.[20] This is one of the reasons why skills training emerged as a signature policy in the 1980s and early 1990s: it was common ground, so long as the government footed the bill.

Clearly, then, the Premier's Council of Ontario was drawing from the same pool of ideas as the New Democrats in the United States. This was hardly surprising given that governments on both sides of the Canada–United States border were reading the same "thought leaders," such as Robert Reich, and turned to the same management consultants to facilitate their economic envisioning and write their reports. The big consultancy firms such as McKinsey and the Boston Consulting Group made a fortune helping governments and businesses respond to the industrial crisis of the 1980s. In turn, the dominance of a handful of consulting agencies in North America led to considerable policy recycling; the same policy prescriptions were recommended from one government client to the next, "resulting in a continual copying and homogenization of policy."[21] Consulting agencies thus transferred the latest and most fashionable managerial ideas and theories between jurisdictions.[22]

The decision to hire the US-based management consulting firm Telesis (Greek for "intelligently planned progress") headed by the well-connected Democrat Ira Magaziner, who had gone to Oxford University with Bill Clinton and Robert Reich (and Bob Rae too, it turns out), meant that the Ontario Premier's Council was tapping into ideas that were just coming into fashion in the US.[23] In 1982, Magaziner and Reich wrote their influential book *Minding America's Business*, which proposed an industrial policy to "ease society's adjustment to structural changes in a growing economy" and to ensure that "no group is driven to oppose economic change because it fears being forced to bear an unfair share of the burden of that change." Retraining was a key part of their strategy. They, too, believed that industrial closures were "the inevitable result of low-wage competition" and should not be interfered with.[24] Magaziner and Reich were described by economist Paul Krugman as "strongly committed to the ideology of competitiveness"; he went on to dismiss them as purveyors of clichéd "pop internationalism."[25] Both men would later become leading members of the Clinton White House, with Reich serving as Secretary of Labour and Magaziner as Clinton's "Health Tsar" with Hillary Clinton.

To advise Ontario, Magaziner sent his right-hand man David Pecaut, who had a strong connection to Toronto, to guide the Premier's Council and write its first report. Pecaut had previously worked with the Canada Consulting Group in Toronto, founded by politically connected Liberals such as Jim Coutts, former principal secretary to Prime Minister Pierre Trudeau, as well as establishment businessmen. According to Pecaut's biographer (and partner in life), "One day he might be advising government, the next day it might be manufacturers, then maybe bankers after that."[26] The Ontario Premier's Council report was thus the vehicle by which the latest US thinking was introduced into Ontario politics, adjusted to some extent through social bargaining, and passed off as homegrown. Such envisioning processes served to build societal consensus about how to respond to the industrial crisis, thereby depoliticizing hitherto contested ideas about the role of the state in the economy. Ontario's progressive competitive strategy was thus very much part of the wider zeitgeist.

I hadn't realized until I interviewed Bob Rae that he had a long association with David Pecaut that predated the Premier's Council. After Rae became NDP leader, he brought a select group of people, including Pecaut, over for regular dinners to discuss new ideas and policy. Rae had originally met him through his old Oxford University chum Ira Magaziner. Rae told me, Magaziner "went through a process not totally dissimilar from mine; went from doing community organizing, he then eventually ended up at the Boston Consulting Group, and did a lot of work on industrial strategy and industrial policy and all that stuff." Anyway, Pecaut was part of Rae's inner circle until the Liberal Premier's Council came calling. Rae told Pecaut that he was fine with him working for the Liberals, saying "we want to be able to give advice to where it needs to be given." They remained good friends. "David was a remarkable idea guy. . . . He had a million ideas, and he worked all over the world for the Boston Consulting Group, so he was always looking at what was happening, what was the worry, and he became a key advisor to Peterson's Premier's Council."[27] These early conversations, as we will see in subsequent chapters, had a lasting impact on Rae and his inner circle.

Most Ontario unions were also "prepared to engage in that dialogue," recalls John O'Grady, a former research director for the Ontario Federation of Labour. O'Grady had previously worked with the International Confederation of Free Trade Unions in

Southeast Asia, where he saw first-hand the scale and rapidity of industrialization in that region of the world. He was impressed and "became much more cognizant of the competition pressure from emerging economies," concluding that there was "no practical possibility of maintaining low-skill, labour-intensive [industries] in North America, or in Canada in particular."[28] There was a growing political appetite inside the labour movement for finding an alternative growth strategy to neoliberalism.

After the release of the first report, the three union leaders on the Premier's Council were criticized by other trade unionists for their participation. Fred Pomeroy admitted to colleagues that there were "a lot of concerns over the thrust of those documents in certain quarters of the labour movement, but we went along with them because we had a certain level of confidence in them."[29] D'Arcy Martin, the education director in Pomeroy's union, similarly observed that the first report had proven "controversial for labour, but [the reports] were well done. They reflected substantial research, raised interesting new questions for policy debate, and came to grips with genuine trends in the economy." The fiercest

We want answers! Angry workers from Pittsburgh Paint in Etobicoke listen at a news conference as provincial NDP leader Bob Rae discusses the sudden announcement that the plant will close. Photo by Jim Russell / *Toronto Star* via Getty Images.

critic of the rhetoric of global competitiveness and the very idea of social partnership was the Canadian Auto Workers, Ontario's largest private-sector union. The CAW had broken away from the United Auto Workers over divergent responses to the industrial crisis on either side of the Canada-US border. In the uncompromising words of Sam Gindin, the CAW's research director: "The American leadership of the UAW chose to sell concessions, and their demoralized membership acquiesced. The Canadian section rebelled, and that rebellion ultimately led to the formation of a new union—that of the CAW."[30] Not surprisingly, the consensual language of the Premier's Council was very much at odds with the union's newly forged identity.

The CAW issued a withering Statement on the Reorganization of Work in 1989, rejecting the language of partnership and the ideology of competitiveness. According to CAW leader Bob White, "True partnership means a measure of equality. None of the examples of the new work organization promoted by management includes workers or their union in any meaningful way in the decision-making process." If the union movement acquiesced to the central logic of the ideology of competitiveness, the CAW reasoned that it would put them "on a treadmill, a rat-race" they couldn't win. The unions needed to "look behind the surface of 'partnership' and ask [them]selves what it really means." Though the Premier's Council was not directly mentioned, the inference was clear. In answering its own question, the CAW maintained:

> For all the talk about jointness and worker control, employers are certainly not putting true equality between themselves and their employees on the agenda. Management will continue to jealously guard the management's rights clause and to unilaterally decide when to modernize, how much to invest, what to produce, with what kind of technology, and so on.

There were, therefore, real limits to the emerging consensus over social partnership and co-determination. There was even divergent thinking on the issue of skills training. The CAW's David Robertson said as much when invited to present to the training subcommittee of the Premier's Council: "It would be wrong to make too much of this consensus—to assume too much agreement. Because there are clear differences between a business-centred and a worker-centred training system. And these differences—these points of divergence—are more significant than the areas of agreement." As Robertson understood it, corporations wanted to "make education more like training," whereas trade unions endeavoured to "make training more like education."[31]

The CAW's criticisms struck a nerve, prompting the unions of Fred Pomeroy and Leo Gerard to issue their own work reorganization statements in defence of social partnership. The May 1990 statement of the Communications and Electrical Workers of Canada opened with: "Instinctively, people resist change." While there were good "historical reasons" for trade unionists to be concerned, it said, the "times are changing, and union members

"War footing"—the United Steelworkers' Leo Gerard, 18 December 1987. Photo by Michael Stuparyk / *Toronto Star* via Getty Images.

are increasingly looking for a new response to work reorganization—one that focuses on intelligent cooperation." The United Steelworkers of America went even further in its 1991 statement, Empowering Workers in the Global Economy, which made the social democratic case for working in partnership.[32]

These fierce debates within the labour movement placed the Ontario Federation of Labour in a difficult position. Its president, Gord Wilson, was one of the three union representatives on the Premier's Council, yet the movement was divided over the progressive competitive agenda. As a quid pro quo for OFL participation in the Premier's Council, the federation received substantial multi-year government funding to run the Technology Adjustment Research Programme (TARP), which funded needed research by affiliated unions.[33] Draft research studies were workshopped each year and the program paid for union study tours to Sweden and Germany.[34] At a critical time, TARP expanded the capacity of member unions to undertake original research. Otherwise, the OFL focused its efforts on formulating a strong union position on training that culminated in its November 1989 Statement on Education and Training. Labour's training agenda aimed to equip workers so they have "more control over their jobs and their work lives," including pathways into better jobs. Accordingly, skills training needed to go beyond any particular job, be available to all, and raise the skill level of the entire workforce.[35] But would this worker-centred vision of training prevail in the second report of the Premier's Council?

PEOPLE AND SKILLS IN THE NEW GLOBAL ECONOMY

Given the divergent thinking on the Premier's Council, the writing of the second report on worker training and adjustment proved to be a fractious process. The Premier's Council had some "pretty serious players on it," according to John O'Grady, such as the president of GM Canada, and was guided by David Pecaut, who "set the table for what we thought was a useful discussion."[36] Everybody I interviewed spoke highly of Pecaut. According to Hugh Mackenzie, Pecaut was retained by the Premier's Council "to be its brains, and David was the guy who was set up to do it."[37] Even so, the three union leaders went "berserk" when they read Pecaut's first circulated draft of the second report. According to David Wolfe, it was "filled with the kind of competitiveness stuff that David did and said, that was his bread and butter, and it was geared towards training."[38] He believes that if you had asked Pecaut, "he would have said he thought that this was a pro-labour document. He didn't intend it to be anti-labour in any way, shape or form, but that's not the way Gord [Wilson], Fred [Pomeroy] and Leo [Gerard] perceived it."

After reading it, a clearly alarmed Fred Pomeroy wrote the two other union representatives to say the draft report was "supposed to deal with the negative impacts that workers will be faced with as the economy is restructured," but it limited itself to "voluntarism rather than legal standards that can be enforced." Legal requirements were necessary to "force employers to bargain over the introduction of technological change, participate in the financing of training through a levy-grant system, and limit their ability to shut down workplaces and move away." As it stood, the draft report leaned too heavily on worker buyouts of struggling factories as a panacea. For Pomeroy, this option should only be "one minor part of a strategy rather than a central part of a strategy." Without substantial revisions, the three labour representatives needed to "very seriously review why we are participating."[39] Pomeroy communicated as much at the next meeting of the Premier's Council. Smartly, Premier David Peterson took this challenge and turned it around, inviting the labour representatives to revise the report and bring it back. It was impossible to say no.

As a first step, three union staff members—D'Arcy Martin (CEW), Hugh Mackenzie (USWA), and John O'Grady (OFL)—reviewed the current draft and agreed that it was "completely unacceptable in trade union terms. It is of lousy quality, laced with anti-union rhetoric, and objectionable in substance." Martin dismissed it as "flimsy, trite, and glib." It was "bad enough to have the earlier documents fixated on competitiveness," he added, but this one "waves many a red flag in front of a labour audience." The three staffers then named several progressive researchers who could help them rewrite the document.[40] They included Pat and Hugh Armstrong, who rewrote the schooling section; D'Arcy Martin, who rewrote the adult education section; and Leon Muszynski, of the Metropolitan Toronto Social Planning Council, who tackled the labour displacement piece.[41] David Wolfe, a political scientist at the University of Toronto who had worked on two influential reports on training for the Social Planning Council of Metropolitan Toronto, wrote the labour board and labour market training section, though he credits John O'Grady for envisioning the proposed Ontario Training and Adjustment Board. Wolfe believed that the training chapter required some cornerstone ideas. As he saw it, the choice was not whether or not to restructure the economy but which path to follow. Skills training promised to redistribute the costs. Indeed, the alternative to neoliberalism was the corporatist model from Sweden and Germany, where the cost of restructuring was socialized to a far greater extent.

Employee adjustment, in turn, was taken up by the Ontario Federation of Labour, which made the case for longer advance notice periods for layoff and plant closure. It rightly argued that advance notice was the linchpin for worker adjustment and retraining. According to the OFL, the key attributes of an active labour force development policy included:

> extended notice periods to permit employment adjustment programmes to be effective; a bias towards retraining or skills upgrading as an integral aspect of employment adjustment, rather than as a reluctant, last ditch expenditure; implementation of employment adjustment programmes through locally responsive bodies with strong input from labour, employers, and the community; recognition that since the benefits of economic restructuring flow to the whole society, its costs should not be borne disproportionately by workers and affected communities.[42]

The OFL also wanted to see Ontario high schools destreamed, as the shunting of working-class children into "dead-end" programs in grade nine served to reproduce class barriers. This essential point speaks directly to my own experience as a high school student in Thunder Bay. White working-class kids, such as myself, were streamed primarily into "level 4," which meant that—unless we went back and took classes over as I did—we would graduate high school and enter the industrial workforce. We were ineligible for university, unlike the middle-class kids in "level 5." Indigenous kids and the poorest whites were usually streamed into "level 3," leading them to exit high school at age sixteen without a high school diploma. Race and class thus structured our life trajectories and horizons at the age of twelve or thirteen.

Labour's "counter-report" was ready to share with the Premier's Council by March 1990; it became the basis for several rounds of social bargaining with the business representatives. There were limits, however, to how far business leaders were willing to go in accommodating labour's training and adjustment agenda.[43] The April 1990 draft thus remained inadequate in the eyes of organized labour, who reiterated the point that they had made in respect of the first draft. "The political credibility of the labour participants is on the line. We understand that the final report will be a compromise and that we will have to defend that compromise within trade union circles."[44] In response, the Premier's Council included more on the Swedish and West German examples.

The Premier's Council defined successful adjustment as more than the placement of a displaced worker into a new job: it was essential that they "do not experience undue stress or health problems as a result of the change, the new jobs use as much or more of their skill levels as the previous one, that workers at least maintain their standard of living and that the adjusted workers consider the new situation satisfying."[45] Yet, how was successful adjustment to be achieved? As employer representatives refused to support the proposed extension of the advance notice period, trade unionists had to be satisfied, like their counterparts in Massachusetts before them, with the inclusion of a list of voluntary best practices. It was a moral victory at best. More substantively, however, organized labour did win a recommendation to expand the coverage of Ontario's advance notice legislation to include smaller workplaces of ten or more workers (instead of fifty-plus). But business members balked at a training payroll tax, something Quebec had just legislated. The federal and provincial governments would need to pay the entire training bill. There was also agreement that collective bargaining should extend to worker adjustment, which, if adopted, would have mirrored the narrow effects-based bargaining that prevailed in the United States after the Supreme Court's 1981 *First National Maintenance* decision ended any legal requirement to discuss the underlying reasons for a plant's closure. The goal, then, was to manage change intelligently and effectively.

Eventually, these negotiations resulted in mutual agreement, allowing *People and Skills in the New Global Economy* to be released just two months before the Ontario NDP's surprise election victory. The "industrial restructuring challenge" facing the province was understood to "require massive shifts of capital and human resources to higher value-added per employee activities in all sectors of the economy." Ontario needed to "manage this restructuring to [its] advantage. This means making major choices about how that restructuring occurs." Embracing the cornerstone ideas of this generational cohort of labour-friendly researchers, the Premier's Council declared that "the choice open to Ontario" was "not whether to restructure its economy, but rather which restructuring path to follow." Skills training would, among other things, enable Ontario to make the transition to a high-technology future.[46]

How, then, should we understand the resulting compromise? Was it a rupture with neoliberalism, as political economist Rianne Mahon once suggested?[47] Certainly, David Wolfe and D'Arcy Martin believed that a "consensus concerning co-determination of decisions, participatory methods, and broadened curriculum" had been forged through social bargaining.[48] Or was it yet another case of organized labour abandoning the politics of resistance in favour of a new accommodation with ascendant capital? Interestingly, the Premier's Council itself came to understand its work in generational terms, observing that "the transition of leadership to the baby-boomers" was driving the new economic thinking. Relatedly, it reasoned that a "more sophisticated understanding of government's role in supporting innovative and prosperous businesses" was emerging. The influence of America's New Democrats is clear here. The Premier's Council went on to say that its primary purpose was not to provide policy advice or even publish reports but rather to "create a mechanism for people from business, labour, knowledge organizations, and government to discuss the challenges of the future, and consider what initiatives need to be taken by each organization individually, and what initiatives should be taken cooperatively, to address those challenges."[49] Hence, it offered a consensus-building process for the province, much as Richard Allen's Hamilton Challenge had done at the community level.

RETHINKING SOCIAL DEMOCRACY FOR A NEW ERA

It was within this wider context that the Ontario NDP caucus initiated an economic policy review in early 1989, led by Floyd Laughren, the long-time MPP for the Sudbury-area riding of Nickel Belt. In the late 1970s, Laughren had been at the forefront of demands to nationalize INCO, the giant nickel mining company that dominates Sudbury's economy, earning him the moniker of "Pink Floyd." However, by the late 1980s, much had changed and Laughren had mellowed. Concern now centred on how Ontario could compete in the new global economy. As he explained to me in our interview, "I had a very clear idea in my mind, that we needed to simplify our economic message. And my solution was, right or wrong, that we will concentrate on import replacement, export promotion, and very selective government intervention."[50]

Laughren was assisted by Riel Miller, a young graduate from the New School in New York City who had spent three years at the OECD in Paris, where he had worked mostly on issues of structural adjustment. Miller's parents had been "political refugees from the Cold War," moving the family from Montreal to work for Tommy Douglas's CCF government in Saskatchewan. They then moved to

Washington, DC, arriving just when the city "was in flames from the assassinations, and then the whole period from '68 to '73 was the Vietnam War," Miller told me. He went on, "And so my whole high school experience was related to the anti-war period, so that was very direct exposure." Soon after returning to Toronto, Miller saw a classified advertisement in the *Globe and Mail* for an economic policy advisor with the Ontario NDP caucus and decided to apply even though he "didn't know a heck of a lot about Canada or Canadian politics because [he] hadn't lived there." He was hired by Robin Sears, another recent returnee, back from a foreign stint with the Socialist International. Miller's OECD credentials made the difference, as the party was looking for someone with professional credentials and who was technically knowledgeable about economic policy.

As Miller explains it, his work for Laughren picked up "on work [he] had done in the OECD on the future of the welfare state and the future of competition." He recalls, "I hope it's not surprising or offensive to say that the Ontario NDP was anti-intellectual and obviously it was anti-communist . . . but there was a part of it that was simply not interested in ideas. . . . So in that sense, I was just a fish out of water."[51] In our interview, Miller admitted that he was highly skeptical of party politics and state power even before he was hired by the party, but he "wanted to get up close and kick the tires and see what it was really like, so those experiences were really invaluable from that perspective." As leader, Rae thus surrounded himself with smart people with international experience, further plugging the Ontario party into wider conversations about what to do about the industrial crisis.

To start things off, Floyd Laughren invited about twenty progressive academics, almost all of whom were based in Toronto or Ottawa, to write discussion papers for the economic policy review. A handful of trusted advisors, also from Toronto, then drafted the report without any regard to the party's existing policy book. Only then were NDP members brought into the process to respond to the articulated vision. The economic policy review was therefore a process undertaken from the top down and from the outside in.

Several key themes emerged from the papers submitted, informing the summary prepared for the Ontario NDP caucus. According to the report by Isabella Bakker, "all the authors recognize that the party faces a tall order. It must present Ontarians with a new economic strategy that protects both working people's interests and offers an alternative which can deliver a better standard of living."[52] The first part of her review grouped several contributions under the heading of Economic Restructuring, Trade and Technological Change. David Wolfe's paper, in particular, caught Bakker's attention, as he explicitly urged the party to come up with a "coherent response to the Premier's Council report and its emphasis on an internationally competitive trade strategy." As isolationism was not a credible option in the free trade era, Wolfe sketched out the core features of the Premier's Council progressive competitive strategy. Rianne Mahon was in substantial agreement with Wolfe, drawing a strong distinction between "good jobs" and "bad jobs." However, she did not agree that the progressive competitive strategy required Ontario to abandon its mature industries.

For his part, the old left-nationalist Mel Watkins advised the party that the "dominant ideology spawned" by the years of economic crisis "has been neo-conservativism as business has tried to force restructuring on its terms and make others bear the costs of slower growth." Watkins urged the NDP to think in terms of the "3 Rs": redistribution (a more egalitarian society), recovery (full employment), and restructuring (economic growth). Yet he, too, was in substantial agreement with the Premier's Council, going so far as to say that there was "nothing inherently wrong with competitiveness through restructuring. The issue is not restructuring per se; it is the need for a left variant of restructuring."[53]

A second theme that emerged from the papers was that of Local Economic Initiatives and Worker Ownership, including contributions from Roger Peters and Ted Jackson on economic democracy and Ethan Phillips on worker ownership. Here, too, the authors agreed that social democratic parties like the NDP needed to recognize the new global economy as an inescapable reality. In doing so, Peters and Jackson spoke of the need to leverage alternative sources of capital and encourage more democratic forms of economic enterprise.[54] Their point of reference was the Labour Party–controlled Greater London Council, a left-wing bastion against Thatcherism in the early 1980s that actively created local investment boards as part of its industrial strategy for the deindustrializing metropolis, and "new enterprises and jobs with the aim of revitalizing the economy and encouraging more local control and democracy in the economy."

Robin Murray, who was a key figure in the Greater London Council, spent the summer of 1990 teaching at Carleton's Institute of Political Economy, putting him into conversation with left-wing political economists in Ontario. David Wolfe, for example, credits Murray for introducing him to the scholarship of Michael Best on sectoral strategies and the "Third Italy." Phillips, for his part, spoke of the value of worker ownership and the ways that labour-managed investment funds "can help the organized labour movement to participate in selected restructuring decisions."[55] The linkage between the two, seen in Quebec's Solidarity Fund, will be something we return to at various points in the coming chapters. Interestingly, several critics of the emerging progressive competitive consensus, such as Leo Panitch, also submitted papers, but their viewpoints were barely acknowledged in the caucus summary document. This dismissal reflected the increasing alignment of the Ontario NDP caucus leadership, and its inner circle of policy advisors, with the underlying assumptions of the global economy and the Liberal Premier's Council.

The policy review also benefited from recent conversations within the Ontario Federation of Labour, which saw a policy statement on industrial restructuring adopted at its December 1988 convention. The statement boldly declared that the "old economy of resource exports and branch plant manufacturing is at a dead point," and the only question was whether the coming wave of restructuring would be market-driven or worker-centred.[56] The "cornerstone of our restructuring programme is a commitment to reverse de-industrialisation," the OFL declared, and the only way to do that would be to actively intervene in the investment process in order to promote "high value-added manufacturing and greater investment in our social infrastructure." Among other things, the OFL proposed development funds, skills training, and labour law reform—the last being cast as essential to a more equitable future, as stronger unions would be in a position to negotiate workplace changes. There was considerable policy cross-fertilization between the party and the labour movement during these crucial years.

With the initial stage of the policy review completed, a preliminary draft statement was prepared by Riel Miller. He would later become a key policy advisor to Laughren when he was Ontario Finance Minister, drafting the famed Budget Paper E in 1991, which laid out the new government's progressive competitive vision. Miller's March 1990 draft document offered a "framework for the development of economic policy." He approvingly quoted John O'Grady's discussion paper when he wrote: "The overriding task of an economic policy statement should be to win for the Party some credibility on the problem of economic management."[57] Mostly, however, Miller looked for inspiration to the Declaration of Principles of the Socialist International, the organization representing social democratic parties around the world, and the policy statements of various European socialist and labour parties. Generally, European socialists conceded that change was inevitable; the real question, therefore, was who was going to control that change and how? The international statements consulted by Miller also placed strong emphasis on extending democratic control to the economy through partnership. A copy of Miller's draft, found in the Bob Rae papers at the Ontario Archives, is lightly marked up with every mention of "democratic socialism" circled in blue pen as one would for a recurring spelling mistake. When I told this to Miller during the interview, he burst out laughing. Democratic socialism appeared nowhere in the next, entirely rewritten, iteration of the statement, this time authored by Chuck Rachlis and David Wolfe, who emphasized the importance of formulating a social democratic economics:

According to popular mythology, the 1980s saw the triumph of liberal, market-oriented policies over interventionist and social democratic ones. This perception is partly ideology and partly a distortion of the facts. Nonetheless, it has convinced many people, both inside and outside social democratic parties, that these parties have little to contribute to discussions of economic policy. The irony is that social democratic positions on economic policy are more crucial now than any point in the past forty or fifty years.[58]

Rachlis and Wolfe also urged Ontario New Democrats to rise to the challenge and fundamentally change "the ways in which investment and production decisions are made" and seek to democratize the economy "to counter the growing concentration of wealth and power and augment workers' equity in the economy and their lives." Otherwise, they sounded a lot like the Premier's Council. For his part, Miller says he was unimpressed by what the Liberal Premier's Council, and its American management consultants, came up with:

> I mean for me that was OECD . . . [pauses] down a notch or two, because the OECD was at a higher level . . . not only do you have [Paul] Krugman and [Joseph] Stiglitz at the table . . . Michael Storper and people like that. Not only do you get the crème de la crème of the academic, but you also have very serious practitioners on the public policy side, who have tangible problems to deal with: housing, inequality, you name it.[59]

It was at this point that Laughren circulated the draft statement to party members in advance of a series of regional "road show" workshops in the lead-up to the June 1990 Provincial Council meeting. Each regional workshop was led either by a member of the policy team who had authored the report or members of the Provincial Executive conscripted to help out. The reports that came back were not encouraging. "They hated it," reported one workshop leader. Another wrote: "People at the school were very, very unhappy with this document." Simon Rosenblum, a party vice-president and a close associate of Laughren, rightly observed that the document "didn't have any clear sense of ONDP policy."[60] The list of key economic policies that were missing was a long one, ranging from regional development to pay equity, which of course reflected who was centrally involved in the process. As I co-led the Ottawa regional workshop with my old friend Christine Lorée, I can confirm that the reception of members in that city, too, was a frosty one. Even Chuck Rachlis, head of NDP Research, had to admit that "the most telling criticism was that the paper fails most of the tests" that had been established for the policy review process in the first place.[61] It was a flawed and disconnected process that ended up going nowhere. The economic policy review, unlike the environmental policy review, did not even result in a final report.[62]

By contrast, *Greening the Party, Greening the Province* provided the party with a compelling environmental critique of capitalism that "today rests on a stunningly false notion of ecology—that the earth's natural resources will always be plentiful enough for human use, yielding more trees, petroleum, fish, with prices rising or falling to self-regulate demand and ensure a continuing supply far into the future." It went on to say that the earth's "most fundamental cycles, such as the global carbon cycle that regulates our climate, are being disrupted by pollution caused by economic activities, with potentially dire consequences for the human race."[63] These were strong words, which have only grown more compelling in the decades since. Interestingly, even here, the party's environmental thinking benefited from parallel conversations within the Ontario Federation of Labour, as the union movement sought to resolve the "jobs versus environment" conundrum.[64] That the Ontario NDP's economic and environmental policy processes were undertaken in parallel reveals some of the conceptual and political challenges we continue to struggle with in today's politics.

Yet, despite its failure, the economic policy review confirmed the profound influence that the Premier's Council was having on the inner circle of top policy advisors around Bob Rae. The progressive competitiveness agenda also resonated with Rae himself; consensus-based approaches and shared communitarian values were integral to his politics. While the focus was primarily on softening the socio-economic impact of displacement, the NDP's emerging approach sought to control the course of economic change itself—an ambitious goal, to say the least. Rae's November 1989 speech to the Ontario Federation of Labour was a case in point. It raised the fundamental issues of who controls economic change, who benefits, and who ultimately pays the price:

> Change can be bewildering. Change can be frightening. Our job, together, is to take as much of the fear and insecurity as possible out of changes in our economy. We must make change our servant, not our master, so that working people and their families can have more control and more power over their lives. Confronting change and giving power to working people require courage and imagination.[65]

Rae went on to argue that society must work to ensure that "change means opportunity for all who would take it. Don't ask workers to bear the cost of change alone. Ask workers to become real partners, real, equal partners, in making change happen." His call for true partnership can be read here as a strategy for achieving expanded industrial democracy. Years later, in his book on the Rae government, Thomas Walkom dismissed the economic policy review as little more than a second-rate "graduate seminar." Floyd Laughren even told Walkom that the draft policy documents were too vague: "There was nothing I felt I could go to the party with; we hadn't been able to come up with anything ... around which people could rally." And yet, almost by default, "it ended up shaping the way the NDP government would approach the economy."[66]

A number of the discussion papers generated during the review were eventually published in a series of books on the future of social democracy in Canada alongside other viewpoints. The first of these, *Social Democracy without Illusions* (1991), edited by John Richards, Robert D. Cairns, and Larry Pratt, originated in a 1988 conference. Marxist analysis was abhorrent to this group of Canadian social democrats. For this reason, perhaps, it is the clearest example of the new emphasis on labour-management partnership and co-determination. For contributor Henry Milner, a specialist on the Swedish labour relations model at McGill University, the "essence of a social democratic—as distinct from a Marxist—credo is faith that a principled reconciliation of classes is feasible."[67] John Richards likewise believed that it was time to go beyond the confrontational industrial relations of the US Wagner Act, with its workplace-based system of union certification based on the closed shop, on which Canadian labour law was based, and explore more consensual approaches.[68] Other contributors emphasized the importance of worker retraining and the search for a political "third option." Former Saskatchewan Premier Allan Blakeney was not alone in turning away from "wholesale protectionism" in favour of "a fundamental change in the relationship among the trade union movement, government, and business."[69] A new post-nationalist social democratic politics was clearly taking shape in the bitter aftermath of the free trade debate.

The second book, entitled *Debating Canada's Future: Views from the Left* (1991), edited by Simon Rosenblum (by then an advisor to Floyd Laughren) and Peter Findlay (head of the Canadian Centre for Policy Alternatives, a left-wing think-tank based in Ottawa), included a number of papers originating in the NDP Economic Policy Review. Organized around a series of thematic debates, the first three head-to-head sections focused on economic issues. According to Rosenblum and Findlay:

> Over the past decade we have witnessed disappointment that France's Socialist Party government was not able to achieve its goals of "transcending capitalism" despite introducing a radical economic program in its early years, and the failure of various Third World governments to find a workable "third way" between capitalism and

communism. The ongoing globalization of the world economy makes it increasingly more difficult to implement a left-wing economic agenda in one nation."[70]

Several contributors also argued that centralized state planning and nationalization were now firmly associated with the failed Soviet model.[71] In his contribution, for example, John Richards equated central planning to the "horrendous cost of lives lost" in the USSR and lamented that "conventional left-wing wisdom has retreated into a protectionist nationalism that equates international competition with loss of social programs, continuing low wages, and lost jobs."[72] In the eyes of Henry and Arthur Milner, a non-Marxist social democratic political economy privileged "partnership and cooperation" between labour and capital.[73]

David Wolfe's own contribution to the volume, originally written for the policy review, is particularly interesting. For him, the "current radical changes in the world economy and technology provide an opportunity to democratize the productive relations, increase our standard of living, and expand the realm of freedom of work through public policy that is open to transnational economic interdependence but commits the necessary resources to training and technological development in Canada."[74] However, he went on to warn: "Many of the economic beliefs held by social democrats for the past four decades have increasingly come open to question, and we are left with the dilemma of clinging to positions in which we no longer completely believe or choosing to sidestep a serious discussion of economic policy altogether."[75] The best way forward, he asserted, was for the NDP to "frame economic policies that are consistent with our traditional political values, yet recognize the changed reality of the global economy." Advanced countries like Canada needed to innovate or die in the economic transition.[76] As Wolfe saw the situation, it was no time to be timid:

> The current wave of radical changes in the economy and technology represents the most significant challenge faced by social democrats since the 1930s. We are confronted

with two options—to sound a cautionary note about the destructive and unsettling aspects of these changes and try to preserve and protect the benefits of the past four postwar decades; or to seize the opportunity that the current wave of innovation presents to improve the quality of life in the workplace through a democratization of production relations, to increase our overall standard of living, and, ultimately, to expand the realm of freedom by exploiting productivity gains to reduce necessary work time.[77]

Wolfe was profoundly influenced by Michael Best's 1990 book, *The New Competition*, calling it his "practical bible" in an interview.[78] He was so enamoured by Best's work on Emilia-Romagna, an Italian region long controlled by the Communists where associational institutions were set up, that he later purchased a dozen copies of the book and "distributed it to bureaucrats throughout the [NDP] government." He told me, "I think people thought I was crazy."

As *Debating Canada's Future* was organized around a series of debates, these ascendant political viewpoints on Canada's social democratic left were pitted against their left-wing critics. Political scientists Leo Panitch and Donald Swartz agreed that the "epochal events of the past year in Eastern Europe ensure that 1989 will now stand with 1848 as a year of revolution when people went to the barricades." However, they were critical of the "old Cold War rhetoric" that equated democratic socialism with Soviet communism. For them, the current restructuring of capital reflected "the working out of global competitive forces in a new era of crisis." Panitch and Swartz also took aim at the social democratic fetishization of the Swedish model, writing: "It has been a constant theme of those who seek to cling to the old politics of compromise to point to Sweden as proof that it still can work. Since the 1930s Sweden has stood as the social democratic equivalent of the communists' Soviet model."[79] Furthermore, they doubted that Sweden's "corporatist approach to state-capital-labour coordination would work in Canada." For them, Sweden's "middle way" was little more than the politics of compromise.

The third collection of essays, published in 1992, edited by Daniel Drache, and entitled *Getting on Track: Social Democratic Strategies for Ontario*, grew out of an Ontario Federation of Labour seminar series on Ontario and the Global Economy between January and March 1990, sponsored by the Premier's Council. It sought to address difficult questions about how to deal with the global economy. The first seminar in the series featured David Pecaut of the Premier's Council as well as John O'Grady and David Wolfe. Another engaged with the idea of a "new bargain with the state." The resulting book suggested that at the heart of the economic crisis was the "imperative to restructure secondary manufacturing."[80] For his part, Hugh Mackenzie called the Premier's Council a "consensual springboard for a new economic direction." Its *Competing in the New Global Economy* report thus "stands virtually alone as a mainstream challenge to the idea that lowest-common-denominator competition is a given against which we must measure our expectations and according to which we must be prepared to trim our living standards." Though in substantial agreement, Drache cautioned that "for the social democratic left, this attempt to escape the neo-conservative ditch and rethink Ontario's future economic and industrial direction needs to be examined critically."[81]

One of the few dissenting voices in the volume was offered by the CAW's Sam Gindin and David Robertson in their chapter on "Alternatives to Competitiveness." They took exception to the emphasis of the Premier's Council on "high-growth" export businesses, lumping mature industries together into one homogenous mass. For Gindin and Robertson, the key was not to fund individual firms, picking winners and losers, but to foster the linkages among them. The goal should be "to develop production networks rather than world-class entrepreneurs." This point would later influence how the Ontario NDP approached its industrial strategy. Ultimately, Gindin and Robertson called the progressive competitive vision of the Premier's Council dangerous:

Once we decide to play on the terrain of competitiveness, we cannot then step back without paying a serious price. Having legitimated the importance of being competitive . . . we would be extremely vulnerable to the determined attacks that will inevitably come in the name of "global realities." . . . That is why, for socialists, competitiveness is not a realistic alternative to the status quo.[82]

Importantly, we can also see the beginnings of a powerful gendered critique of the Premier's Council in the volume, with sociologist Marjorie Cohen writing that the sectors most vulnerable to restructuring were the female-dominated clothing and textile industries. Yet, male policy makers had failed to recognize the ways that industrial restructuring intersected with the gender division of labour. The Premier's Council was similarly silent on pay equity and the ways that Canada's existing training regime served women badly.[83] That there were only a handful of women on the Premier's Council, she added, did much to explain this silence. Six months after the publication of the Premier's Council's second report, another feminist critique emerged, this time from advocates for community-based training and education for women. Echoing some of findings emerging in Hamilton, Advocates for Community-based Training and Education for Women (ACTEW) warned that the NDP's proposed Ontario Training and Adjustment Board was geared to unionized male workers in large industrial workplaces. As women and new immigrants were concentrated in smaller non-union workplaces, they would "continue to fall between the cracks" in the training and adjustment system. The coalition called for OTAB to include equity groups and expand its focus to new entrants in the labour market. Poignantly, ACTEW also objected to the "notion that lack of training education or unemployment is caused by a deficit in an individual. This analysis leads to blaming the economically disadvantaged for being a drain on our economy and our society."[84] It is a compelling critique.

CONCLUSION

The political defeat of economic nationalists during the free trade debate left an ideological void on the left. If central state planning and public ownership were off the policy-making table by the end of the 1980s (the previous two decades had seen the nationalization of a number of mills, companies, and entire sectors by the federal or provincial governments), what, then, was the role of the social democratic state in the economy, especially in a time of crisis? At one point in our interview, John O'Grady declared: "What we're trying to do is shift the debate on economic planning, industrial strategy, from the traditional left-nationalist perspective, which I would say was predicated on high tariffs and Crown corporations, to one that accepted the reality of a more globalized economy, or at least a more open economy. That it was going to be dominated by private capital, not public capital. And that the path to survival would be a high-skills path."[85] However unlikely, the ideological void in Ontario social democracy was eventually filled by a Premier's Council named by the governing Liberals and stacked with business representatives. Political philosopher Nancy Fraser has recently argued that there was a marriage of convenience between an elite-driven politics of diversity and inclusion on the one hand and neoliberal economics on the other, resulting in the hegemony of meritocratic "progressive neoliberalism" during the 1990s and early 2000s.[86] While this formulation captures the post-materialist politics of Bill Clinton and Barack Obama, as well as the Third Way politics of Tony Blair, it doesn't quite capture the "progressive competitive" impulse in Ontario. What was being imagined in the Ontario formulation was an alternative corporatist politics to neoliberal economics, one where trade unions had an expanded economic role to play.

Not everyone, however, was swept up in the enthusiasm for the lofty rhetoric of progressive competitiveness. Looking back, Hugh Mackenzie now thinks the effort to build labour-management corporatism in Ontario was "existing in a parallel universe . . . where plants weren't closing and there wasn't this industrial carnage taking place everywhere you look. It really occupied a parallel universe. I mean, I was engaged with it because every once in a while, Leo [Gerard] would drag me to things. But I really didn't find it very interesting. I certainly didn't find it very helpful."[87] Mackenzie thought the partnership initiatives under the Liberals and NDP were "performance pieces" to show the business sector that they were not a danger to them. But at the end of the day, the business sector remained anti-union. That's why Hugh Mackenzie thought capital mobility rather than trade was a key driver of job losses: "When we were talking about the 1980s, and the impact of free trade, I really framed my thinking about it around capital mobility rather than free trade." It is a critique that I share.

For its part, the Canadian Auto Workers maintained that Ontario needed a rules-based approach to economic change and the plant closing problem. Sam Gindin understood that "competitiveness is a real constraint. We cannot pretend it's not there. But trying to deal with it doesn't help us, it forces us to keep giving things up. . . . It just puts you in that box."[88] Making concessions did not guarantee jobs, "but having rules would." In 1992, Gindin wrote a damning critique of progressive competitiveness for Toronto's *This* magazine.[89] But before submitting it for publication, as a CAW staff member, he had to get Bob White's approval. After reading the draft, White told him:

> "You're going to get us into a lot of trouble. Steel's going to go wild and this is going to be seen as an attack on Steel." And I said, "I just think we're on the cusp of, there's a big ideological battle brewing . . . I have to write it. But I'll write it under another name if you're worried about the impact on Steel." And he came back to me and he said, "I'll let you decide, you do what you want. We'll live with it." And I wrote it under my name. And Steel was furious.[90]

Boldly taking aim at the United Steelworkers' policy statement on Empowering Workers in the Global Economy, Gindin challenged the underlying assumption that "the globalization of the economy is the new and unchallengeable reality Canadian workers must face."[91] Gindin opposed the mantra of "high technology," noting that many so-called mature industries had incorporated advanced technologies. Accordingly, "the very emphasis on high tech diverts attention from, and undervalues, the rest of the economy." Clearly building momentum, he then wrote that those who claim that training is the "answer to our economic problems [are] more than a little naïve." Ultimately, the problem with the Canadian economy was structural, given its reliance on foreign branch plants to serve the national market. Accordingly, capital mobility was the core challenge to Canadian prosperity, not some imagined skills deficit:

> It is crucial to find ways of dealing with the ability of corporations to move wherever they please, and their use of this power to blackmail concessions from the rest of society. Yet the enthusiast of the high-tech strategy rarely raises the possibility of, in some form, re-regulating investments in the Canadian economy. They don't discuss any mechanism to screen investment or even a return to the modest Foreign Investment Review Agency; no rules on plant closures; no direct or joint participation from government; and no Canadian content rules. They also generally ignore or reject any barriers to trade as part of a solution to growing corporate power. In fact, the desire for "responsibility" and "partnership" overrides past criticisms of the free trade agreement.[92]

Gindin was not alone in making this critique. Soon thereafter, prominent US economist Paul Krugman dismantled the idea of national economies competing in the new global economy, calling it a "dangerous obsession." The rhetoric of competitiveness had become "pervasive among opinion leaders throughout the world," he wrote. "People who believe themselves to be sophisticated about the subject take it for granted that the economic problem facing any modern nation is essentially one of competing on world markets—that the United States and Japan are competitors in the same sense that Coca-Cola competes with Pepsi—and are unaware that anyone might seriously question that proposition." Acidly, Krugman added that "every few months" a new bestseller appeared saying much the same thing, calling out Ira Magaziner and Robert Reich specifically. In his mind, they were flat-out wrong: countries are not corporations. In fact, national living standards "are overwhelmingly determined by domestic factors rather than by some competition for world markets."[93] Krugman likewise challenged Magaziner and Reich's association of "value-added" with the high-technology sector rather than with mature industries like steelmaking. It is worth quoting him in full here, as the Premier's Council, and later the NDP government, leaned heavily on the value-added idea in arguing for its embrace of a progressive competitive strategy:

> Ira Magaziner and Robert Reich, both now influential figures in the Clinton Administration, first reached a broad audience with their 1982 book, *Minding America's Business*. The book advocated a U.S. industrial policy, and in the introduction the authors offered a seemingly concrete quantitative basis for such a policy: "Our standard of living can only rise if (i) capital and labor increasingly flow to industries with high value-added per worker and (ii) we maintain a position in those industries that is superior to that of our competitors." ... Economists were skeptical of this idea on principle. If targeting the right industries was simply a matter of moving into sectors with high value-added, why weren't private markets already doing the job? But one might dismiss this as simply the usual boundless faith of economists in the market; didn't Magaziner and Reich back their case with a great deal of real-world evidence? Well, *Minding America's Business* contains a lot of facts. One thing it never does, however, is actually justify the criteria set out in the introduction. The choice of industries to cover clearly implied a belief among the authors that high value-added is more or less

synonymous with high technology, but nowhere in the book do any numbers compare actual value-added per worker in different industries.⁹⁴

In effect, Krugman suggested that the rhetoric of competitiveness was not based on empirical evidence but rather on "predetermined belief." The doctrine thus attracted those looking for "apparent sophistication without the pain of hard thinking" and offered politicians a "good way either to justify hard choices or to avoid them."⁹⁵ These were prescient words, as we now turn our attention to the Ontario NDP's five years in power.

National Rubber Company: Ahmet Dogru, Ismael Sarakiya, and Fernando Rogerio, Sheet press workers, 1993.
Photo by Peter MacCallum.

4

AN AGENDA FOR PEOPLE

> The crowd erupted in a sustained outpouring of exultant, emotion-wrenching cheering and applause. It reflected the sheer elation and pride of men and women whose cause had never before found public sanction. There we all were, 2,000 of us, grown-ups, with a life-time of moral victories and lost crusades behind us, many weeping unashamedly, too choked up to utter a word if our lives depended on it.
> —GERALD CAPLAN's observation of the swearing-in ceremony on 1 October 1990[1]

The Ontario New Democratic Party swept to power on 6 September 1990, taking 74 of the legislature's 130 seats (an increase of 55) with just 37.6 percent of the vote. The euphoria of election night clearly hadn't worn off on 1 October when the new cabinet ministers were led out onto the stage to thunderous applause in the jam-packed Convocation Hall of the University of Toronto and sworn in. This was the moment that New Democrats like Gerald Caplan had been dreaming of for decades: it was their graduation day. No wonder the faithful were choked with emotion. In celebration, the doors to Queen's Park were opened wide in a giant open house.

It had all happened so suddenly, with the NDP winning dozens of seats that had never been in contention before. Many newly elected members had volunteered to be the sacrificial lamb in their riding so the party could field a full slate of candidates. They used to call them "NOBs" for names on ballot, recalls Ross McClellan, "and they all won, right? Every one of them." Now elected, they had to hurriedly make arrangements with their employers. They were blue-collar workers, clerks, teachers, social workers, librarians, and nursing assistants. Fully 40 percent were rank-and-file trade unionists. Occupationally, they were unlike any previous government in Ontario history. "In a very real sense, it's a labor government," observed the interim Liberal leader.[2] He wasn't wrong.

The Ontario NDP had never been close to power before and so never had to wrestle with its constraints. Its policy thinking reflected this lack of context. *An Agenda for People*, the NDP's election manifesto, released mid-campaign, was hurriedly thrown together by a couple advisors in mid-campaign just in time for the televised leaders' debate.[3] While there was relatively little on how the NDP intended to manage the economy, the protection of industrial workers was a clear priority for Ontario's party of labour. Despite its influence on the party's current thinking, the election manifesto avoided any mention of the Premier's Council. To do so would unhelpfully blur the line with the governing Liberals: it was their Premier, after all. The NDP's manifesto also avoided

Happy day for labour: A jubilant Canadian Auto Workers chief Bob White hugs former NDP leader Stephen Lewis at Bob Rae's victory party. Photo by Tony Bock / *Toronto Star* via Getty Images.

mentioning wider neocorporatist ideas of labour-management partnership. Corporatism was strange and complicated, not easily explained in an election campaign or distilled into bullet points. Instead, *An Agenda for People* offered voters something of the "greatest hits" from the party's policy book. The NDP therefore ran on old favourites such as public auto insurance, rent control, and worker protection.

On the industrial crisis, the NDP, once again, promised to force departing companies to justify their plant closing decisions to a public tribunal. If the manifesto was short on details, this promise was an important one, as it suggested that the NDP could protect jobs and industrial communities from the ravages of global capitalism. The party also promised to soften the blow of displacement through a series of enhanced adjustment measures including longer advance notice periods, higher severance payments, and the extension of these measures to smaller workplaces employing ten

New Democrat Team: Plotting the campaign for NDP leader Bob Rae are, from left, director David Agnew, Jill Marzetti, Julie Davis, David Reville, and Ross McClellan. Photo by Ron Bull / *Toronto Star* via Getty Images.

to forty-nine workers. This change would make a real difference for women and immigrants, who were concentrated in smaller workplaces. Additionally, Ontario workers would no longer be at risk of losing their unpaid earnings when their employer went bankrupt. The right of displaced workers to retraining was also listed, though there was little hint that it would become the linchpin to the government's progressive competitive strategy once in power.

There were several key policy differences with the Liberals. For starters, the NDP promised to extend pay equity to all workers and increase social assistance benefits. It also promised to raise the provincial minimum wage from 42 percent to 60 percent of the average industrial wage and eliminate the discriminatory eighty-five-cent wage differential for workers under eighteen years of age. And, most importantly for the labour movement—which was hemorrhaging members, endangering the institutional survival of some unions—the party promised to reform the Ontario Labour Relations Act, making it easier to unionize and banning the use of scabs during industrial disputes. Job, wage, and union security were therefore at the top of the Ontario NDP's agenda for change.

To help pay for these promises, the NDP gamely proposed to tax the rich. At the time, the wealthiest 10 percent of Canadians had 51 percent of the net wealth and the bottom 50 percent had 5.7 percent. Income disparity had grown significantly in Canada over the previous two decades, but especially in the 1980s. The NDP promised a minimum corporate tax rate, something even US President Ronald Reagan agreed to, as well as succession duties for amounts over $1 million (a tax measure that had been repealed back in 1979) and a new tax to deter real estate speculation. If speculators sold a secondary property within one year of purchase, they would pay a 90 percent tax on capital gains, 75 percent in the second year, 50 percent in the third, and 25 percent in the fourth.[4] These tax reforms constituted the crux of the party's envisioned redistributive efforts. All of these promises would have been familiar to voters of the day, as the NDP had campaigned on most of them for years, if not decades. In fact, there was almost nothing new in their 1990 appeal. Even Rae was a known quantity; it was his third campaign as leader.

Over the course of the election campaign, the NDP inched up in the polls. Everyone that I interviewed shared a story about when it became clear that the NDP was headed into government. Frances Lankin, a leading figure in the Ontario NDP, who was running for the first time in the Beaches-Woodbine riding in downtown Toronto recounted this story:

> I think it was three days before the election, my campaign manager said, "Well, why don't you take the afternoon off, Frances." I said, "What are you talking about, Dawn? There's an election on, right?" She said, "Well, I think you've been really going at it hard, and you could use an afternoon off and go shopping." You know, like, I'm not even a big shopper [laughter]. She said, "You have to go shopping for cabinet minister clothes." And I said, "Pfft! Give me my poll stuff" and went out. I wasn't tuned in to it.[5]

Michael Mendelson offers a different perspective. He had served as a senior civil servant in Manitoba under the NDP and then the Tories, before moving to Ottawa to work for the federal Liberal government. Then, in 1989, he was hired as an Assistant Deputy Minister in Ontario under the Liberals. There, he worked closely with Liberal Finance Minister Bob Nixon. Those were boom years in southern Ontario, as the government's revenue was "going up and up." But inflation was also high. "Every few weeks," Mendelson recalls, "we did fiscal updates and in every single update, there was a revenue increase. We had a big surplus for the first time in Ontario in a long time." Then Premier David Peterson called an early election. At one point during the campaign, Mendelson remembers walking with Bob Nixon to see Premier Peterson, when Nixon revealed: "'We are going to announce the reduction of the sales tax.' I was like, we can't do that. He said, 'We are going to lose this election.' I was like, *what!* He said, 'Yeah, we are losing

Bob Rae and Ontario's first New Democratic Party cabinet were sworn in a public ceremony at the University of Toronto. Photo by Patti Gower / *Toronto Star* via Getty Images.

this election, Hail Mary!'"[6] But the political gamble failed and the NDP won a majority of seats.

FINDING THEIR BEARINGS

There are many theories about why the NDP unexpectedly won in 1990. The most popular explanation is that the governing Liberals had become complacent, even arrogant, during their short time in power. They had won a majority in 1987 after governing as a minority for two years with the support of the NDP. The next election was not due until 1992, but with economic storm clouds approaching, and riding high in the polls, the Liberals didn't want to take the chance and went to the polls early. It was an epic miscalculation. In this explanation, the NDP was not so much elected as the Liberals were defeated. While protest voting was clearly the single major factor, and the NDP ran hard against the Liberals, this explanation fails to tell us why the NDP was the default for so many voters for the first time in Ontario history. After all, Ontarians had been bouncing back and forth between the Liberals and Tories since the nineteenth century. What changed in 1990? Bob Rae's leadership was certainly a key factor, and every member of the expanded NDP caucus knew it. It was one of the reasons why Rae was able to maintain a remarkable degree of cabinet and caucus solidarity in the troubled years ahead. As one member of his inner circle told me, Rae was "not a wild-eyed person" and "there was a comfort with him" after three elections.[7] Few accounts, however, have taken seriously the fact that Ontario's economy was already in recession. The province's manufacturing sector had been in decline since late 1989, and the recession had formally taken hold by spring 1990. Howard Hampton, an MPP from northwestern Ontario, recalled that "you could feel the air running out of the [economic] balloon."[8] Others remembered the feeling of economic unease; voters sensed that things were beginning to turn bad, as plant closing announcements became a daily occurrence. Most voters blamed the Mulroney-Reagan Free Trade Agreement with the United States, which made it less likely that they would opt for the Ontario Tories and their new leader Mike Harris.

Politically, the plant closing issue played to the NDP's policy strength. Day after day, before the election was called, the NDP hammered the Liberals on job losses, using the latest closure announcement as a prompt to raise the issue in the legislature. It was an effective strategy that made the NDP much more visible in small-town Ontario, where many of these closures were happening. These were mostly labour-intensive industries that had relocated to rural and small-town Ontario in search of low wage workers back in the 1950s and 1960s. With trade liberalization and free trade, the same economic and political impulse now took these industries to low-wage countries. Ontario's branch plants were fast becoming redundant. Labour was also talking tough. "This is a political issue and workers never make progress until they take it to the streets," Bob White declared in late May 1990.[9] He predicted that Ontario workers would once again occupy their closing plants, just like they had a decade earlier.[10]

Later that summer the Ontario Federation of Labour asked local labour councils to mount protests on the issue in their communities, leading the *Windsor Star* to opine that "there's nothing like a mass rally of angry workers, a plant occupation or some other menacing act of civil disobedience, to put a crimp in a summer barbecue."[11]

During the campaign, Rae framed the party's program as a "New Deal for working people," invoking the progressive agenda of US President Franklin D. Roosevelt during the 1930s. He understood the lingering class appeal of Roosevelt's memory.[12] The NDP campaign's sustained assault on the Liberal government's response to the unfolding industrial crisis is recorded in its media releases. "Nobody can give David Peterson lessons on how to preside over a massive wave of plant shutdowns, jobs loss and the resulting human tragedy," the NDP preached. "While he twiddles his thumbs, free trade is devastating the economy."[13] According to Ross McClellan, the CAW ran a highly effective parallel campaign that involved "setting up a little cemetery with tombstones in each of these towns.... In those days the labour councils could put on a rally, and on the tombstones were the names of the companies that migrated to Mexico.... This had a huge effect on our successful campaign."[14] The leader's tour was similarly anchored in the industrial crisis. Thus, when Rae visited a closed furniture maker in the small southwestern Ontario town of Listowel, he blamed free trade for the displacement of its 137 workers.[15] In one stop after another, the NDP used such local examples to call for improved severance pay and notice as well as new justification legislation. The NDP's promise to economically defend Ontario communities resonated in unlikely places on election day.

That so many of the NDP's candidates from small-town Ontario were trade unionists was no coincidence. Their Wikipedia profiles offer us glimpses into their life trajectories. Shirley Coppen, a registered nursing assistant in a county hospital and president of the Welland and District Labour Council, with a degree in Labour Studies at Niagara College, was elected in the semi-rural riding of Niagara South. In southwestern Ontario, Patrick Hayes, elected in the riding of Chatham-Kent, was a factory worker at Rockwell International in Tilbury, a town of less than five thousand inhabitants, and served as president of his CAW Local, as well as the Chatham and District Labour Council. Then there was Brad Ward, elected in Brantford, located just west of Hamilton, who worked for Bell telephone and served on the town's labour council. He had been named Labour Citizen of the Year for 1989. Others representing small-town or rural ridings, like Randy Hope, elected in Muskoka–Georgian Bay in central Ontario, and Bob Huget, a chemical plant worker in Sarnia, were rank-and-file factory workers and trade unionists.

Bob Rae and the NDP had spent the election campaign raising the hopes of Ontarians, and would spend the next five years trying to temper them. But first they had to calm Bay Street, which was jittery at the prospect of the socialist hordes governing Canada's most populous province. "Business nightmare becomes reality," shouted one headline in the *Globe and Mail*. "Oh-Oh!" declared the *Toronto Sun*, whose business editor predicted "Bob Rae's NDP and recession in Ontario. What a recipe for disaster!"[16] When mainstream economists were asked their advice for the neophyte government, they all agreed that Rae would be constrained in responding to the recession by the fact that it was bigger than Ontario. "He certainly can't spend Ontario's way out of it," said one.[17] Industrial restructuring was necessary and should not be impeded, said another. The economist for the Bank of Montreal cautioned that Rae "faces a skeptical business community that is putting all investment plans on hold in response to both high interest rates and uncertainty over the direction the NDP will follow. Any attempt by Rae to increase expenditures and thus exacerbate the deficit will confirm the worst fears of the private sector that the NDP is fiscally irresponsible."[18] A few days before his cabinet was sworn in, Rae spoke to two hundred Toronto business leaders to allay their fears, saying that the NDP believed in building a partnership with the business community.[19] "No province is an island," Rae insisted in media interviews. "We can't pass laws pretending as if the rest of the world didn't exist."[20]

To say that the NDP was unready for power fails to capture just how fundamentally unprepared the party actually was. The transition team was formed only the day after the election, when Stephen Lewis and Gerald Caplan were put in charge of the process. The NDP had thirty days before the new government was sworn in, not much time to get their bearings, hire staff, appoint cabinet ministers, and so much more. The Lewis family was NDP royalty. Stephen was a silver-tongued former leader of the Ontario NDP, and his father, David, had been the federal NDP leader during the 1970s who had fought the good fight against "corporate welfare bums."[21] Other members of the Lewis family were also key players in the Ontario party. Stephen Lewis's sister, Janet Solberg, who had served as president of the Ontario NDP in the late 1980s, was put to work in the vetting of ministerial staff; their brother Michael had been the party's hard-working provincial secretary and now worked for the United Steelworkers of America. For his part, Caplan, a party insider and a life-long friend of Stephen Lewis, was a former federal party secretary and a frequent media pundit. Neither man had any government experience whatsoever. As a result, they didn't know where to begin.

Michael Mendelson was unimpressed. He had been part of the transition between the NDP and the Tories in Manitoba, so he was stunned when the civil service "never got directions to facilitate the transition. Worse than that the NDP had no clue what they were doing! I would say the Rae government was totally unprepared for it." In effect, Lewis and Caplan "didn't have an effing clue what to do with the government, they didn't know that they should set up an office, a transition office inside the government, in one of the buildings there and take two to three deputy ministers they could reasonably trust and put them on the transition team and they just didn't do that." Mendelson shares a story of when he was finally brought in by the transition team to advise them.

> [It was still] working out of Gerry Caplan's house, with nobody on the public service working with them. They set up a meeting with four to five senior staff who they

thought were compatible with them and I was one of them.
... We met at Gerry's in the evening, and I said, "Why are you operating in secret? You are the transition team. You should be having an office. This isn't a secret! Take over the government for Christ sake!" They just didn't know that.[22]

Stephen Lewis later admitted that he learned more about how government operates in his two-hour meeting with cabinet secretary Peter Barnes, Ontario's top civil servant, than he had in fifteen years in the legislature. David Agnew, Rae's thirty-two-year-old chief of staff, could only shake his head and say "so much to learn."[23]

After this initial meeting, Mendelson was named the Deputy Secretary of the Cabinet Office, and he immediately went to work streamlining the cabinet decision-making process. Under the Liberals, decision-making had been much more decentralized, with strong ministers and their deputies: it was disorganized at the centre as the "cabinet process wasn't well defined." Indeed, it wasn't unusual for cabinet ministers to bring new proposals directly to a cabinet meeting or to come to agreement in the corridor. "Once I was in central government, that was not going to continue," Mendelson told me. Henceforth, he required formal cabinet submissions and thus "almost eliminated all the walk-ins." He believed it important that there be proper due diligence before any cabinet decision was made. He also reformed the writing of minutes in the cabinet: "The minute is going to be the decision of the cabinet. I know that sounds small, but it isn't. From here on, I required all cabinet submissions to clearly state what the recommendation was." Mendelson also set up the cabinet committee system and how their decisions then went to Policy and Priorities, essentially the inner cabinet. Every policy item thus had to come forward from a ministry to one of the cabinet policy committees: "I mean, the process was cabinet committee, then [Policy] and Priorities, and if they involved any fiscal issues they would also go through the managerial board simultaneously, before coming to cabinet or [Policy and] Priorities. But if it was within budget, it would go to the managerial board as a pro forma." He also imposed order on the Cabinet Office: "It was sort of helter-skelter before. We didn't have a clear organizational structure." According to Mendelson, part of the restructuring of the Cabinet Office was intended to take back control from the deputy ministers (who were civil servants but appointed by the government of the day) in the line ministries who had grown used to wielding considerable power under the Tories and were left largely unchallenged under the Liberals.

The Cabinet Office thus supported the decision-making process, set strategic priorities, and managed the policy approval process. There were four policy committees of cabinet including the one on economy and labour. Each one was backed up by a policy unit of five advisors in the Cabinet Office headed by an executive director. Most advisors were career civil servants but a few, like David Wolfe, were brought in from outside by Mendelson. The Policy and Priorities Committee of Cabinet met every Monday, and had its own policy team. During the first two years, the government had a new initiatives process and a special funding envelope. After that point, the fiscal crisis took hold and there was virtually no new spending—just budget cuts and policy implementation. This is one of the reasons why so much of this book is focused on the first two years of the NDP mandate.

In the Premier's Office, Rae retained his closest advisors. David Agnew, the new chief of staff, had worked for him in Ottawa, and moved to Toronto with Rae when he became Ontario NDP leader. The son of the conservative editor of the now defunct *Toronto Telegram* newspaper and a journalist himself, Agnew was extremely well organized. Ross McClellan, who had been an NDP MPP in Toronto's west end from 1975, the chief NDP negotiator of the NDP-Liberal Accord in 1985 as well as NDP house leader, was hired as a senior advisor. Between 1987 and 1990, McClellan had worked for the Ontario Federation of Labour as its legislative director, which meant that he continued to attend caucus meetings. After the election, McClellan attended cabinet meetings as a full participant. He told me, "I think it was because of the bond I had had with the fifteen people, veterans, I mean, we were very close-knit, and I had been their House leader, and so I was able to have a major influence on some of the key debates."[24] He was more circumspect during caucus meetings, however, saying they wouldn't want somebody from the Premier's Office "mouthing off a lot." McClellan was, by all accounts, labour's man in the Premier's Office. Then there was Chuck Rachlis, the former head of NDP Caucus Research, who had worked closely with David Wolfe first at the Social Planning Council of Metropolitan Toronto and then in the NDP Economic Policy Review. After the government's 1995 defeat, the two men co-authored the first "insider" account of the NDP years.

One of the most important decisions that a new government makes is the composition of its first cabinet. A lot of factors come into play, such as experience, geography, gender, ideology, other forms of diversity, and personal chemistry. But there was also the matter of the size of the cabinet. And this was perhaps Bob Rae's second big mistake (after naming the transitional team) as

"Class photo" of the new Ontario NDP cabinet. Members who loom large in this book include the following. Front row: Bob Rae (middle), Richard Allen (second from right). Second row: Bob Mackenzie (third from left), Floyd Laughren (to his right), Frances Lankin (to his right). Back row: Ed Philip (far left), Shelley Martel (third from left), Bud Wildman (two to right, with beard), Allan Pilkey (three to right). 10 October 1990. Photo by Ron Bull / *Toronto Star* via Getty Images.

incoming premier: he decided to name a large twenty-six-member cabinet even though there were few, if any, experienced people inside the caucus. In his interview, Mendelson regretted not having warned Rae that he was making a mistake after it was suddenly announced as a fait accompli at an early planning meeting:

> And I remember thinking to myself in that moment, holy shit that's wrong! You start with the cabinet of ten people and gradually bring people in, as they get more experienced, because they are just inexperienced. . . . I said to myself that I didn't know Bob, I didn't know David Agnew at that time, I said to myself, Should I say something or should I not say something? . . . But then I thought to myself that they had already informed these twenty-six people. I decided not to say anything. I think that was the wrong decision. I think I should have spoken up and if they didn't like it, that's too bad, but then they would get used to a person speaking up.[25]

That said, a majority of the new cabinet had at least served in the caucus previously. This meant that highly unionized industrial areas like Hamilton and northern Ontario had the lion's share of cabinet members. Northern Ontario had long been an electoral stronghold for the party, according to Bud Wildman: "It had elected a lot of MPPs, and re-elected them. And so, we were some of the most experienced members of caucus. When it came to selecting his cabinet, the premier relied on experience."[26]

Critically, Floyd Laughren, the veteran MPP from the Sudbury-area riding of Nickel Belt, was named Ontario Treasurer and the Deputy Premier. The Premier and Finance Minister or Treasurer are central to any government. However, in more ways than one, Bob Rae and Floyd Laughren were a political odd couple. They had very different backgrounds and came from opposite ideological wings of the party. Rae was a party modernizer who had sought to bring the NDP to the political centre, whereas Laughren had co-founded the party's Left Caucus in the late 1970s and was once a strong proponent of public ownership. Rae's father was a career diplomat whose family had a private island on Big Rideau Lake and socialized with members of the economic and political elite. Rae went to the University of Toronto and then Oxford. His brother was a vice-president of Power Corporation, one of Canada's corporate titans during the 1970s and 1980s, and a prominent Liberal. Laughren, by contrast, was born during the Great Depression and grew up in a large family of eight children in the small village of Shawville in western Quebec, before becoming an economics teacher at a Sudbury college. Laughren was soft-spoken and well liked; whereas Rae was said to be aloof and socially awkward. Laughren had even supported Rae's more left-wing opponent during the 1982 leadership contest. And yet, despite their differences, the two men were now very much in sync. According to Bob Rae, "on every issue we faced, I relied on him a lot, and relied on his advice . . . I mean, he went through the same reality check that I did."[27]

Other members of the inner cabinet included Wildman, Lankin, Shelley Martel, Evelyn Gigantes, and Dave Cooke. Only Lankin was newly elected, and she was also the only active trade

Wise words: Treasurer Floyd Laughren (left) and Premier Bob Rae listen attentively as the NDP's agenda is outlined in the legislature.
Photo by Ron Bull / *Toronto Star* via Getty Images.

unionist in the inner circle. The key ministries for the purposes of my study, however, were the Treasury (Laughren), Labour (Bob Mackenzie), Industry, Trade and Technology (initially Allan Pilkey, soon replaced by Ed Philip), Training and Skills Development (Richard Allen), Natural Resources (Bud Wildman), and Northern Development (Martel). Realizing his initial mistake after a lengthy series of costly missteps and mini-scandals, as well as a number of underperforming ministers who had to be shuffled out, Rae belatedly reduced the size of cabinet in February 1993. It was at this point that Lankin took over the expanded and retooled Ministry of Economic Development and Trade. Rae conceded in our interview that he initially "made some mistakes in making appointments of people who were inexperienced and who were thrown into the deep end of the pool and didn't work out."

Although trade unionists made up 40 percent of the caucus, relatively few were named to cabinet. Several strong potential NDP ministers with labour experience, such as Mike Breaugh in Oshawa, had decided not to run again in 1990. "You would've had three or four key ministers who were labour voices," laments Peter Warrian. "And they weren't there. McClellan was in the Premier's Office and he did all he could. I mean, other than Mackenzie, there was virtually nobody in the cabinet with a labour background."[28] This was not altogether true, as Lankin, a senior member of cabinet, had been very involved in the Ontario Public Service Employees Union (OPSEU), and David Christopherson, a former CAW union president from Hamilton who had direct experience with plant closings, was Solicitor General. But the general assessment has considerable merit. If nothing else, the disparity reflected a class-based understanding of what makes a good candidate and cabinet material.

Even before the end of the government's honeymoon, there was growing concern within the NDP caucus about the gulf between backbench MPPs and the cabinet. These concerns were formally raised and discussed within the first eight months, and a committee was struck to tackle the problem. It reported back in September 1991:

After a year of learning the ropes, we know better some of the reasons why relations between cabinet and Caucus can get strained: busy schedules all round, tough decisions that affect some members more than others; overlooked riding concerns; new staff unfamiliar with riding or hot issues; miscommunication (and sometimes just plain noncommunication); stress and strain.[29]

It was agreed that parliamentary assistants, the powerless back-bench understudies assigned to some ministries, would now serve on cabinet committees, and the caucus agreed to explore other ways to tap them more meaningfully. "Too many Minister/PA relationships aren't working," the committee bluntly reported. Ministers were also instructed to have caucus briefings prior to announcing major legislative initiatives, including inviting interested caucus members to provide input at an early stage. These adjustments soothed but did not eliminate the growing pains.

My interview with an anonymous member of Rae's inner circle reveals much about the deteriorating economic situation and the government's thinking. They noted that it was "challenging in those times to make a difference on the economy," especially as a subnational government. The bad news just kept "coming and coming and coming." They then recalled one mammoth new investment of hundreds of millions of dollars at General Motors "and basically, they said this might clean up the layoff list. I mean, that was just our reality."[30] When I asked who had the economic ear of the government, they replied: "There weren't a lot of influential and persuasive voices on the economy." Nor was there a "strong economic bent" among the government's core advisors. They agreed that David Wolfe "was a very important part of the cabinet office," as was Riel Miller in the Treasury, "but they were viewed as being very academic, to be honest with you." Several others shared this assessment. Miller chalked this perception up to a current of anti-intellectualism that ran through the party. Until the appointment of Frances Lankin into a new economic super-ministry in 1993, the same unnamed senior advisor suggested that the cabinet members holding the major economic and labour portfolios were not strong voices. "I am just being blunt," they said.

Veteran members of the NDP caucus had the advantage of having been part of the NDP-Liberal Accord from 1985 to 1987, which saw the party, while still on the opposition benches, negotiate a governing policy framework agreement with the minority government of David Peterson's Liberals. Bob Rae credits the accord negotiations as the "beginning of a serious discussion" about the politics of power. "I worked really hard on convincing the party and the caucus that that's where we had to go," he told me. "And there was a lot of opposition and skepticism to that approach to things."[31] Once negotiated, the NDP and Liberals met regularly to discuss progress on the shared legislative agenda. Jim Foulds, the NDP's then finance critic, recalls that he would meet Bob Nixon, the Liberal's Finance Minister, five or six times before each budget to discuss specifics.[32] He learned a lot in the process. As Rae told me, "It changed the dynamic in the caucus, because people had a much keener sense of how things worked." I then asked him if the experience of the accord years helped the NDP once in power, to which he replied: "It did, it did a lot. It had a big impact on it."

Bud Wildman certainly agrees with this assessment. "Having been in the House, and having been involved in these issues, I was involved with them for fifteen years before I was elected into government," he says. "To be a new member, to be learning how to be an MPP as well as learning how to be a cabinet minister all at the same time, I frankly could not fathom how some of them did very well, others did not."[33]

Rae's third mistake was to rush their return to the legislature, less than two months after the government was sworn in. The cabinet members were still getting a handle on their ministries and the government had yet to finalize its legislative priorities or prepare new legislation. "I think we met the House too early," the anonymous member of Rae's inner circle I spoke to told me. "We were unprepared for it."[34] As a result, the government left itself open to opposition attack for its lack of direction and, just weeks after taking power, the supposed sluggishness in its response to the unfolding industrial crisis. Reflecting back on those early days, Rae says: "There's no textbook that says, 'This is what you got to do. This is how it worked.'" They were all learning on the fly, even the Premier.

The NDP held two cabinet retreats a year, beginning with a start-up meeting in October 1990. These were multi-day meetings where the cabinet reviewed its priorities and made adjustments.[35] The party's provincial secretary, Jill Marzetti, and president, Julie Davis, also attended, as did the OFL's new legislative director, Wayne Samuelson. Here is David Wolfe's account of the first cabinet retreat held shortly after taking office:

> The retreat for the most part consisted of ministers sitting around the table and spending two or three days talking about all the wonderful things that they got elected to do. And if you'd taken everything they mentioned over the three days and made a list, it would have stretched from at least from that door to the other door and been virtually impossible for any government to deal with. So, it was a huge long wish list of things with no sense of priorities, no sense of order, no sense of organization or coherence. So, the Premier's Office, I think, the Premier's staff decided between the first and second retreat that . . . there was a need to organize this a little more coherently.[36]

There were four priority lists, one for each cabinet committee. Some of the items were taken from *An Agenda for People*, others from the line ministries, and still others, according to Wolfe, "quite frankly came from the fertile imaginations of the x number of us sitting around the table and working away. . . . We had a certain degree of latitude to bring forward ideas that we knew there might be genuine interest in the cabinet to look at." Generally, the policy advisors in the Cabinet Office wanted longer priority lists and the political staff in the Premier's Office wanted shorter ones. After considerable back and forth, this list was then approved at the second cabinet retreat in March 1991.

Wolfe suggests, however, that the "least influential" source of policy for the new government was the Ontario NDP's policy book. He wasn't the only one to make fun of it because it still called for the nationalization of a bank and the Sudbury-based mining giant INCO as well as "all sorts of wonderful things." Wolfe insists:

> To the best of my knowledge and my personal experience I never once in the three years I worked in the government saw anyone go off and look up that resolution book and say, "Gee, this is what the party decided in policy convention a couple years ago, why don't we do this." ... I would say those policy resolutions were not a serious source of policy ideas for the government.[37]

The dismissiveness of these comments reminds us that Wolfe, like so many other newly hired staffers, had limited experience within the party itself. They therefore had little investment in membership-driven policy development. As we saw already, the party's economic policy review of 1989–90, led by Floyd Laughren, but which included Wolfe, Chuck Rachlis, and Riel Miller, was totally divorced from the party membership and existing policy. For advisors like Wolfe, who were proponents of European-style corporatism and a progressive competitive growth strategy, most of the economic ideas found in the policy book from conventions past reflected an economic and political world that was now history. That said, Wolfe did suggest to me that *An Agenda for People* "was quite influential in the early going of the government . . . because it was the only indication the bureaucracy had as to what the government's agenda was."

Several key NDP insiders spoke at length of the perceived opposition of senior civil servants to the NDP agenda. The idea that the government was sabotaged from within still resonates thirty years later, as does the convenient idea that the government's problems all stemmed from poor communications rather than anything more substantial. Worried about the loyalty of senior civil servants to the new government, Rae appointed several veteran

NDPers into senior positions. However, the election of NDP governments in British Columbia and Saskatchewan a few weeks after the Ontario victory hobbled the new government, as the coterie of experienced NDP administrators were needed in their home provinces.

Another source of potential staff members was the union movement. Unions did their best, however, to defend themselves against "raiding" from the NDP government. D'Arcy Martin, from the Communications and Electrical Workers union, thought this response was short-sighted at best. In mid-October 1990, he urged his boss, Fred Pomeroy, "We should be placing people where we want them and organizing for ongoing, broad input on the key issues facing workers." He feared that the "risk right now is that we ask for too little and offer too little." After the NDP victory, the union movement had to go beyond the "feeling of 'family celebration'" and use the current goodwill to "establish a political relationship which acknowledges our diverse interests." It was essential, for Martin, that the government not come to view organized labour as just another interest group. Indeed, the "NDP has always been weak on practical economics, while the labour movement has always been strong. This is the area [in] which to push the government in the high stakes area."[38] He told Pomeroy that labour needed to place staff in the key economic portfolios. A few, like the CAW's Carol Phillips, did enter government, in this case coordinating appointments to government agencies. For his part, Ross McClellan tried in vain to convince the "brain trust" of the Canadian Labour Congress in Ottawa to come over: "Well, I mean, they were like hobbits, in their hobbit houses in Ottawa, very comfortable lifestyle in Ottawa, and the last thing they wanted to do was come to Toronto."[39]

Organized labour compounded this initial mistake when it rejected a proposal made by John O'Grady, the OFL's research director, that the large number of trade unionists on the government benches should form a labour caucus. This was, after all, what the union movement did during Provincial NDP Council meetings and party conventions. Issues were debated and positions taken among themselves, after which union representatives voted as a block. It was an effective strategy, though sometimes resented by other delegates. Given its sheer size, a labour caucus of MPPs would have had huge influence inside the new government. However, according to Ross McClellan, CAW leader Bob White spoke strongly against the idea, saying he didn't want anybody to stand in the way between him and Bob Rae. It was a short-sighted stance, to say the least, prompting O'Grady to quit the OFL in disgust.[40] McClellan made the prescient point that in time, many of these same backbench trade unionists formed a rural caucus instead, leading most to take a conservative stance on such issues as extending spousal benefits to same-sex couples. Rae had allowed a free vote on the issue, which the government then lost. These rural and small-town MPPs, according to McClellan, had "lost their connection with their own unions, with one or two exceptions," and were, as a result, another group of victims of "the body snatchers," referencing a popular movie about aliens taking over human bodies.[41] Had these same members formed a labour caucus instead, the internal politics of the caucus might have played out differently. McClellan was convinced of this and I think he is absolutely right.

THE THRONE SPEECH

The inaugural speech from the throne, delivered on 20 November 1990, was sweeping in its ambition. "As a group of people accustomed to being on the outside of the established power structures in Ontario," it began, "my government will open Queen's Park to those who have never before had an effective voice in the corridors of power." Ontario faced many challenges that demanded a "new vision" for the province. With the election safely behind it, the progressive competitive vision of social partnership and consensus building re-emerged as the government's guiding framework:

> As social democrats, my government believes in the need for a new relationship and respect among all the forces in the Ontario economy—labour, business, community

organizations, government—so we can begin to work better together to achieve our common goals. New ways of co-operating will be needed. My government is determined to build a consensual, environmentally responsible economic strategy for the 21st century.[42]

It was an aspirational document, albeit one that emphasized equal opportunities over outcomes, much as Third Way social democracy would do later that decade. "We must build a society in which all Ontarians can achieve the best of which they are capable," the government opined. The signature announcement was the decision to immediately direct $700 million towards new capital expenditures on public-sector building projects to create construction jobs. Regional and community development were similarly emphasized, given that the impact of the recession was falling "unevenly" across the province. Critically, the speech went on to say that "all of us must become open to change and adjustment. But we must ensure that the burden of change does not fall solely upon workers and communities. A fairer and more democratic economy must share both the benefits and the burdens of change arising from the time of major economic adjustment in which we live."

There were some substantive promises in the throne speech: employment and pay equity as well as the promised increase in the minimum wage, revised rent control legislation, more affordable housing, extended child care. Public auto insurance remained a priority. The throne speech also promised that the government would introduce a number of measures to protect workers, including a wage protection fund to ensure those working for bankrupt firms got reimbursed for their lost wages as well as "stronger measures on layoff notice, severance and other adjustment issues." The overall goal, as stated, was to "foster a society where economic change will not mean a dramatic loss of income or self-esteem." Meanwhile, labour law reform would ensure the right to unionize. A Fair Tax Commission would undertake a "fundamental review" of the tax system, thus signalling that no immediate changes would be considered. For better or worse, the new government had decided not to tackle the redistribution of wealth. Naturally, this last decision drew praise from the party's ideological opponents in the Canadian Manufacturers' Association and the Canadian Federation of Independent Business.[43]

It was an ambitious throne speech, but it was telling what was not mentioned. There was no hint of using state power to save jobs. To the contrary, what we see instead is the acceptance of economic change as not only inevitable but necessary for future prosperity. Indeed, the NDP government had turned it into a social virtue. The old left-nationalist politics of resistance to industrial closure, detailed in chapter 1, was entirely absent, as was the New Deal rhetoric of the election campaign. In their place was the consensual language of social partnership, fairness, and the progressive competitive desire to find a high-skill, high-wage niche in the global economy. Expecting something more radical, the media suggested that the first throne speech was a "curiously flat document, which goes drifting off in all directions at the same time."[44] It included twenty-one initiatives, ranging from the "numbingly minor" to others that were "potentially far-reaching." Much of it was "nebulous" enough it could have been written by a Liberal or a Tory, wrote journalist Thomas Walkom, who claimed that Rae looked positively Liberal in his first weeks as premier: "If Ontario voters were worried [that] they had elected the province's first socialist government, they can rest easy. For as Premier Bob Rae's Throne Speech showed this week, whatever the New Democratic Party government is, it is not socialist."[45]

Even so, in the beginning, there was considerable public curiosity and goodwill directed towards the new government. Everybody likes an underdog, at least at first, and the NDP certainly fit the bill. To orient readers to this new political reality, newspapers reprinted long excerpts from *An Agenda for People* or Bob Rae's January 1990 speech "What We Owe Each Other" (which I opened the book's introduction with). Those close to the party were asked for guidance. Two former NDP premiers, Saskatchewan's Allan Blakeney and Manitoba's Howard Pawley, for example, were asked by the *Toronto Star* about what advice they would offer the new premier.

Blakeney cautioned that no provincial government could afford to be "financially radical" as it "cannot print money. It does not control the economy."[46] If it runs a deficit, it must borrow money from the global financial markets; the bond dealers and ratings agencies were therefore a factor. For his part, Pawley advised that Rae's priority should be dealing with the recession: "He needs to develop an over-all economic and job strategy," just as Manitoba did during the previous recession. Unlike Blakeney, Pawley was not afraid of deficit financing during such extraordinary times: "Without action, lack of employment means higher welfare costs, higher health costs, higher justice costs, such as legal aid and courts. So not all the money spent on job creation is lost money."[47] Both former premiers, however, agreed that Rae needed to move quickly on public auto insurance. Every other provincial NDP government had delivered on this promise. It was now part of the party's DNA. In the weeks that followed the election, the party's approval rating skyrocketed to 60 percent. Then all hell broke out.

The NDP was confronted by an economic meltdown in its first months in power. Ontario entered the recession in April 1990, two financial quarters before the United States; the province's unemployment rate climbed from 7.5 percent in June 1990 to 9.2 percent that December.[48] It then reached the double digits. During a January 1991 pre-budget consultation, government experts reported that there were 10 percent fewer manufacturing jobs in the province than the year before, and unlike the last recession, most were being displaced by plant closings rather than layoffs.[49] There was, therefore, no job to go back to once the economy recovered. Even though Ontario accounted for 38 percent of Canada's total labour force, it accounted for nearly 80 percent of the jobs lost during this period.[50] Fully 300,000 Ontario workers lost their jobs permanently.

In our interview, Bob Rae emphasized that the "initial impact of free trade in Ontario in 1990 was terrible. It was a disaster. Because you had all of these companies that were closing down branch plants left and right in medium-sized industrial towns right across the province. It had nothing to do with the provincial

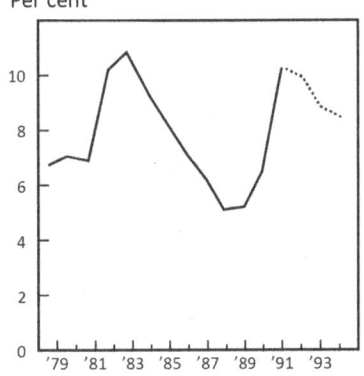
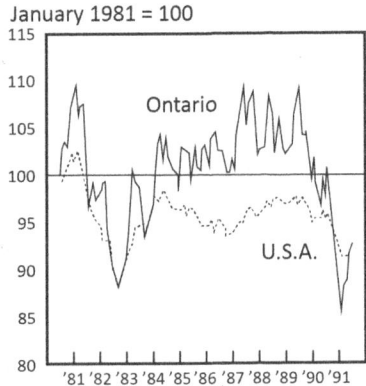

Ministry of Treasury and Economics. Economic Overview. 29 August 1991. File: De Havilland. B368449. Archives of Ontario.

government."[51] The timing could not have been worse for Ontario's manufacturing sector, given the high Canadian dollar, which had risen from 70 cents to the US dollar in 1986 to 89 cents in 1991.[52] There were other factors such as higher interest rates and the imposition of the goods and services tax (GST) by the federal government. The 40 percent tariff reductions as part of the Tokyo Round of the GATT also kicked in at the same time. In short order, Ontario's branch-plant economy was made largely redundant, as multinational corporations restructured their operations in favour of global supply chains rather than national branch plants. Employment in Ontario's manufacturing industries, as a percentage of the workforce, dropped like a stone from 30.2 percent in 1981 to just 18 percent in 1991.[53] No wonder many trade unionists drew comparisons between 1990s Ontario and the 1980s US Industrial Midwest.

Once elected, the Rae government had no choice but to focus its attention on the rapidly deteriorating economic and fiscal situation. Recalled cabinet minister Frances Lankin:

> In the first number of months, we were reeling from the very sudden downturn of the economy, and its effects on

the fiscal situation of the government, and obviously, the economic and job and human impacts and costs within the province and the economy.... Our first couple of initiatives in response were quite short term stimuluses in approach. Traditional short-term job-creation through construction, the anti-recessionary package, to try to get somethings going out there.[54]

Companies were "dropping like flies," recalled Bob Rae. As Ontario's premier, he was briefed regularly and his crisis team put in place a list of companies thought to be in "serious trouble," a kind of early-warning system.[55] Much of the work of the Premier's Office was therefore dousing the economic fires or responding to the many political stumbles of cabinet members. The crisis atmosphere made it difficult to think longer term or see the bigger picture. Under the circumstances, it is hard to imagine how it could have been otherwise.

The rapidly deteriorating situation played havoc on the government's economic forecasts, forcing Floyd Laughren to issue a series of revised Economic Outlooks, each one worse than the previous. The first, dated 4 December 1990, optimistically claimed that the province's overall fiscal position was solid.[56] At this point, Laughren declared that the government "will not sit back and wait for economic forces to take their course. We believe that there are important steps we can take to stimulate job creation, to alleviate hardship among the most disadvantaged in our society and to ensure that the engine of economic growth is primed for an early recover." The $700 million public infrastructure program would, he said, create 14,000 full-time but short-term jobs. The 18 March 1991 Economic Outlook was far more pessimistic, as the recession was much deeper than predicted. Indeed, the release of new job numbers had shown that "Ontario has suffered the worst job losses since the Second World War."[57] The realization that this was not simply another cyclical downturn made the stakes considerably higher.

Business and labour had very different ideas about how to respond to the unfolding industrial crisis. Ruth Getter, a senior economist, told a legislative committee in January 1991: "I am trying desperately to find something good to say," but the declines were generalized across the board—"in our manufacturing, in our construction, in our exports, everything. You name it and we got hit." She urged the government not to get caught up with the idea that jobs were moving to Mexico. Getter asserted that capital flight due to free trade was exaggerated: "We are already so interlinked globally in every possible way. That is where the future is and that is where we are going. If we pretend that the world has not changed, we would be making a big mistake."[58] Getter believed that industrial restructuring, albeit painful in human terms, "does have a positive aspect" in so far as "inefficient and unprofitable firms are forced to compete or else they have to bail out." Putting it frankly, she said that "people get hurt by that, but that is the way it works. ... In a way, it is good for the Ontario economy, because after this recession you are going to be left with efficient and competitive producers." Hence, competitiveness was not only key to Ontario's future, it also made the provincial economy stronger.

The Ontario Federation of Labour, which presented later the same day, countered that the recession was primarily structural, making it different from the last recession in Canada but similar to what the US Midwest experienced between 1979 and 1983. This prospect, the OFL warned, ought to scare Ontarians, as this "was the period in which the term 'rust belt' entered popular economic discourse."[59] Would Ontario become another Michigan? Hamilton another Youngstown, Ohio? It was not enough to sit back and watch it happen.

KEYNESIANISM'S LAST GASP?

The NDP's first budget was delivered on 29 April 1991, containing a projected deficit of $9.7 billion. Much of it was going to be there no matter what the NDP did. Provincial tax revenues were in actual decline for the first time in the postwar era, and the previous Liberal government had handed the NDP a surprise $4 billion deficit. The federal Tories also unilaterally reduced transfer payments to the provinces, substantially worsening Ontario's fiscal situation. Billions more were simply the result of the spike in the number of Ontarians on social assistance: a 40 percent increase in spending in one year. It didn't help that the federal government was restricting the eligibility rules for unemployment insurance, pushing more people onto provincial welfare rolls. As a result, only $1.7 billion was the result of new NDP spending, and much of that comprised the "anti-recession" infrastructure program. Rae later explained in his memoirs, "We felt an overwhelming need to soften the blow of the recession."[60] But it was timid Keynesianism at best: not enough to make a real economic difference but big enough to trigger a political backlash. Given the rapid policy U-turn that followed, it also represented "Keynesianism's last gasp," at least until its resurrection during the 2008–9 financial crisis and, again, during the 2020–21 global pandemic.[61]

Over the summer of 1991, the Standing Committee on Finance and Economic Affairs held budget hearings across the province. To shore up its political position, the NDP mobilized its electoral base in support of its fight against the recession. One of the first to present in Toronto was Mel Watkins:

> As economists, we support the major elements of the recent Ontario budget and reject the view that the degree of fiscal stimulus is excessive or likely to create significant long-term economic problems. Ontario Treasurer Floyd Laughren has rightly noted that he had a choice, to fight the deficit or to fight the recession. He made the correct choice.[62]

In any case, the government's deficit was only 3.4 percent of the provincial GDP, well below recent federal deficits and proportionally smaller than recent ones in Alberta or Saskatchewan. As Ontario had a small accumulated debt, the cost of servicing it was not expected to rise above 12 percent of revenues. Despite having been downgraded, the province's credit rating remained excellent, and so the province would continue to be able to borrow from the international money markets on excellent terms.

Trade unionists, to the irritation of the opposition parties, also presented in large numbers. They defended the government but also urged it to go further. Nick De Carlo, from CAW Local 1967, representing the 3,500 workers at McDonnell Douglas, applauded the government's courage in fighting the recession and not turning to austerity as other governments had done. He praised Laughren's determination to fight the recession, not the deficit. That said, he thought the government should do more to fight deindustrialization: "Let's take a look at plant shutdowns. There have to be legislative changes made to require companies to provide information and to explain the basis for closing down an operation. This would give the community, the workers and the government the right to take a look at it."[63] De Carlo noted that his own aircraft manufacturing plant once employed fifteen thousand people and it had designed and built the most advanced plane in the world: the Avro Arrow interceptor. It now was a sub-assembly plant manufacturing aircraft wings for another plant in California. Conservative Chris Stockwell, a partisan pit bull, was unimpressed by De Carlo's testimony: "You just spent a whole bunch of time talking about crap, in my opinion, and this is pap. All you are missing is the seven-year program, us living on communes and developing a manifesto. Where did you talk about competitiveness? You never even answered the question." When De Carlo asked "which question," Stockwell replied with one word: "competitiveness." To this, De Carlo shrugged. "What about it?"[64]

OFL president Gord Wilson, who presented in the hard-hit eastern Ontario town of Cornwall, similarly defended the government's priorities: The government "made a choice. They decided not to fight the deficit. They wanted to fight the recession."[65] Wilson then said if Ontario is looking for a way to "survive within a global economy," it should follow the lead of Germany and invest in worker training. He credited the Premier's Council, of which he had been a member, for developing an alternative strategy for the province and providing a model of how to build consensus. No fan of the language of partnership, CAW president Bob White's message to the government in Windsor differed: Ontario must act quickly as "the development of the rust belt in the United States a decade ago may now be spreading into Canada." It is worth quoting White's critical assessment of the unfolding industrial crisis:

> Budgets are about choices. They are statements about priorities and direction, about who will benefit and who will pay. They occur in a particular context, which sets some limits on what can and cannot be done. . . . The economic context of the Ontario budget was the deepest recession since the Great Depression. More than a quarter of a million jobs were lost during this recession, almost doubling the numbers unemployed, leading to an explosion of welfare cases and accelerating growth in the dependence on food banks in this, Canada's wealthiest province. An especially frightening aspect of the recession was the parallels to what had occurred in the United States in the early 1980s.[66]

For White, the budget debate was ultimately "about whether or not the economic policy this government has adopted in a time of recession is the correct one, or whether the economic policy of slash and cut is the correct one." He reminded the committee that it was mostly due to the "collapse of revenues" compounded by the reduction in federal transfer payments and the rising welfare case load. Like other trade unionists, White insisted that the budget's social initiatives were "relatively modest" and that future budgets would need to "comprehensively" address the NDP government's mandate.

Yet the wider political reaction to the first budget was disastrous, with the NDP's poll numbers falling off a cliff from a high of 60 percent to 30 percent. In his memoirs, Bob Rae called it a "major setback" for the government, as it enraged business and reinforced the public perception that the NDP were poor financial managers. From then on, the "die was cast."[67] Nearly every NDP insider that I interviewed drew the same conclusion. Ross McClellan told me, "It killed us politically. I mean, from our first budget we were dead."[68] Similarly, for John O'Grady, the "first Ontario budget was catastrophic. Frankly, that's when the government never recovered from that error in economic and political judgment. It destroyed itself from that point."[69] "They never recovered," Michael Mendelson agrees. "The first budget I have to say was a political disaster and to me it's not so much the content of the budget, but . . . the way it was promoted."[70] The NDP had tried to make a virtue of running a deficit.

This political stance was grounded in both the past and present. Canada's political left and the trade union movement had long insisted on the primacy of full employment and had long condemned federal Tory and Liberal governments for prioritizing the fight against inflation instead. In Ottawa, the Brian Mulroney Tories were now prioritizing the deficit to the detriment of working people, who paid the economic price of unemployment. The NDP was going to do things differently, leading the party to lionize its choice to fight the recession. We "took some pride in what that slogan meant," declares Frances Lankin. "I loved it! It's as close to fighting words you can get around a budget."[71] More cautiously, Ross McClellan told me that he had pleaded with Bob Rae to explain the deficit away as something largely inherited from the Liberals (which was true). But the Premier would have none of it: that was the old politics. Michael Mendelson, too, understood it as "both an ideological choice and a political choice. The political choice was made to celebrate the deficit choice and I believe that was politically wrong."[72] The government's rhetoric fired up the party's base, but turned off many other voters.

It appears that the first budget was developed entirely in Laughren's office. Mendelson now wishes he had inserted himself "more forcefully" into the first budget-making process:

> To a certain extent [I] consider it my fault as I was probably in a position where I could have exerted more authority, but I didn't. . . . I don't think I would have won but I would have had some impact. I was aware of it because of my depth of political experience and my attitude, which was

AN AGENDA FOR PEOPLE 145

"All together"—the Ontario NDP cabinet. Frances Lankin sits directly across from Bob Rae (smiling at the camera) and Floyd Laughren to his left. Behind them sits David Agnew, who was Rae's chief of staff. 10 October 1990. Photo by Mike Slaughter / *Toronto Star* via Getty Images.

probably more fiscally conservative than Riel's and Floyd's was at the time.

Burned the first time, Rae's office was much more careful in controlling the preparation of subsequent budgets, but the political damage was done. The business community was out for political blood. In fact, the anti-NDP campaign was already well underway. A November 1990 advertisement in the *Wall Street Journal* warned investors from investing in Ontario. Then, in December, *Barron's*, which Liberal MPP Monte Kwinter called the "bible of the investment industry in the United States," published an editorial warning that a "New Socialist Threat Raises Its Ugly Head."[73] The deficit, which made Ontario the largest non-sovereign borrower in the world, spooked the markets. In mid-May, the bond-rating agency Moody's lowered Ontario's credit rating from AAA to AA2.[74] The treasurer travelled to New York City to calm US investors. In his memoirs, NDP-friendly civil servant Michael Decter recounts another meeting in New York with a senior official of Goldman Sachs about Ontario's borrowing. As he tells it, they tested the waters at ten billion, twelve billion, and then fifteen billion: "When I mentioned the $15 billion a long and uncomfortable silence descended over the table. No one spoke. Finally, Bob Hormats of Goldman Sachs spoke, 'That would be unchartered territory for a non-sovereign borrower.'"[75] This interaction, and others like it, convinced the Ontario cabinet that the risk of crashing into the debt wall was a real one.

The Rae government's first year had not been easy, with the recession dominating all other issues.[76] It didn't help that the government's own emphasis on competitiveness trapped it in the underlying logic of neoliberal thinking. Business climate became a key determiner of what was or was not a policy option and led the government to emphasize consensus making whenever possible. The failure of the Mitterrand government's bold plans in 1981–82 loomed large in the minds of social democrats around the world, including at Queen's Park. The French Socialists had tried to stimulate the economy via redistributive spending but were forced by the international markets to make a policy U-turn within the year, after which they imposed austerity. Riel Miller was still working at the OECD at the time and so had a front row seat:

> I was inside what they call the Working Party Three, which is the top secret—well, secret, very behind closed doors—meeting of the senior finance bureaucrats, who basically told the French bureaucrat, "game over." I mean, you are about to be crushed—the foreign exchange—you can't do Keynesian reflation in one country. It's too porous. It won't work. Your budget will just go out—and the bond market will just kill you, which is what happened, of course.[77]

Given this experience, he was not naive about Ontario's ability to reflate the provincial economy.

> That was obviously ridiculous. But I felt pretty strongly, and this is where ... it made a difference to have somebody from Sudbury, Floyd, and not somebody like Bob,

I suspect, and others. Where I said, "Look, we're not going to do it on the backs of working people," so that was the nuance and the phraseology. The communications person, who was a Liberal Bay Street person who was just being a bureaucrat, who hadn't been replaced at that point in time, was replaced a bit later. She basically said you're going to get killed. You're going to get absolutely wiped out. And Floyd said, "Why did we get elected if we are not going to do this?"

Miller thinks Bob Rae and David Agnew are still angry with Laughren for his first budget, "because they probably felt that that was what catalyzed Bay Street, or helped to legitimize Bay Street to come and protest, because we said we were not going to fight the recession on the backs of working people." Miller strongly disagrees, insisting that it was "complete fantasy" to think that the business-led "counter-revolution" could have been avoided; it was "coming regardless" of any "clever PR or political sloganeering." He credits Laughren for his "integrity and ethics," contrasting his actions to those of US President Barack Obama during the 2008–9 financial crisis: "No, we're not going to bail out the shareholders, so it's not Obama. It's not the 2008/2009. . . . They weren't going to do that. You know, from my point of view, more power to them. Well, more power to us, because I was part of that rump, as it were."

With the party's members strongly in favour of the Rae government's initial approach, the party-government liaison committee reported that everything was going smoothly on the eve of the announced U-turn. Formed after the September 1990 victory, the committee's proactive mandate was to "identify structures and processes for facilitating dialogue and problem solving between the party and the government."[78] Ross McClellan, from the Premier's Office, gave the party's Provincial Executive regular monthly updates and Rae spoke at Provincial Council meetings, giving members the opportunity to raise questions and concerns directly. The party president, Julie Davis, and provincial secretary, Jill Marzetti, both attended caucus meetings.[79] There were therefore structures in place to ensure that the government and the party itself remained in sync. Everything changed in the days that followed.

Unbeknownst to the party, the Ontario NDP government would follow a similar trajectory as Mitterrand's France, concluding over the summer months of 1991 that deficit financing was not a viable option.[80] The fierce backlash against the NDP government, and the abrupt end of its honeymoon period, led to what David Wolfe calls a "subtle but very important change in the priorities."[81] At the third cabinet retreat in September 1991 in Honey Harbour, "the whole priority list was reviewed and reorganized." The cabinet decided to focus on the twin themes of job creation and fiscal restraint; as a result "anything on the original priority list that looked like it had the potential to create a job anywhere in the province of Ontario tended to stay in the top half of the list or to move up. Anything else ... got bumped down to a lower position."[82] The beginnings of austerity were captured in a story shared with me by Bryan Evans, a senior civil servant in the Ministry of Labour. Apparently, after an investigative television program warned that Ontario was in danger of hitting a debt wall, sensationally comparing it to defaulting countries in the Global South, "Bob Rae made everybody watch that. Like deputy ministers, whatever, they all had to watch it. It became required viewing." Evans believes that "from that point on, from when they got the riot act read to them in New York, that was the beginning of the end. Because they had nothing to fight back with and they really believed those bond ratings ... they believed them."[83]

Public auto insurance was the first high-profile casualty of the change in government direction, making Ontario the first NDP government in Canada not to nationalize the industry. British Columbia, Saskatchewan, and Manitoba had all done so, delivering cheaper auto insurance over the long term. To be fair, public auto insurance was never going to be easy in Ontario. Unlike out west, the insurance industry was largely based inside the province and its nationalization would have led to massive layoffs in the middle of a deep recession. That many of these employees were women was also a political factor. "That was their wedge," Bud Wildman insists, "because they knew we were not only an environmental government, we were a feminist government."[84] There was also a fundamental contradiction embedded in the NDP's twofold promise on auto insurance. As Michael Mendelson explained to me, they promised, on the one hand, to "bring in public auto insurance and lower premiums," and on the other, to reintroduce the right to sue. But it was impossible to achieve both objectives: "You can lower premiums and have no-fault public auto insurance, or bring in tort and increase premiums. You cannot have it both ways, so they had made a contradictory promise." The cabinet spent hours and hours "trying to square this circle" to no avail. Eventually, Rae "put an end to this, saying, 'We are not going to do this, we can't do it.'"[85]

If the decision not to proceed with public auto insurance was understandable under the circumstances, given the unfolding economic crisis, there is no mistaking that the announcement was disastrously handled by Bob Rae. He decided to play up his decision, making it public on the first anniversary of the NDP's election night victory. He also took the uncompromising stand that the issue was now off the table permanently, no matter what the party membership had to say about it. Had he simply said that it was being postponed until better economic times, most members would have understood. Instead, many now felt that Rae was rubbing their faces in it. After all, the NDP had run on the issue over multiple elections. Wildman, for one, recalls how divisive the decision was within the party when "the premier finally said, 'No, we're not going to do it.' And he didn't just say we're not going to do it now, he said we're never going to do it. It caused a real division."[86] Only later did Rae come to realize that dropping the auto insurance promise was a political mistake as it "had a significance for all of us" that he "didn't fully appreciate at the time."[87]

The government's unilateral decision to abandon public auto insurance hit the party like a freight train, prompting the party's Provincial Council to defy the government by overwhelmingly reaffirming its policy the next month. Importantly, it went a step further and adopted a resolution put forward by the executive that declared that henceforth, any government proposal that went directly against party policy must be brought to council or convention for full consideration before proceeding. It is worth quoting the resolution in its entirety, so important was this political moment in the party's history:

> Whereas the Rae government has abandoned driver-owned public auto insurance and the Premier has said "we don't intend to revisit this question or return to it or relive it, believe me, over time";
> Whereas this is not the only reversal of Party policy made without full consultation with the Party, contrary to the long standing practice of participatory Party democracy and convention supremacy; therefore;
> BE IT RESOLVED that:
>
> 1. An Ontario New Democratic Party government must follow the established fundamental policies of the Ontario New Democratic Party.
>
> 2. Any proposed variance by the government from established fundamental Party policy must be preceded by the matter being brought before Convention or Provincial Council for full consultation.[88]

To put it another way, the Ontario NDP insisted that "Provincial Council and Convention makes policy. Provincial caucus determines timing and methods of implementing that policy."[89] It is a rare example of a party taking a public stand against its own elected members. The government was stunned by the level of defiance inside the party. To rebuild trust, a caucus strategy document, likely written by Ross McClellan, suggested that future accountability sessions would ideally

> be a discussion which frames the issue in a kind of Talmudic way "on the one hand, on the other hand", which

exposes the trade-offs, the costs, the dilemmas surrounding every initiative that this Government has had to take.
... What I am suggesting is that we talk in real terms about real dilemmas, describing the pros and cons in an honest way, in a thorough way, in a way which reveals the bureaucratic and political and policy implications, so that the inevitable cross currents become obvious. And always in a spirit of openness so that the Party doesn't get the feeling that the decisions have already been made.[90]

The Premier's Office naturally wanted party activists to be confronted by "the complexity of Government initiatives" and for the government to be alerted when proposed government initiatives would be "simply unacceptable to Party activists." Ultimately, the aim was to "help to moderate critical reaction and often painful divisions in the Party." There was also a warning if they didn't get this right: "Then we are not only alienating the people we count on most but we are missing an opportunity to forge a Government/Party relationship unique and meaningful. That would also be an important contribution to democratic socialism in Ontario."

These new consultative measures were put to the test in early 1992 when the government abandoned the party's long-held position opposing Sunday shopping. An extraordinary meeting of Provincial Council was held in May 1992 to debate the government's proposal. "We felt that the party needed to be consulted on this," said party president Julie Davis. "It is an extremely important issue for many of our members, especially retail workers and small business operators."[91] Once again, the Provincial Council voted to reaffirm party policy, but the government proceeded anyway, as it was allowed to do under the new rule. Nonetheless, contributors to the *New Ontario Democrat* newsletter openly asked, "Where does the Ontario NDP stand with the government that it elected?"[92] The party convention that followed "wasn't dull," as delegates "tangled" over auto insurance, Sunday shopping, and government accountability.[93]

The chasm between the Ontario NDP and the government it elected continued to grow wider as the government slid deeper into austerity politics. The party was in virtual rebellion, with members openly debating the extent to which the government is "obliged to follow the policies that party members have democratically adopted."[94] The November 1992 Provincial Council was another heated one, with the *New Ontario Democrat* running the headline "Party and Leader lock horns." The editor of the party's newsletter freely admitted that the "continuing tension between the government and the party has been no secret." Rae's personality didn't help. Several people told me, off the record, how Rae would signal his displeasure at these council meetings by performatively burying his head in his hands or dismissively reading the newspaper during debate. Most importantly for the purposes of this book, there was growing concern about the "economic stance" of the Rae government, as "deficit control appear[ed] to take precedence over the sufferings that follow from unemployment and economic disparity."[95] The Provincial Council, heretofore indecisive on the government's U-turn, demonstrated "new resolve" at its November 1992 meeting, overwhelmingly adopting two motions put forward by the party's executive. One called on the government to "declare war on the recession" again, and the other "stressed that ours must be a 'different vision' of the economic future."

Bob Rae's incomprehension at the party backlash was shared by others in his inner circle. According to advisors Rachlis and Wolfe, "The ideological fireworks were blinding. Key party spokespersons decried the flip-flop, the timidity, the sell-out, the betrayal, the turning away from fundamental principle, the cowardly flight from confrontation with the insurance industry." They explained away the divergent views as merely the result of "the different demands of opposition and government. The logic of opposition, at least as the NDP had defined it, was rigidly black and white."[96] In Rae's own mind, auto insurance fed into the "myth of betrayal" that took hold in much of the party.[97] The auto insurance issue, like others that followed, speaks to the fundamental challenge for parties on the left that claim to be membership driven. What happens when the party is elected into office? It also speaks to the ways that the economic conversations within government diverged from those in the party's grassroots.

CONCLUSION

The actions of the Rae government must be understood within the context of a quickly deteriorating economy. The recession was longer and deeper than anyone had expected, bottoming out only in August 1992. By then, Ontario's economy had shrunk almost 3 percent and provincial revenues declined by $3 billion: the first actual decline in a half century.[98] As Bob Rae explains it:

> We were facing a crisis of deindustrialization: we lost 300,000 manufacturers [jobs] in a year, which was incredible. We were having to deal with that, and putting out fires on a constant basis, but also dealing with them. And as Premier, I was deeply involved and engaged in every one of the major restructurings that we did. As were the people who worked in my office.[99]

The government spent the first year trying to deliver on its wide-ranging election promises. Its initial focus on the recession instead of the deficit recognized that working-class and other marginalized peoples were always the ones paying the price for economic change. One can therefore understand why Floyd Laughren's office initially made a different choice. But claiming the deficit as their own damaged the government, unfairly reinforcing the perception that the NDP was not a good fiscal manager. The far bigger mistake, however, was the hasty political U-turn that followed and the subsequent slide into austerity politics. In Rae's mind, this was when the NDP government came of age, moving from a party of protest to a party in power. Much of his own party clearly did not agree.

By all accounts, the decision to make a political U-turn emerged over the summer months of 1991, as the budget hearings were still underway. Rae credits David Agnew, his chief of staff, as the one who first understood "the need for a major turn in government policy on the economy."[100] Others around him say much the same thing. Michael Mendelson, for example, recalls that "the U-turn took place in the Premier's mind after the budget" when he and a small circle of cabinet ministers "realized that, 'Oh no, this isn't really working out and we have to figure out what to do.'" To Rae's critics, however, the political U-turn revealed a panicking government in full retreat. Thomas Walkom paints a portrait of a cabinet "united in its fear that Ontario was going to hit a 'debt wall.'"[101] In his view, Rae was too easily spooked:

> Take his U-turn on the budget. In April, Treasurer Floyd Laughren brought down the first NDP budget in Ontario. It was not radical. In fact, it was mildly conservative. But it did deliberately avoid the shibboleths of contemporary fiscal wisdom: it included no massive spending cuts.... But then it changed—dramatically, suddenly, for no apparent reason. There were no new arguments, little new information. But at some point in mid-summer, Rae decided to do a U-turn. The deficit—the difference between what the government spends and what it takes in—would become the single most important target for government. Not unemployment, not bankruptcies, but the deficit. This had implications.[102]

Likewise, in Sam Gindin's oppositional telling, the Rae government "met with the trade union leaders and tried to intimidate them—'We're hitting a wall, we can't do anything.' 'We're not going to be able to borrow money'—and the trade union leaders, of course, didn't listen." Instead, they "called in the researchers" and asked them to dig up the "facts." Those facts told a different story: "I mean, they might have to pay more, but it was ludicrous to think that global finance is going to say 'We're not giving Ontario any money.' And Rae was intimidated by that." But even Gindin has to admit that "competitiveness is a real constraint. We cannot pretend it's not there. But trying to deal with it doesn't help us, it forces us to keep giving things up . . . it just puts you in that box."[103]

While there is considerable truth to this criticism, I also think John O'Grady was right when he insisted in our interview that "fiscal crises are real. Recessions are real."[104] Laughren remembers "feeling very strongly that we couldn't let the deficit go up. . . . we really had to fight hard to make sure it didn't go up."[105] He still believes that the government was "flirting with danger, if you will, in terms of our bond rating, and so forth."

When I asked Bob Rae about the change in direction, he explained it mainly in pragmatic terms. The government was trying to do too much, citing specifically the restructuring of Algoma Steel (chapter 6), Spruce Falls (chapter 7) and De Havilland (chapter 8). His office was integrally involved in each of these efforts. He is not wrong. But Rae went on to also suggest that the policy change was the culmination of the government's steep learning curve over its first year in power. According to him, the first signal of the coming course change occurred in January 1991 during a speech he gave to the Rotary Club at the Royal York Hotel, when he "started talking about how creating wealth is just as important as distributing it; and if you don't create it, you can't distribute it, and these are lessons you have to learn to be practical about." The policy shift was justified in terms of pragmatism, but as we will see in the coming chapters, the triumph of the pragmatic politics of progressive competitiveness over an older labourist politics was incomplete.

National Rubber Company: Nivia Simao and Natalia Raposo, 1993.
Photo by Peter MacCallum.

5

BOB MACKENZIE'S LABOURISM

> Bob Mackenzie has been in the House for a long time and I will respect the fact that he really cares. That is one thing about the member for Hamilton East, something you cannot attack. He has views that you cannot agree with because they are extremely radical. He is extremely devoted to the labour groups, and that I respect.
>
> —BOB CALLAHAN, Progressive Conservative Party, 1991[1]

Bob Mackenzie worked his way up from the shop floor to become a trade union organizer and an elected member of the provincial parliament for the NDP in 1975, where he represented the working-class district of Hamilton East until his retirement in 1995. He spent his years in opposition hammering away at the governing Tories and Liberals on labour issues, so his appointment as Minister of Labour was a dream come true. It also signalled to the union movement that the newly elected government intended to deliver on its promises to workers. Mackenzie often referred to himself as the Minister *for* Labour, though Rae forced him to give up his United Steelworkers membership in the name of the appearance of neutrality. But there was no doubt that he was labour's man in the cabinet. He was known to end internal ministry meetings with "I need to check with Gord," before proceeding.[2] That's Gord Wilson, president of the Ontario Federation of Labour. Hitherto a fairly minor portfolio in the provincial cabinet, the Ministry of Labour gained new prominence under the NDP. Symbolically, Mackenzie was seated in the second row in the legislature—a row ahead of Oshawa MPP Allan Pilkey, the hapless new Minister of Industry, Trade and Technology (MITT). Historically, Pilkey's ministry was the high-profile voice of the business sector inside cabinet, making his appointment, as the son of a recent president of the Ontario Federation of Labour, and his seating placement, doubly symbolic.

While more educated members of the NDP government's inner circle later whispered that Mackenzie was not the sharpest tool in the toolbox, there was no doubting his determination or commitment. Jim Foulds fondly recalls that "he was a bit of a bull in the china shop, but he was a good bull in the china shop. He was the kind of guy you should have in your caucus because he actually knew the working-class experience, because at fourteen he started working on boats."[3] In truth, I came to like Mackenzie a great deal over the course of my research. He was a straight shooter. One oft-told story about Mackenzie's years in government speaks to this deeply felt working-class sensibility, which is too often missing in the upper reaches of power. The story originates in the early days when the cabinet was wrestling with how to extend the life of uranium mining in Elliot Lake in order to buy the isolated town of fourteen thousand inhabitants some time to transition to a non-mining future. The fledgling government had inherited the problem after Ontario Hydro, the province's arm's-length public utility, ended its contract to purchase Elliot Lake uranium, which was grossly overpriced. The deposits in Saskatchewan were of higher grade and considerably cheaper to mine. Indeed, as Bud Wildman explained to me: "The problem with the operations in Elliot Lake was that they were underground mines, and they were competing with open pit operations in the West, which are a lot less expensive to get the product out." It was therefore the worst of times for the northern Ontario mining town, located midway between Sudbury and Sault Ste. Marie, forty-five minutes' drive north of the Trans-Canada Highway. Its unemployment rate had already soared to 60 percent by the time that the NDP came to power, and there was real concern that it would become a ghost town unless the government intervened.[4] Once dubbed the "uranium capital of the world," Elliot Lake only existed as a town because of the uranium mines, though it was the historic homeland of the Anishinaabe of Serpent River First Nation. The environmental and health legacies of uranium mining were far-reaching and long-standing.[5]

Members of the NDP's Northern Caucus were committed to helping Elliot Lake in its economic transition. Floyd Laughren recalls that the United Steelworkers were "at us all the time," wanting the government to intervene energetically:

> I remember, I had a meeting at a hotel with the Steelworkers, and we were talking away and . . . I came up with a number. I said 250 million. And it was sort of a gasp in the room. And one said, "Can you deliver on that?" And I said, "Well, if I can't, you won't be talking to me as a finance minister." And so, Bob was good that way. He was a bit surprised, I think, at the number too. But you know . . . in the overall scheme of things . . . it wasn't just the town, it was the surrounding area and all that, but it was the right thing to do.[6]

Shelley Martel, the new Minister of Northern Development and daughter of Elie Martel, the veteran NDP MPP who had served with Mackenzie on the Select Committee, was able to finalize the promised $250 million adjustment and diversification package, including $65 million from Ontario Hydro in recognition that the community had fed the province's nuclear reactors for decades. The financial support was used to reduce municipal debt, expand the airport, and purchase empty residential housing for the town's ambitious plans to become a centre of assisted living for seniors. Ontario Hydro was also convinced to extend its wind-down until 1996, enabling 750 miners to work a few more precious years. In sum, the government refused to let the town die overnight, giving it the breathing space necessary to diversify. According to Martel, "We had a choice in Elliot Lake. We could have told Hydro: 'Cancel the contracts. Walk away. Leave the community in absolute crisis,' and it would never have been able to be in a position to make the kind of transition we are convinced it will make."⁷ Not only did Elliot Lake make that transition, but it also became a beacon for other single-industry towns across Canada looking for a new beginning.

But Elliot Lake's success was not a given and there were real concerns about nuclear energy within the NDP cabinet. The deadly Chernobyl accident in Ukraine occurred in 1986, hardening opposition to nuclear power. The new Minister of Energy, Jenny Carter, an anti-nuclear activist and secondary school teacher from Peterborough, froze the building of new nuclear reactors in November 1990. However, during one cabinet discussion about saving Elliot Lake, Carter reportedly declared: "Why bother? They'll all be dead of cancer soon anyway."⁸ Mackenzie was so upset by the unfeeling remark that he instinctively lunged across the table. The table was wide and Carter was in no danger, but his visceral reaction speaks to a deeply felt class sensibility. Carter was quietly dropped from cabinet soon thereafter.

At one level, this story reveals the political cross-currents within the Ontario NDP. The party united the post-materialist politics of many urban middle-class progressives and the redistributive politics of many working-class voters. Not surprisingly, the two groups did not always see eye to eye. We sometimes forget that the politics of any individual are not simply a matter of ideological choice, but also derive from the felt knowledge accrued over a lifetime. Race, gender, class, and region infuse, but do not predetermine, people's sensibilities and political outlook. At another level, Elliot Lake revealed something important about Mackenzie himself, beyond the masculinist rough-and-tumble politics of trade unionism and working-class ridings like Hamilton East: he was hot-wired to do everything he could to implement his party's ambitious agenda on labour issues.

To that end, Mackenzie was aided by the fact that labour matters were where the NDP had the most policy expertise. No other political party had more. Mackenzie could also count on the civil servants in his ministry who, according to most observers, "responded enthusiastically to the election of the new government and rushed to cabinet with proposals to implement a wide range of new initiatives."[9] Bryan Evans, who worked as a civil servant in the Employment Standards Branch of the ministry, recalls the party atmosphere at the office the morning after the NDP victory. "We were all pinkos," he says, laughing.[10] The coming of the NDP meant new programs, increased budgets, and more staff for the Ministry of Labour. Indeed, its budget estimates jumped from $154 million (1990–91) to $356 million (1991–92), given its oversight of a new wage protection program.[11] Labour matters were therefore at centre stage during the government's first throne speech, as it declared its intention to proceed with its campaign promises to expand pay equity, revise the workers' compensation system, improve parental leave, reform labour relations, hike the minimum wage (and eliminate the discriminatory two-tier system for those under eighteen years of age), provide wage protection, offer longer notice periods for plant closures, improve severance pay, and reimagine skills training. Accordingly, the *Toronto Star* declared that organized labour was the "big winner" of the throne speech.[12] Over at the *Globe and Mail*, a journalist similarly concluded that "most of the new initiatives are directed at embellishing the rights of workers and the disempowered."[13]

While there was considerable backsliding and watering down of these policy initiatives, mostly because of the fierce, some would say hysterical, opposition of the business community, aided by the long delays in introducing and passing legislation, these promises were mostly kept. There were two notable exceptions. First, the party's long-standing promise to create a job protection board to review plant closing decisions was quietly dropped in the first weeks without explanation, and so did not even make it into the throne speech. Job protection quietly became wage protection in government press releases. The long fight to regulate plant closing decisions therefore died quietly. More surprising, perhaps, was the eventual decision not to proceed with the twice promised changes to advance notice and severance pay. That these changes were important to the labour movement and popular among the trade unionists in the caucus made the decision even more curious. In fact, a June 1991 private member's bill from George Dadamo, NDP MPP for Windsor-Sandwich, proposed to substantially increase notice and lower the minimum threshold.[14] Several NDP members in the legislature spoke with real pride about the proposed legislation. "We have waited too long for this," declared backbench MPP Randy Hope from Muskoka–Georgian Bay, adding that it would give unions the ability to "sit down and discuss with management the possibilities and alternative routes other than being terminated."[15] But it was not to be; as we will see, the matter was referred, studied, and ultimately rejected.

Bryan Evans, now an anti-austerity scholar, understood the cabinet's unwillingness to follow through on its promises to displaced workers as the result of having been severely burned by the fierce opposition of business to the wage protection and labour relations laws. The archival record supports this conclusion. The general feeling was that organized labour had got what it most wanted; it was now time to move on. That these plant closing measures had been largely agreed to by the Liberal Premier's Council in its consensus report of July 1990 no longer seemed to matter for a cabinet taking heavy fire from the media and opposition parties. In any case, the Ministry of Labour's regulatory approach was falling out of favour with a government fixated on social partnership and consensus building. Instead, as we will see, the Rae government opted to extend the duty to bargain to plant closings under the Ontario Labour Relations Act and require that labour and management consult on a regular basis during the life of a collective agreement in the hopes that a less confrontational atmosphere emerged. Accordingly, the recession of the early 1990s, unlike those of the early 1970s and 1980s, would not see substantial improvements in Ontario's existing plant closing legislation. There was a clear cost to this shift away from a more regulatory, rules-based approach and it was paid by workers in smaller, mostly non-union shops who continued to fall outside the province's advance notice and severance pay laws. That women were concentrated in these very workplaces speaks to the ways that the gender division of labour worked against women in the industrial workforce. In 1993, the Ministry of Labour's adjustment functions were transferred to the Ontario Training and Adjustment Board, a multipartite body at arm's length from government.[16] With the shifting balance of ministerial power, Bob Mackenzie increasingly found himself on the outside looking in. Bud Wildman, a good friend, recalls that Mackenzie "found his experience in some ways quite frustrating."

TURNING THE TABLES

With the November 1990 throne speech, a new session of the legislature threw the inexperienced cabinet into the day-to-day pressure cooker of legislative debate. As it takes time to prepare legislation, the rushed beginning delayed the introduction of promised legislation and gave the opposition parties the public platform they needed to pummel the NDP on the unfolding industrial crisis. The defeated Liberals quickly adopted the old NDP parliamentary tactic of using the latest plant closing announcement to regularly attack the government.[17] One day it was the closure of Fedders in Orangeville, during a strike, no less, and the next it was Fiberglas Canada in Sarnia, with the loss of 191 jobs. Small-town Ontario was hemorrhaging jobs. When Harding Carpets closed its Collingwood plant, on 29 November, the Liberals noted that "within the span of a year, the town has been forced to look on in horror as one third of its workforce joined the unemployment rolls courtesy of industrial layoffs."[18] When would Bob Mackenzie and the NDP deliver on their promises to Ontario working families? It mattered little that the NDP had only been in power for two months.

That same day, Liberal Remo Mancini, who had earlier served with Mackenzie on the Select Committee on Plant Shutdowns, solemnly read onto the legislative record the names of dozens of recent closures across southwestern Ontario and how many workers had lost their jobs in each instance. He worked his way from one town or village to the next, prompting jeers from the NDP benches.[19] Dave Cooke, an NDP cabinet minister, loudly heckled: "What are you doing?" To which, Mancini explained:

> I am cataloguing for the new government the pain that is being felt by real people, the suffering that real families are going through, the bleak Christmas and the bleak new year that hundreds of families will be facing. Some of these people faintly remember the promises that were made by the new government during the last election campaign. I will continue to stand in my place and speak for these people who are suffering, who have received their pink slips, who have been told that they are no longer useful at their place of employment, for whatever reason. They will have a voice in this Legislature.

Getting the rise from the government benches he hoped for, Mancini continued to work his way through his long list of closures, including those in Cooke's own Windsor riding, before turning to the individual stories of those displaced. For good measure, he then read back Mackenzie's own words while in opposition in support of a job protection board. Mancini wanted to know if the NDP would follow through on its promise to stop closures from happening. Mackenzie had little choice but to respond vaguely, as his legislative proposals had to be vetted first by the cabinet committee responsible for economic and labour issues before going to Policy and Priorities for final approval. The devil was in the details and the throne speech only offered the broadest of brush strokes. The public perception that the government was slow to respond to the industrial crisis was thus first established by the premature return to the legislature.

Interim Liberal leader Bob Nixon could smell blood in the water. He urged the government to be more specific and to move quickly to introduce legislation to help those being displaced.[20] On 6 December, another Liberal MPP noted that *An Agenda for People* "stated quite clearly that they would establish a job protection board to establish whether plant closures are justified."[21] Was it still the government's intention to legislate plant closure justification? To this direct question, Mackenzie could only say that "plant closure justification is but one of a number of suggestions . . . that we will be bringing in when we bring in the labour adjustment programs and the amendments to the Employment Standards Act."[22] Similarly, when asked the same question by the *Financial Post*, Premier Rae replied: "'We are committed to the principle of job protection . . . How we do it and how justification happens' is an issue under study by the Ministry of Labor."[23] Meanwhile, the NDP's election promise that it could somehow prevent plants from closing was being proven false almost every day. By March, six months after the NDP's election victory, one Liberal declared that "the promises [to those laid off] sit gathering dust on some obscure shelf, hoping they will be forgotten and go away. This province needs leadership; these people need direction."[24]

From the start, there was little hint of the old left-nationalism in the government's responses to plant closing questions. Instead of multinational corporations, they blamed free trade as well as high interest rates and the higher value of the Canadian dollar. The policies of the federal Tories and the Bank of Canada were held primarily responsible for job losses in Canada's export industries. There was no doubt that these were key drivers of manufacturing job losses in Ontario. However, the government's failure to also hold departing companies to account for relocating production to lower-wage countries effectively let them off the political hook. If they were not to blame, why force corporations to justify their decisions to shut plants? Left-nationalism, however, still framed how much of the trade union movement saw these issues. The Ontario Federation of Labour thus continued to reiterate its strong support for regulating plant closings as well as measures to control capital mobility. In January 1991, it succinctly declared: "Notice is the foundation of adjustment policy. Justification is the foundation for intervention."[25] It is as good an articulation as I have seen.

The government's shift away from a rules-based approach was reflected by the fact that in May 1991 Allan Pilkey, not Mackenzie, began taking most of the plant closing questions in the legislature. Unfortunately for the Rae government, Pilkey quickly established himself as one of the government's worst performers. After he awkwardly responded to a question in a glib and partisan way, the Liberals' Monte Kwinter went for the jugular: "There are three kinds of people in this world: Those who make things happen, those who watch things happen and those who do not even know something is happening. This minister epitomizes the third one. . . . he is a disgrace to this province."[26] At this point, Liberal David Ramsay, a former New Democrat who had crossed the floor in the mid-1980s, sought to "give another chance" to Pilkey "to show that maybe he cares and is concerned about jobs in Ontario."[27] He hoped that the minister was aware that Abitibi-Price had just closed its Thunder Bay Division, displacing four hundred paper workers: "What is it going to take for the minister to wake up and start to be proactive, rather than reactive, and come out with some innovative plans to help jobs in northern Ontario?" As it turns out, Pilkey was shuffled out of the ministry that summer, replaced by the diligent Ed Philip, who sought to mend relations with the business community.

The June 1991 announcement that Uniroyal-Goodrich was closing its Kitchener tire plant, displacing another thousand workers, hit the government hard. The rubber and tire industry had a long history in the city, dating back to 1890. Bob Rae met with

Ready and waiting: Ken Nichols spends his day at a union hall training centre with other unemployed tradespeople, 27 March 1992. Photo by Al Dunlop / *Toronto Star* via Getty Images.

the company to see what could be done, but to no avail. Despite the fact that Uniroyal-Goodrich gave Kitchener tire workers eighteen months' advance notice, thanks to the collective agreement, the announcement drew considerable media attention and tough questioning in the legislature.[28] When the Liberals charged that the government was doing "absolutely nothing" to help those displaced in Kitchener, Finance Minister Floyd Laughren insisted that the tire plant was an "outdated facility" and that it closed due to market conditions.[29] "In this province," he declared, "we cannot replace the private sector every time there is a problem. We will do whatever we can as a government to help in adjustment programs for those workers, to help in any kind of negotiations between the union and the company. If there is any meaningful role we can play, we will play it." Even the old "Sudbury Red" was bending to the new political order:

> It is fine for the member opposite to stand in his place and in some strange kind of logic say that because a large company such as this, with worldwide operations, decides to downsize its operation and rationalize it, somehow we are to blame. For heaven's sake, go and talk to the Uniroyal people.... Now surely to goodness the member is not suggesting that in situations like that we move in and guarantee employment for all the people in that plant. Is that what the member is implying? Because if he is, that is not our intention. We simply could not afford to do it, and quite frankly it would not be the right thing to do.[30]

The exigencies of governing, combined with the logics of neoliberal globalization, were fundamentally changing how the NDP leadership understood and spoke about plant closings. But as we saw in previous chapters, they were already primed for this shift. Laughren now thought that the "reality of the world out there is that in many cases there has to be downsizing for all sorts of reasons." There would be no more calls to nationalize troubled sectors from the government benches. These were new times.

The September 1991 policy U-turn worked against the Ministry of Labour, as various promises were delayed, dropped, or watered down. Mackenzie did convince his cabinet colleagues to proceed with the first installment of the promised minimum wage hike as part of the government's wider anti-poverty strategy, making an immediate difference in the lives of 160,000 Ontario workers. In 1991, the NDP increased the standard minimum wage by 60 cents to six dollars per hour as a first step towards its goal of pegging it at 60 percent of the average wage rate (as opposed to 41 percent), and reduced the student differential to 45 cents an hour, down from 85 cents, promising to eliminate it altogether the following year. At the time, Mackenzie maintained that the student differential "just cannot work in a society that promises equality and fairness. In fact, the existence of the student differential is currently before the courts in a challenge under the Charter of Rights and Freedoms, and recently our neighbouring provinces, Manitoba and Quebec, recognized this inequality and eliminated their differentials."[31] The double increase for those under eighteen years of age represented an immediate pay raise of one dollar per hour, a hefty sum considering how little they were being paid in the first place.[32]

But even there, the NDP had a change of heart over the summer months of 1991, as it decided to prioritize economic renewal and jobs over everything else. It therefore decided to slow future increases in the standard minimum wage and to maintain the reduced 45-cent wage differential for young workers. Having helped initiate the original court challenge myself on the two-tier minimum wage, I have long wondered what happened. Thanks to cabinet minister Richard Allen, who donated his records to McMaster University, I discovered that the Ontario Restaurant Association and other employer groups lobbied hard to convince the NDP cabinet to reverse itself, arguing that the "student minimum wage category should not be seen as discriminatory against young inexperienced workers, instead it should be viewed as an affirmative action initiative which assists young inexperienced workers in gaining employment."[33] These were tough economic times and the youth unemployment rate was a dismal 18 percent.

To find out more, I filed an Access to Information request to see several key files in the Premier's Office. What I discovered was that a decision was made in September 1991, the same month that the NDP abandoned its long-standing promise to deliver public auto insurance, to hold off on the elimination of the two-tier minimum wage until the issue could be studied. The Ministry of Labour then formed a Student Minimum Wage Consultation Group with representatives of the four main employer groups in the hospitality industry, all with a strong vested interest in maintaining the differential, as well as two service-sector unions, with a tangential interest, and an obscure student group. They agreed to maintain the reduced differential, giving the government the excuse it clearly wanted and arguably manufactured.

In its April 1993 cabinet submission, the Ministry of Labour conceded that the reduced differential was discriminatory but recommended its maintenance anyway: "Clearly, the student minimum wage does discriminate on the basis of age and student status. The student component does not appear to present any legal difficulties, but the age discrimination is a complex legal issue." The ministry's legal counsel "concluded that if a Charter challenge were to be raised again there is a risk that the student differential could be found to violate the Canadian Charter of Rights and Freedoms on the basis of age discrimination. . . . Other provinces have considered this and concluded the opposite. There is no legal ruling directly on this issue and no current challenge."[34] The NDP cabinet agreed with the warped line of reasoning that paying *less* to an identifiable category of Canadians was a form of affirmative action. Decades later, young people in Ontario are still paying the price.

WAGE PROTECTION

With the promised job protection board all but abandoned, the NDP's signature response to the plant closing problem became the Employee Wage Protection Program, which would compensate workers for unpaid wages, vacation pay, severance pay, and pay in lieu of notice when employers went bankrupt and shut down. The maximum compensation for an individual was set at $5,000. Otherwise, according to federal bankruptcy law, workers were unsecured creditors and thus received very little, if anything. Signalling its legislative importance, the proposed amendment to the Employment Standards Act was announced on the first day in office by Bob Rae himself, with seed money coming from the Ontario government's settlement with Varity Corporation. Formerly the storied Canadian farm machinery manufacturer Massey Ferguson, Varity had received a $200 million bailout from the provincial and federal governments in 1981, followed by a second restructuring in 1985–86 that led it to close its Toronto plant and consolidate operations in Brantford. Varity also spun off the Massey Combine Corporation as a subsidiary that went bankrupt soon thereafter, displacing 3,500 workers. When Varity then decided to relocate its corporate headquarters to Buffalo, New York, it first had to be released from its contractual obligations as part of the earlier bailout agreement. It therefore agreed to pay Ontario $5 million in compensation for moving its corporate headquarters and another $375,000 for its failure to meet its job guarantees.

Massey Ferguson North Combine Plant, Toronto: Portrait of some of the last workers, June 1986. Photo by Peter MacCallum.

With the compensation agreement in place, the NDP cabinet had to decide where to direct the settlement money. Three options were laid out to cabinet by the Cabinet Office. First, the money could be directed to the workers displaced at Varity and its wholly owned subsidiary Kelsey-Hayes in Windsor. This had the value of being consistent with the treatment of Massey Combine workers, who were scheduled to receive $12 million in severance in a negotiated settlement between Varity and the Canadian Auto Workers. But the worker adjustment committee reported that most of those displaced had already found jobs. Second, the government could invest the money in community economic development programs in Windsor and Brantford to help the two hard-hit industrial towns adjust. But this option might set an unwanted precedent. Or it could direct the Varity settlement towards the proposed wage protection fund, as it would send a clear and unambiguous signal of the government's determination to adopt a systematic approach. The only downside was that the NDP might be criticized for not doing more for impacted workers and hard-hit communities. It was this last option that the cabinet agreed to in its first two weeks in power.

The proposed wage protection fund, as it was originally conceived, would pay employees' claims for unpaid wages and seek to recover these funds from company directors and officers. Wage protection funds were essentially insurance schemes. Manitoba's wage fund offered a straightforward model whereby the government investigated the claim and ordered payment. By contrast, Quebec's plan, limited to the construction industry, was funded by a payroll tax on employers. Wolfe estimated that Ontario would need $135 million a year to run the program, depending on what was covered and how high the maximum cap was per claimant. The Ministry of Labour then distributed a discussion paper on the issue on 31 December 1990 and held hearings over January and February prior to the introduction of Bill 70.[35]

Wage protection should have been a slam dunk for the NDP, especially after it opted not to fund it via an employer payroll tax, which would have been strongly opposed by the business lobby.

That it was fumbled and allowed to drag on until October 1991 speaks to wider problems within the government. Mackenzie was right to express early concern that the government's commitment to consultation not end up "just delaying or stalling legislative changes."[36] The NDP's uncertainness and lack of experience, and its desire to build consensus, led it to undertake lengthy consultations before and after each bill was introduced. Even Rae's closest advisors came to realize that they were "consulting people to death!"[37] The NDP's closest allies were soon telling the government that it was all too much. Opposition centred on Bill 70's extension of liability to corporate officers such as CEOs as well as the inclusion of the directors of non-profit corporations. The government's rationale was that company officers participated in decisions that led to the non-payment of wages.[38] Eventually, under pressure, the government dropped the offending clauses, even though the change limited the state's ability to retrieve the money owed from defunct companies.[39]

Opposition members welcomed the changes to the bill, saying the original proposal was "so badly flawed and so ill-conceived that one has to wonder how it ever got through cabinet in the first place."[40] Not to be outdone, one legislator even said that Bill 70 "would have shocked even the greatest socialist."[41] Meanwhile, the forces of political reaction were growing stronger outside the legislature. In June 1991, the Toronto Board of Trade suggested that, even as amended, the wage protection fund would help make "Ontario far too uncompetitive on the world market." Globalization and the political neo-realism that it produced were imposing new limits on democratic action. To these barbs, Mackenzie reminded the bill's opponents that nearly three thousand companies had been forced into bankruptcy the previous year and that in many cases workers had not been paid: "This government is not prepared to stand by and watch as workers are denied the money they have worked for. It is legitimately theirs and they need it. Losing your job for any reason is a rather traumatic experience."[42]

Over the summer months, the Standing Committee on Resource Development held hearings on the amended legislation.

Not surprisingly, unions spoke out in strong support of wage protection. "Working people are the ones who pay the price for corporate restructuring, sales, mergers and takeovers, and companies going out of business," declared Kip Connolly from the United Food and Commercial Workers. While his union was "not opposed to change," he said that Ontario must find "more effective and more equitable ways of dealing with that change." The union expressed concern, however, with the $5,000 individual cap, as it would be insufficient to cover unpaid severance pay. To ground his point, Connolly cited the example of Royal Dressed Meats, a slaughterhouse in Guelph, that went bankrupt in 1987, putting fifty-one union members out of work. The amount owed to these workers ranged from $500 to $10,000.

The International Ladies' Garment Workers' Union (ILGWU), for its part, spoke to the devastation caused by plant closings in the textile and clothing sector. In Toronto, for example, 3,500 garment-sector jobs were lost between 1986 and 1990; and since 1988, fully one-third of the union's Ontario membership were unemployed. This was no small matter. Ontario's apparel, textile, and leather industries employed 12 percent of all manufacturing workers in the province and constituted the single largest industrial sector in Toronto.[43] According to Alexandra Dagg, "if this situation persists much longer, the garment industry will be annihilated." She, too, grounded her case in example, citing Best Outerwear, which closed in July 1988 without notice and without paying its twenty employees wages or vacation pay. Nothing remained in the bankruptcy proceedings nor were they eligible for severance pay anyway, as the shop fell below Ontario's minimum threshold. For good measure, the ILGWU cited three more Toronto closures since the NDP took office. In the case of J. H. Warsh, which had operated on Spadina Avenue since 1917, its one hundred employees received no notice or severance pay whatsoever and the company even owed money to the pension fund. Nota Havaris testified that she had worked there for thirty-three years as a sewing machine operator after coming to the city from Greece. She had been legally entitled to eight weeks' termination pay and 4 percent vacation pay but got nothing back. As a result, Havaris's daughter had to suspend her university studies.[44] These real-life examples hit home.

The wider argument for the wage protection legislation was made by D'Arcy Martin and Leo Dowhaluk of the Communications and Electrical Workers of Canada, a union representing twenty thousand Ontario workers, of whom fully 20 percent had already lost their jobs during the current recession. "What we are arguing is that the distribution of risk needs to match the distribution of power, that those who have authority over a workplace need to carry some particular responsibility in terms of the social costs of mistakes that happen." Martin went on to say that the legislation, as amended, failed to include some key provisions sought by the union movement. They wanted the fund, for example, to be paid by employers, not ordinary taxpayers. It ought to be as expensive as possible for employers to shut plants:

> Is there a union agenda developed with our members around enhanced job security and greater compensation? Absolutely yes. We believe there should be disincentives to employers to shut down. But the social costs of shutdowns should be carried more proportionately by employers than is now the case. That is true in much of western Europe, for example. It does not introduce rigidities. What it introduces is a situation where employers think twice before they toss people on the street.[45]

Martin's comments were not well received by the opposition parties. Tory Elizabeth Witmer thought Martin's presentation was "actually rather confrontational" and took exception to the idea that businesses leaving the province were speculators rather than investors. For his part, Liberal David Ramsay wondered if the union felt that "we can insulate ourselves from the vagaries of economic downturns, or any other conditions and daily challenges that the world presents us. What you are saying basically is that people should be guaranteed employment."[46] To this, Martin replied: "I would say that the quid pro quo for the kind of self-reliance you are talking about would be an inclusion of workers and their organizations in economic planning. Now, if we can talk about that, then we can talk about sharing risk. Until we do that, I think it is incumbent on employers to offer a degree of insulation."[47] Now reluctantly supporting Bill 70, the Liberals focused their questioning on the length of time it took the government to deliver on its promise. Where was the government's sense of urgency, they asked? After a year of indecision and debate, the wage protection bill was finally adopted with retroactive coverage to 1 October 1990.[48] It was the first major piece of labour legislation passed by the NDP majority government.[49] As of March 1995, 57,080 Ontario workers received $133 million in wage protection funding, for an average of $2,300 each.[50] The legislation made a real-world difference until it was quickly repealed by the Tories after their election victory.

Lost jobs: Protesters hold tombstone-shaped signs, each listing the number of jobs lost when a firm folded or left the country. 16 March 1991. Photo by Bernard Weil / *Toronto Star* via Getty Images.

EXPERIMENTS WITH UNION-LED ADJUSTMENT

Bryan Evans, a senior policy advisor in the Ministry of Labour, headed the Employment Standards Act Review that put forward a comprehensive series of recommended changes that would have increased the cost for employers to close plants. He likened the proposal to the workers' compensation system, which makes unsafe working conditions financially costly for employers, incentivizing them to take safety seriously. "A handful of us were sequestered away from the hurly-burly of the ministry, where we worked for about eight to nine months on a broad review, and then it was all, well, not all, but 95 percent of it abandoned," Evans recalls.[51] The reform package was killed by the cabinet. He recounts how one cabinet minister apologized to them, saying, "I'm sorry, we put all of our capital into the Labour Relations Act and we have nothing left." The only legislated outcome of the review was a new homeworker regulation for those in the garment industry. Homeworkers had previously been excluded under the Employment Standards Act regarding regulation of the hours of work, overtime, and holiday pay. The changes ended their exclusion and imposed a special 10 percent minimum wage premium to cover their overhead costs.[52] Grassroots pressure on this issue had made the difference. The Coalition for Fair Wages and Working Conditions for Homeworkers drew inspiration from similar campaigns in the UK organized by the Leicester Outworkers Campaign and the West Yorkshire Homeworkers Unit to demand government action. It was even one of the themes for the 1994 International Women's Day in Toronto.[53]

There was growing awareness of the ways that the gender division of labour served to render women working in manufacturing more vulnerable to displacement. Thanks to the Canadian Advisory Council on the Status of Women, a series of research reports on the impact of the Canada-US Free Trade Agreement on women was commissioned in 1987. In their contribution, Ann Porter and Barbara Cameron concluded:

Free trade presents the women's movement in Canada with an important question: should organizations committed to advancing women's right to equality become involved in debates over general economic strategy? The tendency of women's organizations during the last two decades since the re-emergence of the women's movement has been to make equality demands within the framework of the existing strategy of economic development. The debate in Canada during the 1960s and 1970s over the issues of foreign ownership and industrial policy, for example, took place without the intervention of organizations representing the specific interests of women. During the past year, however, the attitude has developed among certain sections of the women's movement that free trade is, in fact, a women's issue.[54]

Having established this, Porter and Cameron showed that many of the sectors most likely to lose out in trade liberalization and free trade were the labour-intensive clothing (74% women), textile (43%), leather (52%), and electrical (33%) industries. These sectors were the first to move to low-wage countries in the Global South. Fully 281,000 manufacturing jobs in Ontario, or 31 percent of the total, were thus in "highly sensitive" industries that were vulnerable to free trade.

With research like this in mind, the Ministry of Labour initiated a union-led sectoral pilot project for garment workers in Toronto.[55] We know a bit about it thanks to sociology professor Roxana Ng, who deposited her records to the University of Toronto Archives. The Apparel Textile Action Committee (ATAC), spearheaded by the International Ladies' Garment Workers' Union and the Amalgamated Clothing and Textile Workers Union, was established in the summer of 1991 to serve the adjustment needs of unemployed workers in the garment and textile industries of Metropolitan Toronto "due to the massive downsizing and restructuring of this industry."[56] Plants were small in this sector, leaving most workers ineligible for legislated severance pay and advance notice. ATAC therefore sought to coordinate worker adjustment for workers in smaller plants. In a break from existing practice, the storefront operation did not include employer representatives but rather the representatives from the community-based Women Working with Immigrant Women (WWIW) and the Chinese Garment Workers' Association (CGWA) as well as George Brown College. Ng served as ATAC's chairperson and researcher.

As a sectoral-based committee, ATAC had the advantage of developing an overall picture of wider trends and helped provide a coordinated response. Its three-year mandate was longer than the one-year mandates of most workplace adjustment committees. However, it was more distant from the shop floor, making it difficult to forge connection with workers in closing plants. According to Ng, "it takes more time to establish trust and smooth working relations with displaced workers." Workplace adjustment committees have a clearer mandate and can recruit from the factory floor, which facilitates rapport and closes the distance. In the words of Ng: "Workers are helping themselves. This is important if workers are to empower themselves."[57] Yet adjustment requires skills not always available on the shop floor, limiting these committees' effectiveness.

Ng's final 1994 report pointed to "unequal power relations" among ATAC members, given differences in their "language facility, educational level, gender, race, knowledge base, as well as the official positions they hold within the organizational hierarchy."[58] She also noted that there was a "high level of frustration" within adjustment committees and between displaced workers and action centre staff. While often cast as personal conflicts, the report suggests that the problem was in fact structural, given the violence of the plant closing process and the resulting sense of helplessness. As the economic situation in the industry worsened far "beyond original predictions," it proved "unrealistic to re-train workers for an industry whose long-term outlook is one of major re-organization, if not decline."[59] Much of ATAC's work therefore focused on their "immediate plight" rather than on "developing long-term training needs." In its second year of operation, the committee counselled workers and referred them to appropriate services and training agencies such as George Brown College and the Metro Toronto Labour Education Centre.

Between 1987 and 1993, the labour adjustment program of the Metro Toronto Labour Education Centre, which was union-led, worked with more than four thousand workers in 130 workplace closures. According to Jennifer Stephen, who led these efforts, labour-led adjustment programs "must encourage critical thinking, to identify collective approaches as an alternative to the correction of alleged personal deficiencies. This includes identifying the real reasons for lack of access to training, services and jobs." In an October 1993 paper, Stephen observed that most governments had abandoned the goal of full employment as well as "any notion of industrial strategy and planned economic development."[60] She was highly critical of the new emphasis on labour-management

La Ping Fashions, 96 Spadina Avenue, Toronto: Ironing garments, 1991. Photo by Peter MacCallum.

partnership in adjustment, writing: "A great deal of energy has gone into facilitating a process of apparent negotiation between labour and capital—working toward bringing labour into a series of structures and processes where the rules of the game have already been decided, the objectives and outcomes already determined. Nowhere is this more clear than in the process of adjustment." Stephen believed that the government's emphasis of skills training, and its commitment to outsource training and adjustment to a multipartite board, effectively depoliticized industrial restructuring. Trade unions therefore had good reason to be wary of the government's training mantra. It is a powerful critique, one we will return to later.

LABOUR LAW REFORM AND THE DUTY TO BARGAIN

There was no question that substantial changes to the Ontario Labour Relations Act, making unionization easier and prohibiting the use of replacement workers during strikes, were the overriding priority of the Ontario Federation of Labour. Plant closings and layoffs were decimating private-sector unions, threatening their institutional survival. Between 1979 and 1985, for example, North American membership in the United Auto Workers, United Steelworkers of America, and United Rubber Workers fell 32.6 percent, 40.6 percent, and 32.9 percent, respectively.[61] Hundreds of union locals were merged or rendered defunct. Trade unions also had to lay off staff members, given the contraction in membership. D'Arcy Martin's memoir reveals the onset of these years of crisis:

> The collapse of the US steel industry was like a rock dragging down the union's membership figures. With the income from membership dues declining, expenses had to be reduced and staff had to be laid off. The experience would take its toll on the confidence of activists and the openness of the leadership.[62]

The United Steelworkers' layoffs were undertaken by seniority without regard to the Canada-US border, even though membership decline at the time was less severe in Canada. In fact, the percentage of the Steelworkers membership who were Canadian climbed significantly, given the enormous declines south of the border. Martin was one of the lucky ones. With the 1990s downturn, unions were again laying off lower-seniority staff. Had Hugh Mackenzie not been appointed to run the Ontario Fair Tax Commission, he would likely have been laid off by the Steelworkers from his staff position.

Concerned, industrial unions responded to the industrial crisis by diversifying out of declining core industries and merging with other unions. In this regard, they mirrored the actions of many multinational corporations. Not everyone agreed with

Union Density in Ontario by Sector and Major Industry (1991)	
Sector	Union Density (% of Employment)
Ontario	30.6%
Public Sector	70.0%
Private Sector	19.1%
Agriculture	—
Other Primary	40.4%
Manufacturing	41.6%
Construction	45.5%
Transportation, Communication, and Utilities	53.0%
Trade	10.1%
Finance, Insurance, and Real Estate	1.5%
Services	27.8%
Public Administration	72.0%

Statistics Canada, CALURA, Union Membership Survey and Labour Market Activity Survey, 1991.

this institutional response. Sam Gindin saw union mergers as a "bureaucratic response" to the crisis "rather than saying, 'What's wrong with us, why are we getting nowhere, what do we have to change?' It became, 'You have to become bigger.'"[63] His own union brought in East Coast fishers, electrical workers, and railway workers such as my father. Even so, the promise of labour reform remained essential to future union security and promised to counter declining union density in the private sector.

When he presented his ministry's early achievements to the Standing Committee on Estimates in June 1991, Bob Mackenzie declared that "labour and management must work together in a spirit of partnership and must have the necessary framework in place to do so."[64] His ministry aimed to "reshape the long-standing confrontational approach to labour-management relations," nothing less. Our future depended on it, he argued. At the same time, Mackenzie expressed ambivalence about some of the new ideas emerging out of the government's inner circle. On worker ownership, he cautioned: "I have said many times that it is likely to never reach even 1% of closures. Maybe I am just picking a figure out of the air, but I know it is never going to be a major tool."[65] He was even more reticent about the wider conversation about labour-led venture capital funds initiated by the Premier's Office, saying it would interest some trade unions, though not all, as it was a "desperation move and a recognition, in terms of some of the closure and some of the potential worker buyouts, that there has to be an investment fund they can turn to."[66]

The NDP government's inaugural throne speech promised comprehensive labour law reform, as had the election manifesto. To that end, in March 1991, the Ministry of Labour initiated a social bargaining process between two parallel teams of management and union labour lawyers with a neutral chairperson. In theory, "rather than being dictated by government, the new legislation would reflect a consensus between the private sector actors."[67] But the process quickly broke down. According to insiders Chuck Rachlis and David Wolfe, "the union lawyers drafted an enormous wish list of reforms that proposed to rectify through legislation every arbitration case they had lost in the past decade and the management team called for no change at all."[68] To make matters worse, the labour side's maximalist proposal was leaked to the press, sparking a media firestorm and a ferocious business backlash. One of Rae's advisors recalls how politically damaging the leak was to the government: "I mean, it was just infuriating. It was just a wish list, there was no filter on it. And it was very hurtful."[69] No fewer than three business coalitions formed to fight labour law reform. The ensuing fight was long and ugly.

Kevin Burkett, a career labour arbitrator who had the misfortune of chairing this failed experiment in social bargaining, was left embittered by the experience. He was placed in an impossible situation. Years later, he reflected back on it in his 1998 Sefton Lecture at the University of Toronto. Burkett initially thought it possible to find middle ground between the two negotiating teams, but soon realized that he "had badly misread the situation."[70] Ontario politics had swiftly polarized after the NDP's election. Burkett now regretted being co-opted into a flawed and, to his mind, partisan process. Bob Mackenzie had identified thirty topics for negotiation, "constituting significant areas of change, all seen by the management side as being in favour of unions."[71] By tipping his hand, Mackenzie had made the labour team feel emboldened, with no appetite for compromise. While I am sympathetic to Burkett's predicament, he fails to recognize that the NDP won office on the promise of undertaking a major overhaul of Ontario's labour relations system, including the prohibition on the use of scab labour. Yet Burkett personally opposed this measure, calling it out of step with the rest of North America. In saying this, he conveniently ignored the fact that neighbouring Quebec has banned strikebreakers since 1977.

Despite this debacle, the idea of social bargaining continued to blossom within government circles. Peter Warrian and John O'Grady, two of its most knowledgeable advocates, were invited to write a paper on "Human Resource Development, Labour Adjustment, Work Organization and Labour Relations." The paper, circulated within the Premier's Office in July 1991, recommended that the government require employers to formulate and implement, jointly with labour, social plans for human resource development and labour adjustment.[72] These social plans would then be enforced by the Ontario Labour Relations Board (OLRB). Warrian and O'Grady believed that the government's initial focus on the Employment Standards Act was a "clumsy instrument for dealing with human capital issues and with many aspects of labour adjustment." They recommended, instead, the extension of the duty to bargain to plant closures and layoffs, as well as the requirement that labour and management consult regularly during the life of the collective agreement. These two changes, they hoped, would provide the basis for a more collaborative and less confrontational labour relations regime in the province. Optimistically, they proclaimed that a "new model or paradigm" based on "negotiated adjustment" was emerging in Ontario.[73] But there were real limitations to this approach: labour standards covered all workers in the province, whereas unions represented a declining minority in the private sector. With reason, Bryan Evans called the Employment Standards Act the collective agreement of the unorganized. The shift to negotiated adjustment therefore left a majority of workers high and dry, especially women and new immigrants, who were concentrated in smaller, unorganized workplaces.

Informed by these internal discussions, Mackenzie prepared a submission to cabinet, dated 7 August 1991, with sixty-one proposed changes. These ranged from barring scabs to encouraging sectoral bargaining. The proposals, if adopted, would have made union recognition, the conclusion of the first contract, and the organization of smaller shops considerably easier for trade unions. The proposed legislation would also require companies to negotiate plant closing agreements, extending the duty to bargain. It was equivalent to effects-based bargaining in the United States after the First National Maintenance decision (1981) removed the duty to bargain over plant closing decisions. Why it did not extend to the decisions themselves, something that would have approximated long-time union demands for justification, is unclear to me.

There was considerable internal debate over labour law reform within cabinet, including resistance to the anti-scab provision. Wolfe remembers "sitting through a lot of P&P [Policy and Priorities] committee meetings debating the strikebreaker stuff."[74] Warrian, by then the government's chief economist, concurs, saying it was "far from unanimous. But Rae was behind it, you know. Being premier's not easy... you have to decide what are you going to put your weight behind, and he was behind this one."[75] Warrian went on to suggest (in an obvious reference to Marion Boyd) that there were a "bunch of ministers" for whom "this is probably inappropriate, but—all they had ever done is run a women's centre in Chatham, okay?" Fierce business opposition was also having an effect. One close advisor to Rae suggested, probably unfairly, that Mackenzie was to blame for "an awful series of cabinet meetings and discussions with him and some of his folks."[76]

The Ministry of Labour then prepared a discussion paper, a draft of which was, once again, leaked in September 1991, causing more uproar. The finished draft was only released in November 1991, minus several contentious features such as sectoral bargaining. Even the anti-scab law was watered down.[77] Naively, perhaps, the government sought to forge a consensus, arguing that the changes would provide stability and an environment more conducive to labour-management partnership. Given the growth in global competition, which "has contributed to unprecedented pressure for change in workplaces in almost every sector of Ontario's economy," new "cooperative approaches" were needed to "respond to the restructuring." Accordingly, the government proposed a new Work Organization and Adjustment Service run jointly by the ministries of Labour as well as Industry, Trade and Technology, as there was "no mechanism for constructive dialogue during the term of a collective agreement, nor expectation that this will occur." This new service would work with employers and unions to "respond positively to pressures for change through cooperation and innovation rather than conflict." The multidisciplinary team would provide expert advice, mediation services, brokerage, and information. The discussion paper also explained that the government had decided "not to deal at this time with forms of statutory notice and severance pay requirements in mass layoffs; establishing new requirements for notice of, and bargaining over, technological change; or mechanisms for reviewing alternatives to plant closures and other mass layoffs." Instead, it was prepared to extend the statutory duty to bargain in unionized establishments, but this provision "would neither affect the employer's prerogative to close or carry-out layoffs nor create a right to strike or lockout over the plan."[78]

If the wage protection bill was controversial, that was nothing compared to the furor caused by labour law reform. Hundreds of newspaper articles pounded the government. Predictably, business mogul Conrad Black, later jailed for mail fraud and obstruction of justice, blasted the "innumerate Luddite biases of the NDP" and Rae's "submissive bondage to Bob White." For good measure, he dismissed the government as a "babel of single-issue fanatics: militant homosexuals, feminists, abortionists, eco-geeks, worker radicals and social agitators, standing and shrieking on each other's shoulders."[79] The National Citizens' Coalition, a far-right pressure group, even put up incendiary billboards comparing the Bob Rae government to Salvador Allende's Chile.[80] That Allende was killed in a bloody coup that toppled his elected government in 1973—the original 11 September—made the message all the more threatening.

Alan Ernst, who calls himself "more of a Rosencrantz and Guildenstern type figure" insofar as he "wasn't really in the front of the room and where the decisions were [made]," was the executive assistant for Sharon Murdock, the backbench MPP for Sudbury, who was the parliamentary assistant to the Minister of Labour. Generally, PAs got the "easy, boring, boilerplate type meetings," he says. "You're just going out to fly the flag or you go into shitstorms that you don't want to send the minister—'Let's just send the PA.'" This was "second tier stuff" where you go "speak the lines." Ernst remembers labour relations reform as a political firestorm. Murdock was responsible for the northern Ontario hearings on the controversial legislation. "Those were pretty ugly consultations," he recalls. The NDP got "the crap kicked out of us" and the Minister of Labour was being pushed by the government's "centre" to dilute the legislation further. Ernst remembers once sitting at a table alongside Mackenzie, who sat right across from a bunch of business representatives who "were literally shouting in his face. And I thought, Mackenzie twenty years ago would have gotten out of the seat and punched the guy out. And I don't know how he could just sit there. How is he doing this with a poker face? But that was the tone. The tone was horrific."[81]

The union movement was taken aback by the ferocity of the business backlash. Incoming Canadian Labour Congress president Bob White called the business reaction to labour law reform "the worst kind of insanity I've seen in 30 years. It made them look as if they had just come out of the caves." He didn't think the legislation was revolutionary at all. "If I had been Bob Rae," White mused, "I would have had a much tougher labour reform bill and I would have done it in the first couple of months. I think the government made a mistake in allowing wide consultation, but it wanted to be fair."[82] Ross McClellan came to the same conclusion, saying: "We knew what we wanted to do. We had so much expertise in the labour movement. And two or three people outside that could have drafted the legislation in forty-eight hours. . . . Instead we built this elaborate process, blah blah blah, while the employers are busy organizing across the province."[83] For his part, Leo Gerard of the United Steelworkers of America expressed his dismay "at the level of attack on the trade union movement itself and the concept of unionization by the business community."[84] He reminded opponents that it took twelve to eighteen months for workers to gain union certification and almost as long to get their first contract: "Workers have to sneak around in back alleys and washrooms in the dark of night to sign a card to join a union, which is recognized as an expression of democracy, for fear of getting fired, harassed and punished. Don't talk to me about tipping the balance of power, please." Some employer groups argued in the early 1970s that Ontario's economy would be destroyed if joint health and safety committees and the right to refuse unsafe work were legislated.

More concessions to the proposal's critics followed the three-month-long consultation period, and the Labour Relations and Employment Statute Law Amendment (Bill 40) was finally tabled in the legislature in June 1992 and adopted that November, two years after it appeared in the NDP's first throne speech. According to Bud Wildman: "Bob [Mackenzie] worked very, very hard . . . [pause] on two things: health and safety issues, and anti-scab legislation. And I think he was very disappointed that we never went as far as he thought we should go on anti-scab legislation."[85] But there were other interests putting pressure on the government and it sought political consensus where there was none. Frankly, these delays were a gift to the opposition parties and the business lobby.

Looking back thirty years later, John O'Grady laments the bounded horizons of the labour reform proposals. From his perspective, the pro-union labour lawyers who drafted the NDP legislation had a narrow view: "Most of them, this is the only labour relations system that they can imagine. It's like they've never travelled. They don't know that the only two places, well, three places in the world that have it like this [were] Canada, the United States, and the Philippines. Nobody else does it this way."[86] The government's willingness to drop the sectoral bargaining component particularly hurt. It was considered "too novel" within the North American context, he laments: "Labour lawyers couldn't understand it." Peter Warrian agrees, suggesting sectoral bargaining would have been a game changer, as smaller workshops would have become organized.[87] O'Grady adds that the mainstream trade union movement was, itself, "deeply conservative" with respect to labour relations reform: "They don't actually want it reformed. They want it tinkered with."[88]

Albeit watered down, Ontario's labour law reforms made some difference for unions. There was a small but significant jump in the number of Ontario workers joining unions in the years that followed, climbing from 15,253 (1992) to 24,180 (1993) and 24,464 (1994).[89] But it was not the tipping point that proponents of sectoral bargaining had hoped for. In any case, the labour reforms were quickly rolled back by the Tories in 1995, and the window to organize the unorganized was quickly slammed shut.

CONCLUSION

While the union movement eventually got only a watered-down version of comprehensive labour law reform, it still represented the most pro-union legislation in North America. In return, the government got the stuffing kicked out of it, casting a pall over the rest of its agenda. Chuck Rachlis and David Wolfe later wondered if it had all been worth it. In their view, labour law reform had burned the government's bridges with the business sector. Their reticence speaks to a tension within the government between an older class-infused labour politics, represented by Bob Mackenzie and the Ministry of Labour, and the newer progressive competitive desire to make common cause with the business community through social partnership. Rachlis and Wolfe were heavily invested in the neocorporatist approach. It is this fundamental tension between the two impulses that was the source of some of the contradictions and mixed signals coming out of Queen's Park.

What is clear from the historical record is that, as time wore on, the Ministry of Labour became an outlier in the NDP government. Institutionally, it was a product of an older regulatory politics rather than the new emphasis on consensus building and partnership. It was no coincidence that the NDP moved worker adjustment and training, once the purview of the Ministry of Labour, to the new arm's-length multipartite Ontario Training and Adjustment Board (discussed in chapter 9). It is also why the NDP ultimately failed to bolster plant closing regulations as promised, preferring to leave the issue to the stakeholders to hammer out. When I raised this idea with Bryan Evans, he immediately concurred:

> The Ministry of Labour was the institutionalization, maybe fossilization, of a politics of another era: call it '45 to '75. ... So, you had a situation where the Ministry of Finance [and] the Ministry of Industry were constantly

vetoing the Ministry of Labour. When I was here, that was the end of the golden age. Because the world had changed ... the world had changed, and it took time for that to catch up to the Ministry of Labour.[90]

He laments the fact that the Ministry of Labour was "no longer about protection of workers, it [was] no longer about workers' rights. I call it rebuilding the nineteenth century." To make his point, Evans recalled how he and a colleague in the Ministry of Labour put together a proposal to develop a "high-end monitoring unit, two to three people, which would report on the shifting terrain of free trade, investment flowing in, flowing out, restructuring of the economy, but the executive committee of the Ministry of Labour and its Deputy Minister said, 'Why would we do that?' I'm not kidding." Instead, their work at the ministry remained "very much reactive, we called it 'firefighting.' As issues emerged every day, we'd spend all of our time in issue management. And there would be no planning, there'd be no long planning horizon. It would be, what shit hit the fan today? ... It's kind of like watching the provincial state shut down its ability to think."

It is an essential point, one that speaks to a much wider reorientation of the provincial state. Despite his frustrations, or perhaps because of them, Bob Mackenzie remained very much beloved within the party in the decades after the government's 1995 defeat. When he died in January 2011, the tributes from party members were glowing; people remembered him as a fighter for working people. Amid all of the broken promises of the Rae government, his anti-scab law stood out as a signal achievement.[91] Symbolically, at least, Mackenzie represented the NDP government that might have been. Where the Rae government excelled, however, was in its ad hoc response to the industrial crisis in northern Ontario.

National Rubber Company: Ling Co die-cutting radiator baffles, 1993. Photo by Peter MacCallum.

6

WORKER OWNERSHIP AND LABOUR-LED VENTURE CAPITAL

> Algoma [Steel] could be used as a model for the development of a distinctly Canadian approach to encouraging and facilitating worker buy-outs as a tool to be used in restructuring.
> —USWA Staffer to Ross McClellan, Premier's Office, 30 January 1991[1]

On 23 January 1991, Dofasco announced that it would write off its $740 million investment in Algoma Steel, Canada's third-largest steelmaker, leaving its six thousand workers at the mercy of its creditors.[2] The integrated steel mill's demise would have devastated the northern Ontario community of Sault Ste. Marie: fully one-third of the city's employment would have been lost immediately, with more to come from the knock-on effect on suppliers and small businesses.[3] The urgency of the moment was recorded in the archival records of Ross McClellan, a senior advisor to Premier Rae. On 24 January, the day after the shock announcement, it was noted that "tomorrow's payroll is safe," as was that for the next week, after which all bets were off. One senior civil servant from the Ministry of Northern Development estimated that Algoma needed $200 million to pull through: "All they need is an optimist with $200 million in the bank." This joke prompted another senior advisor to say that "one way or another, we were about to acquire an industrial strategy," while another "made a strong pitch that it was vital that we move quickly to begin assembling criteria by which this and other industrial assistance issues, not least because the lineup for help will only grow as time passes, and because the government's financial resources are under tremendous strain." Despite the uncertainty, the Premier's Office remained optimistic. "For all the gloom, there was a strangely positive tone to the meeting, produced ... by the sense that this group and this government have what it takes to deal with the crisis at ASC [Algoma Steel Corporation]."[4]

One of the reasons for optimism was the fact that the United Steelworkers of America had far more experience with worker buyouts than any other union in North America. Faced with a crisis in the US steel industry in the early 1980s, the Steelworkers had brought Ron Bloom, a Wall Street investment banker, on as an advisor for industrial restructuring and worker ownership. "There was a period of time when Bloom's firm was working almost exclusively for the Steelworkers in the States on various industrial restructuring projects," recalls Hugh Mackenzie, the former research director for the Canadian section of the union.[5] Bloom would become a key architect of the union-led Algoma buyout.

Towering giant: Algoma Steel dominates the skyline of Sault Ste. Marie in the same way it dominates the city's economy. 10 March 1983. Photo by Pat Brennan / *Toronto Star* via Getty Images.

Sault Ste. Marie was "an obvious place to move," according to Mackenzie, especially with the NDP in power. With Algoma, "you had a willing former owner, you had a union that had some capacity to deal with these things, mostly American, but Ken Delaney, on the [Canadian] Steelworkers staff, really developed a lot of expertise in that world as well. And you had a single-industry town with a long history with the union, so you put all those things together and you've got a critical mass."

Bob Rae agreed with this assessment, writing in his memoirs that there were "too many jobs at stake for everybody to just walk away."[6] He had a strong connection to the United Steelworkers, having worked for them briefly before entering politics. Thanks to a chance encounter with Peter Warrian, Rae had been hired by the union to help with some legal cases, starting with the proposed closure by Falconbridge of a mine site. He then attended the union's 1976 convention, which was the year of Ed Sadlowski's failed rank-and-file insurgency within the Steelworkers.[7] Thereafter, the union was one of Rae's strongest political backers. The Premier was therefore personally involved from day one in the effort to save Algoma. There were two key factors driving the union-led worker buyout of Algoma, according to Rae:

> The first was the experience of the union itself in the US. A dramatic downturn in the American steel industry a decade earlier had forced the union to become partners in business, and sometimes owners, of their own jobs. Employee ownership was not the product of some abstract ideology of worker involvement. It was the result of economic necessity and political will on the part of the union. A new philosophy of unionism and economic partnership followed on from this. . . . The will of our government was the second critical ingredient in finding a solution.[8]

It is a fair assessment. The NDP brought the parties together and arbitrated a deal. Its insistence that any solution had to include the union was pivotal, as was its commitment to guaranteeing bridge loans to keep the steelmaker in operation while negotiations dragged on. As we will see in this chapter and the next, worker ownership became a major plank in the government's emerging economic renewal agenda. The rescue of Algoma required extraordinary political will, and looking back, there is every reason to believe that Algoma Steel would not have survived had any other political party been in power at that moment in history.

SAVING ALGOMA STEEL

Sault Ste. Marie is located on the St. Marys River where the waters of Lake Superior descend into Lake Huron on the long journey to the Atlantic. The river's enormous water power drew Francis Hector Clergue to the Sault with the dream of developing a massive industrial complex on the northern frontier. Before his corporation collapsed in 1903, he had built a paper mill, a steel mill, and a railway to bring iron ore in from a mine near Wawa.[9] But his industries lived on. Mounting economic problems in 1986 led the mill's owner, Canadian Pacific, to demand steep wage concessions. The union responded that it needed to see the financial books before it would consider such a demand. Granted access, it commissioned a trusted labour-friendly consultant to prepare a report. While there was no immediate threat of bankruptcy, the consultant concluded that Algoma "could drift into such a crisis within the next 1 to 2 years."[10] The primary sources of danger were identified as the bleak sales outlook for the mill's main product lines, its operating revenue and debt servicing payments, as well as its product mix. "Algoma Steel faces a fundamental structural problem," the consultant concluded. Changes to the collective agreement would be required in the near future to keep the mill afloat. In exchange, the union should demand a substantial equity share in Algoma and representation on the company's board of directors. Indeed, "the solution to the current problems of Algoma Steel will require nothing less than a New Deal between the union, management and the government."

That new deal was deferred when Dofasco, Canada's second-largest steelmaker, but non-union, purchased Algoma in 1989, promising to modernize the Sault Ste. Marie operation. Dofasco immediately collided with the United Steelworkers, resulting in a 112-day work stoppage in retaliation to downsizing, contracting out, and other issues. When Dofasco suddenly announced that it would walk away from its investment on 23 January 1991, the future of Algoma was put into doubt. In our interview, Bob Rae recalled: "I got the call from the president of the company, from Dofasco, saying we're going to do this, and I said, 'You're not doing anything without talking to us, and you're not doing anything without talking to the union.' I said, 'My door's open to talk to you, but if you think you're going to be able to close this place and walk away, you're wrong.'" Rae then met with local union officials on 29 January to discuss how best to save the mill, and then with company officials the next day. The sequence of meetings is important here. The situation was dire. Ross McClellan relates a story of how the CEO of the Royal Bank, a major creditor, advised that the blast furnaces should be shut down for the interim to save money:

> And Bob [Rae] had to point out to them, if you shut down a blast furnace in winter, it would create an explosion that would take out the entire north of Sault Ste. Marie; it would be like dropping a dummy bomb. So, these guys . . . are the ones controlling investment in the province of Ontario, and all they wanted to do was shut down the blast furnace, shut down Dofasco, and throw how many thousands—basically destroy the Sault.[11]

After Algoma was put under the Companies Creditors Arrangements Act, a federal law that gives troubled companies time to restructure without going into bankruptcy, the United Steelworkers insisted on a long-term fix. If Dofasco "succeeds in getting short term relief, the problems won't go away. The next time there is a crisis, Dofasco's responsibility will be diluted even from what it is now. Responsibility will be shared by all those who help short term." The union called it a trap, adding that it was "interested only in changes that address the problems of long-term viability."

From the outset of the crisis, the Steelworkers saw a worker buyout as being their preferred option. In a 30 January letter to the Premier's Office, the union noted that it had developed "significant expertise both internally and in the consultant community in the U.S. on these matters. Our union is uniquely placed to place the worker ownership option on the table in the case of Algoma and is in a position to offer valuable assistance based on our extensive experience." Not surprisingly, the union's primary objective was "to maintain as much of the operation and as many of the jobs as possible consistent with maximizing long term competitive viability." On this basis, they were willing to consider "any kind of configuration," including major restructuring.[12]

Rae brought all the parties to Queen's Park in March 1991 where he "told them that the Ontario government was not going to bail them all out, that they had to find a co-operative and market-based solution, and that we would do everything we could to broker a solution."[13] To that end, the Ontario government created a task force, chaired by Tim Armstrong, the new Deputy Minister of the Ministry of Industry and Trade, which included representatives of Algoma, Dofasco, the Steelworkers, the creditors, and of the wider Sault Ste. Marie community.[14] Dofasco was convinced to remain involved in the process, and even to develop a new restructuring proposal, given its sizeable environmental and pension liabilities. Relying on his close relationship with Leo Gerard, the district director of the United Steelworkers, Bob Rae told me he had to convince the union that deep concessions would be necessary:

> I think Leo, Leo Gerard was instrumental in that, although I have to say [chuckles] I had one of my toughest conversations with him [when] he and I went out for a walk. I remember we were down by the Park Plaza Hotel, and we went out for a walk together, and I said, "Leo, this isn't going to happen without some pain, it's going to be hard." And he said, "Oh, why do we have to?" and I said, "No, we're all paying up. We're going to pay up too, but it's going to take some difficult decisions." And eventually he came

around to that idea, but I don't think it was something any of us enjoyed doing.[15]

The federal Tories were of little help. They contributed financially to the first bridging loan to keep Algoma running, but not the second. The issue of bridging workers to retirement, key to avoiding layoffs and getting union members onside, was complicated by restrictive federal rules. The union wanted the bridging to start at age fifty instead of fifty-five, as only 800 workers would be eligible at fifty-five. The number eligible shot up to 2,600 at age fifty, more than enough to cover the needed contraction of the workforce. Ken Delaney informed Rae that the federal government "has not yet demonstrated a willingness to do anything creative." Delaney conceded it was politically difficult for the union to talk about restructuring to its members when mass layoffs were still on the table. Their ultimate goal, naturally enough, was to save the mill while avoiding outright layoffs. Delaney and the Steelworkers were convinced that there were "forces inside the Federal Government that believe Algoma should not be saved. We have nothing tangible to demonstrate this, but we do hear rumors that we believe."[16]

Dofasco's May 1991 restructuring proposal would have seen the radical downsizing of the plant with the termination of three of the mill's four product lines as well as the closure of the iron ore mine in Wawa. Three thousand jobs would have been lost and the wages of those remaining would have been rolled back by 14 percent.[17] In this scenario, mill workers would have received minority share holdings in exchange for their wage concessions but no control over their investment. Dofasco also wanted to shift some of the company's pension liability onto workers by converting the liability into Algoma shares, thereby exposing workers to enormous risk. The United Steelworkers rejected the proposal. Leo Gerard called it a "blueprint for confrontation," arguing that it served Dofasco's interests rather than Algoma's or Sault Ste. Marie's.[18] There was a dramatic showdown between the union and the company at a task force meeting in Toronto. The union brought Ron Bloom, the Wall Street investment banker who regularly advised the Steelworkers.

Bloom later recalled that Dofasco's proposal was "a pretty draconian thing" as it "imposed all the pain on the workers."[19] The *New Republic* provided an account of what happened next:

> Management, flanked by its bankers, lawyers, and a team of McKinsey consultants, put its official proposal on the table. When it was Bloom's turn to speak, he casually dismantled the McKinsey case with a rapid succession of questions. How, he wondered, could the owner justify taking the biggest stake in the new company when the union was contributing far more through its wage concessions? "The McKinsey advisers couldn't defend the numbers. Ron showed them they were phony," says Leo Gerard, then the union's district director. "The whole thing collapsed like a house of cards."[20]

With Dofasco's restructuring proposal dead on arrival, worker ownership emerged as the last best hope for the mill's survival.

The union's willingness to experiment and take risks led it, with the help of its Wall Street banker, to develop the voting trusts strategy, first developed after Wheeling-Pittsburgh Steel faced bankruptcy in 1982. Concessions were negotiated in exchange for preferred shares that carried full voting rights. By 1990, roughly one-quarter of the US steel industry was under some measure of employee ownership and it had become the central job-saving strategy of the union, at least in the US.[21] By then, the United Steelworkers of America had developed guidelines for union locals thinking about pursuing the idea. Thereafter any proposal must first go through a full feasibility study, the resulting arrangement must give worker-owners full voting rights, and it must never replace a pension plan.[22] Lynn Williams, a Canadian, who had replaced Lloyd McBride as United Steelworkers international president in 1984, advocated "participation more boldly than most American labor leaders, challenging companies in a way they rarely had been challenged before." When feasible, Williams strongly supported worker buyouts as a last resort to keep troubled plants open. In so doing, according to John Hoerr's book on the decline of the US steel industry, Williams enunciated "a politics of hope, not of despair, a policy that would enable him to restore institutional pride in the USW and individual pride in members."[23]

To be sure, Ron Bloom was uniquely positioned to lend organized labour a helping hand. He was what they call a "red diaper baby," as his parents had met in Habonim, the socialist Labour Zionist youth movement in the 1940s. As a boy, Bloom was sent to the movement's summer camp each year before graduating to camp counsellor. He recalled, "We sang the songs, but it wasn't about that. It was a broader sense of identifying with the underdog, and of observing the world through a lens, through people who don't have as much and aren't as lucky."[24] After graduating from university in 1977, Bloom worked for the Jewish Labor Committee and then joined the Service Employees International Union (SEIU), where he soon concluded that the trade union movement needed to better understand the workings of business if it was to survive. To acquire these skills, he went to the Harvard Business School, graduating in 1985, and then made a name for himself at Lazard Frères, a Wall Street investment bank. Soon thereafter, he engineered a hostile takeover of Wheeling-Pittsburgh in order to achieve the desired result. Bloom described his approach as "dentist-chair bargaining," in which he "grabs the dentist by the balls and says, 'Now let's not hurt each other.'" By all accounts, he was a brilliant negotiator. "Ron has what I refer to as ass power," suggested one observer. "He'll continue to talk about things, explore them, work on them, not letting the other side see what's really important to him. Even if it's important, he'll bargain it away early and work on getting it back."[25] The Algoma Steel buyout was Bloom's first big assignment after starting his own firm.

We are fortunate to have access to an oral history interview conducted with Bloom by Yale University, as he later became a key figure in Barack Obama's response to the 2009 financial crisis, becoming the administration's "Manufacturing Tsar." In 2018, he told his interviewer:

If you go back and read the history of the bankruptcies of the steel companies around the year 2000—and there were many, many of them, and I was intimately involved in each and every one of them—there are numerous cases, in fact, all cases, in every single steelworker bankruptcy, [in which] we did better than similarly situated creditors.[26]

He also noted that in 99 percent of bankruptcies, new ownership results and the existing shareholders are "wiped out, and the people who are the owners are typically the predators. They're the guys whom the company owed money to." The United Steelworkers, out of necessity, became one of those predators, using its leverage to win control of failing steel mills. Bankruptcy was "a combination of law and politics," Bloom explained. "By politics, I mean power. Creditors get their way because they have the leverage to get their way. It's, as they say it, 'an adults only game.' Everyone is out for themselves, which is fine, but if you have leverage, you use it."

The worker ownership idea had broad cross-party support in the Ontario legislature. Tony Martin, the NDP MPP for Sault Ste. Marie, moved a non-binding resolution that called on the government to support worker ownership, an idea "whose time has come."[27] Martin explained in the legislature the particular vulnerabilities of northern Ontario, where one-industry towns were the rule rather than the exception: "Living in a smaller, one-industry community and having friends in many small, one-industry communities in northern Ontario, one gets the feeling sometimes that maybe we are developing a Third World economy up there too." One by one, members of the opposition rose in support of the motion, noting that uncertain times required creative responses.

After considerable preparation, the union's restructuring plan for Algoma was ready by August 1991. Leo Gerard, a former hard-rock miner from Sudbury, made the public announcement. It included long-term wage concessions, the elimination of 1,600 jobs, mainly through early retirement and natural attrition, and capital investments of $500 million over the first five years. In return, the new Algoma would be employee owned and controlled.

The union's restructuring proposal, based on "German and Scandinavian models of codetermination between workers and industries," proposed to expand labour-management partnership in the operation and governance of the restructured plant.[28] After releasing the union's restructuring plan, Gerard said, "I'll stand or fall on that."[29] As Ken Delaney from the Steelworkers further explained to me, a "particular set of circumstances" made Algoma Steel "the right candidate for an employee buyout."[30] There was no corporate white knight waiting in the wings prepared to invest real capital. Dofasco wanted everyone else to "take a haircut" (an analogy I heard repeatedly over the course of my interviews), except itself: "If Dofasco had been prepared to invest money, this might have gone completely different. But nobody was prepared to step up." Creditors were therefore convinced to go along with the worker buyout. "We were the only dance partner available, to be blunt," Delaney told me. "It doesn't matter how ugly you are, if you're the only dance partner available, you get the dance."

To support the union, a Community Action Team was formed, signing up 22,000 members in Sault Ste. Marie.[31] The union brought Bloom to town in August 1991 to speak to the viability of the union's proposal, and eighteen local leaders were sent by the Steelworkers union to visit worker-owned Weirton Steel in West Virginia and McLouth Steel in Michigan.[32] The community campaign gave the union's proposal added legitimacy and political backing. Pushed into a corner, Algoma's management eventually agreed in principle with the worker ownership model, but the details needed to be ironed out. Multipartite negotiations dragged on into 1992, and there were moments when these talks threatened to break down. The breakthrough came at the end of nine days of around-the-clock negotiations at Toronto's Park Plaza Hotel led by George Adams, a judge of the Ontario Supreme Court, who had been brought in as arbitrator.[33]

The deal was announced by Bob Rae at Queen's Park on 28 February 1992, ending more than a year of uncertainty. Algoma's new board of directors now comprised the CEO, five employee nominees (two selected by the national union, two by the local union, and one by salaried employees), along with seven independent directors, including the former premiers of Ontario (Bill Davis) and Saskatchewan (Allan Blakeney). In exchange, unionized workers gave up $2.89 per hour in wages and salaried staff lost 14.5 percent. Algoma's new mission statement read: "As equal partners, Algoma and the United Steelworkers of America make as top priority, the creation of an organization that is dedicated to economic security and empowerment of employees and to continuing improvements in productivity and quality."[34] The new era at Algoma Steel was symbolically marked by the elimination of punch clocks for employees and the suspension of its membership in the local chamber of commerce. On the shop floor, the worker buyout ushered in a period of experimentation.[35]

A number of initiatives were undertaken to increase employee involvement in mill operations, including the creation of self-directed work groups that reduced the level of supervision required. Workers were also invited to suggest how the company could reduce operating costs and better use equipment. Algoma's annual reports claim that these ideas resulted in savings of millions of dollars.[36] These same reports emphasize labour-management partnership at all levels within the organization. Not surprisingly, changes to shop-floor relations were not always welcomed by managers. As the top two executives admitted at the time, "Cultural change in a large and long established organization is often a difficult and lengthy process. Through vehicles such as workplace restructuring and employee empowerment, the cultural change taking place at Algoma is well under way and is real."[37] The saving of the plant generated considerable community pride in Sault Ste. Marie with the inauguration of a monument to the successful effort called *Spirits Rising*.[38] Located on the waterfront, and built by local tradespeople working as volunteers, the steel and glass pyramid-like structure was meant to represent the three-way partnership between management, labour, and community.

The worker buyout garnered international attention, with the union being invited to speak around the world, and it hosted a steady stream of visitors. Ken Delaney had "no shortage of speaking invitations" as "everybody wanted to know about it. So, we were happy to share," Delaney says. "I was happy to share."[39] In 1995, the Steelworkers and Algoma Steel organized a conference on The Changing Workplace: A New Frontier, drawing two hundred people from companies and unions across North America. According to researcher Linda Savory-Gordon, there was a new pride among Algoma Steel workers and new stature for Steelworkers in the community. One employee was quoted as saying: "My daughter now wants to know what's going on at the plant. She's going to be going on a tour of it next week. I also took her over to the union hall so she knows what's going on there. So now these kids are starting to ask questions. What's going on?"[40] There were other, more tangible effects. Algoma saw a huge drop in the number of workplace injuries after the buyout, declining from three hundred employees on workers' compensation at any given time to just thirty or forty.[41]

Within three or four years, however, there was a sense that the joint labour-management decision-making process within the plant was eroding. When it was revealed in 1994 that 130 salaried employees had received substantial retention bonuses, there was an explosion of anger and a wildcat strike.[42] Here is Savory-Gordon's exchange with one steelworker:

> *Steel worker:* When it first started I was very proud to be part of the restructuring programme. When I learned more about it and discovered that the rumours were true—how much the upper level took out of this restructuring in bonuses—it became a total negative for me, and I'll tell you I was very ashamed that that was allowed to happen.
>
> *Linda Savory-Gordon:* So that overshadowed the positive?
>
> *Steel worker:* So the positive was gone in my mind. How the top level could possibly have done that when we sacrificed so much.

Linda Savory-Gordon: Do you think that that is a factor in why the changes at Algoma are not talked about more?

Steel worker: Only hearing the negative now. When news of the bonuses first came out it was known as the "swindlers' list"—when the individuals were given the bonuses, like Hopkins (CEO) being made a multi-millionaire. How many millionaires were made?[43]

There were also wider lessons. The Algoma Steel buyout helped Ron Bloom to appreciate just how much leverage trade unions can have during bankruptcy proceedings. For him, the buyout yielded two key insights:

First, you can typically show that liquidating a company is a lousy deal for everyone involved. Second, once you've convinced stakeholders that they're better off with a living company, labor has enormous leverage. The law technically gives lenders and suppliers priority over workers, but you can usually find new lenders and suppliers. The workers, on the other hand, are virtually irreplaceable.[44]

If Bloom's role was crucial, so too were those of Leo Gerard and Ken Delaney, as the three men worked out the union's successful strategy. According to Peter Warrian, Gerard's "act of absolute genius" was to use the bankruptcy court so the "union comes out with greater powers, because the pension liability exceeded the capital base of the company, and they used it." But it wasn't the only factor. The NDP government was crucial at every step. Without question, the Rae government invested considerable time and energy into the buyout of Algoma and, according to Warrian, expended valuable "political capital" in the process. Though a success, as the mill continues to operate thirty years later, albeit under private ownership, the worker buyout has been all but erased from political history. Or as Warrian puts it, it was as though someone pressed the "delete button of history."[45] For him, Algoma Steel represented "the high-water mark achievement of the industrial policy that we [the NDP government] had in mind." The single greatest challenge facing worker-owned industries, however, was how to find the capital for ongoing mill modernization. "The problem, which we all knew at the time, was that steel plants need capital," recalls Hugh Mackenzie. "And it would have taken a rebound in steel prices in the 1990s, which didn't happen, to generate the capital that would have been needed to make it work."[46] Without access to capital, the new Algoma was forced to recapitalize by going public in 1994, reducing the workers' share in the company from 57 percent to just 30 percent. In anticipation, additional job security guarantees were added to the union's collective agreement, ensuring union members their jobs or 90 percent of their income if laid off.[47] The resulting infusion of capital was directed into the construction of a new thin-slab caster, positioning Algoma as one of North America's leaders in the hot rolled sheet market.[48] But there were technical problems with the cutting-edge technology, and the employees' share of the company continued to shrink until Algoma got into financial trouble again in 1998. As a result, older production lines were closed and there was another round of layoffs. The iron mine near Wawa was finally shut, but displaced miners were able to transfer into the steel mill. In June 2007, Algoma was acquired by Essar Steel, an Indian-based multinational, for US$1.63 billion. While no longer employee owned, Algoma Steel survived and modernized thanks to the 1992 buyout. Ken Delaney thinks "the biggest legacy of the employee buyout is that Algoma is as large as it is. And to be honest with you, that's the legacy we were looking for."[49] He, for one, favoured employee ownership as a pragmatic response to impending closure rather than as an alternative economic model, and I tend to agree.

For his part, Gerard went on to become international president of the United Steelworkers, only the second Canadian to do so. A few weeks after Obama's 2008 election victory, Gerard received a call from Obama's transition team asking for advice on the automotive crisis. He put Ron Bloom on the call, who impressed the presidential aid with his blunt assessment.[50] Bloom ended up managing the restructuring of GM and Chrysler for the US government, after which Obama named him his "Manufacturing Tsar." "He may only manufacture deals, but that's been more than enough to retool the Rust Belt," declared *Time* magazine in 2010, naming Bloom one of its one hundred world changers.[51] But as Ross McClellan quips, "He was our czar first, we beat Obama."

LABOUR-LED VENTURE CAPITAL

Worker ownership appealed to Bob Rae's NDP, as it offered a third way between public ownership and private enterprise. It also seemed to combine the party's commitment to economic democracy, labour-management partnerships, and community-led economic development. However, a major stumbling block for worker buyouts in Canada, as elsewhere, was access to capital. Inspired by the example of the Solidarity Fund held by the Fédération des travailleurs et travailleuses du Québec (FTQ), the NDP introduced enabling legislation for labour-sponsored venture capital funds, despite the vocal opposition of the Ontario Federation of Labour and major unions such as the Canadian Auto Workers. The legislation had two parts. The first provided a tax credit to workers buying out the companies they worked for. The second enabled the formation of labour-led venture capital funds that gave investors generous tax credits. Subsequent debate over the legislation revealed much about the NDP's thinking on economic democracy and industrial restructuring.

Financing was a key challenge facing worker ownership, both in terms of incentivizing worker buyouts and satisfying the recapitalization needs of worker-owned firms. The NDP was strongly opposed to the US employee stock ownership plan model of directing tax credits to employers willing to sell shares to employees. Thus, when the Liberals introduced their own Ontario-light version of ESOPs in early 1987, NDP finance critic Jim Foulds informed the government of the party's strong opposition to the legislation. "Instead of democratizing the workplace ESOPs only serve to perpetuate a society divided into two classes: those who control and those who are controlled. The only difference will be that workers will have to risk their savings in return for the right to be controlled and quite possibly lose their collective bargaining rights."[52]

The FTQ's much-praised Solidarity Fund, established in 1983, was an attractive alternative model. It originated out of the union movement's frustration with the refusal of banks to bail out troubled companies and the danger of employee buyouts when the risk fell only on the shoulders of employees. There was also nationalist concern in Quebec over a perceived capital gap for mid-sized companies. John O'Grady, the then research director of the Ontario Federation of Labour, told me that Jacques Parizeau, Quebec's Finance Minister, was "effectively the tutor to the Quebec Federation of Labour. He literally held seminars for them. He taught them their economics. He was an economics professor, and he taught them their economics."[53] The FTQ's Louis Laberge officially proposed the Solidarity Fund to the Parti Québécois government, which quickly passed enabling legislation and provided $10 million in start-up funds as well as generous tax breaks for investors. Its stated objective was to promote "job maintenance and job creation, stimulating the economy and training workers in economic matters."[54] The FTQ controlled seven of the Solidarity Fund's thirteen board members, and by 1989 there were 68,000 shareholders, fully 70 percent of whom were union members. Within a few years, the Solidarity Fund's assets had grown to $215 million. By this time, the labour federations of British Columbia and Saskatchewan as well as the Canadian Federation of Labour (a small breakaway union central representing the construction trades) created their own labour-led venture capital funds based on the Quebec model. But the funds were tiny in comparison. Ontario trade unions proved to be far more resistant to the idea.

Initially intrigued, the Ontario Federation of Labour's executive board decided to explore the idea of a Quebec-style Solidarity Fund after meeting in January 1988 with Ontario Liberal Premier David Peterson, who was supportive of the idea. FTQ leader Laberge was then invited to speak about the Quebec model at a board meeting in Brockville. Interested in exploring the idea further, OFL president Gord Wilson informed Bob Rae in March 1989 that it was "on the verge of some serious dialogue as to whether or not to proceed to engage the provincial and federal governments in discussion as to the establishment of a fund somewhat similar to the currently constructed Solidarity Fund within the province of Quebec."[55] A committee was formed with representatives from key unions as well as the Ontario NDP. It included Wilson, OFL vice-president Julie Davis (who was soon to become the president of the Ontario NDP), and then OFL research director John O'Grady, as well as Sam Gindin from the Auto Workers, Hugh Mackenzie from the Steelworkers, and Robin Sears from the Ontario NDP.[56]

In a draft background paper, O'Grady warned that they needed to avoid "economic romanticism," as any labour-managed fund could not "redress the imbalance of power between communities and multi-national corporations." However, he wrote:

> if there is a legitimate trade union *economic* interest in a development fund, it will lie in a fund's strengthening of the collective bargaining position of workers in at least some types of workplaces. And if there is a legitimate *political* interest to be served by a fund, it will be its role in building coalitions around restructuring issues and in supplementing our movement's technical capacities and overall leverage.[57]

While the idea of a labour-led venture capital fund potentially offered a way to politicize "the restructuring question" and to develop "countervailing expertise on restructuring questions," O'Grady worried about the resulting "ideological confusion" that would result and the "gross distortion of our energies and resources." Moreover, the Quebec Solidarity Fund's approach was difficult for O'Grady to comprehend, as it did not "attempt to alter the way in which management runs a business." Indeed, it "deliberately refuses to take a majority stake in any enterprise." You could almost see him shaking his head as he wondered aloud what the point was:

> To our thinking this amounts to divorcing the strategy of the Solidarity Fund from the broader strategy of the labour movement. We believe that a fund is only of interest if it goes in the opposite direction. To be of use to the trade union movement the financial strategy of a fund must be joined to our overall strategy to establish collective bargaining in the small and middle sectors of the economy. And to be of value to our members who are employed there, the fund must use its financial leverage to both improve their conditions of employment and to increase the say which they have in their workplace.[58]

The group as a whole agreed that the Solidarity Fund had "met with near unanimous praise within Quebec." However, while the fund gave the FTQ "some control over the direction of investment" in the province, it was "an illusion to believe that workers can mobilize, through their savings (even if supplemented by tax loopholes), the funds that come anywhere close to matching the resources of the major corporations in the economy." Fully three-quarters of the Solidarity Fund's assets, at the time, were invested in traditional bonds, stocks, and mortgages, with just $50 million directed towards fifty-two investments that, the fund claimed, created twelve thousand jobs. The Ontario group thought the job creation number was grossly inflated, and only a couple of the early investments actually involved troubled mills or factories. I've written elsewhere that the reopening of Truscon Steel's plant in Montreal was one of these exceptions.[59] Otherwise, the Solidarity Fund behaved much like any other venture capital fund. The Ontario group therefore concluded: "As a response to economic crisis, solutions like the Solidarity Fund are simply marginal to the overall picture." Furthermore, unless we address the basic issue of the corporations' unilateral right to restructure the economy as they see fit, and the power of the banks to mobilize our savings and invest them as they see fit, proposals like the Solidarity Fund remain marginal to the real problems facing working people.

To make matters worse, the return on investment in the early years was "very low even in terms of its own expectations," with yearly growth of only 5 percent between 1984 and 1988. This amounted to less than the interest rate at the time and considerably less than what investors would get back if they had instead purchased Canada Savings Bonds. The FTQ's Solidarity Fund was, they concluded, more a tax loophole than it was a serious investment vehicle: "Claims made on behalf of the Quebec Solidarity Fund have been wildly exaggerated. Nor is there any evidence that it has in fact strengthened worker solidarity and union strength."[60] The committee therefore unanimously rejected the Solidarity Fund model, believing that a venture capital fund was inappropriate for saving plants threatened with closure.[61] To truly influence the economy required controlling major corporations, "not ignoring them and trying to concentrate on the smaller businesses on the fringe."

Instead the OFL proposed a social investment fund that would "channel a portion of workers' weekly savings into socially advantageous economic projects such as non-profit housing and environmental projects."[62] The idea was then adopted by the OFL executive board and by delegates at the labour federation's November 1989 convention. Delegates reaffirmed the policy in November 1991, which called for a social investment fund that would forefront "socially useful investment" and include some types of community economic development. Saving failing plants should be dealt with "through other mechanisms" and as part of a "broader strategy."

Despite the devastating assessment, Quebec's Solidarity Fund continued to inspire dreams of industrial democracy in the minds of some sections of the union movement and among many of the top economic advisors in the NDP government. For them, tax credits offered a powerful incentive for worker ownership and a way to influence the restructuring process.[63] The NDP's first budget mentioned that it was considering "freeing up pension funds and establishing investment pools" along the lines of the FTQ's Solidarity Fund. "We want to channel the capital resources of Ontario to finance restructuring and promote regional development," said Floyd Laughren in April 1991.[64] "We are all aware that the Ontario economy is undergoing fundamental restructuring as a result of changing markets and growing international competition," Laughren told the media a couple months later. "To meet these new economic challenges, businesses need better access to sources of capital and employees need to be full partners."[65] The proposal, modelled on existing legislation in Saskatchewan and British Columbia, would enable the public to receive a tax credit for investing up to $15,000 per year in labour-sponsored venture capital funds. Laughren suggested that it was possible the legislation could help the worker buyout of Algoma Steel, but it wasn't specifically designed for that purpose. "That would not be acceptable under the free trade agreement, anyway," he said. The government had to be careful not to aim the legislation at any one industry, as doing so could trigger countervailing duties from the US. "The seeds for a worker buyout have been planted," Leo Gerard enthused. "Now the government has made it possible for a viable proposal to be developed."[66]

The new legislation was announced in June 1991, a month after Dofasco's restructuring proposal was shot down by the United Steelworkers. "We are all aware," Laughren told the legislature, "that the Ontario economy is undergoing fundamental restructuring as a result of changing markets and growing international competition. To meet these new economic challenges, businesses need better access to sources of capital and employees need to be full partners."[67] A discussion paper was then released in August 1991, the same month as the Steelworkers' restructuring plan for Algoma was made public, sparking a wave of media interest. "Ontario unions and workers are expected to become major investors in the province under a worker ownership program," wrote one journalist. As Bob Rae explained, these labour-led investment funds would be a source of "patient money—investment money that's prepared to be patient—that's prepared to really look at the long-term picture of our economy."[68]

While Bill 150 was supported by the United Steelworkers, other parts of the union movement opposed the linkage of worker ownership to labour-led investment funds. Trade union opponents at first voiced their concerns privately to the government. In September 1991, for example, Bob White wrote to say:

> We want to emphasize our opposition to the worker-financed venture capital fund. There has been no research presented to indicate that a lack of venture capital is a principal problem in the province and if it were, why workers—rather than those with the capital and those who are in the business of "risks"—should be placed at the centre of the solution.[69]

The Canadian Auto Workers, White said, remained unconvinced that tax breaks have "either saved more jobs, or done more to strengthen Quebec's economic structure, or encouraged any more meaningful worker input. The point of such funds is to get workers to 'buy into' capitalism and the culture of tax breaks. They mean playing at the margin of the economy and divert attention from the real (complex and difficult) problems of economic strategy." White then reminded the government that the Ontario Federation of Labour had already rejected labour-led venture capital funds.

These clashing perspectives only became public over May and June 1992, when the Standing Committee on Finance and Economic Affairs held hearings on the proposed legislation. This was the second round of consultations and most of the technical issues had been resolved.[70] The OFL thought Algoma was a "valuable experiment and perhaps . . . the only way to save people's jobs. It perhaps will lead to some interesting experiments in technology and work design as well," so the federation was "very much in favour of that." However, the OFL still had doubts about the overall value of worker ownership as an economic strategy and expressed concern that industrial workers were being asked to carry the risk: "It is . . . difficult to see how this can form the basis for a widespread alternative to an increasingly unregulated market economy."[71] Otherwise, it focused its criticisms on the second half of the legislation on labour-sponsored venture capital funds. Even if there was a "capital gap," why should union members take the risk? The OFL remained unconvinced: "In our view, while majority ownership may well be an option for workers, minority ownership venture capital funds are not. They amount to buying into the margins of the economy without having any say over how it operates or how it is structured." The OFL urged the NDP government to substantially amend the legislation along the lines of its social investment fund idea.

Hearing this hard-hitting testimony, opposition members on the standing committee asked if it still made sense for the government to proceed with the legislation. The OFL's Chris Schenk coolly replied, "That would be something you would want to ask the government." Liberal Monte Kwinter agreed, saying, "It doesn't do what it's supposed to do, that is, to help small and medium-sized businesses, it doesn't deal with the social fund labour wanted. It's neither fish nor fowl; it doesn't serve the purpose and doesn't answer the need."

Next, the Canadian Auto Workers presented to the committee, with Jim O'Neil, the union's secretary-treasurer, in attendance, as well as Sam Gindin. O'Neil pointedly asked if labour venture funds would actually contribute to job creation or worker control. He suggested that the FTQ's Solidarity Fund has been a "bit player in the overall scheme of things." The Caisse de dépôt et placement du Québec, which manages the Quebec Pension Plan, was another matter—it was a major economic player, but it was a different kind of investment vehicle. The CAW then questioned whether the proposed fund would be a good investment for working people: "The tendency to erode future pensions in favour of venture funds is, for working people, a dangerous mistake." The union therefore urged "the government to withdraw its current proposal and seriously consider introducing an alternative based on the OFL model." To this, Kwinter expressed his bewilderment that the government was proceeding with its labour-sponsored fund even though much of the labour movement was lining up against the legislation. Why would they proceed under such circumstances? Gindin responded that he was in complete agreement with Kwinter for once:

> I think the Ontario government is basically following the Quebec model. It looks like that's what's happening across the country. . . . From our perspective, we really don't understand why, if this is supposed to be a labour-oriented fund, the alternative put forth by the labour movement isn't what we're discussing today. Maybe somebody else can answer that question. I can't answer that question.[72]

Gindin noted that nobody from the government had approached the CAW or the OFL to find an acceptable way forward. In fact, the unions were only given ten days' notice to prepare their briefs. Asked who was driving the legislation forward, Gindin said that the CAW was "less interested in who's doing it and more interested in stopping it and getting it changed." Later, Kwinter suggested that the "whole project is doomed to failure. How could you possibly encourage an employee to buy into a program where the two major entities in the labour movement are saying, 'This is of no consequence, a terrible deal, and we don't think it should be done'? How do you deal with that?" It was a remarkable exchange, to say the least.

The Steelworkers were next up. Surprisingly, even this union had substantial concerns with the proposed legislation. In a letter tabled to the committee, Leo Gerard expressed his disappointment that the union was not consulted earlier in the process: "In fact, we did not get the invitation to attend tonight until Tuesday, and unfortunately this week, starting yesterday and going until tomorrow, is the national policy conference of the Steelworkers and all the senior members of the union are down in Hamilton attending that conference." The union was therefore represented by its lawyer, Robin MacKnight, who emphasized that there was a real danger that the legislation, as currently written, could trigger countervailing duties over perceived subsidies, as there was too much government discretion:

> When we raised the concept of a cabinet order in council being the final decision generating a tax credit, we almost had to peel our trade lawyers in Washington off the ceiling. In their view, there could not be anything clearer than a cabinet order in council as an indication that there is some kind of government intervention in the marketplace here, and that means countervails, and that means a lot of the companies who probably need worker ownership and need the assistance of this bill will not be able to access it simply because their foreign competition will take them to whatever trade tribunals are appropriate in the foreign countries. That is a serious problem with this bill, and I can't overemphasize that point.[73]

Not surprisingly, opposition politicians seized onto Gerard's letter. "We used to have a bit of a standing joke around here that we saw more of him here for a while than we did cabinet ministers," Tory Gary Carr laughed. Liberal Gerry Phillips then observed: "These hearings are proving far more interesting than we thought. ... I thought it would be fairly routine, but so far we're running into an awful lot of major comments. Your comments really struck a responsive chord. We've been talking about the order in council, the implication being that the government is backing it. It's not just the free trade agreement, there's probably some GATT stuff involved in this."[74]

The Standing Committee on Finance and Economic Affairs continued to consider Bill 150 on 4 June 1992. At this point, the government shared a set of six new amendments to the legislation based on the specific concerns raised by the Steelworkers. Civil servants then went over the changes. But Kwinter still couldn't get over the earlier testimony:

I was stunned sitting here the other day when the Ontario Federation of Labour came in and the Canadian Auto Workers came in and announced that this bill is not going to have their support, that it does not address the intent of their initiative. I was the minister at the time when they came in to see me. They told me that they wanted to get the support of the government for a fund to address social matters, to be sponsored and backed by labour. I said I had no problem with that and, "If you can go out and get it organized, great," and they went ahead and did it. Somewhere along the line—when I spoke to Mr Gindin and I said to him, "Where did this this go wrong?" He said, "I don't know where it went wrong, but it has absolutely gone wrong." We have a bill that is supposed to be sponsored by labour and benefit labour and two of the largest constituencies in the labour group are saying, "Not only are we not going to support it, but we are going to actively encourage our members not to support it."[75]

This time, however, the NDP members on the committee jumped to the defence of the legislation. What followed would be laughable if it wasn't so sad. NDP backbencher Paul Johnson from eastern Ontario declared, "Let's get one thing straight. This is not a labour initiative; this is a government initiative."[76] To this, Kwinter simply read out the title of the bill: "An Act to provide for the Creation and Registration of Labour Sponsored Venture Capital Corporations." Undeterred, Johnson insisted the title was "open to interpretation," and that "the focus of this bill isn't on labour. This is not a labour bill. This is a bill that allows for investment in small and medium-sized businesses in the province, and not investment from just labour but from people who have capital they would like to invest. To suggest that it's exclusive to labour and that it was a labour initiative is wrong." Kwinter coldly retorted: "I think your whole statement is absurd. If that is the case, then I would suggest you change the title, because I can read as well as you can and the title says it is labour-sponsored." At this point, the NDP's

Kimble Sutherland jumped in to minimize the importance of the Ontario Federation of Labour, dismissing it as "an overall umbrella group." These acts of political contortionism speak to the growing divergence between the NDP government and much of the labour movement on how best to respond to the industrial crisis.

Next, the legislative committee on Bill 150 heard from the Minister of Revenue herself, Shelley Wark-Martyn.[77] All evidence to the contrary, she insisted that there was strong labour support for "the concept of worker ownership and venture capital investment," citing specifically the Steelworkers' restructuring of Algoma Steel and the small breakaway Canadian Federation of Labour. She acknowledged that the OFL and CAW "expressed some reservations" about the venture fund side of the bill, endorsing "a rather different type of worker investment than that contained in Bill 150."[78] Wark-Martyn then insisted that the bill wasn't simply aimed at organized labour but "for the participation of all working people and all Ontarians in the economic regeneration of our province." Who else might lead these labour-led venture capital funds remained unclear.

The Liberals and Tories present were incredulous. Elinor Caplan, a Liberal from Toronto, asked why the minister was invoking Algoma Steel, as the legislative model being proposed was not at all the same. To this, Wark-Martyn responded that the "Algoma Steel workers and the union people were very much a part of why this bill was created. . . . So, although they are not now using this plan, they are still very supportive and were very much a part of the concept of having this sort of plan in Ontario's economy." Caplan then pointed to the strong opposition from "some of the organized labour union leadership" to the model being proposed. Wark-Martyn replied that they were in favour of the worker ownership half, just not the other half on labour-sponsored investment. Wark-Martyn was a weak performer and clearly did not have a strong handle on the file; as a result she constantly tried to deflect questions to her technical staff. The opposition parties would have none of it: "Minister, you are a member of the cabinet that made the policy decision here at committee. As you defend your legislation, I'd like you to explain your policy decision to us. It's the government's policy decision, not the Treasurer's, and you're a member of the government."[79]

With the committee hearings concluded, the debate shifted to the legislature with the third reading of the bill in July 1992. Wark-Martyn drew members' attention to the leadership of the fringe Canadian Federation of Labour in the visitor's gallery of the legislature, proof positive that at least some trade unionists were in favour of the legislation.[80] No other union group appeared to be present for the occasion. For his part, Bob Rae argued that the legislation "puts democracy into the economy. It gives workers a chance to participate. It gives them a chance to participate as equity partners. It's clearly an idea whose time has come."[81] If so, "surely," Liberal Greg Sorbara retorted, what the government should have done was "halt consideration of the bill and redesign it in consultation with the Ontario Federation of Labour before proceeding to third reading and royal assent of the bill."[82] I have no straightforward answer as to why the government stayed the course, except that it was locked into the idea, but we will return to this point later.

CONCLUSION

When the United Steelworkers of America and the Ontario NDP government engineered the worker buyout of Algoma Steel in 1992, Algoma became the largest worker-owned industry in North America. The Algoma Steel buyout was a "bold social experiment" in two respects: it successfully saved the mill and it was a rare experiment in economic democracy.[83] The NDP government's energetic response to the Algoma Steel crisis therefore made the difference, as did that of the United Steelworkers. Alone among North American unions, Steelworkers had developed the internal capacity to undertake large-scale worker buyouts. Accordingly, this chapter unsettles the usual bifurcated understanding of trade union responses to the industrial crisis in North American labour studies. The dichotomy between defiant "social unionism" and tired or corrupt "business unionism" conceals as much as it reveals. Concessionary agreements were sometimes more than capitulation, as unions experimented with new ways to save jobs at a time when their memberships were in free fall. Employee buyouts were one such innovation. For trade unionists, it was a pragmatic response to a rapidly deteriorating economic situation rather than an ideologically driven one. This was not necessarily the case with NDP politicians influenced by New Left ideas about economic democracy.

How, then, should we understand the Algoma experiment? In his memoirs, Bob Rae portrayed Algoma Steel as a central achievement of his government. I could not agree more. Even so, we need to recognize that worker ownership did not take hold outside of northern Ontario and its long-term viability was undermined by the continuing need for capital investment. Tim Armstrong, the government's point person on the Algoma buyout who later served on the steelmaker's board of directors, noted that majority employee ownership was short-lived. But "the real achievement at Algoma was not only survival—a quite remarkable consequence in itself—but also the fact that Algoma was in the forefront of the restructuring which has subsequently been found to be essential in many sectors of the 'old' economy. The result is that there is now in Sault Ste Marie a modernized and efficient mill capable of producing quality steel at relatively low costs per tonne." That said, he thought that "whatever the future may hold, employee ownership will remain a ripple on the surface of Canadian industrial relations, at least for the foreseeable future." He was certainly proved right. Even at Algoma, worker ownership did not fundamentally change how decisions were made on the shop floor or in the boardroom.[84]

If worker ownership got some traction in recession-battered Ontario, the NDP's experiment with labour-led venture capital quickly turned into a fiasco. When he introduced the legislation in November 1991, Floyd Laughren claimed it represented "an important step on the road to rebuilding the economy," as it would provide businesses with a new source of financing and offer workers "an opportunity for greater participation and increased decision-making in the places they work."[85] The legislation failed on both counts. Ken Delaney, who was later involved in a labour-led fund, remains "unconvinced" by their value to the trade union movement. In Ontario, these were smaller funds than Quebec's Solidarity Fund because the Ontario Federation of Labour was divided on the issue, leaving it to affiliates to decide. A much more critical assessment is offered by Hugh Mackenzie, who says the NDP "basically opened a cafeteria" that inaugurated a "sad period" of "rent-a-unions." Traditional venture capitalists "would sign up a union to skim off basically to get graft from the fund, and they would run it, and they were running it strictly for the basis of extracting the tax credit." These were small funds and "as soon as the tax credit was gone, that was it." They all disappeared, and "it was embarrassing." For his part, Ross McClellan says he "wouldn't have gone there with a ten-foot pole. I wouldn't buy a nickel's worth of that stuff. It gave the impression, almost, of being a Ponzi scheme!" No wonder Rae didn't mention the labour-led venture capital scheme in his memoirs. One wonders what would have happened had the Ontario NDP listened to its critics in organized labour and embraced the alternative model of social investment.[86]

National Rubber Company: Alti Jones, a fork lift operator, 1994.
Photo by Peter MacCallum.

7
NORTHERN EXCEPTIONALISM

> It doesn't matter whether the commodity is nickel, lumber, pulp and paper, iron ore or the gold from the new boom in Hemlo the correlation between resource development and regional disparity is a fact of life in the north. And in the vocabulary of economic life resource development becomes synonymous with dependency and dependency is just another word for vulnerability.
>
> —Floyd Laughren, 1983[1]

Northern Ontario comprised everything north of the French River, accounting for 80 percent of the province's landmass but only 10 percent of its people. Its proportion of Ontario's population is considerably less today, even though the region's southern boundary has been pushed southward to hide the region's declining political clout. With the expansion of the railway in the late nineteenth and early twentieth centuries, and the extension of the highway system in the 1930s and 1940s, resource towns were strung across the Canadian Shield like so many Christmas lights. These were economically dependent places, subject to decisions made outside the region. Even the Ontario Liberal Party came to understand that the North had been "treated as a virtual colony of the South."[2] This was true in more ways than one. Northward expansion was very much tied to the dispossession of the Anishinaabe and Cree peoples. Industrial colonialism thus put its stamp on the region.[3]

Northern Ontario has a long history of trade union struggle and radical class politics.[4] Vestiges of the Old Left were still visible when I was growing up in Thunder Bay in the 1970s and early 1980s. My hometown had a Red Ukrainian Hall with the portraits of Marx, Lenin, and Stalin on the walls as well as "big" and "little" Red Finn Halls, standing side by side, built by the syndicalist and communist lefts. But more importantly there was a strong working-class sensibility.[5] My long-time local NDP MPP, Jim Foulds, credits the 1952 railway strike, which saw his father, a section man, go out, for politicizing him at an early age:

> The local paper—the *Chronicle-Journal*—wrote editorials calling these people, these strikers, enemies of the people. And when you're fourteen years old, you don't have a great opinion of your old man. But I knew my old man was not an enemy to people . . . and that made me susceptible to being on the left.[6]

He calls it "both an emotional and intellectual conversion." A similar story unfolded in towns and cities across the region. However, the Cold War hunt for communists, real or imagined, scarred left politics in the nickel mining and refining centre of Sudbury. Bryan Evans grew up in that city at around the same time that I did. His was a proud "Mine Mill family," referring to the left-wing union that was eventually driven out of INCO by the anti-communist (but social democratic) United Steelworkers.[7] The conflict between the two unions was still quite raw when Floyd Laughren ran for the first time in 1971. As a relative newcomer, he was well positioned to be the NDP's compromise candidate in the Nickel Belt riding:

> There had been huge battles between the unions, Sudbury Mine Mill versus Steel [Steelworkers]. And the Steelworkers had put forth a candidate to run in for the NDP in the '70–71 election. And Mine Mill had done the same. We had two opposing candidates. And they knew they couldn't win the election with a vote split that way. So they needed somebody who had a foot in neither camp. And I'd only been in town for less than about two years. And so I talked with my wife, we had three little kids. And she said, "Come on, let's do it." She was good that way.[8]

Once elected, Laughren had to walk a fine line. On Labour Day, for example, there were separate union picnics and he was inevitably asked if he had attended the other one first. It paid to be honest about the little things. There were other stories. One day, while canvassing, Laughren encountered two elderly couples playing cards:

> I introduce myself. "Oh, yeah, we know, we heard, yeah." And I said, "So, I'm here to ask for your support in this election," and they said, "Well, okay, but you have to answer a question." I said, "What's that?" "Are you a socialist?" I said, "I would call myself that, yes, and be proud if somebody else did." "Well," the guy said, "you got a vote, thank you."[9]

They were Red Finns. The NDP, and left politics more generally, was deeply embedded in much of the region. "It was very much a neighbourhood-rooted, working-class party," recalls Evans. So much so, in fact, that his mother simply referred to the NDP as the "labour party."

While the entire province was hurting, the North was hit especially hard in the early 1990s. A leaked memorandum from the Deputy Minister of Northern Development revealed the "degenerating state" of northern Ontario's resource-based economy.[10] A perfect storm of aging mills, resource exhaustion, a high Canadian dollar, corporate consolidation and rationalization, and trade liberalization threatened to sink northern Ontario's economy. We already heard about the successful effort to keep Algoma Steel in operation, and the length to which the government went to support a just transition for the uranium mining town of Elliot Lake, but the region's forestry industry was also in trouble. A paper mill in Thunder Bay, one of four, closed in 1991. It looked likely that others would follow in Kapuskasing, Sturgeon Falls, Sault Ste. Marie, and a second in Thunder Bay. Sawmills were also suffering from the long-running softwood lumber dispute with the United States that saw, in 1986, the imposition of a 15 percent export tax in lieu of import duties.[11] Bud Wildman, the new Minister of Natural

Resources, remembers that it was as if the entire regional economy was in a state of collapse: "The whole economy of northern Ontario was threatened. We couldn't allow it to happen."[12]

New environmental standards likewise put northern Ontario mills into jeopardy, as corporations refused to invest more into aging mills.[13] In fact, the pulp and paper industry was—and is—one of the worst polluters in the country. The 1970s mercury poisoning of the Anishinaabe community of Grassy Narrows in northwestern Ontario, which remains a live issue, was part of a much longer history of environmental racism and industrial colonialism. The forests were also being cut at unsustainable rates, sparking confrontations with environmentalists and Indigenous peoples. A blockade of Red Squirrel Road near Temagami became a flashpoint in 1989, leading Bob Rae, while still in opposition, to be arrested by the police after he joined it in solidarity with Temagami First Nation. His action proved controversial within some sections of the Ontario NDP, especially in northern Ontario. In this, however, Rae had a strong supporter in Bud Wildman, whom he appointed as the NDP's first Minister of Natural Resources and the minister responsible for Indigenous issues.

Temagami protest: Ontario NDP leader Bob Rae is photographed just before his arrest during a September 1989 protest over the building of a logging road. Photo by Darcy Henton / *Toronto Star* via Getty Images.

A regional development mindset continued to frame the province's approach to economic issues in the North, setting it apart from how the industrial crisis was increasingly understood and responded to in the rest of the province. The 1985 Ontario Royal Commission on Northern Environment had concluded after eight years of study that the people who live in the region are extremely vulnerable and that they have been historically excluded from the major decisions related to the region's development. Regional devolution of decision-making and community-controlled forestry were among its many recommendations. The late 1980s therefore saw the relocation of several branches of the Ontario civil service, involving thousands of public-sector jobs, from Toronto to northern communities in an effort to diversify the region's economy.

We also see the same regionalist impulse in the 1986 report of the Advisory Committee on Resource Dependent Communities in Northern Ontario, chaired by Robert Rosehart, which recognized that the region's economy had historically "been tied to the natural resource sectors of forestry and mining and [was] heavily dependent on the activities of large corporations."[14] The committee identified over fifty resource-dependent communities in the region, defining them as communities where there existed "dominant resource based economic activity with a single employer or group of employers in that activity and which [were] not within commuting distance of another area or areas offering alternative employment opportunities." Over 60 percent of these communities had fewer than 2,500 inhabitants. Even before the recession, the statistical portrait of the region the committee offered was "horrifying," with skyrocketing unemployment, depopulation, and youth out-migration. In response, the Rosehart Committee (which included Wildman) recommended the creation of a northern Ontario regional development fund along the lines of the Swedish model, as well as longer notice periods for plant closures in the region, community adjustment funding, mandatory adjustment committees, compulsory severance pay in the resource sector, early retirement schemes, and relocation assistance for workers and other residents.

With the election of the NDP in 1990, the region enjoyed a level of influence inside the provincial cabinet never seen before or since. Not only did northerners represent one-third of the inner cabinet, but they controlled many of the key ministries: Floyd Laughren in Finance; Shelley Martel in Northern Development and Mines; Bud Wildman in Natural Resources and later Environment; Howard Hampton as Solicitor General, then Natural Resources; Gilles Pouliot in Transport; and Shelley Wark-Martyn in Revenue. There were five others on the NDP backbenches. The Northern Caucus, according to Wildman, met regularly to "work out what the issues were, and what [they] felt [their] position should be." If they reached a consensus, they'd "take that to cabinet—or if not to cabinet immediately, through to the caucus."[15] The NDP's northern MPPs and their senior staff worked closely together to find ways to keep the region's mines, mills, and factories open. Had these shut permanently, "the whole community would be dead," Wildman adds, so they "were determined in the Northern Caucus to get assistance to save the communities." The Northern Caucus also provided feedback to other ministers contemplating new legislation or regulations that would affect the North. Ruth Grier, the Minister of Environment, thus visited to get feedback about accelerating new pulp and paper pollution standards. This proposal prompted general concern about possible mill closures. According to Laughren's handwritten notes, Grier feared a slower implementation timeline would be unacceptable to the militant environmental group Greenpeace. To this, Tony Martin from Sault Ste. Marie suggested that "realism is needed—cannot be dictated to by Greenpeace."[16] They also discussed the possible impact of pulp pollution to male sperm counts, presumably as an argument to counter those opposed to the new environmental standards.

The election of the Ontario NDP saw the rapid expansion of worker buyouts of closing plants across northern Ontario. That these efforts were mostly located in remote single-industry towns, where the future of the mill and that of the surrounding community were one and the same, was not coincidental. While Algoma Steel was the largest of these, by far, the paper mills in

Kapuskasing (Spruce Falls), Thunder Bay (Provincial Paper), and Sault Ste. Marie (St. Marys Paper) were also saved with various configurations of worker, manager, and community ownership. Spruce Falls, the first of these, emerged out of the crisis 52 percent employee owned, with another 7 percent owned by other Kapuskasing residents, and 41 percent owned by Tembec, which also operated the plant.[17] Tembec had originated in the worker-manager buyout of the mill in Témiscaming, Quebec, in 1972–73, but had since become a publicly traded company. Provincial Paper, in contrast, was a management-led buyout, even though unionized workers owned 75 percent of shares.

While this chapter focuses on Spruce Falls and Provincial Paper, the NDP government was active across the region in saving mills from closing. As we will see in the next chapter, there were few equivalent efforts in southern Ontario, though the province did take a minority stake in De Havilland, a global leader in the manufacture of regional commuter aircraft. Clearly, then, the NDP proved far more willing to step in to stop industrial sites from closing in northern Ontario than anywhere else. When I asked Bud Wildman how this bifurcated approach to plant closures was received by the rest of the cabinet and caucus, he replied: "They recognized that the resource industries in the North were a basic part of the overall provincial economy."[18] The regional framing of economic issues thus helped insulate the North to some extent from the progressive competitive agenda that increasingly recontextualized industrial closures as not only necessary but a positive good in themselves.

SAVING THE NORTH

Bob Rae appointed Bud Wildman as the NDP's first Minister of Natural Resources, a high-profile ministry in northern Ontario, as it managed the province's Crown lands and forests. Historically, the MNR was dominated by foresters with close ties to the lumber and paper industries. Fish and wildlife officials had less influence. Charged with the management of the forests, the MNR had—in reality—little idea of the actual extent of timber resources or the health of wildlife habitats or of non-extractive species of plants and animals. When they were still in opposition, the NDP's Northern Caucus called for the reform of forest management; among its recommendations was a proposed independent audit of Ontario's forests.

At first, there was some concern that Wildman was being placed into a conflict of interest in serving as minister of both Natural Resources and of Native Affairs. There was a long history of conflict between the MNR and Indigenous peoples exercising their treaty rights to hunt and fish on their traditional territories. Several Indigenous leaders told him that, as a result, Wildman would not be able to advocate on their behalf. Some non-native anglers and hunters also feared that this combination might work against their own interests. Some forestry boosters feared that he was too much of a conservationist. When confronted by these concerns, Wildman would jokingly retort that "every morning the Minister of Natural Resources would confront the Minister of Native Affairs in front of the mirror. And there we would resolve these thorny issues."[19] Many were not reassured at first, but Wildman earned grudging respect in these dual portfolios.

Wildman pushed the MNR to move to an ecosystem approach that would take into account all interests and Treaty rights. In an email exchange following our interview, Wildman called it a "tall order" and equated it to "trying to turn a mammoth sea-going oil tanker around." The first step was the promised independent audit:

> An audit, it had never been done in the history of Ontario! So . . . the ministry really didn't know what they had, and how they could issue licences without knowing what they had, was . . . [brief pause in incredulity] beyond me. So my priority there was to have an audit, the first public audit.[20]

He recounted how he was challenged, at first, by some senior MNR officials who opposed this reorientation, at which point he held up the NDP report on forestry and said it was to be "the bible" for the years to come. It was a very different "bible" than the one that David

Wolfe distributed to key policy makers after he joined the Cabinet Office. The resulting audit was completed by a panel chaired by a retired forestry professor, who had been a long-time critic of the MNR's forestry practices, giving the government a much better picture of where things were at. Not great, as it turned out.

Wildman and the NDP took a more holistic approach to managing the region's forests, as something more than simply wood fibre "but for all of the species, animals and plants. And for other values, like recreation, spiritual value of the forest, fish and wildlife." He worked to effect a change of mindset inside the MNR. Wildman's efforts found strong supporters within the middle echelons of the MNR as well as from his deputy, George Tough. This was the first step in the NDP's effort to "green" the MNR. The Crown Forest Sustainability Act subsequently required that "land use planning consider all forest values, not just timber." The act "sets out measurable indicators of sustainability, sets up local citizens' committees for forest management, and guarantees that logging companies will pay the full costs of forest renewal."[21]

In our conversation, Wildman proudly recalled listening in the front row to Bob Rae's inaugural speech after being elected Premier, which committed his government to recognizing First Nations as a third order of government. It was shortly after the Oka standoff in Quebec and Indigenous issues were on the political front burner. The government's new approach was later enshrined in August 1991 in the Statement of Political Relationship between First Nations and the Provincial Government. The NDP government broadened its approach to northern development to recognize the co-delivery of programming with Indigenous communities. Wildman pushed hard to deliver on the NDP's promises to First Nations, fast-tracking the many unresolved land claims, starting with two in his own constituency of Algoma. He faced down angry white protesters in the small community of Iron Bridge, located east of Sault Ste. Marie, who feared their access to the land was now being denied. His community forestry program, which sought to give forest-dependent communities some say in the management of the surrounding forests on which they relied, also extended to Indigenous communities. Historically, Indigenous communities were treated by the province as someone else's problem: namely, the federal government's, as it had constitutional jurisdiction.

While the MNR was key to the long-term management of Ontario lands and forests, it was the Ministry of Northern Development and Mines that took the lead in the government's regional response to industrial closures. As the new minister, Sudbury East MPP Shelley Martel noted that her ministry was "unique because it's the only ministry that has very specific roles and responsibilities for a geographic part of the province."[22] It did much to resist the industrial crisis by bolstering the economies of northern communities, both Indigenous and non-Indigenous. The creation of the Northern Ontario Heritage Fund provided Martel with the financial means to intervene in the regional economy. Though considerably less than the $100 million per year promised during the election, the $30 million per year Heritage Fund represented a substantial new commitment to the northern economy. Its board members saw their responsibility as not only to encourage the diversification of single-industry resource towns, but also to secure existing jobs in order to stabilize these hard-hit communities. We already saw an example of this in chapter 5 when the uranium mining town of Elliot Lake needed government help to facilitate its transition to a non-mining future. It was not the only success story.

Martel offered a good overview of the early work of her ministry at the Standing Committee on Estimates in November 1991, where she reported that the restructuring of the northern economy was underway and that the government needed "to be part of this transformation to manage it as well as possible."[23] For example, the Heritage Fund directed loans and loan guarantees to the two major employers in Atikokan, a former iron mining town in northwest Ontario that had transitioned to lumbering in the early 1980s. The regional fund also supported the Sawmill Adjustment Initiative, which financially supported eleven other sawmill communities. Martel told the standing committee that her ministry's priority was to "deal with the very difficult conditions imposed by the recession and fundamental restructuring of the economy in as humane a way as possible and, second, to foster development in a manner that creates co-operation among business, labour, first nations and municipalities, while respecting the environment and aboriginal rights."[24]

Martel's work with sawmill communities began in March 1991 after her ministry was approached by "a number of groups, and the former Minister of Northern Development as well, at a meeting in Hearst to try and provide some assistance particularly to the small local sawmillers. These are people whose family operations have gone on for years through difficult times. They are the last people to leave the community. They are the last people to pull out when everyone else has." In response, the Ministry of Northern Development and Mines put together a package targeting small sawmill communities by "going to the bank with them and negotiating a further line of credit or increased credit from the bank to the particular corporation." Government involvement helped these companies leverage needed funds to keep their sawmills running. In Atikokan, as we already heard, it involved reopening the local sawmill and a waferboard plant that used the sawmill's waste product. It was a matter of life and death for this hard-hit town, as its unemployment rate had skyrocketed to well over 60 percent. Martel recounted in the legislature how she first travelled to Atikokan with Howard Hampton, another government minister and the local MPP, to see what could be done:

> The people who met with us on that day told us how this crisis was affecting their lives. They wondered if the town would survive and they turned to this government for help. Since that time, the community of Atikokan has received good news. Last spring, the Northern Ontario Heritage Fund Corp and the Ministry of Industry, Trade and Technology through the Northern Ontario Development Corp, provided $1.5 million in loans to Atikokan Forest Products. The Sapawe sawmill resumed operations and

put 160 people back to work. Today I have more good news. I am pleased to inform the House that the heritage fund has secured a loan guarantee of $3.6 million for Proboard Ltd. This will give the company the working capital it needs to start up again, restoring 190 direct jobs in Atikokan and 143 indirect jobs throughout northwestern Ontario.[25]

There were many such small, but locally significant, examples across northern Ontario. Overall, the Northern Ontario Heritage Fund invested $130 million in 1,233 projects during the NDP's years in power, resulting in an estimated 6,870 jobs created or retained.[26] In addition, fully one-third of the province's anti-recession capital spending in 1991, totalling $230 million, was directed by the government to the North.

There was the specific case of the corrugated paper mill in Sturgeon Falls, which was given a new lease on life when the province funded a new pulping facility for recycled paper, placing it under the dual ownership of the local community and the company. Macmillan-Bloedel had no intention of investing any more in modernizing the mill, and it faced certain closure with new environmental regulations coming into effect in 1993. Luckily, as I wrote in my earlier book *One Job Town*, the local mill manager was a go-getter and came up with a plan for converting the mill to recycled paper. It would require a $13 million to $15 million investment, but the union was unwilling to consider concessions. As the NDP government sought to avoid a direct subsidy to the company, the idea of a community partnership emerged. To sidestep the legal prohibition against Ontario municipalities entering into joint ventures with for-profit companies, the province turned to the West Nipissing Economic Development Committee to co-own the new pulping facility within the larger Macmillan-Bloedel mill. It was a creative response to threatened closure. The capital funding came from a variety of public sources, primarily a $4 million grant from the Ministry of Environment and a $4 million loan from the Northern Ontario Heritage Fund. Another $1 million was raised

The Sturgeon Falls paper mill, 2006. Photo by David W. Lewis.

by the community pledge campaign. Everybody chipped in, except the company.

When the new facility went into operation in June 1993, it incorporated cutting-edge technology. So good, in fact, that Macmillan-Bloedel took what it learned in Sturgeon Falls and applied it to its much larger mill in Henderson, Kentucky. According to my sources, the partnership had five good years, during which community representatives were involved in the decision-making. But once the loans were paid off, there was some confusion about whether the partnership still existed. A new mill manager, a new provincial government, and a municipal merger brought new players and the partnership faded away. After Macmillan-Bloedel was purchased by the US-based multinational Weyerhaeuser in 1999, the company convinced the municipality to sell its interest in the joint venture for one dollar, clearing the way for it to close the mill in 2002.[27] Like Algoma Steel, the period of co-management and creative renewal was relatively short before the mill reverted to business as usual. Ultimately, community co-ownership did not shield Sturgeon Falls from corporate decisions made south of the Canada-US border.

SPRUCE FALLS, KAPUSKASING

The government's interventions in Atikokan and Sturgeon Falls played out mainly on a local stage, generating few news headlines outside of the immediate area. Not so the sustained effort to keep Kapuskasing's giant Spruce Falls newsprint mill in operation.

Kapuskasing is a small Franco-Ontarian town of twelve thousand on the remote Northern Highway in the upper reaches of the region. It was built as a "model town" in the 1920s, complete with a giant traffic circle at its commercial centre with roads radiating outwards like so many spokes in a wagon wheel. The town is located in the great clay belt, an expanse of fertile soil that drew settlers after World War I in search of free or affordable land to farm. But the growing season was short in this northerly climate, and the ruins of old farm houses that now dot the roadside attest to their collective failure. What remains are the string of resource-dependent communities and a wider web of small Cree and Anishinaabe communities. The highway literally wraps around the Kapuskasing mill, which still employed fifteen hundred workers in 1990. Its closure would have threatened the town's continued existence and driven a stake into the economic heart of this French-speaking region.

For its sixty-five years of existence, the Spruce Falls mill was jointly owned by the *New York Times* and Kimberly-Clark, a highly profitable and diversified US-based multinational that made a range of products from Huggies diapers to Kleenex tissues. Spruce Falls itself produced newsprint, mainly for the world's English-language paper of record. The times were changing, however, and the owners put the mill up for sale. They reached a tentative deal to sell the mill, but it fell through just days after the NDP victory.[28] With no other potential buyer on the horizon and the co-owners wanting out of the newsprint business, an employee group formed to buy the mill. The Purchasing Employees Group (PEG), chaired by Kapuskasing mayor T. K. Jewell, and supported by four of five unions, including the International Woodworkers Association / Syndicat des bûcherons et des employés de scieries (IWA), which represented those employed in the mill's woods operations, as well as the foremen's association and local managers. However, the Canadian Paperworkers Union, which represented the majority of the mill's unionized workers, declined to be part of the group.[29]

Darwin Smith, the CEO of Kimberly-Clark, encouraged the worker buyout, promising to hand over the mill for free as a gift.

It was a misleading promise, as Smith's chief condition was that (government-owned) Ontario Hydro complete its $133 million purchase of the Smoky Falls hydro dam, built by Spruce Falls in 1928, which would have been paid—in its entirety—as a dividend to the two departing shareholders. The sale of the hydro dam had been agreed to the year before, but on the condition that its proposed expansion be first approved under the province's environmental assessment regulations. Any decision was years away, as Smoky Falls had been folded into a comprehensive watershed-wide environmental review with Ontario Hydro's other expansion plans to increase the generating capacity of its existing dams. This delay was unacceptable to Smith, who insisted either Smoky Falls that should be exempted from review or that the transaction be finalized immediately. Ontario Hydro, however, was only interested in Smoky Falls if it could be expanded.

The Mattagami River flows northwards into the Moose River shortly before it reaches James Bay. The Ontario Hydro complex consisted of three dams—Little Long, Harmon, and Kipling—located sixty to one hundred kilometres north of Kapuskasing.[30] Ontario Hydro built the dams in the 1960s without consultation or approval of area First Nations. Historian Jean Manore testified during the environmental hearings that, after the construction of the three dams on the Mattagami,

> fish became smaller, rarer and often inedible—the meat was brown and smelled like mould or rotten earth. Some of them had to move their traplines because the dams lowered the waters, causing certain areas to become too dry. Other elders noted that the changes in the water levels made travelling treacherous. The ice was only half as thick as previously and became unsafe to cross because the water, when rising and falling, produced a pothole or false ice. Also, during the summer, the rivers became muddy. The silt build-up affected the ducks and other feeders of the river bottom.[31]

Ontario Hydro's dams had also destroyed Indigenous historic sites, portages, and cemeteries. Given this recent history, Chief Randy Kapashesit pointedly told the environmental assessment board: "Justice requires that . . . past grievances be settled before future projects are even considered. It is immoral for Ontario Hydro to be talking about future projects when they have not entered settlements to compensate for the damage they inflicted by past projects."[32] Cree and Anishinaabe leaders demanded a moratorium on any further development on the Mattagami and other northeastern Ontario rivers.[33]

Politically, the NDP government was caught between a rock and a hard place. On the one hand, the future of Kapuskasing now depended on the rapid sale of Smoky Falls to Ontario Hydro. On the other hand, the dam's expansion was in real doubt due to Indigenous opposition. The Oka standoff outside Montreal had occurred the summer before, and some feared that it was going to be another hot summer of confrontation in 1991. To get a better sense of the political moment, I browsed the bi-weekly newspaper *Windspeaker*, the closest Canada had at the time to a nation-wide Indigenous newspaper. It was filled with stories about Oka, the confrontation over the Oldman dam in Alberta, and opposition to Quebec's James Bay II, the Great Whale project.[34] In March 1991, Cree Chief Billy Diamond warned of violence in northern Quebec, suggesting that helicopters could be shot out of the sky and power poles blown up unless there was a settlement.[35] The Quebec Cree barricaded the airport in Whapmagoostui on 25 June, turning back a delegation from Hydro-Quebec and resulting in the cancellation of scheduled public hearings. The protesters were opposed to Quebec's greenlighting of road construction and site preparation before the new dams had received their environmental approvals. According to *Windspeaker*: "The standoff was reminiscent of the confrontation between Mohawk and police at Oka last summer."[36] It then editorialized that "the days of building dams to create jobs and to satisfy the never ending thirst for electricity belong in the past. Damming rivers does have serious consequences."[37]

These developments weighed heavily on the minds of the NDP government, particularly given their declared commitment to a new political relationship with Indigenous peoples. The Statement of Political Relationship, which promised that "no developments occur in the Territories of the First Nation of the Coalition without the consent of these First Nations,"[38] was approved by the Chiefs of Ontario and the Ontario government in early June 1991, and signed in Thunder Bay in early August 1991. The effort to save Spruce Falls unfolded at precisely the same time.

True to his word, Bob Rae steadfastly refused to exempt Smoky Falls from environmental assessment or carry the entire risk should it result in a decision that prevented the planned expansion. "The government simply cannot bail out or solve all the problems of industries," Rae told the media. "There has to be some give from all sides. We can't just be expected to pick up the entire tab."[39] He was acutely aware, he told me, that Indigenous communities in the Mattagami watershed were demanding a moratorium on further power developments in the watershed.[40] At the same time, the prospect of the mill's closure, deep in the NDP's northern heartland, was politically difficult, to say the least.

Meanwhile, Darwin Smith mobilized the Purchasing Employees Group in his campaign to convince the Ontario government to pick up the tab. He flew up to Kapuskasing between Christmas and New Year's in 1990 to meet with them, giving the PEG a copy of the mill's prospectus with vital financial information. The PEG then notified all Spruce Falls employees that a working group had "spent the last two weeks investigating the feasibility of employee participation in the purchase of Spruce Falls, as well as the elements of a preliminary business plan for the next 7 years. The group has developed a growing understanding of the factors involved in an employee participation buyout and its inherent opportunities and risks." It concluded the letter by saying that employee ownership was the "best option available," even though they still needed strategic outside investors "who possess industry expertise."[41]

The archival records of the Syndicat des bûcherons et des employés de scieries, held in Hearst, located just down the highway, offer a comprehensive record of these initial efforts. On 20 January 1991, Darwin Smith sent Mayor Jewell updated information and again raised the issue of the purchase of Smoky Falls. Playing hardball, Smith suggested that the closing of this sale was necessary if the transfer of the mill to its employees was going to happen. The only alternative on the table, Smith insisted, was the so-called Amos plan—modelled on the earlier restructuring of the newsprint mill in Amos, Quebec—which would see the dramatic downsizing of the Kapuskasing mill, with the loss of 1,200 of the mill's 1,500 workers. To avoid this eventuality, Smith insisted that government subsidies were needed, "depending on its commitment to your part of Northern Ontario."

When the Purchasing Employee Group met again with Smith on 21 January, he promptly opened the meeting by expressing his "deep concern for the people of the community." Smith then reiterated that the "success of [their] efforts" was contingent on the Smoky Falls deal. According to the minutes of the meeting, "Mr Smith stressed how important the meeting with Bob Rae would be; we will only get one shot so we must be very convincing."[42] The language here is telling. Darwin Smith and Kimberly-Clark were clearly using the community to pressure the government. Rae's "first impression of Mr Smith," according to his memoirs, "was that he was Darwin by name and Darwinian by nature." He developed, however, "a grudging respect for Darwin Smith, who was a rough but fair negotiator."[43]

The PEG dutifully demanded that the Smoky Falls expansion be exempted from the environmental assessment and sought the province's financial support in the form of loan guarantees, loans, or grants.[44] In Jewell's words:

> Solutions are urgently called for if we are to avoid a situation similar to that which is unfolding at Sault Ste. Marie. The high level of fear and apprehension in Kapuskasing and its six sister communities in northern Ontario arise

over the possibility of a total or massive partial shutdown of Spruce Falls Power and Paper Company, Limited, Kapuskasing's only industry.[45]

Jewell also informed Rae that the PEG had "formed an excellent working relationship" with Smith. One might even call it cozy, after Smith flew the mayor and other members of the PEG on his corporate jet to see Kimberly-Clark's big modernized mill in Coosa Pines, Alabama, providing them with free accommodation and meals. As designed, the tour also made it clear to Jewell how much "Canada has been left behind, and will continue to be so unless some changes are accepted and put into practice." Jewell wrote, "We conclude that some work practice changes are inevitable, but that they can be made to the benefit of all concerned."[46]

It is important to remember that the two Canadian Paperworkers Union locals at the mill, which represented the lion's share of the mill's workforce, had so far refused to join the PEG. The CPU had a much more adversarial relationship with the employer. In one union update, for example, it complained that "Mr Darwin Smith shows up . . . and apparently tells the people present that early in 1985 Kimberly-Clark made the decision that it no longer wanted investment in Canadian newsprint." The union invited readers to look "at the simple facts. We were not notified of Spruce Falls' intentions for over 5 years. The only time the membership is ever contacted is when the Company wants something, others want something, the Company is in trouble, or others are in fear of their future."[47] After being put on the spot, the CPU agreed to join if the PEG's governance structure reflected the relative weight of each participating group. Why should the foremen's association have the same voting power as the union representing over half of the mill's entire workforce? The mayor dug in his heels, however, insisting that it was the practice of the group to come to a decision by a majority vote, with all unions having one vote each.[48] Rebuffed, the CPU remained outside the PEG.

In March 1991, the same month as the NDP government formed a working group to deal with the Algoma Steel situation, it directed management consultants Ernst & Young to develop a strategy to "secure the best practical solution for the Kapuskasing community and its major employer." The consultants reported that the government was "as much a stakeholder as K-C and PEG and should take a lead role" in securing a "credible strategic buyer/operator." It was noted that Kimberly-Clark also owned the Terrace Bay mill in northwestern Ontario, giving the province some potential leverage. Even though the company "chose over the years not to re-invest to modernize sufficiently (the root cause), it has now shifted the 'blame' for this to Government."[49] Among the "critical areas" to be resolved were the Smoky Falls transaction, the modernization of the mill, and finding a credible buyer/operator. The government already had an inter-ministerial group working on a solution, but a wider task force (as at Algoma) that included the company and community was also recommended.

But Kimberly-Clark's Smith would have none of it. Instead, Darwin Smith ratcheted up the political pressure. On 13 March, he sent a video cassette to every Spruce Falls employee where he reiterated that the plan "to give the company to its employees" was conditional on the sale of Smoky Falls.[50] "We don't want an Algoma Steel situation in Kapuskasing," Smith said in justifying his decision to impose a deadline. He ended the video by saying: "Are you willing to change the way you work? Are you willing to help reduce costs? Are you willing to lay the 'Uncle Spruce' syndrome to rest? If you are, then the government must be persuaded to close the Smoky Falls contract by April 30."[51] By invoking "Uncle Spruce," Smith was clearly denigrating the community's long-standing dependence on his company. According to *Le Régional*, Smith's ultimatum had the "effect of a bomb" in a community that had already lived under a cloud of uncertainty for a year.[52]

The urgency of the April deadline was felt immediately. The Friends of Kapuskasing et ses ami-e-s, led by Wayne Major, a journalist for the *Northern Times*, piled additional pressure on the government, mobilizing for a mass rally in early April.[53] Photographs of the thousands of area residents filling the traffic circle at the centre of town sent a clear message to the NDP government.[54] PEG could also report that they went to Toronto to meet with their legal and financial advisors, namely Orenda and NLK Engineering, who had been "developing plans for the modernization of the mill's wood-handling operations."[55] One of the key questions that the worker buyout faced was where the capital was going to come from to modernize the mill. The proposed woodyard modernization alone would cost $50.9 million with the legislated ending of river drives in 1992.[56] No longer would rivers be used to transport pulp wood to the province's mills. There were no specific plans to replace the four paper machines, but they would require another $12.8 million in investment just to keep them running. Improved secondary treatment of waste water was also required. Meanwhile, demand for newsprint was in steady decline and Spruce Falls was forecast to lose $10.2 million in 1991, despite the fact that the long-term contract with the *New York Times* had so far insulated the mill from market changes.[57]

Again and again, Mayor Jewell wrote to Rae, insisting the government finalize the sale of the dam so the community could save its mill. Ignoring Indigenous concerns entirely, he argued that there was little risk that the expansion would not be approved: "We do not see this future project as being a gamble."[58] The grand public announcements from the mayor even began to grate on Smith, who characterized the PEG's proposed operating plan as "acceptable when viewed as a sincere effort by affected parties whose principal purposes are to prevent an immediate and material reduction of jobs at Spruce Falls and serious effects on the community of Kapuskasing."[59] On the basis of this faint praise, the PEG triumphantly declared that Kimberly-Clark had accepted its ten year business plan.[60] This mental leap prompted an exasperated Smith to remind the mayor that he still needed written confirmation that the NDP government was closing the Smoky Falls deal. He also noted that the two CPU locals did not favour the PEG's plan "and, without support from these unions it would appear that the plan will almost certainly fail."[61]

Only after Smith agreed to extend the deadline was there a breakthrough: Tembec came forward on 17 June as a strategic investor willing to take a minority stake and operate the mill.[62] Two days later, Shelley Martel released a statement that the NDP government accepted the employees' proposal in principle, but there were still many challenges ahead before an agreement could be finalized. Again, she insisted that the "government will not agree to an exemption from an environmental assessment for the Smoky Falls power facility because 'there are real environmental and First Nations concerns surrounding this project which require further study and consultation.'"[63] Ultimately, the deal foundered in a telephone call between Martel and Smith in the late afternoon of 25 June over Smoky Falls. The government had no intention of plunking down another $136 million up front for a dam it might never use.[64] It was only fair that the risk be shared. But this was not enough for Smith, who gave the government fifteen more days to reconsider. On 28 June, Martel told the public that Kimberly-Clark's conditions were impossible to meet. "There are legitimate environmental and native concerns that must be addressed," she repeated.[65] In refusing to buckle under the pressure, the NDP government showed considerable political backbone.

The government's decision hit Kapuskasing hard, but again the community rose to the challenge. The KAP (Kill Amos Plan) was formed by community leaders across the political spectrum, including René Piché, a former mayor and Liberal cabinet minister; Len Wood, the local NDP MPP; and Enzo Altobelli, vice-president of the local Canadian Paperworkers Union who also served as president of the Kapuskasing and District Labour Council. Mayor Jewell was conspicuously absent from the leadership. KAP worked to restart negotiations and carry on the fight to attain "local ownership."[66] This could only be accomplished, they now realized, by resolving the Smoky Falls issue. For the first time, Kapuskasing contacted Indigenous leaders "to determine what specific objections they have to modernization of the Ontario Hydro power plants on the Mattagami River and to resolve any policy differences in a reasonable and cooperative manner."[67] They also approached nearby municipalities and tried to mobilize support from national unions.[68] Full-page ads were placed in Toronto newspapers and one hundred Kapuskasing residents camped out on the lawns of Queen's Park in downtown Toronto. Within two weeks of the dissolution of the PEG, the Employee Ownership Group emerged, representing the entire workforce.[69] André Foucault, an assistant to the president of the CPU, played a key role in its formation. Each union representative was now given a number of votes based on their membership. Thus, the Syndicat des bûcherons et des employés de scieries received three votes, the foremen's association one, and the two CPU locals eight. This second effort paid off, as an agreement was finally reached on 12 August. The comprehensive environmental assessment would proceed as planned, but Ontario Hydro would buy Smoky Falls from Spruce Falls for $34 million upfront and a decade of free hydroelectricity for the worker-owned mill. It was the compromise that the government needed. The deal meant considerable sacrifice for mill workers, who agreed to deep cuts in their wages and benefits. They had a lot to lose, but if they were lucky, they could make history and "end up as folk heroes, like the guys who saved the Temiscaming mill."[70]

The Smoky Falls redevelopment received its environmental approval in 1994, but Indigenous leaders vetoed it, as they had said they would. The next year, Ontario Hydro finally signed a settlement agreement over past environmental disturbances. As Chief Kapashesit had said, justice required that past grievances be settled before future projects could be considered. Ontario Hydro's modified plans were eventually approved by area Anishinaabe and Cree communities. In Kapuskasing, meanwhile, the period of worker ownership was relatively short-lived, as Tembec purchased their shares in March 1997 for $170 million.[71] Mill workers and community investors got eighteen times what they initially paid. Many a truck and motorboat were bought with this windfall. And most importantly, the Kapuskasing mill is still in operation today. The worker buyout is today remembered as a community victory. For example, Ontario's French-language TV network produced *Sauver Kapuskasing !*, which aired on the twenty-fifth anniversary of the worker buyout, telling the story of how the community pushed a reluctant NDP government to the bargaining table.[72] Notably, it overlooked Indigenous resistance to the expansion of Smoky Falls or the government's efforts to balance the needs of the two communities, which would have complicated the uplifting narrative.

PROVINCIAL PAPER, THUNDER BAY

A very different story unfolded at Provincial Paper in Thunder Bay. Originally built in 1918, the mill on the north shore of Lake Superior was unionized four months later. As part of an ill-timed buying spree, Abitibi purchased it in 1929, operating the maker of fine coated paper for promotional flyers and magazines until 1993. After sustained losses, it tried to find a buyer but none came forward. Taking a page out of Darwin Smith's corporate playbook, Abitibi then offered to sell the mill to employees for one dollar and set a firm deadline of 31 January 1993 to finalize the agreement.[73] From the start, the buyout of Provincial Paper was driven primarily by local management. The negotiations were arduous, as labour and local management wrestled for control.

Bud Wildman had recently appointed John Valley as Assistant Deputy Minister in charge of the forest industrial action group, with the mandate to address economic challenges in Ontario's forest-products industry.[74] Unprompted, Bob Rae also named Valley in our interview as one of the "unusual people" the government brought into government to manage the industrial crisis.[75] Originally from Thunder Bay, Valley was a former vice-president of a major forestry company and was therefore in a good position to be the government's point person on the effort to save Provincial Paper. While he worked mainly with mills in northwestern Ontario, Valley was also tasked by Wildman with establishing a sawmill in Wawa, as its underground iron ore mine was on its last legs. Wildman reassigned timber limits from another sawmill community (Chapleau) after deeming it surplus, which did not go down well there, to entice US multinational Weyerhaeuser to establish a new sawmill just outside of town, thereby throwing "an economic lifeline to miners in Wawa who did not transfer to the Sault to take positions in the steel mill," once the mine closed for good in 1998.

Negotiations at Provincial Paper bogged down on the twin issues of governance and shop-floor control. The Communications, Energy and Paperworkers union (by this time, the CPU had merged with two other unions to form the CEP) was strongly opposed to "another Spruce Falls" and favoured the "Algoma" cooperative model, where unionized workers controlled the company they owned. However, there were deep philosophical divisions between hourly and salaried staff. Management wanted to retain control and introduce more work flexibility on the shop floor; the CEP countered that management's proposal was "as Bay Street as you can get."[76] Ten days before the deadline, Valley reported that the talks had broken down and that the mill's closure was now a "very real possibility."[77] A special mediator was brought in by the province and an agreement was finally reached that "effectively gave management the right and the obligation to manage the employee owned company."[78] Local managers also won equal representation on the new board of directors. The seven-member board therefore comprised two union representatives, two non-union representatives, and three independent directors.[79] It was nothing like the Algoma model.

The financial contribution from Ontario consisted of a $6.5 million direct loan and a loan guarantee for another $11.5 million. Abitibi, for its part, provided $20 million in cash and guaranteed a twenty-year supply of wood fibre, a key issue for the mill, as it had no woodlands of its own. One hundred jobs were eliminated and the remaining 704 employees accepted a wage rollback of 15 percent to 20 percent as well as a five-year wage freeze. It was not a great deal for unionized workers, but they still had their jobs. Workers voted 87.5 percent in favour of buying the mill, but they felt they had no choice but to vote in favour. "If you want to work, you have to take it. It's either half a loaf of bread or no loaf," said one worker.[80]

By contrast, news of the worker buyout was heralded in the hard-hit city. "Mill buyout a triumph in the making," shouted the headline in the Thunder Bay *Chronicle-Journal*. It pointed to Kapuskasing as "proof the idea is not crazy. It's admirable, it's bold and it represents the best of what human nature and determination can achieve."[81] On CBC Radio, former NDP MPP Jim Foulds struck a similarly enthusiastic tone, telling listeners how much he admired the mill's employees:

> With the help from their unions and the provincial government, they took control of their own economic future last week. Saturday's headline said it best: "Abitibi workers save mill." That's spelled W-O-R-K-E-R-S. Workers. There's an exciting lesson to be learned here. When all else failed—it was the workers who came through.[82]

Abitibi had already closed its Thunder Bay Division mill across town, something Foulds was intimately familiar with, as he had chaired the adjustment committee. Decades later, Foulds still teared up recalling the paper workers he'd helped. Provincial Paper was therefore a good news story. Foulds told his radio listeners to remember that "in the crunch the mill wasn't rescued by an outside white knight. No flood of investment came from international capital in Zurich, Hong Kong, or New York. Or Toronto, for that matter. No. The mill, and just maybe our city's economy, was saved by its workers. And they were given a huge assist by their unions and the provincial government." He also credited the "unsung achievements" of the NDP government in "the saving of jobs in places like Sault Ste Marie, Kapuskasing, and now at the Provincial Mill in Thunder Bay." Here too, without the NDP's persistence, the mill would have closed.

During our interview, I asked Foulds how he came to be named to the board of employee-owned Provincial Paper. As he explains it, he was walking by the Canadian Paperworkers' office inside the Thunder Bay Labour Centre and the union representative popped his head out and said:

> "Hey, Jim, you got a minute here?" He said, "You would like to be on the board of [Provincial Paper]?" I said, "Oh shit, yes I would." And you know, Steve, it's an experience

I wish I'd had twenty years earlier, before I went into politics, 'cause if I'd understood really how a business worked, even a small one like that, I would have been much cleverer in devising industrial policy and taxation policy for the NDP. Ah, it really opened my eyes . . . You need to be able to stand up to the bluffing that they do, and that's what I learned.[83]

Union concessions had made Provincial Paper more competitive, but it was still an old, high-cost mill. To improve its position further, management sought to rationalize production, concentrating on fewer high-end niche products. Provincial Paper was worth putting money into and saving because it specialized in fine paper, including what Foulds calls "the best beer label in the world." There was only one other company, based in Europe, that could compete. Benefiting from a lucky rebound in the market, C. Ian Ross, the CEO, reported in March 1996 that the company's revenues had climbed from $123 million to $211 million over the previous year, with a pre-tax profit of a record $17.3 million.[84] In recognition of this achievement, Ross was named Ontario's "Turnaround Entrepreneur of the Year."[85] But it was not nearly profitable enough. The age of the mill—with its narrow paper machines, slower speeds, and excessive waste levels—meant that it needed a $25 million loan to modernize for the short term and a new $500 million paper machine over the long haul. But the mill could not offer its timber rights as collateral, as other mills did, as it had none.[86]

We have a pretty good idea of what happened next thanks to Foulds, who donated his papers to the Thunder Bay Historical Museum, offering us a unique inside look at this worker-owned firm. Concerned about its long-term outlook, Provincial Paper hired Orenda and NLK Engineering, the same two consulting firms employed earlier by the PEG in Kapuskasing, to conduct a review of its operations in January 1996. Six months later, the consultants reported that should the company remain as it was, it would not survive another recession "of any severity." It needed a new paper machine and to make the full transition to specialty papers. The consultants quoted one unnamed employee to illustrate their point: "We can clean and polish the machine so that it shines. We can repaint it to look beautiful. We can work on it until it runs like a clock. However, when I walk to the back of the machine and read the label, it still says '1924.'"[87] The long-term capital requirements were such that "under any scenario, control of the Company will almost certainly pass into the hands of whatever new investor provides this equity. Without significant capital, the Company seriously risks bankruptcy in the next recession."[88] That said, Orenda believed that the recent success of the company had created "an opportunity for the Company to secure its future" by finding a new corporate buyer. Based on the report, the board of directors determined that the sale of a significant equity interest "of up to 100%" was required.[89]

With the search for a buyer underway, labour-management relations inside the plant took a turn for the worse.[90] The board received worker "petitioners" who were concerned about the perceived overuse of consultants "taking their exorbitant fees with them" as well as a more generalized concern about how management "handled the employee/owners of this company." Trade unionists also lamented their lack of direct access to the CEO and board, suggesting they should "go out in the Mill and talk to people that make our products."[91] The concerns raised speak to a deeper frustration that they did not control the company they owned. In May 1996, the board of directors received an external report from consultants Ernst & Young on how shop-floor relations might be improved. As a result, the board formed an Operations Steering Committee, chaired by Foulds, responsible for improving the workplace environment. His role was to be seen as neutral and spend time with the unionized workforce as well as middle and senior managers. These simmering tensions exploded a few months later when management unilaterally offered large incentive bonuses to supervisory staff, sparking fury among unionized workers whose lowered wages were still frozen. The Union Coalition now insisted on changes to how the company was being managed. Conrad

Fournier, the coalition's chairperson, could not understand how managers justified a raise for one group at a time of a wage freeze for another. He also claimed that senior management never truly bought into employee ownership.[92]

In response, senior managers met to discuss their demands, rejecting the idea that compensation policy should be co-governed. Managers were mobile and the bonuses were the only way to retain needed talent. They then discussed their "options for a consistent and effective management philosophy," concluding:

> Management should show leadership by developing its plans first and then, as appropriate, arrange for some form of participation accepting input to finalize the plan. The concept of the Coalition having a veto over management decisions in major areas of the company's business was not acceptable. It was felt that the Board of Directors with its representatives elected by Union and Non-Union employees and the joint appointments is a form of co-governance.[93]

The next Operations Steering Committee, held on 18 November and chaired by Foulds, focused on the issue of governance. It was an explosive meeting. The unions tabled a proposal that they be more involved in the areas of compensation, discipline, capital expenditure, hiring and firing, investment opportunities, and contracting. The motion sparked "considerable discussion" on the differences between governance and co-management. One board member said it "was imperative that management manage the organization and some of these proposals would limit that ability."[94] It was agreed that the Union Coalition would be consulted in all future capital purchases of more than $100,000. Foulds also wrote down his impressions of the meeting, noting that the anger and bitterness of unionized workers over the management bonuses was "deep & profound." He quoted one worker as saying, "You can move, we can't."[95] Foulds also raised wider questions about the board of directors' decision to proceed with the search for a strategic investor. Only now did he realize that the CEP "doesn't want to give up control," prompting him to write in his notes: "We've made a fundamental mistake—when I asked the questions at the Board level and was told that 'yes, the employees wanted to seek a strategic investor which might result in their loss of control'; I was told wrong." He then resolved to ask the CEO how far along the search for a strategic investor had gone and if anyone would be willing to buy a minority interest in the company. What the union's two representatives on the board were doing during all of this is an open question.

A Strategic Investment Committee of the board was also created to oversee the search for a buyer and to "develop a consensus as to the appropriateness of various strategic investors."[96] Eighty potential buyers were solicited and the company's financial advisors soon identified Rolland, a division of Cascades, as the best bet. Rolland took the bait and announced its intention to purchase 100 percent of Provincial Paper in February 1997. Two months later, the $26 million sale was recommended and then unanimously agreed to by the board of directors.[97] If accepted, unionized workers would get a lump-sum payment of $17.25 million and management another $5.75 million, with the average worker receiving $30,000 tax free. Some took away as much as $60,000. Not surprisingly, workers enthusiastically voted 97.8 percent in favour. For the local president of the CEP: "The workers—the employee owners—have worked hard and turned it around. It's a major, major victory for all the employees and the union people."[98] He could not help adding that "there's no sweetheart deal for the management people." But it was not all good news for organized labour. There would be another 20 percent rollback in the number of jobs at the mill, and ten years later, the company closed the mill for good.[99] "My heart just sank when that happened," whispers Foulds.[100] As previously forecasted, without substantial new capital investment, Provincial Paper could not survive the next major economic downturn. Northern Ontario's mills needed to modernize or die. And die many did over the next twenty years.

CONCLUSION

Worker ownership in northern Ontario was weakened by persistent shop-floor tensions and the resistance of local managers to doing things differently. How far unions were able to redistribute power depended, in large part, on their institutional capacity to counter managerial arguments. The CPU/CEP had no Ron Bloom on retainer and left these things mainly to local leadership. Nor was worker ownership the magic wand that the NDP hoped it would be. Unfortunately, labour-led venture capital funds were of no help whatsoever. Nonetheless, the government's record of saving single-industry towns from economic ruin was rightly touted as one of the NDP's greatest achievements. Indeed, I would argue that the NDP has much to be proud of in terms of how it responded to the industrial crisis in northern Ontario. Its use of the sovereign debt "as bait," as Ross McClellan put it, helping industries get cheaper loans thanks to government guarantees, succeeded in stabilizing the region's economy at very little cost. It also did so without sacrificing Indigenous communities in the process. And a more sustainable forest management policy and the community forests

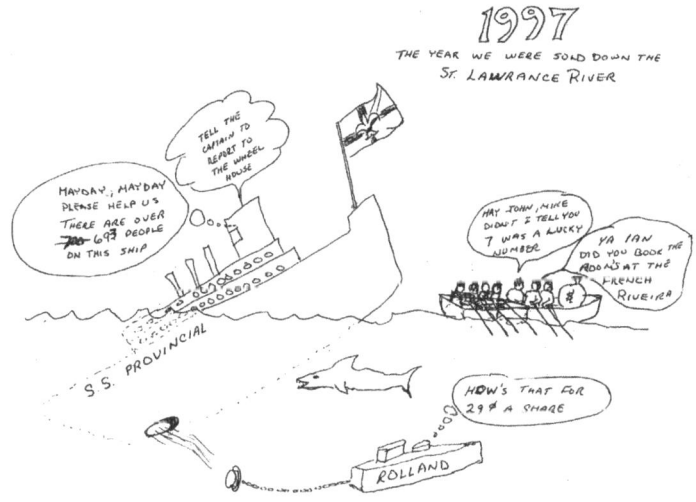

"S.S. Provincial [Paper]." A worker's drawing. Thunder Bay Historical Museum. B39-14-1-4.

program introduced by Wildman promised longer-term benefits for northerners.

At Queen's Park, northern Ontario was treated as a special case, even by the opposition parties. Their legislative attacks were directed not so much at state intervention in the North, though there was some initial opposition, but rather at the ad hoc and reactive nature of the NDP's plant-by-plant approach. Liberal Michael Brown, representing Algoma-Manitoulin, which included Elliot Lake, likened the NDP's response to "plugging holes, kind of sticking fingers in dikes." He wanted to see policies that would serve the region over the long haul: "We have to know our mills are competitive and viable."[101] But Hugh Mackenzie makes the essential point that the NDP government's "willingness to engage on Kapuskasing and Algoma in particular, but more generally on the industrial crises, created space that actually the Harris government [1995–] used to keep doing some of that stuff."[102] It is perhaps one of the NDP government's few lasting economic legacies, as the Tories rolled back virtually all of its long-haul policy work. That said, worker ownership was a flawed model. While the worker buyouts proved successful in terms of saving mills from closing in the short and medium terms, they ultimately failed as an experiment in worker empowerment and economic democracy. For workers, the buyouts were a half-a-loaf solution to the immediate problem rather than an ideological choice, especially as they required painful wage and benefit concessions.

Near the end of our interview, Hugh Mackenzie credited the persistent "sense amongst northerners of solidarity. You could help Algoma, and everybody in Sault Ste. Marie would thank you for it. You could help Kapuskasing and everybody in any of those mill towns in northeastern Ontario would recognize that it could have been them, and they'd thank you for it. In a way that doesn't happen with a foundry in St. Catharines." This observation aligns well with the experience of Bud Wildman. When I asked him why he was re-elected in 1995 when so many New Democrats went down to defeat, he immediately credited the saving of Algoma Steel and St. Marys Paper, as well as extending the life of the underground iron ore mine in Wawa and ensuring the town's transition to forestry. After all, Tony Martin, a backbencher from the Sault, also won again. Wildman recounted how "Bob Rae and his wife Arlene came into the Sault riding, and we were going to a function, and it was near the end of the [1995] election campaign, and he was pretty discouraged. And he said to me, 'Well, how are you guys going to do?' I said, 'We're going to win.' I said, 'This community owes our government, and they know it.' And they did." Wildman followed up this story with another one from decades later. He was making a dinner reservation one day in the Sault:

> This man, I don't ever remember seeing him before—big, tall fellow, over six feet. And he walked in, and I was talking to the person about making a reservation. This guy was wearing work clothes, and she said "And your name is?" to me, and before I could say Bud Wildman, this man turned around and said, "This is Bud Wildman! Don't you recognize him? He's the man who saved Wawa!" [laughs] So obviously he was from Wawa. I don't know who he was. And this is thirty years later![103]

These stories point to a key regional difference in the subsequent verdict of voters on the Rae government. While the NDP was routed in the 1995 election, only a couple of the weaker members of caucus from northern Ontario were defeated. Everyone else was re-elected. Clearly, the government did something right in the region. Why the Rae government did not extend this winning approach to southern Ontario is a question that we will grapple with in the next chapter.

National Rubber Company: Prudence Osman, 1993. Photo by Peter MacCallum.

8
FROM DOWNSVIEW TO DAVOS

> The aircraft industry in every part of the world is a heavily subsidized industry. That is true. It is true in Europe. It is true in the United States, only they do not call it subsidization; they call it military contracts. It is true in Quebec. It is true in every part of the world that has an aircraft industry. It has been subsidized by taxpayers in this province to some extent, but not to the extent it has been in other jurisdictions, either by us or by the feds. The question we have to ask ourselves, and this is really the important question, is how critical is this industry—not just this company, but this industry—for the industrial future of Ontario?
>
> —Bob Rae, 22 October 1991[1]

Bob Rae's pointed question to Mike Harris, the leader of the opposition Tories, about troubled De Havilland, a manufacturer of turboprop commuter aircraft based in the Downsview district of Toronto, speaks to the importance of an industry's *perceived centrality*, now and in the future, in determining how governments responded to its decline or threatened closure. Over the last two chapters we have seen that the centrality of local mills to the futures of Sault Ste. Marie and Kapuskasing, located in the NDP heartland of northern Ontario, mattered. In southern Ontario, the bar was set much higher, as the industry had to be viewed as central to the future of the province or country as a whole. When governments in the post-1945 period nationalized the "commanding heights" of the economy, they focused their attention on coal mining, steelmaking, auto manufacture, shipbuilding, and eventually, aeronautics. These industries had three things in common: (1) production was concentrated in massive workplaces (or concentrated coalfields) employing thousands; (2) the industries were viewed as central to national economic and military power, with words like "strategic" often being used in reference to them; and (3) they employed mostly the classic male proletarians, or breadwinners, of lore.

While perceived centrality did not ensure special treatment, one only needs to visit the hollowed-out steel valleys of western Pennsylvania or the "motor city" of Detroit to know its limits; the best examples of state-managed industrial decline involved these same sectors. Coal mining in particular had a softer landing than most, except under Margaret Thatcher. Many deindustrialization scholars have come to call this the "moral economy of the coalfields," as coal miners successfully pressured the state to soften the socio-economic blow by nationalizing the mines, slowing the pace of pit closures, allowing displaced miners to transfer to other mines, and directing new manufacturing plants into coalfield areas. We see this pattern around the world, including in industrial Cape Breton.[2]

Canada's aeronautics industry was also a special case. The federal government rescued Canada's two major aircraft makers, Canadair in Montreal and De Havilland in Toronto, operating them as Crown corporations between 1974 and 1986, before selling them to Bombardier and Boeing, respectively. De Havilland was no branch plant. It was a fully integrated manufacturer, producing popular short takeoff and landing regional aircraft.[3] Indeed, it ranked ninth in terms of private-sector research and development expenditures in Canada.[4] It was also the single largest industrial employer in Metropolitan Toronto, employing 5,600 workers. A briefing note for a federal Tory cabinet minister thus declared that De Havilland's popular Dash 8 passenger planes were "among the most visible and prestigious symbols of Canada's standing as an advanced industrial economy."[5] De Havilland also had a "long and glorious history," recalled Liberal MPP Monte Kwinter: "Some members are old enough to remember the Second World War, when they were building the Mosquito bomber."[6] For others, the De Havilland name was "synonymous with the evolution of flying to remote parts of the world."[7] Its bush planes were legendary.

Politically, in the early 1990s, De Havilland was just too big and too important to fail.

De Havilland thus stood apart from the hundreds of other manufacturing plants that were shutting down across southern Ontario during what Richard Allen provocatively called "the great displacement."[8] During its second throne speech in April 1992, the NDP declared that "Ontario lost more than an argument in the free trade deal. Implemented without adjustment measures, free trade has devastated Ontario's manufacturing base, costing tens of thousands of jobs in Ontario communities."[9] Fully 80 percent of the job losses across Canada in the first twelve months of the recession were concentrated in Ontario, where one in ten factories closed between 1989 and 1996.[10] The deepest pain was felt in the electrical and electronics industry, which saw employment drop 59.9 percent during this short period, and the clothing sector, which declined 49.7 percent.[11] Both employed mainly women, a bitter reminder that gender was centrally implicated in economic

Mr Suli Dress Factory, 119 Spadina Avenue, Toronto: Machine operators, 1984. Photo by Peter MacCallum.

restructuring.¹² Between 1985 and 1992, International Ladies' Garment Workers' Union membership dropped 60 percent, slashing the rate of unionization in the garment sector from 80 percent to 20 percent.¹³ If De Havilland was the single largest industrial employer in Toronto, Ontario's apparel and textile industries as a whole employed 12 percent of the city's manufacturing workers.¹⁴ Yet the rapid destruction of this female-dominated sector passed largely below the political radar.

The absence of a southern counterpart to the Ministry of Northern Development and Mines meant that the NDP government had very little capacity to respond to industrial closures across southern Ontario, even if it had wanted to.¹⁵ With Algoma, Spruce Falls, and De Havilland already on its plate within four or five months of being elected, the Premier's Office was quickly overwhelmed. Deindustrializing small towns such as Collingwood, Cornwall, Cambridge, and Brantford didn't stand a chance. In the larger scheme of things, these communities hosted small or medium sized factories employing hundreds, not thousands, of workers. Nor were these places so remote as to be considered towns of single industry. Nonetheless, in the legislature, Liberal Murray Elston suggested that the signage on the exit ramps on Highway 401 through southwestern Ontario should now indicate these were "ghost towns."¹⁶

To build its capacity to do more, the government sought to reorient the Ministry of Industry, Trade and Technology to make it more purposeful in its approach to economic development. Ed Philip explained his ministry's new mission this way:

> A top priority for my ministry was to work in partnership with business, unions, communities and investors. I want to emphasize the word "partnership" because it underscores the entire philosophy of our ministry. We recognize that the government by itself cannot make Ontario more competitive. We have to pool our strengths with those of our economic partners; we have to make the best possible use of the resources available. We used a partnership

approach in Kapuskasing when the Spruce Falls pulp and paper mill was threatened and as a result, we were able to usher in a new worker-ownership arrangement and a mill modernization program.

He went on to say that the restructuring of De Havilland would not only save a "great number" of jobs, but it would "strengthen Ontario's position in the strategically important industry, namely the aerospace industry."[17] Tim Armstrong was brought in as the new Deputy Minister, after Bob Rae personally invited him to return from his position as Ontario's Agent General in Japan. He would be Rae's point person on the government's industrial rescue efforts as well as the reorientation of the ministry. It was a tall order, to say the least.

Born in 1931, Armstrong had worked in the Toronto labour law firm of Ted Jolliffe, a former leader of the Ontario CCF, and David Lewis, a future federal NDP leader (and father of Stephen Lewis). In 1974, he joined the Ontario civil service under the Tories first as the chairperson of the Ontario Labour Relations Board and then as Deputy Minister of Labour from 1976 to 1986. There, he was an early proponent of labour-management cooperation, forming the Ontario Labour Management Study Group—a precursor to the Premier's Council. Armstrong brought this sensibility with him to the Ministry of Industry, Trade and Technology and, then, after November 1992, as special advisor to the premier on the automotive sector. His newest appointment was part of a wider shuffle that saw David Agnew, Rae's chief of staff, controversially named Cabinet Secretary, the top job in the civil service, and its previous holder, Peter Barnes, become the deputy of the expanded and retooled Ministry of Economic Development and Trade led by Frances Lankin.[18]

Despite these changes, the NDP government seems to have largely accepted the inevitability of industrial closures in southern Ontario. It was here where the progressive competitive agenda reigned supreme. The only two exceptions, given their economic and political centrality, were the aeronautics and automotive sectors. We will take a closer look at the specific cases of De Havilland's Downsview plant and the General Motors complex in St. Catharines before examining the government's wider efforts to attract new automotive investment. The Canadian Auto Workers' strong opposition to worker ownership, and to concessions more generally, precluded worker buyouts in the southern half of the province. In any case, worker buyouts were not an obvious option in the case of closing branch plants. Departing multinationals left with more than the client list; they usually left with the legal patents for the consumer products they produced. The government therefore had to find other ways to respond to the unfolding industrial crisis, starting with De Havilland.

DE HAVILLAND

On the first day of the 1990 election campaign, Bob Rae participated in a plant gate at De Havilland's Downsview plant, shaking hands with hundreds of workers during the shift change. As he wrote in his memoirs, the fate of the company became a major preoccupation for his government from day one. De Havilland, a

NDP Solidarity: Ontario NDP leader Bob Rae—joined by flag-carrying Auto Workers' union leader Bob White and federal NDP leader Ed Broadbent at strike-bound De Havilland plant in Downsview. Photo by Boris Spremo / *Toronto Star* via Getty Images.

high-profile company, had been saved by the federal government when its original owner, Hawker-Siddley, walked out. In 1986, it was then sold by Prime Minister Brian Mulroney to Seattle-based Boeing, the largest aircraft maker in the world. Boeing quickly closed all of the De Havilland production lines except for its popular Dash 8 turboprop regional passenger planes, putting all of its eggs in one basket. Over the next five years, Boeing injected $1 billion into De Havilland in an effort to turn it from a "craft shop" into a "flow-based manufacturer" with an assembly line.[19] It needed to do something, as De Havilland was manufacturing forty to fifty airplanes per year but needed to make and sell seventy in order to break even.[20] Some have suggested, perhaps unkindly, that Boeing purchased De Havilland mainly to politically position itself to bid for a big Air Canada order for jets, as the airline was still a Crown corporation. Europe's Airbus won the competition, though allegations of bribery, known as the Airbus scandal, marred the result. Coincidentally or not, Boeing put De Havilland up for sale shortly thereafter.

A CAW media backgrounder on the "Future of De Havilland," released days after the NDP election victory, noted that under Boeing, the Toronto manufacturer was fast becoming a final assembly operation, with much of the engineering and design work centralized in Seattle. It warned that De Havilland had gone, in four short years, from a "crown corporation performing complete design/build on three popular aircraft, to a branch plant of an aerospace multinational doing final assembly of a single product."[21] The CAW wanted the Canadian government to take an equity stake and get a written commitment from any buyer that it would proceed with the launch of the long-delayed Dash 8-400 Series aircraft.

Boeing proposed instead to sell De Havilland to the European consortium of France's Aérospatiale and Italy's Alenia (A&A), sparking controversy, as A&A's aircraft were the direct competitors to the Dash 8.[22] Naturally, the CAW feared that the consortium would, in short order, turn "a fully integrated airframe manufacturer with complete design/build capabilities, to an offshore production subsidiary of a government-owned European aerospace consortium."[23] From the start, the NDP government insisted that the deal must have a Canadian partner if Ontario was going to put money into it. As Rae later recalled, he was "reluctant to buy the company for the province" on its own. He wrote:

> I was not impressed by the federal experience of the 1970s. The idea of an open-ended subsidy was anathema. We suggested another route: a partnership between ourselves, Aerospatiale (the French consortium), and Bombardier, the Canadian company which had been so successful in its purchase of Canadair in Montreal. The Canadair privatization was the beautiful twin when the Mulroney government got out of the airplane business.[24]

Quebec-based Bombardier was the logical choice as A&A's Canadian partner. It had acquired Canadair in 1986, expanding its workforce from five thousand to eight thousand. Canadair produced business and regional jets as well as water bombers. Over the previous year, Bombardier had been on an acquisition spree, buying the state-owned Belfast aircraft maker Short Brothers in 1989 and then Learjet in Wichita, Kansas, in 1990.[25] These acquisitions had left Bombardier cash poor by the time that Bob Rae came calling. That said, Rae had developed a close working relationship with Bombardier's Laurent Beaudoin as a result of that company's purchase of the Urban Transit Development Corporation, a former provincial Crown corporation that made subway and rail cars in Thunder Bay and light rapid transit systems in Kingston. It had been sold to Lavalin, another Quebec company, by the Liberal government of David Peterson, but the parent company quickly fell on hard times and the province was left "holding the bag, with good technology but virtually empty factories in both cities."[26] Bombardier took them off of Rae's hands for a price.

The NDP's hard line with A&A came under fire in the legislature from the opposition parties. Interim Liberal leader Bob Nixon suggested that the government's stance put five thousand jobs in danger.[27] Monte Kwinter noted that Boeing, "the largest and most successful aircraft company in the world," wanted to "get rid of that company, and the question has to be, why?" He then answered his own question, saying:

> The sad part about it is that every time they build an airplane, they lose over $1 million dollars. . . . The new buyers, Aérospatiale from France and Alenia from Italy, have taken a look at it and said: "We are certainly not interested in buying this company just to lose money. We will buy it on the condition that we can restructure it, which means we are going to have to do some very radical things. We are going to have to cut down on the work force. We are going to have to out-source some of our materials. We are going to have to get competitive. That is what we are talking about when we talk about competitiveness. If we cannot compete, there is no reason for us to buy it." Immediately, the response of this government is: "No way. You have to keep those jobs. You have to be uncompetitive because we are not prepared to let you buy that company and be competitive. We insist that you pay for the honour of losing money and staying uncompetitive." That is a silly kind of argument.

Not stopping there, Kwinter then drew a connection to the government's earlier insistence that any proposed restructuring of Algoma Steel must have union support:

> We are getting exactly the same thing at Algoma. I have great sympathy for the workers who are there. It would be a terrible thing to have people lose their jobs, but let us not continue to kid the troops. Dofasco, which is one of the most successful and the largest steel company in Canada, just bought it three years ago. They have decided they are going to write off $700 million. They did not say, "We are going to sell it to somebody." They have determined that

they are taking their investment, they are writing it off and they are not going to support that company any more.

He ended his speech by invoking Sydney Steel, which became a "sink-hole for years and years" after it was saved by the Nova Scotia government in 1967. He called on the NDP to "change its orientation," by which he meant letting the market do its dirty work.[28]

Investment Canada's decision to deny A&A's initial application until such time as it lined up a Canadian partner bolstered the NDP's position. Rae then directed Tim Armstrong to be the government's point person in the negotiations. His regular reports back offer us an inside look at the NDP's efforts to save De Havilland. A couple weeks after Investment Canada's decision, Rae met with Bombardier's Beaudoin to discuss the matter, after which Beaudoin drafted a letter to the European consortium outlining his conditions for participating as a full one-third partner, along with Aérospatiale and Alenia.[29] Soon thereafter, A&A replied that it was agreeable to the idea and that they should meet. But Bombardier had no intention of being the silent partner, proposing instead that key management decisions be made by consensus.[30] In effect, Bombardier wanted a veto. Once A&A made it clear that it was not interested in losing control, negotiations quickly broke down. Armstrong reported to Rae that "events have been moving quickly, although not, I regret, in a positive direction."[31] A&A proceeded to apply for approval from Investment Canada, undertaking to use its "best efforts" to avoid reducing employment levels below 3,700 employees and 430 engineers.[32] By then, De Havilland's financial position was rapidly deteriorating.

Without Bombardier in the ownership mix, the federal government was also concerned for De Havilland's long-term prospects "as an integrated designer and manufacturer of complete aircraft."[33] Indeed, what A&A was proposing was a "fully government supported operation" involving $750 million in financial support over the next decade and guaranteed purchases of their product, "which is what we are supposed to have left when de Havilland was

STRUCTURE OF THE CANADIAN AEROSPACE INDUSTRY

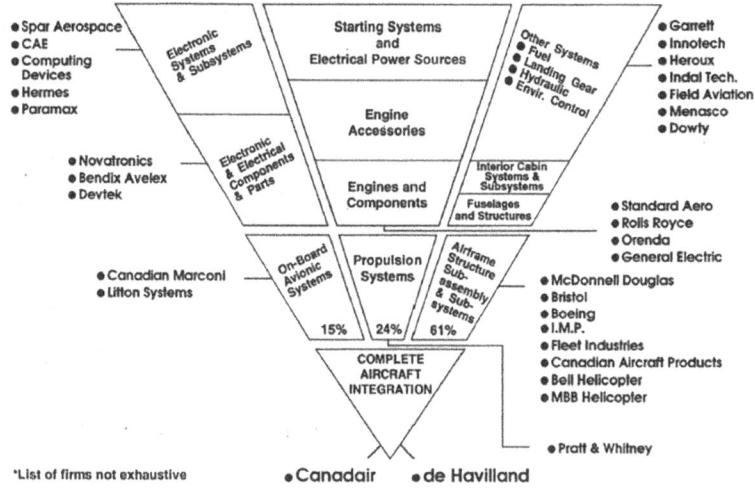

Aerospace—Stanley Ing, Office of Aviation and Space, 21 January 1994. B353188 Davos—World Economic Forum. WEF 1993. Archives of Ontario.

sold to Boeing."[34] Ontario was now faced with a choice. It could agree to take an ownership stake in the company, becoming the de facto Canadian partner, drop the condition, or let De Havilland die. It chose the first option. Smiling, Ross McClellan recalls that the decision to "partially nationalize" De Havilland "was taken on the sidewalk in front of Bob [Rae]'s house. Me and Floyd [Laughren] and David [Agnew]. And Bob. Bob said, 'You want to own an airline company?' We all say: 'Of course we do!' And then the rest is implementation, right? So that's how a lot of those decisions get made."[35] As a first step, the government hired the accountancy firm of Arthur Anderson to undertake a due diligence review of De Havilland's finances. Its report found that sales of the Dash 8 had flattened out since 1990 due to the recession and uncertainty over the company's future.[36] Ontario pushed the A&A consortium to provide guarantees: if not fixed employment levels, at least targeted levels of capital investment.[37] And on this basis, a modified proposal with Ontario as junior partner was approved by Investment Canada.

Just when Rae thought the crisis was over and he could concentrate on tackling other economic wildfires breaking out across the province, the European Economic Community (EEC) unexpectedly ruled against A&A's application to purchase De Havilland on 2 October 1991. The merged company would have controlled 60 percent of Europe's turboprop market.[38] It was a stunning setback. That same day, Armstrong shared some of the government's first thoughts during his appearance before the Ontario legislature's Standing Committee on Estimates:

> One could go on and on about the state of play in each of those major restructuring efforts, but it is almost like collective bargaining.... We have now a new element over which we have very little control. The European commission has made a ruling and we now have to make a determination as to the effect of that ruling on our effort to bring a successful conclusion to the de Havilland problem. ... I would be less than candid if I told you that we were not somewhat concerned and perplexed by this unexpected development.[39]

After the EEC ruling, France's Aérospatiale now proposed to take a 35 percent stake in De Havilland if Ontario took majority ownership. The next day, Ontario's negotiating team received the green light from Rae to proceed with negotiations with Aérospatiale. Armstrong met with Aérospatiale on 12 and 13 October, when draft Principles of Agreement were drawn up that provided that the equity partners would share losses on a 65/35 basis.[40] Rae wanted Bombardier in the mix, but Beaudoin made it perfectly clear that his company would remain on the sidelines. He told Armstrong that life was "too short" to waste it on Aérospatiale's management, whom he considered too arrogant to work with. According to Armstrong, a "legacy of bitterness, and the markedly different objectives and corporate cultures, militate against any grand alliance." A "shotgun marriage between Aérospatiale and Bombardier" was therefore "not in the cards."[41] However, Beaudoin now proposed that Ontario purchase all of De Havilland and let Bombardier manage the business on its behalf. Having no real money to contribute, Bombardier wanted De Havilland essentially for free. It was becoming abundantly clear that Ontario would need to take a majority stake if De Havilland was to survive.[42] Boeing also piled on the pressure after it threatened to close out the operation, as it wanted out now.[43]

The pressure on Ontario from all sides was enormous. It is a wonder that Bob Rae had time left over to run the province. With two bona fide potential partners in Bombardier and Aérospatiale, Ontario needed to assess the merits of each option. However, Rae had never been keen on the European consortium. His frank memorandum, dated 2 December 1991, detailed a private conversation he had had with federal Finance Minister Michael Wilson:

> Experience with A&A led me to believe that they were arrogant, and wanted Ontario's money but nothing else. I don't look forward to more of this if they are the owners, and industrial relations could also be very difficult. . . . There is no particular strength in the guarantees allegedly being negotiated with Ottawa, and the assumption, again, is that Ottawa will negotiate away and simply present us with the bill. The bill is unconscionably high from our point of view in any event; it far exceeds anything we have done in any other sector, comes with us as the junior banker in every respect but with all the liabilities and in fact with more of the political responsibility.[44]

Public ownership of De Havilland was never Rae's preferred option, but he was cornered. "Quite bluntly," his memo continued, "if Ontario is being expected to provide millions anyway, as they are in all options seen so far, I don't see the philosophical objection to some of that being in the form of equity. With Bombardier we buy some expertise and credibility in the business, but no deep pockets, or no pockets deep enough to operate with continuing losses."

In the meantime, Rae was having "full and frank" conversations with Beaudoin. Bombardier was willing to give the Ontario government assurances on a "sincere good faith effort to make a success of the DASH 8 program."[45] And to consider whether or not it made business sense to proceed with new versions of the aircraft.[46] To Rae's relief, a deal was struck whereby Bombardier took majority (51%) ownership with Ontario as minority (49%) stakeholder. Ontario spent $49 million on its equity share and another $300 million to cover expected losses over the first four years as the company restructured.[47] In return, Ontario would get three members on the board of directors. Another $240 million was contributed by the federal government.[48] When judged next to the public contribution of nearly $600 million, Bombardier's $51 million investment for majority control was almost a steal. Armstrong conceded that the proposed investment of the two levels of government was "very high," working out to $240,000 per job saved.[49] It only made sense if those jobs were saved over the long term. At the January 1992 ceremony marking the purchase of De Havilland by Bombardier and the Ontario government, Beaudoin promised

Joining hands, from left, Ontario Industry Minister Ed Philip, Bombardier chairman Laurent Beaudoin, Premier Bob Rae, Canadian Auto Workers secretary-treasurer Jim O'Neil, and federal Trade Minister Michael Wilson, 22 January 1992. Photo by Boris Spremo / *Toronto Star* via Getty Images.

that De Havilland would "retain its identity and carry on as an integrated design and production unit here in Downsview."[50] By 1994, the government could report that De Havilland had made real progress and that the company's losses were less than anticipated.[51]

As a new member of De Havilland's board of directors, Tim Armstrong continued to report back to the government. At first, Bombardier treated De Havilland as if it was its wholly owned subsidiary. Even though De Havilland had its own president, Armstrong made clear that "the company is being run by [Bombardier's] Messrs. Beaudoin, Brown and Royer. De Havilland's President, while knowledgeable and apparently intelligent, takes his directions from Bombardier."[52] Important decisions were made by senior Bombardier managers before the board meetings, leading Ontario's representatives to insist that meeting materials be provided in advance.[53] Armstrong even wondered how committed Bombardier was to turboprop aircraft. That said, he believed that the company seemed "to be managed efficiently." Writing in June 1993, he noted that "cost savings over the past year, as reflected in the financial statements, are quite impressive." Armstrong urged Ontario to assert its interests more effectively, perhaps establishing "a mechanism for assessing its objectives and developing an effective technique for asserting them, at the Board of Directors, the Steering Committee and, presumably, at the political level."

Two years after the defeat of the NDP government, the Tories would sell Ontario's stake in De Havilland over the protests of the CAW. In the years that followed, the Downsview plant manufactured Bombardier jet aircraft as well as the Dash 8 turboprop. In 2018, however, Bombardier announced that it would move production of its Global series of jets to a modern new facility located at Toronto's Pearson Airport. It then sold its 148-hectare tract of land at Downsview for US$635 million to the Public Sector Pension Investment Board, one of Canada's largest pension investment managers, for commercial and residential redevelopment.[54] Bombardier then sold its turboprop program to Longview Aviation, controlled by the billionaire heiress of the Thompson family (who once owned many of Canada's newspapers), for $300 million in

June 2019. Many feared that the new owner intended to move production to Alberta, leading seven hundred Unifor (the CAW merged with the Paperworkers union to form Unifor in 2013) members to strike for three months in 2021. The union tried to negotiate "scope clauses that would limit production to somewhere in the GTA [Greater Toronto Area]," but to no avail.[55] The new contract was essentially a close-out agreement, as production of the Dash 8 ceased. On 11 June 2022, De Havilland organized a closing event at Downsview that featured ten "iconic models" of aircraft once manufactured there.[56] Hundreds of former workers and their families, plus airplane enthusiasts, came out. At day's end, the aircraft took off in the order they were manufactured: The last to go was the Dash 8-400, which had been manufactured at Downsview earlier that year. Thus ended Downsview's long history of aviation and Dash 8 production.

PROMOTING THE AUTOMOTIVE SECTOR

With the De Havilland deal in place, Tim Armstrong turned his attention to the automotive industry and met a variety of industry leaders to gain a handle on the massive sector. Fully 88 percent of the Canadian auto sector's 152,000 employees in 1989 were located in Ontario.[57] Canada's automotive industry had weathered the early 1980s relatively well thanks to the Canada-US Auto Pact, which guaranteed that the same number of vehicles sold in the country would be manufactured here.[58] There were also Canadian content rules in place for component parts. Of forty-six auto assembly plants in the United States in 1980, only eighteen were still operating a decade later.[59] By contrast, only one Canadian auto assembly plant closed in this period. Instead, this was a time of expansion (see Canada Auto Industry Employment graph) as Canada tied auto bailouts to new investments, rather than to union concessions, as the US Congress had done. As a result, Canada's proportion of the North American industry actually increased during these years.[60] In 1993, a record 2.24 million vehicles were manufactured in the province.[61] By 1995, Ontario produced 13 percent of the vehicles sold in North America, second only to Michigan:

Canadian Auto Industry Employment 1972–1993

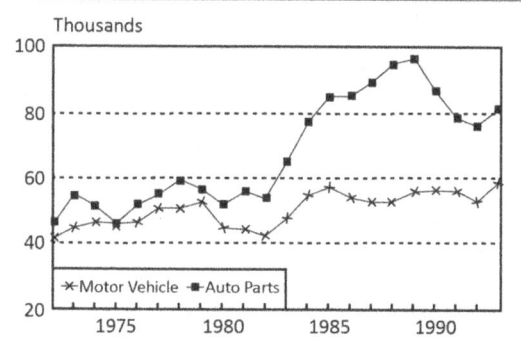

Source: Statistical review of the Canadian Automotive Industry. Industry Canada. 1992 and 1993 figures are Industry Canada estimates "Quarterly Automotive Circular" – 3rd QTR, 1993

Aerospace—Stanley Ing, Office of Aviation and Space, 21 January 1994. B353188 Davos—World Economic Forum. WEF 1993. Archives of Ontario.

an increased proportion for the province. Three Ontario assembly plants eventually closed between 1989 and 1994, first Chrysler's Brampton facility, then GM's Scarborough van plant, and finally Mack Truck's Oakville plant.[62] The province's five hundred auto parts plants were scattered across the region.

When the NDP came into office, General Motors employed eight thousand people in St. Catharines, representing half of the city's manufacturing workforce. It then began to close significant parts of this vast industrial complex. Just a month after the De Havilland signing ceremony, GM announced in February 1992 that its foundry, which made engine blocks and other components, would close in three years' time, displacing 2,315 workers. As the CAW viewed plant closures through the political lens of free trade, its first reaction was to launch an aggressive "fightback" campaign to convince the company to reverse its decision.[63] There were resolutions and protest rallies, leading the legislature to pass a symbolic motion urging GM to continue its operations in St. Catharines. The effort got support from the party itself. In March 1992, the NDP Provincial Council called on the government to intervene to save the "world class" GM foundry in St. Catharines.[64] It also endorsed a resolution on capital flight to low-wage countries, which called for the government to develop an economic plan for the province that includes direct government intervention to save jobs. Both motions were later endorsed by the 1992 Ontario NDP convention.

Even then, the Save the Foundry Committee of CAW Local 199 failed to convince the NDP government to politically respond to the foundry's closure. As Sean M. DiGiovanna showed in his excellent PhD thesis, Bob Rae came to St. Catharines and "told the foundry workers that convincing GM to change its mind was an 'illusion.' This angered many in the community who felt that the Ontario government had given up without really trying."[65] Rae's initial reaction was badly received by Buzz Hargrove, the CAW's new leader:

> The premier's statement ... does a major disservice to a lot of concerned people who are fighting like hell to defend their jobs. Instead of throwing cold water on people who are trying to keep this important facility open, the premier would better serve his constituents by reminding GM of the important contribution Ontario plants make to the overall success of GM.[66]

The CAW's Sam Gindin, for his part, remembers a meeting that Rae convened with the union and GM. The first thing Rae apparently said was "about what we were ready to give up. You know, we expected him [laughing] to hit GM a little bit. First question he asked was, 'Well, what are you guys ready to give up?'"[67] In response, GM's president turned to Rae and said, "Excuse me, Premier, we haven't asked the workers to give up anything ... they're not the reason for this."

Armstrong, who had accompanied Rae to St. Catharines, was directed to explore ways to save the foundry. On 29 October, he met with a group of local managers who were putting together a proposal for a downsized foundry. He wrote Rae to say that while "a long shot, perhaps, and would involve external financing (including, undoubtedly, some government money) I don't see how we can decline to examine the plan and determine whether it is feasible, and more importantly whether GM would be prepared to entertain a buyout." On 2 November, Armstrong reported that CAW officials were treating the foundry closure as a "fait accompli and believe that there is little if any possibility that GM's decision will be reversed."[68] The next day, GM announced it would also close the city's axle plant unless it found a buyer. It was part of a wider series of "plant utilization decisions" that saw the company close plants in Delaware, Michigan, Ohio, New Jersey, and New York. These were in addition to the twenty-three other GM plants closed in the previous year.[69]

Acknowledging the devastating news, Ed Philip told the legislature that it was "a tragic day for the people of St. Catharines, it's a tragic day for the workers of St. Catharines and it's a tragic day for the workers in the nine plants in North America, of which one happens to be in St. Catharines, because they are losing their jobs or will eventually lose their jobs. The fact is that the Premier is in St. Catharines today meeting with the workers and with the company."[70] By framing it as a human tragedy, Philip sought to depoliticize the announcement. However, the likelihood of a second GM closure struck fear in the community. James Bradley, the local Liberal MPP, strongly urged the Ontario government to "intervene in all possible manners to stop the erosion of jobs and the economic base of our province, and in particular the Niagara region."[71] For his part, Hargrove insisted that Rae do more in response to the unfolding crisis. "To your credit, you went directly to St. Catharines to hear and respond to the pain, frustration, anger, and growing fear that even the closures to date are just steps towards the total closure of the entire GM engine complex in St. Catharines," he said. "But something more must be done; we must try to reverse this."[72] Concerned that the entire GM manufacturing complex in the city was now at risk, Hargrove called on the NDP government to send a strong message to GM that it had a responsibility to the community.

Unwilling to pick a fight with General Motors, perhaps because its president served on Bob Rae's new Premier's Council on Economic Renewal, the government limited itself to quiet diplomacy and continued support of the local management group interested in buying the foundry. Amstrong met with all of the parties on multiple occasions, but everything depended on GM remaining the foundry's major customer.[73] At one point, Armstrong let Rae know that the interests of the CAW's national office and the local union were "not entirely congruent," making it difficult to know what the CAW position would ultimately be.[74] On 4 February 1993, Rae convened a meeting of General Motors, the CAW, and the buyers' group. Very quickly, however, it became clear that GM and the national CAW had met previously to settle on their response.[75] As a result, the buyers' group never even got the chance to make a full presentation of their revised proposal, which notably called for a wage rollback of 25 percent to 30 percent. GM simply restated its intention to close the foundry and the CAW reiterated that it would not consider wage concessions. Armstrong felt both parties had "taken unnecessarily rigid positions, to the detriment of 876 St. Catharines families." He wrote, "I hope that this is not symptomatic of the difficulties we can expect to face, as we move forward with other restructuring situations."[76] A corporate buyer for GM's axle plant was eventually found, but it then promptly consolidated production at another plant in the US, closing the St. Catharines facility for good. Capital flight remained a key issue.

What the government did do for St. Catharines was announce in April 1992 the relocation of a branch of the public service to the city. As Floyd Laughren explained, St. Catharines was chosen because its "economy has been rocked by major plant closures. A total of 1,400 jobs [were] moved to that community."[77] Other hard-hit industrial communities—such as Windsor, Chatham, Brantford, Peterborough, and even Elliot Lake—also benefited from the relocation of civil service jobs from Toronto. Thanks to the efforts of local cabinet minister Dave Cooke, Windsor got its casino, beating several other hard-hit towns in the running. As sociologist Alissa Mazar notes, the Windsor Casino was the very first resort casino built in direct response to deindustrialization in

North America.[78] With the North American Free Trade Agreement (NAFTA) coming, Windsor feared another round of industrial closures as the automakers moved production to low-wage Mexico. During our interview, I asked Bob Rae about the seemingly divergent approaches to plant closures in northern and southern Ontario. His immediate reaction was to point to the ideological divisions within the trade union movement and how they played out geographically. There was a "greater flexibility on the part of the leadership of the unions and the industrial workers in northern Ontario, partly because they knew that everybody else in town was worse off than they were. And I think that affected the environment in which people were willing to make a sacrifice."[79] Not so the Canadian Auto Workers, which was the major private-sector union in southern Ontario. They "had a different view, and they kept saying, 'Oh, we're not going to make any concessions, no concessions on bargaining.' So that made it a little bit more difficult for us politically in terms of how can we make this happen."

This may be true, but Ontario's unwillingness to respond politically to the closure of GM's foundry had everything to do with growing concern in NDP circles over the province's business climate. By 1993, ministerial briefing notes were regularly suggesting that "in our global economy, every jurisdiction needs to compete for investment. Ontario is no exception."[80] The new Ministry of Economic Development and Trade, headed by Frances Lankin, regularly issued its Ontario Competitiveness Report that trumpeted all the new investments in the province. These good news stories, meant to counteract the bad news of layoffs and plant closures, included Ontario's $30 million contribution to Chrysler's $600 million investment in its Windsor assembly plant, securing the jobs of four thousand auto workers; and the government directed another $26.9 million for worker training and $7.2 million for infrastructure improvement at Ford's Oakville assembly operation that led the company to invest another $1 billion and deliver a new product mandate. The NDP's Manufacturing Recovery Program also provided financial assistance to firms experiencing difficulty. Through the Ontario Development Corporation, it "moved to make industrial assistance programs more strategic with an emphasis on supporting firms whose activities generate benefits for the wider economy."[81] In all, the program supported 220 firms between 1990 and 1995, helping to secure up to 14,300 jobs.

The list of major private-sector automotive investments in the province, totalling $5.53 billion, was impressive (see table of Major Automotive Investments). Windsor and Oakville came out the big winners, but substantial investments were also directed towards the Chrysler assembly plant in Bramalea, the new Freightliner assembly operation in St. Thomas, and a new Toyota engine assembly in Cambridge.[82] We begin to see here a union strategy of negotiating new investments as part of the collective bargaining process as a way to secure jobs.[83] But these new investments mostly involved the renewal or expansion of existing facilities, not the building of new ones. Armstrong tried in vain to convince European automakers to locate in the province. Ontario lost to South Carolina for a BMW plant and to Alabama for a Mercedes one. The NDP was able to secure new product mandates for Oshawa's two GM car assembly plants after it had been informed that one of these plants was in danger of losing its allocation. As a result, employment in the transportation equipment sector increased as a proportion of all industrial employment in the province from 32 percent in 1985 to 38.4 percent in 1995.[84] These were no small victories. Nor were they cheap.

Despite business opposition to the NDP's labour law reforms, some CEOs came around to what the NDP government was trying to do in other areas. In one of those stories that no doubt has been told and retold, Rae told me about when the CEO of Ford Canada phoned him up one Thursday afternoon in 1992:

> He said, "I've got to come in and see you tomorrow." And I said to him on the phone, I said, "Oh, shit." I said, "Don't tell me—don't—don't tell me." He said, "No no no no, it's good news, it's good news, it's good news." So I said, "Fine, you're welcome—if it's good news, I'm glad to see you." So he came in, and we chatted about making a decision about

MAJOR AUTOMOTIVE INVESTMENTS IN ONTARIO

COMPLETION DATE	PROJECT	INVESTMENT ($ MILLIONS)
1992	Ford - new Oakville Paint Plant	439
1992	Chrysler - retooled Bramalea Assembly Plant	600
1992	Freightliner - new St. Thomas Assembly Plant	30
1993	Ford - new Windsor Cosworth Aluminum Casting Plant	200
1993	Ford - retooled Oakville Assembly Plant	560
1994	GM - retooling Windsor Transmission Plant	300
1994	Ford - expanding Windsor Essex Aluminum Casting Plant	100
1995	Ford - reopening Windsor Ensite Engine Plant	1,000
1995	Toyota - new Cambridge Engine Assembly Plant	30
1995	Chrysler - expanding Windsor Assembly Plant	600
1996	Honda - expanding Alliston Assembly Plant	20
1996	Ford - expanding Oakville Truck Plant	400
1997	Toyota - expanding Cambridge Assembly Plant	600
1997	Ford - expanding Windsor Engine Component Plant	650
	TOTAL:	**5,529**

Ross McClellan, "The Story of Ontario's First NDP Government," Draft #12, 30 March 1995. In the possession of the author thanks to Ross McClellan.

the Oakville plant, and he said, "Look, we're not doing this because we're in love with you, or we're in love with everything you do, but we're doing this for a couple of reasons. One is because the way you work, effectively, with the community colleges in providing training inside the plant makes a huge difference. We're working on a longer-term deal with the unions, which we think is going to be helpful, and will allow us to provide some stability, and frankly, the competitiveness on health care was a huge advantage for you guys, and so we're going to make a major announcement. But it's going to require some commitments from you and from the federal government."[85]

Given the dire times, one can understand Rae's initial reaction: bad news was not in short supply. In this case, they got the job done, but not every industry had this kind of political access.

By the time that Rae attended the World Economic Forum (WEF) in Davos, Switzerland, in 1993 and 1994, it was regularly bringing together two thousand leading business and political leaders from around the world for six days of plenaries, receptions, and private meetings. The themes of these two years were, respectively, "Rallying all the forces for global recovery" and "Redefining the basic assumptions of the world economy."[86] Economist Klaus Schwab had originated the idea of an "annual exercise in business-government summitry" in 1971, first as the European Management Forum, and after 1987, as the World Economic Forum.[87] According to the Ontario Premier's briefing notes, Davos offered participants the opportunity to meet "with a high-level international audience and to convey the advantages of Ontario as an investment location and technology transfer partner."[88] But Rae's presence was about more than meeting with potential investors; it was also an opportunity to be *seen* back home actively promoting the province.

Rae's itineraries for these two editions of the World Economic Forum reveal back-to-back meetings, mostly with corporate Canada, with the odd meeting about investing in Ontario with a foreign multinational such as Mercedes-Benz, Siemens, or Volkswagen.[89] Rae and Frances Lankin, the Minister of Economic Development and Trade, seem to have attended only a few of the plenary sessions. A dinner hosted by the Toronto power couple Peter and Melanie Munk included a clutch of corporate CEOs and the labour movement's arch-nemesis himself: Thomas D'Aquino of the Business Council on National Issues, who had made a name for himself during the free trade debate. One wonders if they talked over dinner about one of the preoccupations of the 1994 World Economic Forum: the supposedly urgent need to reform welfare systems, which "had become a disincentive for employment and a burden on economies."[90] The ideas in circulation in Davos and their underlying assumptions were no doubt important in forging an elite consensus. Working closely with preferred corporate leaders such as Bombardier's Beaudoin thus became the government's primary response to the industrial crisis in southern Ontario. Financial incentives to big business rather than worker buyouts were, at least in the automotive sector, the order of the day.

CONCLUSION

De Havilland stood alongside Algoma Steel and Spruce Falls as among the NDP government's greatest achievements. Added to this, the ability to secure major automotive investments for plant modernization made a real difference to auto towns such as Windsor, Oshawa, and Oakville. The government's record in St. Catharines was far less impressive, as it was constrained by the CAW's unwillingness to contemplate concessions on the one hand and its own unwillingness to respond politically to plant closures. Despite the government's best efforts, General Motors also closed its Scarborough van assembly plant on 7 May 1993. It was a slow-death closure; the initial announcement had been made in October 1989 with no clear timetable. The union sought to negotiate the best possible closure agreement and launched an extensive lobbying campaign to apply pressure on GM to reverse its decision. As the months wore on, and turned into years, there was considerable labour turnover in the plant as workers found other jobs. Large groups of workers displaced from other GM plants in Ontario came to work at the van plant from Windsor, Oshawa, and St. Catharines. Several hundred francophones came to work there after GM closed its Sainte-Thérèse assembly plant in Quebec. With the closure approaching, the van plant did not "explode like Houdaille or Bendix [when workers occupied those closing plants in 1980]. The death watch had been too long and the closure package was, in context, reasonable."[91] Instead, there was quiet resignation. A few days before the final closure, a protest rally was held in front of the Scarborough plant, where defiant speeches were given. When it was the turn of Gord Wilson, president of the Ontario Federation of Labour, shouts of "Where's Bob Rae?" could be heard. Wilson could only nod his head in agreement.

The closure of the Scarborough van plant was unusual only insofar as CAW Local 303 was able to get some funding from the Ontario Ministry of Culture and Tourism for a heritage project to document the history of the union local and record the dying days of the sprawling plant. Workers collected union records and conducted oral history interviews. One worker in the plant, Gayle Hurmuses, was a gifted photographer who took three thousand pictures. The booklet that resulted, entitled *You Can't Bring Back Yesterday: A History of CAW Local 303*, captures the hurt and pain felt by displaced workers but also their pride at the long history of union militancy in the plant. It opened with a letter addressed to the members of the local union from CAW president Buzz Hargrove, who spoke of his anger and sadness at the closure. He went on to say that in "most closures, the history and memory of the local and its members have disappeared with the jobs." However, "this has not happened here. You have found a way to salvage your history and ensure that it is remembered. This is not an alternative to fighting for jobs and a working future. It is a way to learn from our experiences and history. Your work recognizes the important role history plays in the life of our union today." In the main text, the members of the heritage committee noted that the closure of the van plant had been in the news: "The coverage was 'better' than most closures." They worked hard to ensure that the union's history, and their workplace community, would not be erased from history:

> It is no accident that these stories are unknown and forgotten. The achievements of the trade union movement have been pushed to the margins of public perception and in the process, outside the realm of public memory. . . . The erasure of places like these from the landscape in both communities and memory ties into the current economic war being waged against working people. It is part of the political and ideological campaign currently being waged against unions. In writing this history we assert the social and political value of the union as an institution.[92]

It was, therefore, much more than a souvenir book; it was a reminder of the human cost of each and every mill and factory closure.

This was not the only project of its kind. The NDP government launched the Ontario Workplace Heritage Program, delivered through the Ontario Heritage Foundation, which gave out grants for small projects that documented "economic and technological changes affecting workplaces in the province."[93] The Workers' City Project in Hamilton, for example, developed labour history walking tours of the city that highlighted the histories of many of the city's secondary industries that had recently closed. According to Robert Kristofferson, "It was based on the concern that the rapid erosion of the city's industrial base and surrounding residential districts is endangering the heritage of its working people."[94] Ottawa trade unionists, led by my friend Ken Clavette, received a $27,000 workplace heritage grant to undertake an oral history project on Beach Foundry, which shut in 1980, despite its CAW members occupying the closing plant, as well as Ottawa Car and Aircraft, which closed back in 1948. According to the final report of the heritage project, "Both of these companies are prime examples of Ottawa's, indeed Canada's, disappearing industrial and manufacturing sector." The local workers' heritage committee produced a video, display, and leaflet featuring the oral history interviews collected. As part of their efforts, they also recovered fifty items related to the histories of the two workplaces including photos, company and union newsletters, documents, and other materials. All of these were deposited with the City of Ottawa Archives.[95] This, too, countered the erasure of working-class people.

The culmination of these efforts was the creation of the Workers Arts and Heritage Centre (WAHC) in Hamilton's former customs house thanks to funding from the NDP government.[96] It is a museum like no other in North America, as it centred the history of trade unionists and workers' struggle. It therefore differed from the global industrial heritage movement with its more consensual narrative anchored in material culture and architecture.[97] Nor was it quite like the ecomuseum movement that emerged in deindustrializing France, which established an outpost in 1980s Montreal at the Écomusée du fier monde, as it was focused on citizen activism in a given locality.[98] Every curatorial project at WAHC, at least in its first five years, was undertaken in partnership, often with unions, but also other community organizations.[99] Its stated mission was to "preserve, display and communicate the heritage of Ontario workers and their unions, reflecting fully the broad cultural and racial diversity of Ontario and the role of women' and to 'foster the display and interpretation of the creative expression of work as depicted through the fine, decorative, and performing arts.'" Until the NDP came to power, there was little recognition of working-class or trade union heritage.[100] You might say that workers' arts and heritage emerged out of the ruins of Ontario industry.

What do we make of this attention to workers' heritage, given the government's wider response to the industrial crisis in southern Ontario? With deindustrialization, historians have long observed that "the urge to reaffirm or celebrate the industrial past seems to grow stronger."[101] One strongly suspects that, like elsewhere, Ontario government funding of these trade union–led heritage projects aimed to "sooth concerns" and, in so doing, sought to further depoliticize industrial decline.[102] It can even be read as a form of symbolic compensation. Either way, it doesn't change the fact that, to some limited degree, workers' heritage funding empowered workers like Gayle Hurmuses and Ken Clavette to counter the cultural and historical erasure that is an integral part of deindustrialization.

National Rubber Company: Susi Chow operating a stitcher, 1993.
Photo by Peter MacCallum.

9

CORPORATISM'S MOMENT

> Arriving at a social contract, as other socialist parties have discovered, is not an easy task. In the past, in national rather than provincial arenas, the contest has often been an unequal fight between governments and trade unions over wages and inflation. Too often these one-sided social contracts meant that workers lost and eventually, where socialists were part of such deals, the socialists lost as well.
>
> —RIEL MILLER, March 1990[1]

In September 1991, as part of its political reset after its ambitious first year, the Ontario cabinet opted to make economic renewal its top priority. By economic renewal, the government was referring to its progressive competitiveness agenda, namely "those policies and programs with the potential to promote the long-term restructuring of the provincial economy towards the creation of more well-paying, high value-added jobs."[2] Some members of the inner circle had grown concerned that restructuring situations like Algoma Steel, Spruce Falls, and De Havilland were being dealt with only on a case-by-case basis. One senior advisor told me that Bob Rae "would get very focused on an individual plant . . . and he'd want to know what we can do to solve this problem." Accordingly, Michael Mendelson advised Rae in October 1991 that there was far too "little assessment of the implications of the proposed solutions for the industry or sector as a whole. Decisions on fiscal allocations are being made in isolation from each other, without consideration of the global budget for restructuring or the opportunity cost of funding one case at the expense of several others."[3] These rescue efforts, he added, were "absorbing an inordinate portion of staff time" and "diverting those resources from the development of other initiatives" in the government's new agenda.

Two senior advisors, in particular, made the case that time and money should be directed towards the new economy, not wasted on the old. For Riel Miller (Treasury) and David Wolfe (Cabinet Office), the election of the NDP created an unprecedented opportunity to forge a new social consensus on the direction of economic change itself. Within weeks of taking office, Miller was already urging the government to link key economic and policy issues as part of a wider social bargaining process aimed at achieving a new social contract. Though the cabinet ultimately decided against this grand idea as too complex, the aspiration for societal consensus lived on as the central impulse of the NDP government, infusing its political rhetoric on everything from labour law reform to training and adjustment.[4] The single most important articulation of the NDP's emerging progressive competitive vision can be found in *Ontario in the 1990s: Promoting Equitable Structural Change*, released as Budget Paper E in Laughren's controversial first budget in April 1991. Written primarily by Miller, with the assistance of Wolfe, it recognized that the economy was "undergoing profound and far-reaching structural change" and that the economic transition needed to be equitable so workers were not "left to carry the burden of adjustment alone."[5] Technological change, not capital flight, was understood to be the primary driving force of the unfolding industrial crisis. Ontario's future prosperity would therefore depend on the flexibility and skills of the labour force. Budget Paper E declared that Ontario's successful transition would depend "on the ability of business, labour and government, working together, to increase the flexibility of our economy, its supporting institutions and society in general." The NDP government would therefore seek to become a "facilitator of structural change, not only to minimize the costs of transition and distribute them more fairly, but actively to promote the development of high-value-added, high-wage jobs through strategic partnerships."[6] Only a "new economic strategy based on broad social partnerships" would position the province for success in the new global economy. The corporatist vision of Budget Paper E differed from the Liberal Premier's Council insofar as it privileged cooperative, community, and worker-led approaches to value creation in society.

The economic renewal agenda appealed to Rae, who used the opportunity of the Cunningham Lectureship at Queen's University in March 1992 to call for a stronger consensus on Ontario's economic future. Rae reminded his listeners that there was once a time when such a consensus could be built around the idea of national self-sufficiency. Canada's first prime minister, for example, pursued a national policy of import substitution to industrialize the country in the late nineteenth century. But those days were gone. According to Rae, Sir John A. Macdonald's old tariff wall had been largely levelled by free trade and the GATT. To make his point, Rae once again referred to the experience of the Mitterrand government in the early 1980s. When the French Socialist and Communist parties bravely tried to "reflate an economy in recession," they were brutally disciplined by the international markets: "A national, or regional, or local, economy can only go its own way if it is sufficiently strong to dictate the terms on which it will relate to the rest of the world." All it seems Ontario could do was invest in skills training, education, and infrastructure to create a locational advantage for new investment in a rapidly restructuring world. Rae argued that we needed to break through the binary thinking that leads us to falsely conclude that we have no other option but to choose between the economy and the environment or between efficiency and fairness. That is why, he said, "institutions that bring people together are so important.... We need more of them, not less."[7] Rae ended his speech by saying that "economic renewal, social justice, and fiscal responsibility are natural and necessary allies." The challenge, he said, was "to find the balance that will work and be most productive."

With the postwar compromise in tatters, a rising chorus of voices called for a new social compact to replace the old. Since the 1970s, governing social democratic parties had sought to leverage their close relationship to the trade union movement to negotiate wage restraint in the fight against inflation or the deficit, as the case may be, in exchange for wider social gains. Here we can point to the ruling British Labour Party's "social compact" with labour between 1974 and 1979 or the "Statement of Accord" between the Australian Labour Party and organized labour in 1983. Both proved bitterly disappointing for the trade union movement. Writing in 1994, political economist Bennett Harrison noted that social contract experiments had become quite common in "many places across the industrialized world" including "at least a dozen states" in the US.[8] As early as 1987, Chuck Robb, the former Governor of Virginia and leader of the Democratic Leadership Council, had called for a "profound change in our capitalist culture." Indeed, he said, "just as we did in the New Deal, the time has come for Americans to negotiate a new social contract, to insist on economic growth with economic equity."[9] Other Democratic Party modernizers such as Bill Clinton, and his friends Ira Magaziner and Robert Reich, used similar language in the years that followed.[10]

Social democrats in Canada were also drawn to the idea, beginning with a national conference on the pros and cons of a new social contract held in 1984.[11] Simon Rosenblum, a key advisor to Floyd Laughren, co-edited a 1991 volume on the future of social democracy that included an entire section on the idea.[12] In his contribution, union researcher John Calvert suggested that demands for a new social contract were based "on certain assumptions about how a mixed economy can be managed by a left-leaning government intent on pursuing equality and full employment."[13] It is clear, then, that the social contract idea was now bound up in efforts to more equitably share the pain of industrial restructuring. Even the US Rust Belt offered up its share of hard-earned lessons. Rae told me that he was influenced by United Steelworkers' Lynn Williams, the first Canadian to become the union's international president. Rae had talked to him "a lot about how he had had to go through a real process of internal change to say, 'Okay, how do we save these jobs? How do we save some of these jobs? And how do we provide people with the kind of adjustment that's going to be required?'"[14]

Since 1993, however, the idea of a social contract in Ontario has been tainted by its association with the Ontario NDP's failed experiment in negotiating deficit reduction with public-sector unions. Collective agreements were forcibly opened and unions told to renegotiate or face unilateral action. The NDP's Social Contract did not end well politically, although layoffs were avoided and $2 billion saved. Unpaid "Rae Days" joined the "Bennett Buggy" of the 1930s in the Canadian lexicon of derisive political vernacular, and the party's special relationship with the union movement was largely ruined. Trying to make sense of it all, Ross McClellan recalls that the longer the NDP was in office, the more the fight against the deficit took over. The Ministry of Finance, which he calls a "complete nest of neoliberals," was "having an increasingly strong impact on government decision-making."[15] This chapter explores how such a lofty idea as a new societal social contract was reduced to little more than social democratic high diction for the politics of austerity.

DREAMING OF A NEW CONSENSUS

The Liberal Premier's Council, supplemented with the new scholarship on flexible production and industrial districts focused on Italy, provided the NDP with its intellectual framework for understanding the significance of the economic changes sweeping the province and an alternative progressive competitive economic strategy to neoliberalism. Soon after its election victory, the new cabinet discussed the future of the Premier's Council under the NDP. Bob Rae wanted three advisory councils, focusing on economic renewal, health strategy, and the environment. As under the Liberals, they were considered central to the government's wider efforts to forge a consensus on key challenges and put senior cabinet ministers into sustained dialogue with different stakeholders. Some concern was expressed, however, about the perceived exclusivity of the Premier's Councils, so they were opened up to a wider diversity of members. But there was never any doubt that the NDP would seek to build on their success, with one senior advisor recalling that Rae loved them as they "embodied his approach."[16]

The Premier's Council on Economic Renewal, launched in late 1991 with thirty-one members, focused on strategies to support industrial and economic policy. It included cabinet ministers Bob Mackenzie and Ed Philip, as well as Leo Gerard and Gord Wilson from organized labour and several business CEOs, with Peter Warrian as one of its facilitators.[17] Ambitiously, the council's mandate was to "accelerate the process of economic renewal in Ontario, acting as a change agent, in addition to advising government."[18] Instead of working together as a single body, the government opted for task forces, or subcommittees, to develop targeted "consensus-based solutions for achieving economic renewal and restructuring."[19] It launched, for example, a project to identify the economic and social indicators "helpful in positioning Ontario's performance within North America." Essentially, this project compared the skills level and educational attainment of Ontario's workforce to other jurisdictions to ascertain if the province had a competitive advantage.[20] For its part, the task force on the organization of work investigated the main characteristics of "innovative workplaces and empowered workforces." When the newly elected Clinton administration appointed a commission in May 1993 to look into the future of worker-management relations "to do what we have been doing for some time now," task force members were told that "the fact that the Americans have entered the race means that we can't rest on our oars" in developing a "vision statement for the workplace of the future."[21]

Overall, the tangible achievements of the Premier's Council on Economic Renewal are difficult to see. Certainly, Ross McClellan was no fan; he told me it was a "cosmic waste of time" that only served to "push people to the right." McClellan went on to call it an "appallingly bad exercise," but he couldn't say much at the time, as "Bob [Rae] was so enthusiastic about it." He would make "the occasional disparaging remarks" and leave it at that; to him, "it was a toxic exercise, there were better ways of relating to the private sector."[22]

With Ontario grappling with the worst economic downturn since the Great Depression, there was never any question that the economy would be front and centre. It was not predetermined, however, how the government would approach these issues, given the party's fluid thinking on economic issues. Yet a strong progressive competitive vision soon took hold, guiding government actions in a host of areas. Political economist Rianne Mahon was one of the few to call the Rae government's emerging economic strategy "relatively coherent," pointing to Budget Paper E as an example.[23] Even so, there was a fundamental tension between labourism, with its working-class sensibility and emphasis on the rules-based regulatory state, and the new progressive competitive politics of consensus building and social partnership. As early as February 1991, Riel Miller and David Wolfe were expressing their concern that the government's "labour agenda" was interfering with their efforts to forge connection with business.[24] Alan Ernst, who worked for the parliamentary assistant assigned to the Ministry of Labour, noted that there were internal "divisions within the government and labour over the tactics and substance of 'social bargaining' and social partnership with business."[25] Wolfe and Chuck Rachlis offered their own insiders' account of the internal struggle for policy coherence:

> One of the ... challenges for the NDP was coordinating its longer-term economic strategy with the more immediate crises of the recession and its fiscal constraints. In part, the government was fighting a battle on two fronts. One involved a long-term structural adjustment of the emerging, technology-intensive economy, a wrenching change that was magnified by the impact of the Canada-US Free Trade Agreement. The other and more immediate challenge was responding to the devastating impact of the recession.[26]

In their estimation, the government tried to do both and failed. As a result, "the gains from its longer-term initiatives were slow to develop and hard to discern."

Just days after the NDP took office, Miller was urging the new government to make wage increases to public-sector unions "contingent on a general, publicly declared social contract" that would hold down the higher wage categories but let the lower ones climb in the name of fighting inflation. He also thought it wise to make the proposed increase in Ontario's minimum wage part of a wider package "to move the labour force to a higher skill level, ie. as part of a strategy to alter the sectoral and occupational composition of the economy towards a higher proportion of high-value added activity."[27] He was convinced that the only way to share the pain of industrial restructuring was to move quickly to forge a new social contract:

> If we are to take on the recession and restructuring at home and try to provide leadership on the national stage then we need to begin practicing the alternative—ie the social contract approach. I think we need to convene a working group of Ministry, trade union, academic and business economists to begin hammering out the features of this national alternative to high interest rates. I think if we don't Herbert Hoover will be eating with us in the afterlife. Ciao.[28]

You might well wonder what Miller meant with this final turn of phrase. Hoover, the Republican US President during the first three years of the Great Depression, has been widely condemned by history for not responding effectively to the economic crisis. It was only Franklin D. Roosevelt's New Deal that restored hope to America. Miller's comment thus revealed the high stakes as the NDP faced its own moment of reckoning. The Miller-Wolfe tandem is key to understanding corporatism's moment in Ontario, as they sought an "overarching vision/framework" for the many "worthwhile initiatives" that the government intended to undertake. Without this, Miller cautioned, the new government ran the "risk of foundering on the obstacle of confusion and contradiction." To hammer home his point, he referred to the "mistakes of some previous socialist administrations dealing with recessions, like Mitterrand in 1982," suggesting that the Ontario NDP needed to "pursue a carefully balanced package of positive adjustment policies aimed at building a coalition of labour, business and community interests for change." He thought such a "positive adjustment framework" would integrate fiscal, social, and educational policies within a single "vision of labour market and industrial change." Indeed, Riel Miller added:

> Our goal is to recognize that change is taking place and to direct this change towards high wage, socially useful and healthy areas of activity. However, we must be very explicit that this means that many low wage occupations and sectors of the economy will be actively phased out. (Consequently, many of those least well off—youth, working poor, immigrants, and women, will be called upon to adjust).... For this type of socially directed restructuring to take place workers, capitalists, and government must be willing to take risks together.[29]

The economic framework that Miller had in mind would ease "transition costs" and share the socio-economic burden. Miller understood that significant labour law reforms, a cornerstone of the party's electoral platform, would trigger a business backlash that could threaten the government's efforts to achieve consensus on a common response to industrial restructuring. He pointed to the experience of Dave Barrett's BC NDP government in the 1970s as evidence of what might happen: it is commonly remembered as having tried to do too much too quickly, and as a result was a one-term wonder. Labour law reform therefore needed to be "integrated into an overall approach towards economic and social changes aimed at equity and prosperity." In making his argument, Miller leaned heavily on "public antagonism" towards trade unions and how "business unionism" was "seen/depicted as greedy and job destroying." Ontarians needed to be convinced that labour law reform was in the wider public interest, and only a wider social bargain could do that. Labour reform might then contribute to, rather than undermine, the transition to a social partnership approach along the lines of the Swedish model.[30]

Meanwhile, a background research paper on "Competing Socialist Strategies for Economic Change," written by David Wolfe, suggested that "a clearly developed social contract between the state and its social partners provides a negotiated platform of policies concerning how we work and live. It is the essential underpinning of a coherent and directed economic development strategy."[31] For Wolfe, much as for Miller: "If we are to proceed to develop a new social contract—that not only embodies efficiency and equity values—but also embraces a new kind of socialist economics and popular planning a number of options, including those previously untried, must be raised and discussed." Wolfe maintained that the restructuring of the global division of labour made "worker participation/control in layoff and plant closing situations an important variable to consider in any negotiated social contract."

When Miller's initial push for a social contract failed to convince the Cabinet Office, which argued that making trade-offs was "too complex," he asked Laughren to make the case to cabinet anyway. The "bone of contention," he wrote, related to linking initiatives. Should the government "link the various items which make up our overall economic strategy" or not? Miller insisted that linking labour law reform to the government's wider partnership approach would provide "incentive to compromise" and make consensus possible. Labour law reform, employment standards amendments (advance notice, severance), training and adjustment, as well as ways to finance industrial restructuring (pension fund investments, labour-sponsored investment funds, etc.) were all listed as good candidates for linkage, as they would send the message that the government was adopting a "balanced strategy" as part of its "overall social partnership approach to facilitating economic and social change." Together, these measures could form the core of a "new social contract."[32]

There were other proponents in the cabinet of the wider social contract idea. Bud Wildman, for example, recalls that he had told his cabinet colleagues right from the start that "no social democratic government in Europe had survived without a social contract with the labour movement." Others around the table, he recalls, looked at him strangely, as though they were thinking "where on earth are you coming from?"[33] While the cabinet concurred with the Cabinet Office that the linkage idea was too ambitious, the debate may have contributed to the government's eventual effort to negotiate austerity under the banner of a new Social Contract.

The government committed itself to developing an industrial policy almost immediately. To jump-start the process, the cabinet approved the creation of a series of inter-ministerial working groups on industrial restructuring, training, and adjustment, as well industrial and technology policy.[34] All of the working groups were to complete their work by June 1991 so their findings could be integrated over the summer months in order to develop options for the cabinet. The Working Group on Industrial Restructuring, chaired by the Ministry of Treasury and Economics, presumably Miller, prioritized its work on the financing of worker ownership through labour-led venture capital, promoting community-based financial institutions such as credit unions, and the possible development of a Caisse-like institution for Ontario. The Caisse de dépôt et placement du Québec was founded in 1965 with the creation of the Quebec Pension Plan, after the province opted out of the Canada-wide plan. The majority of its portfolio was managed conservatively to ensure a good return on investment, but it was sensitive to government priorities in terms of economic development, and it was widely credited with being an important catalyst for Quebec's entrepreneurial dynamism. Talk included undertaking a "full-fledged copy of the Quebec caisse, consolidating Ontario public sector pension assets" into a single massive unit with a mandate to support economic development in the province, but the working group admitted that the idea would likely meet stiff resistance from business and public-sector unions.

Some senior advisors also believed that public funding should not simply go towards labour adjustment and training but also to managerial efforts to restructure. By March 1991, their work was becoming urgent given the unfolding industrial crisis, especially the events surrounding troubled Algoma Steel, Spruce Falls, and De Havilland. It was noted that:

At the recent Cabinet retreat, there was a lot of discussion on economic problems and awareness that the government needs to take action. It is also important to note that business will find it hard to accept the labour initiatives to be announced this Spring if these are not followed up with a coherent industrial strategy. The rule-of-thumb that the working group was advised to follow is: provide clearly structured decision options for Cabinet to consider; and not to be afraid to provide (small "r") radical options (avoid gravitating towards options that represent the common lowest denominator).[35]

In mid-April 1991, there was a meeting at Bistro 990, a posh Bay Street restaurant popular with celebrities, about the core problem the industrial restructuring working group was trying to resolve. The government's "clear priority" was saving the *next* 200,000 manufacturing jobs rather than "recreating" the 100,000 jobs already lost. The obstacles were enormous. Those in attendance felt that there was a need "for long term patient capital which will wait for the time necessary [to] restructure" and to finance "community development." They also discussed "risk diffusion," by which they meant the political risk "if it rescued sunset industries it would be horrible—and if it didn't it would be horrible." They then noted:

> Many of the elements of the [social] bargain are floating around—pension funds, training, social programs, labour relations amendments, worker ownership and equity, limits on capital mobility, workplace flexibility, sectoral technologies, tax burden shifts environmental policies; but each individually is a recipe for dissention and a loss in the next election; however taken together the whole might be quite acceptable to most collectives and most people individually. We should be asking what we want collectively and how to give each other what we want. This has been called a process of social bargaining; we will have

to think of a new name. It is clear that there is no such atmosphere in the labour movement or the popular sectors for this negotiation. Focussing on the Caisse makes it tangible and pragmatic and gets people to the table who might otherwise not come; however it should be treated as a stepping stone to the big social bargain conversation and not as an end in itself.[36]

For this group of senior policy advisors, at least, a social contract remained an active option. It also helps us understand how worker ownership became linked to labour-led venture capital and why the government paid no heed to the OFL's proposed social equity fund.

Ontario already had an alphabet soup of investment mechanisms such as the Ontario Development Corporation, to which was added the Ontario Lead Investment Fund, one of the first "fund of funds" models in Canada. David Wolfe thought it ahead of its time, as it aimed to direct public-sector pensions towards in-province investment. Voluntary, it was a fraction of the

Premier Bob Rae working on TV speech, 16 January 1992. Photo by Tony Bock / *Toronto Star* via Getty Images.

originally envisaged size and largely failed to attract public pension plans, leading some independent analysts to call it a "dismal failure."[37] Wolfe notes that the banks blocked its efforts at every turn. There would be no Ontario Caisse under the NDP thanks to ministers like Marion Boyd, who counted blocking the idea as one of her most significant accomplishments in government: "Getting the teachers in charge of their pension plan, turned out to be probably one of the most lasting things because that was a real burr under the saddle of most teachers and I mean the fiscal return from that plan was just disgraceful. It was awful."[38] The Ontario Teachers' Pension Plan was restructured so that its investments were no longer limited to government securities. Operating as "conventional finance capital," the now jointly administered plan quickly became "an important force for continuing the neoliberal privatization revolution."[39] The same is true of the other public-sector pension funds.

The growing ideological hold that progressive competitiveness had on the government's inner circle was on display during an internal seminar on economic partnerships organized on 30 July 1991. Those present included the Premier, cabinet ministers Floyd Laughren, Frances Lankin, Bob Mackenzie, and Allan Pilkey, trade union researchers D'Arcy Martin, Sam Gindin, Peter Warrian, and Ken Delaney, and various senior policy advisors as well as Judith Maxwell of the Economic Council of Canada. Laughren opened the conversation by stating that the government was interested in "forming partnerships with business, labour and others" as "a sign that we want to do things differently." He went on to say that the government's role was primarily as "facilitator of these relations." What becomes clear in reading the resulting conversation summary is the fundamental tension between the old class-infused politics of the party's election manifesto, and the new politics of social partnership. Someone said, for example, that the NDP government needed to "have a tough-minded discussion of taxation, auto insurance, etc, to see if these are compatible with its long-term partnership objectives." Those present also wondered how much

Ontario could realistically diverge from the rest of North America on economic matters and feared that the proposed labour law reforms might damage the government's ability to build business-labour partnerships over the long haul. There was even push-back on the government's early efforts to save Algoma Steel, Spruce Falls, and De Havilland from closure. For some, there was "too much emphasis" on "mature industries, and not enough on partnerships to develop future industries." They feared that "Ontario could be the Rust Belt of the 1990s if we don't invest in innovative firms" instead.[40]

There was general agreement by those in attendance that some instances of restructuring should be "facilitated, but others counteracted, in order to support the people who are being devastated by them." How the government was to determine which course of action to take, however, was left unsaid. But there seemed to be agreement that the government needed to respond strategically if Ontario was going to compete in the new global economy. The overall objectives of any NDP industrial policy thus needed to be geared towards competitiveness and the facilitation of restructuring. Finally, in an early sign of the government's slide into austerity politics, the group discussed how the government could leverage the NDP's reputation as a defender of the social safety net to make it "more efficient and productive, since it won't be accused of trying to dismantle the safety net."[41] It was a remarkable conversation, coming as it did during the fierce political backlash against the NDP's first budget, offering us a better understanding of the ideological underpinnings of the government's U-turn that September. What they were trying to do, explains John O'Grady, was to "shift the debate on economic planning, industrial strategy, from the traditional left-nationalist perspective, which [he believes] was predicated on high tariffs and Crown corporations to one that accepted the reality of a more globalized economy, or at least a more open economy. That it was going to be dominated by private capital, not public capital. And that the path to survival would be a high-skills path."

ONTARIO TRAINING AND ADJUSTMENT BOARD

The Ontario Training and Adjustment Board was supposed to be the cornerstone of the NDP's economic renewal strategy to position Ontario as a high-skilled competitor in the new global economy. Building on the foundational work of the Liberal Premier's Council, and drawing from the wisdom of other countries as well as the earlier work done in Hamilton, the government proposed to build an entirely new training and adjustment regime that combined sectoral and communitarian approaches within a multipartite agency. Its ambition was to transform Ontario into a model "unparalleled" in Canada or even North America. Not surprisingly, the government saw OTAB as the best candidate for its new partnership approach; it was a win-win for labour and business, as long as the government footed the bill. According to its chief architect Richard Allen, the Minister of Skills Development:

> The only way we can compete is to go in the direction of the most highly trained, best educated workforce we can produce in order to produce the finest, most competitive products in the most efficient fashion possible. Translated into principles, training for economic renewal means that training programs must be based . . . in the view of this government, on joint responsibility and co-operation between governments and labour market partners, and between employers and employees in the design, implementation and evaluation of training initiatives.[42]

If the original bipartite concept was very much tied to workplace training and adjustment, the NDP government broadened its scope enormously after three feminists in cabinet—Zanana Akande, Marion Boyd, and Elaine Ziemba—expressed their concern in May 1991 about OTAB's lack of inclusiveness and representation.[43] The OFL tried to make the case that the proposed labour-management bipartite structure could still reflect Ontario's diversity, but it was never simply about the social profile of board members, as these ministers wanted the community sector at the table as well.⁴⁴ They successfully made the case that traditional training and adjustment programs served women and racialized minorities badly, something we recognized in previous chapters. OTAB under the NDP would henceforth be a multipartite structure with representation from equity groups and community-based trainers as well.

With this shift, OTAB's mandate quickly expanded outward from workplace training and adjustment to cover workforce entry/re-entry, "multicultural" programming, literacy, help centres, English as a second language, and student training as well. But even this listing does not quite capture OTAB's extraordinarily broad mandate. Its enabling legislation, not passed until July 1993, indicated that it would "promote, support, fund, co-ordinate, design, provide and evaluate labour force development programs and services for the private and public sectors," carry out research and development, advise the Ontario government, enhance skill levels, develop common standards, and eliminate discriminatory barriers in training and adjustment.⁴⁵ That was a tall order, to say the least. Complicating matters further, OTAB would also coordinate a network of local training boards jointly with the federal government's own newly established Canadian Labour Force Development Board.⁴⁶ According to John O'Grady, who is said to have originated the idea for OTAB, the concept morphed to the point that it "was quite different from what had been originally envisioned." As a result, OTAB's governance structure became more and more elaborate.

The devolution of authority over training and adjustment was never going to be easy. Neil Bradford, a junior policy advisor in the Ministry of Labour during the NDP years, has since posed challenging questions about the feasibility of creating corporatist structures in North America, where there was "little history of collaborative planning and power sharing."⁴⁷ Not only that, but these were also highly polarized times. "Consensus among business, labor and social equity groups proved elusive," he wrote. That is putting it mildly. Instead of building consensus, OTAB only seemed to generate more polarization. It didn't help that the government let the labour market partners refine their own mandate "using the government's draft of the proposed mandate as a base," which led to months of infighting.[48] Soon enough the cabinet, too, became "frustrated with the ideological differences, protracted disputes and slowness of policy progress" in the new corporatist body.[49] Ultimately, Bradford contends that "the lack of tangible results in the face of a rapidly deteriorating economy eventually relegated it to the margins of the government's agenda." Given its organizational paralysis, OTAB ultimately collapsed "in part due to the weight of its own structural and policy complexity."[50] It was overly ambitious, ponderously developed, and incomplete by the time the government was voted out of office, and the board was put out of its misery by the incoming Tories. If the OTAB was an unmitigated failure, what is useful here is to ascertain the underlying reasons why the signature initiative of the NDP's economic renewal agenda went so terribly wrong.

When the Ontario cabinet adopted a strategic focus on economic renewal at its September 1991 retreat, it directed the OTAB design team, led by Minister of Skills Development Richard Allen, to prepare the consultation document and to bring it back for approval. The NDP's model, released as *Skills to Meet the Challenge: A Training Partnership for Ontario*, included a twenty-two-member board comprised of labour (8), business (8), equity groups (4), and trainers (2), as well as one representative each from the provincial and federal governments.[51] It was essentially the same breakdown as the federal Canadian Labour Force Development Board. There were also stakeholder steering committees and reference groups, which tended to harden the divides, delaying things further. The inclusion of equity groups opened a Pandora's box, as a succession of other groups demanded representation, eventually raising questions about the representativity of the Ontario Federation of Labour itself, since only 19.1 percent of Ontario's private sector was unionized. Business and private trainers demanded to know why non-union workers were not represented, and organized labour demanded that OTAB should extend to the public sector too. Questions were also raised about how decisions would be made.

Would there need to be a double labour-management majority, or perhaps a triple majority, with the inclusion of equity groups? Years were wasted trying to negotiate a governance structure and other process-related issues, delaying implementation. More than one person lamented that these meetings rarely talked about training itself, never mind adjustment.

At various points, there was real concern that the Ontario Federation of Labour would boycott OTAB. In July 1992, for example, OFL president Gord Wilson insisted that the federation's continued participation was now conditional on the inclusion of public-sector workers.[52] This prompted Richard Allen's staff to produce a confidential memorandum outlining options should the OFL walk away: it could delay implementation, concede the issue to labour, or proceed without them. Should it concede, the confidential memorandum cautioned that it would "leave the impression that the government's decisions are dictated by the OFL or suggest that conditions and ultimatums are useful forms of labour market partner behaviour." However, the staff found a lot of positives in proceeding without the OFL, as it would discourage ultimatums and reinforce "the view that the government is not captive to labour."[53] Allen phoned various union leaders, including Leo Gerard and Buzz Hargrove, to clarify the OFL's decision to only conditionally participate.[54] In the end, they agreed to set the public-sector issue aside for future negotiation.[55]

Meanwhile, business representatives were also unhappy with the trajectory of OTAB, fearing labour and equity groups would gang up on employers. Any possibility that a payroll training tax could be imposed at some future date was strongly resisted.[56] Most observers also suggested that the government's labour reforms further "soured" the climate at OTAB.[57] The Canadian Federation of Independent Business, for example, quit in protest in July 1991.[58] The increasing dysfunction at the Workplace Health and Safety Agency (WHSA)—another corporatist body, started under the Liberals, which certified and set training standards for job safety staff—led most of the business representatives on that board to resign. The Ontario Chamber of Commerce could therefore point to the WHSA as evidence that "a badly designed system of stakeholder representation can cause serious problems."⁵⁹ To avoid this fate, the chamber of commerce made the case that a double-majority at OTAB was needed, giving employers a veto. With the inclusion of community-based trainers, the proposed devolution of government responsibilities for training and adjustment also caused growing concern that it would undermine Ontario's network of community colleges and school boards.⁶⁰ Under the 1985 federal Canadian Jobs Strategy, community-based training organizations for women were integrated into Canada's training system.⁶¹ They were underfunded and usually paid their own staff low wages. Business representatives also pushed for the inclusion of private for-profit trainers.⁶² Richard Johnston, a former NDP MPP and chairperson of the Ontario Council of Regents, which was responsible for the college network, made the essential point that fully two-thirds of Ontario's training dollars had until then flowed to the colleges.⁶³ Naturally, he expressed concern that OTAB could "produce a balkanized and privatized product, which would be counter to the education and training interests of the government."⁶⁴ The community trainers, who were competitors for training dollars, then refused to accept the college network's nominee for the OTAB board, prompting Johnston to quit the steering group.⁶⁵ The OFL, for its part, sought to limit training funding to public educational institutions, as it, too, was concerned by the prospect of privatization.⁶⁶ Women's organizations, however, strongly opposed that position, as it would threaten the flow of future funds to their own "network of agencies in place to serve women, which are community based."⁶⁷ Private trainers and trade unionists were also at each other's throats during the lengthy province-wide consultations, as private trainers wanted access to government training monies, arguing that consumers should have choice. They also called for non-union worker representatives on the local boards to dilute the influence of the union movement.

If this sounds like a mess, it was. In his memoirs, Thomas R. Klassen, a senior policy advisor on labour market policy, blamed a lack of leadership, warring interest groups, and a focus on process rather than on training itself.[68] According to Neil Bradford, "the most notable outcome was a protracted, ideologically charged dispute among the social partners that prevented meaningful policy development."[69] Even John O'Grady, the originator of the OTAB idea, had seen enough. "Nobody there was interested in the training system," he told me. "They were interested in their own particular stake in the training system."[70] But it was Bill Thompson, the Hamilton union leader at Canadian Porcelain who subsequently worked for Richard Allen, who said it best: "The result has been the Wars of the Roses between training empires, local political fiefdoms, agents of the crown, and anyone else interested in a good, nasty, brawl. The players we most want to draw into the process (people of vision from business, labour, and the social action groups) are repelled by the minutiae of the debate and the obvious self-serving positions of most of the players."[71]

By 1993, even NDP-friendly journalist Judy Steed was calling this "noble experiment in power-sharing" a "nightmare on wheels."[72] It had become a "more bureaucratic, less effective training system than the one we currently have."[73] No wonder Rae never mentioned OTAB in his memoirs. In the cabinet shuffle of February 1993, Richard Allen was demoted and Windsor's Dave Cooke took over OTAB as part of his new education mega-ministry. Enabling legislation was only adopted in July 1993, more than two years after it was announced, and it wasn't fully implemented by the time the NDP was voted out of power. If any good came out of the OTAB fiasco, it was that the failed process sharpened the labour movement's own thinking on training and adjustment. The OFL adopted a policy statement at its November 1993 convention insisting that worker adjustment should be rules-based rather than something "voluntary," "consensual," or "cooperative."[74] Moreover, the OFL now believed that labour adjustment needed to be grounded in workplace dislocation and provide a strong disincentive to major layoffs and closures by requiring that employers cover more of the social costs. Some labour movement researchers even called the government's approach a "training trap," where adjustment and training became an "ideological legitimation device" that "blames the victim rather than the system."[75]

AN INDUSTRIAL POLICY FRAMEWORK FOR ONTARIO

Learning from the unfolding OTAB fiasco, the NDP's effort to develop an industrial policy for the province was a much more streamlined process. Flanked by the presidents of the Steel Company of Canada and the Canadian Auto Workers, Minister of Industry, Trade and Technology Ed Philip launched the forty-three-page *Industrial Policy Framework for Ontario* in July 1992, which aimed to promote "continuous innovation" and raise skill levels to help Ontario compete in the global economy. "It means working smarter," he declared.[76] The document set out the overall procedure for developing labour-management sectoral strategies that would help move Ontario to a high-value-added economy with the assistance of a $150 million fund. Developed by senior staff in the ministry, the framework was built on the analysis of the Liberal Premier's Council but was supplemented with some of David Wolfe's insights about sectoral strategies "drawn from the experience of some US states and the more innovative subnational jurisdictions in Europe" such as London's Greater London Council in the early 1980s.[77] According to Wolfe, the "approach to economic renewal" was "based on the premise that the traditional dichotomy between competition and cooperation is outmoded."[78] Hence, the purpose of industrial policy under the NDP was "not to substitute the plan for the market, but to shape and use markets. The focus of industrial policy should be on strategic sectors—those where an international competitive advantage can be secured by gaining organizational superiority."[79]

After interviewing Wolfe early on in my research, I had my homework given to me, as he helpfully recommended a long list of influential books from the late 1980s and early 1990s. Three stood out. The first, Michael Porter's *The Competitive Advantage of Nations*, published in 1990, had a huge impact on North American policy makers at the time.[80] During his previous work on President Reagan's Commission on Industrial Competitiveness, Porter had come to the conclusion that the national environment played a key role in the competitive success of firms. He offered a new theory of comparative advantage tied to education and training, infrastructure-building, and research and development. However, it was the other two books that primarily influenced Wolfe, starting with Michael Piore and Charles Sabel's *The Second Industrial Divide* (1984). The authors popularized the idea of "flexible specialization," a return to flexible manufacturing and craftsmanship, as well as the sustained innovation that results from having a network of such firms in close proximity, as in central Italy.[81] Michael Best's *The New Competition: Institutions of Industrial Restructuring* (1990) also impressed Wolfe, as it emphasized the importance of building cooperative relationships between firms and between management and labour.[82] Interestingly, Best himself worked for the UK's Greater London Council at the same time as Robin Murray, whom we will discuss in the next chapter. This constellation of ideas informed the NDP's Industrial Policy Framework, as the government attempted to "forge a new analytic and policy framework for the delivering of economic development policy— one which diverged from the traditional command and control form of policy implementation and from the use of traditional policy instruments such as tax incentives and direct subsidies to accomplish its goals."[83]

The Sector Partnership Fund, with a budget of $150 million over three years, applied some of the insights from regional innovative strategies already adopted in the European Union.[84] Instead of funding specific firms or troubled industries, the new focus was on self-identified economic sectors and cooperative linkages between firms. The government avoided the problem of picking winners by letting corporations and labour self-organize. It was a smart decision, as it shifted the onus onto unions, employers, and trade associations in a given sector. It was, therefore, voluntary, straightforward, and flexible. It sought to extend interaction within a sector, building linkages and leveraging private funding to match Ontario's contribution. According to Wolfe, the "overall goal of the framework was to promote the transition of the Ontario economy towards those sectors and firms with the capacity to generate higher wage, higher value added and environmentally sustainable jobs."[85] The fund was in operation within a year, and twenty-six sectors ranging from telecommunications to plastics and furniture-making had developed strategies by the end.

How successful, then, was the NDP's initiative? Not very, it seems, but to be fair it was cut short. Generally, business had no interest in partnering with labour in most industrial sectors. Just half of the $150 million budgeted was allocated by the time the NDP was voted out of office. A couple of the functioning sectoral initiatives, especially in auto parts, were also highly conflictual.[86] According to political scientist Douglas James Hall, strong business opposition to the initial draft led Rae to direct staff to create business focus groups to provide feedback, and the industrial framework document was significantly revised: "By May of 1992 they produced another draft and it went back out once or twice to these business people to see if it was getting more acceptable to them and each time it did it got a little more right-winged in slant." When Rae's office saw the new draft document, it had to be substantially revised again, as it had strayed too far to the political right. For Hall, it had become a disconnected, incoherent mess—trying to be all things to all people: "As a written document, it bore the scars of the ideological battle waged in its preparation."[87] Rae admitted as much in his interview with Hall, saying the Industrial Policy Framework had "too many objectives, and too many targets, and tried to do too much."[88] Hall therefore concluded:

> In the attempt to incorporate competing visions into a single document, the [Industrial Policy Framework] failed to articulate clearly a cohesive vision, and risked alienating constituencies in both the labour community and the business community. The document became a virtual "catch-all" for the articulation of bureaucratic and political views on economic development and its role in shaping society.[89]

It's a harsh assessment, but a compelling one. Wolfe blames business hostility to labour law reform for undermining the effort.[90] But Wolfe still maintains that the sectoral initiatives undertaken saw "a gradual evolution towards a more reflexive and comprehensive approach to managing the process of technological change."[91] Bradford largely agrees with this more positive assessment, suggesting that there were "two years of modest, incremental progress" and that Industrial Policy Framework's achievements "resided more in the process it engaged than in the products it delivered."[92] At the very least, the Sector Partnership Fund proved useful when the government needed to deflect opposition criticism for not doing enough on the economy. For example, Frances Lankin waved it around in the legislature as proof that the NDP government was planning for Ontario's economic future:

> The members opposite are talking and waving around the *Agenda for People*, which is a book. There's another book as well: *Industrial Policy Framework for Ontario*. This is the one I would like people to read. It's about two years old and it is the blueprint for what we're doing here in the province of Ontario, which is in fact turning around this province, which is contributing to economic renewal, to the creation of jobs and to creating a new framework for the future: an investment in jobs now, an investment in jobs in the future.[93]

The idea of an industrial policy was thus politically important to the Rae government's claim that it was managing the crisis, even if it delivered little in reality.

THE SOCIAL CONTRACT

Fighting the deficit took over much of the government's attention by 1992, eclipsing everything else. Ontario had become the world's largest non-sovereign borrower, drawing more than $1 billion on average per month.[94] Peter Warrian was at an OECD meeting in Paris in 1992 as part of the Canadian delegation when he received a phone call from Leo Gerard, his boss at the United Steelworkers, who playfully told him he'd been traded. Warrian recalls: "I said, 'What, you could? [laughing] Who'd you trade me to?' He says,

'Rae.'"[95] With that, at least in this perhaps fanciful telling of the story, Warrian became Ontario's new chief economist. He then recounts the chain of events that led to the Social Contract. Ontario's revenues were collected by the federal government. As a result, the province didn't find out until February each year what its fiscal position was for the previous April. There were, therefore, surprises:

> We're sitting in a room, trying to work on the coming budget, and we find out that we're $3.7 billion, the wrong way. And this is like, Laughren, me, David Agnew, Ross McClellan. Four of us. And we have to walk across the road, to the premier's office. Said we don't care what meeting is going on, here's where we are. And we started to get refusals in the bond market. They had to do something. And that's the middle of February, so what you see come out in March, in the Social Contract, is how to manage that.

For his part, Floyd Laughren recalls one pivotal meeting with the leadership of the Ontario Federation of Labour: "I don't know who all was there, I know Bob [Rae] was there. And one of the labour leaders said, 'Listen, private sector goes bankrupt all the time. So, what's to stop us from defaulting on some of our debts?' I thought I was going to come across the table at him."[96] Still shaking his head decades later, Warrian calls that meeting "sheer madness." If Ontario defaults, the "Americans will close the border, we'll have a 143,000 auto workers laid off, and these same guys will be in here, calling for us to be hung."

By 1993, the Rae government was increasingly feeling under siege. In Walkom's remarkably candid book *Rae Days*, we hear devastating on-the-record comments from a who's who of the Ontario NDP, calling the Premier's Office dysfunctional, that it was locked in a "bunker mentality," and most devastatingly, that it demonstrated "arrogance under siege."[97] Fighting the deficit took over their thinking, shaping the government's approach to

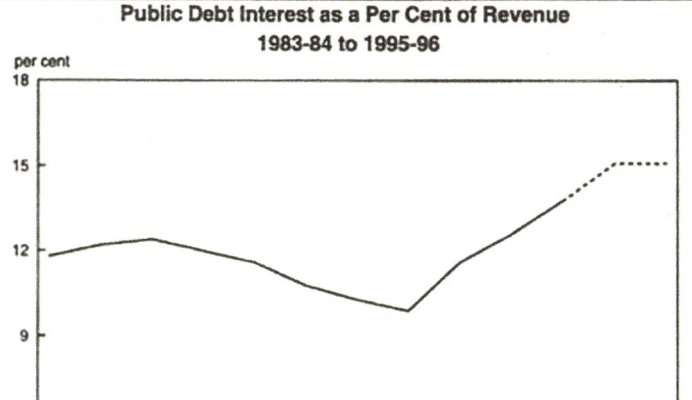

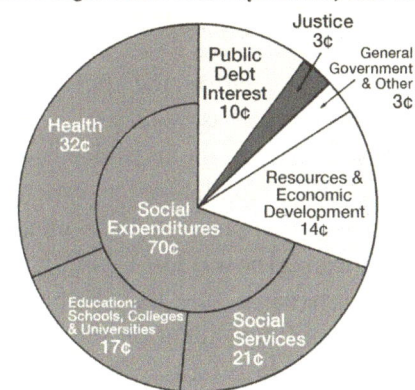

Floyd Laughren, Treasurer and Minister of Economics, *1992 Budget: Meeting Ontario's Priorities* (Toronto: Queen's Printer for Ontario, 1992).

welfare reform—one of the largest government spending areas. Initially, the NDP saw welfare as a form of income support rather than as a mechanism for labour market adjustment.[98] In its first year, it therefore increased social assistance funding substantially. McClellan speaks with real pride about this achievement, but others thought it a costly mistake. For his part, Laughren remembers "being very unhappy with the increase in the social assistance. But you were made to look like an ogre if you stated that."[99] However, attitudes hardened as the province's welfare rolls rose to 12 percent of the population. By 1992, there were 558,400 recipients of social assistance and 1,086,800 Ontarians, including children, "dependent" on social assistance.[100] Another 509,000 were on unemployment insurance, with 30,000 to 40,000 exhausting their benefits each month. Ontario's welfare spending thus skyrocketed from $2 billion to $6.2 billion. It didn't help that the federal government was restricting eligibility for unemployment insurance, pushing many people onto the already overstretched provincial welfare systems. To make matters worse, Brian Mulroney's federal Tories capped the transfer payments, reducing the federal government's share of Ontario's welfare spending from 50 percent to 28 percent between 1990 and 1993.[101]

In response, Laughren announced in his 1992 budget that the NDP would improve "mechanisms for the prevention, detection and recovery of overpayment and fraud" from social assistance recipients. The 1993 budget revealed even greater focus on the dramatically rising social assistance costs. The government now promised to reform the social assistance system itself, "linking people on social assistance to the workforce and hopefully as well doing something about child poverty in this province." Year by year, Laughren noted that welfare expenditures increased 20 percent in 1989–90, 37.9 percent in 1990–91, and 43 percent in 1991–92.[102] The industrial crisis was fast becoming a fiscal crisis.

At the same time, Rae also began to speak of welfare recipients as lazy and dependent on the state. On one occasion, he reportedly told business students that it made "little sense" to him to "be simply transferring monies to people so they can sit at home."[103] The government even hired 270 new inspectors as part of a new anti-fraud campaign, which uncovered very little.[104] When I asked McClellan how the NDP went from raising the welfare rate by 22 percent in its first year to joining the public witch hunt against welfare cheats, he returned to his favourite analogy of the "invasion of the body snatchers."[105] It could have been even worse. A leaked cabinet document from January 1993 revealed that the NDP seriously considered substantial cuts to social assistance, but the idea was quietly dropped as it proved internally divisive.[106] Instead, the government imposed new eligibility restrictions. Notions of underclass and cultures of poverty contributed to the growing moral panic, serving to blame the poor for being poor rather than the structural forces that were displacing hundreds of thousands. Nancy Fraser and Linda Gordon have rightly suggested that "dependency" is a moral stigma and thus, an ideological term.[107]

Launched as part of the 1992 budget, one of the major objectives of the Ontario Jobs Strategy was to reduce the projected growth of social assistance.[108] Writing to his federal counterpart, Laughren expressed concern at the prospect of their "potential permanent detachment from the labour market," noting that this was what happened after the 1981–82 recession when welfare case loads never settled down to their pre-recession levels.[109] Jobs Ontario directed funds towards training ($1.1 billion over three years to create 100,000 jobs for the "long-term unemployed"), capital ($2.3 billion over five years to build new economic infrastructure that generated 10,000 jobs in year one alone), and homes (construction of 20,000 non-profit housing units). Under Jobs Ontario Training, employers received a $10,000 training credit for each eligible worker hired. Twenty thousand child-care spaces were also promised to help single mothers re-enter the workforce. The Ontario Coalition for Better Child Care was highly supportive of the initiative, but pointed out that the principle of "first come, first served" for those on wait lists was well established in many communities.[110] There was, therefore, a danger of a parental backlash to perceived queue jumping. Expanding Ontario's child-care system was no easy task, as it took up to two years to license a new daycare in the province.

To move quickly, the government identified a network of local or regional brokers who would coordinate the training of those on social assistance for new jobs. Brokers were existing community organizations, thus keeping additions to the civil service to a minimum. The brokers ranged from community colleges to school boards, private trainers, and a variety of other community groups: "With the credit, employers, assisted by the community broker, would purchase training from their choice of trainers. Emphasis would be placed on the use of public institutions and community-based trainers." Employers had to declare that they had not laid anyone off to benefit from the financial incentive and needed to submit a detailed training plan with the assistance of the broker. The use of community-based brokerage agencies was justified on the basis that it contributed to community economic development and more community "buy-in."

The implementation of the brokerage system immediately ran into problems. Howard Hampton, the NDP's Solicitor General, wrote Richard Allen in June 1992 to complain about the unfolding process, in which he'd initially had such "high hopes" for the constituents in his sprawling northwestern Ontario riding. He noted that the area has "traditionally and systematically been the hardest hit by unemployment, recession or no recession," and thus needed the training funds on offer. Hampton had been told that the province-wide network of brokers would include a wide range of possibilities. But he now felt "cruelly misled," as organizations in his riding were contacted at the very last minute, too late for almost all to submit an application. As a result, only two did so, despite the great geographic distance that separated localities in the riding: "What happened to this much touted, ambitious outreach plan boasted about by your ministry??" Hampton's letter did not end there; he went on to say:

> As a government, we have often declared that one of our priorities was economic diversification and stability in Northern Ontario. While in opposition we long portrayed ourselves as a party that understands the factors that make the North special ie: community size, cultural sensitivity, aboriginal needs, access to health care facilities, geographic impediments, and dependence on resource and tourism based industries. As a result of this "understanding" we have been blessed with significant support in the North. These are the people who voted for us long before we became government. And here we are, once again, leaving them out in the cold.[111]

Hampton went so far as to complain that he had once thought it would become easier to represent his riding while in government but he was "dead wrong." Indeed, he continued: "What's the point of being in government if we can't even fulfil the meanest of our goals? It's more of a struggle for me now than it was then! This is very frustrating to put it mildly. It is my considered opinion that your ministry failed to execute its mandate. They did not make an effort to reach the people and organizations who would implement the goals of the JOBSONTARIO program. In my opinion a very cursory job was done." It is a remarkable letter, revealing some of the tensions within cabinet and the wider caucus.

Publicly, Richard Allen insisted Jobs Ontario Training was no "make work project," but rather a needed investment in the training and placement of the long-term unemployed.[112] Business representatives agreed that welfare caseloads needed to come down and strongly supported the training component as well as its linkage to economic development. Community-based trainers were also very supportive of the proposed brokerage delivery system, "in which a community agency takes responsibility for the development of a proposal which integrates the various program options (employment incentives, training, child care, etc) at the local level."[113] Both these groups, of course, had the most to gain from the government-funded program. Other voices were more critical. There was considerable concern that the training program would simply dump participants into low-skilled jobs, and in so doing exert "downward pressure on the labour market."[114] The Association of Municipalities of Ontario cautioned that some municipalities might see the program as a "workfare initiative and may coerce clients in a way that the program does not intend."[115] Trade unions, for their part, feared that the program would displace those already in the workforce unless employers were policed closely.[116] Even the government conceded that similar programs in the past had a 50 percent displacement factor and that it was difficult to police employer behaviour.[117] Yet nobody demanded the hiring of dozens of fraud inspectors to track down business cheats.

Soon after the program began, the CAW's Buzz Hargrove cautioned Allen that "good intentions can be easily derailed, on the one hand, by an overriding fiscal imperative to get people off the welfare rolls and, on the other hand, by an institutional process whose objective is to justify its own programs."[118] Hargrove argued that the jobs program was "poorly designed and runs the risk of being cynically implemented," claiming that subsidized trainees were already replacing existing workers in some companies. He cited Chrysler's assembly plant in Bramalea as a case in point, after it added a second shift. Chrysler was going to hire 1,300 people anyway, only now 650 of them were government subsidized. Hargrove then suggested that Jobs Ontario Training was making it more difficult to negotiate preferential transfer rights for CAW members laid off at other company plants, who were ineligible under the training program. It also bothered him that the first big government training announcement involved Linamar, a non-union auto parts plant in southwestern Ontario. Hargrove insisted that the government's initiative favoured non-union employers, as they didn't have to respect layoff lists when recalling workers. It was an essential point. Ultimately, the government's own research found that two-thirds of the job placements under the training scheme were in the lowest-skilled job categories.[119] This finding reinforces the impression that the program was more about the government's fight against the deficit than training people upwards.

At the same time that it was targeting those on social assistance, the NDP government decided to substantially lower the corporate tax rate from 14.5 percent to 13.5 percent and raise personal income taxes.[120] This was certainly not the kind of tax fairness that the party had promised during the 1990 election campaign. Initially, the NDP was going to set up a couple of joint working groups on each of the promised tax changes. The proposal then went to cabinet, where the property tax issue was added. According to Hugh Mackenzie, "at some point somebody decided, 'We've covered most of the waterfront, let's just cover the whole waterfront.'" The government therefore created the Ontario Fair Tax Commission to study the matter in depth. According to Wolfe and Rachlis, the commission produced "a mountain of quality research, analysis, consultation, and recommendations, the NDP government failed to deliver on large-scale reform of the tax system—wages went down, taxes went up (no fairness delivered)."[121] McClellan directs blame towards the commission itself, which produced a final report that was a "useless thing, hundreds and hundreds and hundreds and hundreds of pages. And it really had almost no impact."

My interview with Hugh Mackenzie, who served as the Fair Tax Commission's executive director, offers another perspective. Within three months of starting, Mackenzie realized that the commission had been "asked all the wrong questions. But we were stuck. We were stuck with the questions that we'd been asked."[122] He always believed that to focus on tax fairness without considering the expenditure side was "not even asking half the question. And it's profoundly misleading." A more useful question, he muses, would have been: "How do we build the fiscal capacity to create the state that we need to be able to deliver on social democracy?" A second question he would have asked related to the radical changes underway to the economic structure of North America and the world, yet the state's understanding of industrial development was rooted in the time before trade liberalization and free trade. As it stood, the "top of the house" question was "How do you do tax policy in a non-sovereign sub-national jurisdiction?" The commission also thought a lot about the relationship between tax policy and capital mobility: they tried "to dig into the underlying reality behind the threats of corporate capital mobility, and exploring the limits." How do you structure Ontario's tax system "so that you can defend your tax base"? They found that tax policy was not the most important factor in corporate investment and disinvestment decisions. Whether or not a jurisdiction could offer a non-union future was far more important. Over time, Mackenzie came to think of the temporary advantage that came with building new mills and factories: "Nobody builds an obsolete steel plant, right? You ask me the question, 'What is the most efficient steel plant in the world?' My answer is, 'The one that was built most recently.'" Expectations of many so-called experts were upended when low-wage countries also invested in the latest technologies instead of simply relying on lower wages to give them a competitive advantage. The combination of high technology and cheap labour in emerging economies had a devastating effect on North American workers. It was an interesting conversation, although it doesn't explain why the government balked at increasing corporate taxes or introducing new wealth or succession taxes.

The Ontario NDP's failure to tax the rich led the government to take a three-pronged approach to fighting the deficit in 1993: it would reduce its expenditures by $2 billion, raise an additional $2 billion from taxes and user fees, and save another $2 billion by reopening the collective agreements of public-sector unions.[123] This, in Laughren's mind, was analogous to a three-legged stool. As part of the Social Contract process, the government asked unions to voluntarily agree to a three-year wage freeze and twelve days of unpaid leave each year in order to avoid outright layoffs. The negotiations were prolonged and ultimately failed, leading the government to break the seal of collective agreements in order to legislate austerity. Laughren recalls:

> We tried very hard, and I give Bob a lot of credit for that. We tried very hard to sell that idea, that concept, and had a number of meetings where it was like a brick wall. And no, there wasn't that same sense of "we're all in this together" which you might get, say, in Sweden . . . And we weren't getting any headway, and yet, we couldn't back down.[124]

When I asked Rae about internal fault lines and debates within cabinet, he replied that they "really took shape over the Social Contract, which was a very difficult discussion for everybody. And I think, in the end, the fact that we held cabinet together, and a caucus with some dissenters together" was "kind of remarkable."[125]

Riel Miller says he wrote the original briefs about a negotiated Social Contract, circulating them "very quietly" six months before the "whole thing happened."[126] However, in our interview, he lamented how the big idea "descended into who's going to make the sacrifice to save the government." Once it went into collective bargaining mode "it was game over," he says. Ken Delaney has a somewhat different take on it. He thought the Social Contract was a mistake but for a different reason: "It was just bargaining 101 . . . like they thought it was such a good idea, giving workers these unpaid days off, that they presented it to the public as their idea. Like, man, bargaining 101. You bargain quietly and you let the other side get the credit. Yeah, I think they kind of blew that."[127] As for Peter Warrian, who helped lead these negotiations, he still thinks it was the right thing to do even if Laughren and Rae "were signing our death warrants politically, when we did it."[128]

Bob Rae's own views have softened over time. He told me that the "schism in the labour movement over the Social Contract" was because the government was trying to apply to the public sector what was already going on in "industrial contexts." After Algoma and Spruce Falls, Rae and his inner circle had "become very committed to the model," but it didn't work when they "tried to inject that model into the public sector." It was "in the end, very painful, and very difficult," he says. "I mean, it was a bridge too far in terms of the impact it had on the government." Smiling ironically, Rae remembers watching Barack Obama's inaugural speech as incoming US President and "he started talking about, it was a great thing when workers gave up a day's pay in order to save jobs in their factories, and he gave a shout-out to the American workers who'd done this. And I said, Here, it's the Social Contract. 'Rae Days,' you know?"[129]

A PARTY IN CRISIS

The Social Contract blew apart the Rae government's relationship with much of the trade union movement and nearly did the same with the party itself, prompting mass resignations and the disaffiliation of numerous union locals. Party membership fell from 31,791 in 1992 to 14,674 in 1994.[130] With membership collapsing and many unions breaking their formal ties, the Ontario NDP was thrown into financial crisis. Staff in the party headquarters even had to take unpaid leave to avoid layoffs. The Ontario Federation of Labour's statement in support of public-sector workers challenged the government's fixation on the deficit and its too-ready abandonment of long-standing NDP policies: "If there is to be a fight, it will be with the Premier of the province and those elected representatives who are not living up to the policies of the NDP and the labour movement."[131] Gord Wilson, OFL president, then requested that time be set aside at the next NDP Provincial Council meeting to discuss the "failure of the provincial government to implement our Party's policy."[132] The "dark and stormy" March 1993 Provincial Council meeting had already seen a clash between the party and the government.[133] Things quickly deteriorated from there. In late April, popular Windsor MP Steven Langdon was stripped of his role as finance critic in the federal NDP caucus because he forcefully criticized the Ontario government's fixation on deficit reduction.[134] Furious, Rae had phoned federal NDP leader Audrey McLaughlin demanding immediate action and got it. The disciplining of Langdon added fuel to the fire of outrage already burning brightly within the Ontario party and its union allies. For example, Arlene Rousseau, a member of the Ontario NDP's Provincial Council from Windsor, captured the rapidly deteriorating situation in her angry letter to Bob Rae:

> A lot of Ontario ridings are having problems renewing members. . . . An eighty-year old woman, who joined as a CCFer, would not renew her membership because she has had it with you and your government. In two days of calling, approximately two hours each day, I had twenty members quit with words for you. A host of other people will not renew at this time, as they want to see a change for the better in this socialist government. Members are angry over issues such as unaccountability.[135]

At its May meeting, the Ontario NDP executive discussed the latest wave of protest letters and resolutions from riding associations and union locals.[136] A Toronto local of the United Association of Plumbers and Steamfitters, for example, expressed its outrage that the "Government of Premier Rae has embarked on a course of conservative economics, in fighting the 'Deficit' and not Unemployment" and had abandoned a string of important party policies, culminating in the Social Contract. It demanded an emergency convention be held to "address the widening gulf between the direction of the Government and the programs and policies of the Party" and to consider the "demoralization of party membership" that has resulted. Other letters followed. A local of the Service Employees International Union, based in London, Ontario, notified the party that it was withholding its affiliation fees for three months in protest, suggesting it might formally disaffiliate at a later point if the government failed to change its current direction, a decision reached "after much soul searching and discussion," the local wrote. "We feel very strongly that this provincial government has betrayed our rights as trade unionists."[137] Clearly, then, the party's leadership was under intense pressure from below to stand up even more firmly to the Rae government.

The Provincial Executive met on 15 June to decide on a series of emergency motions submitted by affiliated unions and various riding associations. The most important of these, submitted by the Ontario Federation of Labour, called on the party to "demand that the government respect free collective bargaining and signed collective agreements, and provide public sector workers with the job security they are seeking." It also called for the Rae government to "shift direction away from the emphasis on reducing the deficit through reducing the size of the public sector, and adopt a 'jobs first' economic strategy."[138] Two emergency resolutions were then forwarded to the June 1993 Provincial Council meeting in the small eastern Ontario town of Gananoque, including the endorsed OFL resolution. The Provincial Executive demanded that the Rae government respect the integrity of free collective bargaining and shift its focus back to employment from deficit fighting.

By all accounts, the June Provincial Council meeting went to "the brink and back" with an all-day accountability session with cabinet ministers.[139] The council then passed the two emergency resolutions, with the OFL's resolution winning by a two-to-one margin.[140] The momentous day ended with Bob Rae's address. He began by making light of the perceived threat to his leadership, saying, "I have read my obituary in the newspapers, probably more often than Mark Twain." Rae then recounted the moments in his political career when the naysayers thought he was finished, but he'd surprised them every time. He trumpeted the achievements of his government, referencing De Havilland and worker ownership in the North as well as the wider "program of jobs and of justice."[141] He proceeded to list the many items in the *Agenda for People* that had been, more or less, delivered over the past three years. Yet, even now, he remained unapologetic about the Social Contract, telling delegates:

> I happen to believe not that we should be pulling back from the social contract, but that we have to extend it. We have to extend the idea behind it, and we have to extend it across the province and we have to extend it nationally. What it is about—hear me out please. We do have a debt problem in Canada, and we have one in Ontario. People may disagree with that statement, but I really fundamentally and profoundly believe that we do.[142]

At one point, Rae briefly recognized the "very strong and passionate views" expressed earlier in the day, but refused to engage further with the pain and hurt in the room. Instead, he dug in, saying the government was faced with difficult but necessary decisions. He had no intention of changing direction:

> I believe if we were to govern oblivious of the deficit—hoping it would go away, trying to ignore its impact on social programs, on job creation, on our children and on our future generations—I think we might avoid an argument internally. Sure, we might be successful in avoiding that, but I do not think we would be credible as a group of people who truly want to govern, which means taking responsibility.

A vast political gulf had opened up between government and party. However, the combined efforts of the union movement and the party's grassroots leadership failed to convince the government to change course: there would be no second U-turn.

Over the summer, Wayne Samuelson, the Ontario Federation of Labour's legislative director who regularly sat in on caucus meetings, drafted a discussion paper for the OFL executive board on "Labour and the New Democratic Party."[143] It spoke of how their histories were interwoven and why the legislative agenda of the Rae government had "resulted in a profound sense of betrayal." But Samuelson was quick to credit the party itself for standing in solidarity with the trade union movement and called on the OFL to take back "our party" by increasing, not decreasing, its participation. After the paper was circulated for comment, Jim Woodward, of the Canadian Union of Public Employees (CUPE), called it "extremely weak, both in terms of its analysis of the problems and the proposed solutions. It does not accurately outline the sense of crisis that exists in the progressive movements in Ontario because of the actions of the Ontario Government. Furthermore, it does not reflect the sense of outrage and betrayal our members feel over the manner in which this government has bought into the right wing agenda."[144] Woodward ended by saying that delegates at the upcoming OFL convention would be "looking for a paper that truly reflects the anger and frustration that is out there." Other comments were similarly critical. Jim O'Neil, the CAW's secretary-treasurer, thought the draft reflected "both a dangerous insensitivity of what is actually happening at the membership level, and a disappointing underestimation of how serious the present situation is for the 'labour movement.'"[145] Its general thrust, he suggested, missed "the depth of the crisis we face." O'Neil feared that "if not responded to properly, we may be at one of those turning points which signal a decline in unions (it happened in the US; it can happen here). Workers are frustrated in bargaining and, after the high of electing a 'friendly' government, even more frustrated with politics." O'Neil believed that the union movement was at a crossroads.

At its fall 1993 convention, the OFL voted to withhold support from any NDP candidate in the next provincial election, still a year and a half away, who had voted in favour of the Social Contract. Moreover, because the Rae government had "not respected the historic relationship" with the union movement, the OFL declared that it would "no longer depend on direct political involvement to ensure a progressive political agenda" and instead build coalitions around its agenda.[146] It was a pivotal moment in Canadian labour history, as ascendant public-sector unions flexed their collective muscle at a time when private-sector unionism was weakening due to plant closings and layoffs. The CAW's decision to support the hard-line position of public-sector unions was enough to decisively tip the balance on the OFL convention floor. In protest, thirteen private-sector unions, known as the "pink paper group," walked out of the convention and issued their own public statement of continued support for the Rae government.[147] They pointed to labour law reform, worker buyouts, pay equity, and other advances for labour.

Union affiliation with the Ontario party plummeted between 1992 and 1996 (see table of Trade Union Affiliation). CAW Local 222 in Oshawa was the single biggest loss to the party, with its 12,000 dues-paying affiliated members.[148] Overall the number of CAW locals affiliated with the party fell to 47, less than half of the previous figure, with another 10 locals directing their fees exclusively to the federal party and 10 in arrears. The Steelworkers were now, by far, the largest affiliated union in Ontario. Not

Ontario NDP Trade Union Affiliation, 1980–1996		
Year	Affiliated Locals	Affiliated Members
1980	562	225,185
1992	503	200,827
1996	369	136,681

Various Unsorted Union Affiliation Records for the Ontario NDP. Box 2003-027. 5/8. ONDP Fonds. Queen's University Archives.

surprisingly, the situation was even more dire in the public sector. Before the Social Contract, CUPE was the fourth-largest union in terms of the number of members affiliated with the Ontario NDP. No longer. Numerous CUPE locals voted to disaffiliate, including one Toronto local representing 9,200 workers. Quiet quitting led many others to go into arrears. Indeed, of CUPE's remaining 18 affiliated locals in November 1994, fully 13 were in arrears.[149] The party struggled to keep track of the quickly deteriorating situation (see pictured list with deletions). In fact, only 435 CUPE members were in affiliated locals in good standing. The situation was not much better at OPSEU (1,799 workers remaining) and the SEIU (6,300 workers).[150] The Ontario NDP's special relationship with the union movement lay in ruins.

In the face of growing opposition, NDP caucus members struggled to maintain control over their own riding associations. A motion, for example, was brought forward by a member of Hamilton West in May 1993 urging the party not to "scapegoat public sector workers in times of economic difficulty" and to instead implement fair taxation policies such as corporate and wealth taxes. The handwritten notes of Richard Allen, who represented the riding, suggest that the motion was "clearly set up against future contingency of failure of social contract, otherwise

```
CUPE Ontario Division                                              17
CUPE Toronto District Council                                     133
CUPE A/D       4045           Islington                         1,163
CUPE            -1-           Willowdale                        1,253
                  6           Sudbury                             241
                 45           Oshawa                              221
                -68-          Kitchener                           239
               -134-          Toronto                             500
                170           Elliot Lake                          76
               -185-          Etobicoke                           985
               -218-          Oshawa                              754
               -250-          Oshawa                              214
                771           Toronto                             200
                -801-         Kitchener                          -133-
              -1000-          Toronto                            -0,300-
               1023           Sudbury                             252
               1140           Timmins                              76
               1369           Val Therese                         198
```

Excerpt from New Democratic Party, Organizations Affiliated at 31 December 1992, with Changes to November 1993.

motherhood and no need."[151] If the motion had passed (it was ultimately tabled), Allen intended to move a second motion that the riding association urges the broader public sector to cooperate with the provincial government in the current Social Contract negotiations. His hostility towards public-sector unions came through in a letter to a disaffected party member: "The government has since 1990 been fighting to keep a healthy public sector afloat—to the tune of $28 billion of debt keeping public sector jobs afloat. That cannot go on. No, you *alone* are not the cause of this debt, but the entire public sector has been living off it, you included, and the entire public sector will be affected as we adjust our scale of operations a little closer to our means."[152]

Trade union anger at the Rae government even extended into the United Steelworkers of America. One of its largest locals in the province, Local 6500, representing INCO miners in Sudbury, saw a grassroots push in 1994 to disaffiliate from the party. Barry Tooley, chairperson of the local Political Action Committee, made the case for maintaining the formal link in a passionate two-page letter to members. He emphasized the "fighting record" of local NDP MPPs on meat-and-potato issues such as worker health and safety. "Ever since the sixties," he declared, "our Union has raised hell in Queen's Park over Inco's lousy safety practices and we have won lots of changes. We did so because we had a team of committed allies in the NDP." Otherwise, he wrote, "we would still be drinking dirty water underground [and] sintering plant widows would still be uncompensated." Notably, Bob Rae's name was not even mentioned in the letter. Indeed, Tooley's defence of the current NDP government was carefully worded and limited itself to the NDP's actions in northern Ontario:

> No government is perfect. But for workers in northern Ontario, this NDP government has demonstrated time and time again—by saving Steelworker jobs at Algoma, by saving paperworker jobs in Kapuskasing, by pumping money into Elliot Lake—that they are the only political

party that we can count on to put the interests of workers in the front of their agenda."[153]

This line of argument proved to be enough, as the local remained affiliated to the party, but one can once again see how the Rae government's bifurcated response to the industrial crisis played out regionally.

The federal NDP was annihilated in the October 1993 federal election, losing all of its Ontario seats and receiving just 7 percent of the vote Canada-wide.[154] It was a historic defeat. It was also the election when right-wing populism broke through in Canada. The Reform Party under Preston Manning had established its protest credentials honestly, by being the only major party to oppose Brian Mulroney's latest effort to resolve Canada's constitutional impasse. The Charlottetown agreement gave something to everyone in an effort to break the deadlock and bring Quebec back into the fold. The deal then went to a national referendum in late 1992, where it was promptly killed, despite the elite consensus. Bob Rae had invested considerable time in helping to negotiate the would-be accord and then campaigning for it, taking him away from other pressing issues. In truth, it drove his staff mad. When I suggested to a close advisor that Rae was a federal politician trapped in provincial politics, they replied: "One hundred percent, I don't think your characterization is unfair." Rae was most passionate about issues under federal jurisdiction, such as the Constitution and Indigenous rights. If the Charlottetown negotiations and referendum drew much of his attention, Rae acknowledges, "that's part of who I was, and part of who I am. I was concerned about that."

There was much finger pointing among New Democrats after the landslide victory of the federal Liberals, which reduced the governing Tories to two seats and the NDP to a rump group. Mel Swart, the beloved former NDP MPP for Welland-Thorold and the party's long-time champion of public auto insurance, held a press conference at Queen's Park to demand that Rae resign or be kicked out of the party. He blamed Rae's "union bashing in the

Social Contract and his hijacking of the party to the right" for the party's dismal showing: "Simply, Bob Rae, as Premier, has undermined, torn apart and trampled on the basic principles, policies and integrity of the NDP causing its members and supporters to turn away."[155] Soon thereafter, the media reported that unnamed "Rae backers" were "now talking about the need to rebuild the party without the labor movement, and without the one-third of the membership that has quit" in the past year alone.[156]

CONCLUSION

Neocorporatism's moment in Ontario was a brief one. The corporatist agenda was first destabilized by the labourism contained in *An Agenda for People*, especially the commitment to proceeding with labour law reform, and then the exigencies of the fight against the deficit, which resulted in the infamous Social Contract and the rupture with much of the labour movement. The rise of post-materialist politics further destabilized corporatism, shifting it from a labour-management partnership to a multipartite model, making it much more complex to implement, and distancing it from the very workplaces that it was designed for. The Ontario Training and Adjustment Board thus fell victim to long delays and a multi-directional tug-of-war. Further polarization resulted. No wonder David Wolfe, Riel Miller, and Chuck Rachlis all exited the government a year or two before voters delivered their verdict. By the end of the Rae government's five years in power, *Agenda for People* had quite literally become the punchline for a joke within governmental circles. When Rachlis, the advisor who had written much of the election manifesto, left the government in 1994, Ross McClellan organized a celebratory roast where all he did "was to read sections of the *Agenda for People*, which had people howling with laughter."

National Rubber Company: Maria Novias operating the multi-daylight sheet press, 1993. Photo by Peter MacCallum.

10

NEW LEFT COMMUNITARIANISM

> At its most basic level, community economic development is the community helping itself and investing in itself. It's a participatory process involving all community interests, founded on the development of a long-term plan, a commitment of resources and an accessible base of services that help to prioritize and address a community's needs.
> —FRANCES LANKIN, 1994[1]

In the bitter aftermath of the Social Contract, community economic development emerged as one of the distinguishing features of the Rae government's economic policy.[2] It offered an alternative to the old labourist politics, now in ruins, and the failed neocorporatist experiment, while still being grounded in the New Left's ambivalence or outright hostility towards the centralized state. New Left ideas about grassroots democracy and decentralized decision-making infused the rhetoric of community economic development.[3] As Hilary Wainwright, a British socialist feminist writer, has suggested: an "important, if implicit, dimension of the new left's radicalism since 1968 has been a rejection of the social wisdom of the all-knowing, social-engineering state. New movements have asserted a knowledge and an awareness of needs over which state institutions in their ignorance trample."[4] Local communities and marginalized "communities of interest" now became a central policy focus of Frances Lankin's new Ministry of Economic Development and Trade. Community economic development also had the virtue of being relatively cheap, making it a worthy handmaid to austerity politics. Ontario, Riel Miller explained, "faced with the first decline in absolute tax revenue in forty years and a limited capacity and scope for macro economic policies at the sub-national level, shifted emphasis to the micro level and supply side policies. This was the beginning of the CEDS [Community Economic Development Secretariat] story."[5]

But there were other, more tactical, reasons why the Rae government now turned to communitarianism. Stefano Harney, for example, has suggested that the government's CED initiatives "put public investment dollars directly into the hands of core NDP constituents, like grassroots women's groups, the environmental community, ethno-racial organizations and advocacy groups." Having been a member of the government's Anti-Racism Secretariat and then the CED Secretariat, Harney had seen how these groups failed to benefit directly from the previous emphasis on public works and worker buyouts. Now, he enthused, "these groups suddenly were to be treated as full partners in an economic program, not just social and cultural programs, and that meant in economics

There's just too many miles to walk yet to know what will happen, says Health Minister Frances Lankin, seen canvassing her Beaches constituents, 1 June 1991. Photo by Peter Power / *Toronto Star* via Getty Images.

ministries rather than just social and cultural ones."⁶ The women's movement played a key role in this policy shift towards a decentralized politics of diversity and inclusion.

When the NDP won a majority in 1990, it elected more women to the Ontario legislature than ever before. Bob Rae's appointment of eleven women to cabinet was unprecedented, leading *Chatelaine* magazine to publish a group photo of them on its front cover with the headline "Yes, Eleven Ministers." Most of these women, representing 40 percent of cabinet, came out of the women's movement and had direct experience running daycare centres or women's shelters or directing grassroots political action campaigns.⁷ Lankin recalls that it "made a real difference at the table in the discussions that we had around policy issues."⁸ My research certainly supports this claim. Feminist cabinet members were vocal in their criticism of the initial anti-recession investment in construction jobs, correctly noting that it benefited male workers almost exclusively. They were also effective in opening up the Ontario Training and Adjustment Board from a bipartite to a multipartite body, as well as the adoption of the "community broker" model for the Jobs Ontario Training program. Lankin herself cites pay and employment equity as well as certain changes in the health sector (specifically the new midwifery program and access to abortion) as key examples of their collective influence in cabinet. She then settles on the Ontario Jobs Strategy as the best economic example:

> One really interesting one is when we launched Jobs Ontario—we are in a recession, so we are trying to do some stimulus at local levels. The discussion around the table, because of the presence of women, acknowledged that most of the jobs are created in these kinds of programs are men's jobs. Well, what about women? And we began to do some more work.... As an example, I remember Evelyn Gigantes and I, and couple of others, put forward a proposal that we had to look at social infrastructure as much as physical infrastructure, and so that meant, you know, child care and expanding child care, and a few

other things. It was that marrying together of physical infrastructure and social infrastructure and working at the deficit of social structure in parts of the province that I thought was so cool at that point in time.[9]

The feminist reconceptualization of public infrastructure spending so that it included social infrastructure such as daycares constituted a key political innovation, helping to gender the government's overall economic renewal agenda. Government spending on child care increased 62 percent, mainly because it was tied to Jobs Ontario Training, given the government's efforts to bridge single mothers back into the labour market.[10] Community economic development also resonated with other so-called interest communities formed around race and ethnicity who had been largely locked out of economic decision-making in Ontario. Unfortunately, the trade union movement was almost entirely absent from these conversations, as the new approach centred on where people lived rather than where they worked.

After serving as Health Minister, Lankin's February 1993 appointment as Minister of Economic Development and Trade, a new economic mega-ministry in a reorganized and much smaller cabinet, signalled that the government was going all-in on community economic development. Lankin recalls that Rae told her that she would "bring an interesting perspective as both a trade unionist, a feminist—someone that fights for gender equality—and all of [my] activity before coming into government was volunteering and organizing at a community level."[11] She was steeped in the women's movement, having been a founding member of the Ontario Coalition for Better Childcare. After university, she had gone to work at the Don Jail as a correctional officer, becoming one of the first three female jail guards in a male prison in the province. Lankin then got involved in her union as its equal opportunities coordinator at a time when the labour movement was "really focusing on women's involvement and women's voices." Rae, she said, was therefore "fully aware of the kinds of sensibilities I would bring to thinking about the job." Once there, Lankin pushed hard not to just deal "with the Bombardiers, you know, all the big plants . . . but also a focus on community economic development and community loan funds, and working with finance cooperatives." The NDP's retooling of the Ministry of Economic Development and Trade reflected a new emphasis on developmentalism, whereby the state "plays an active role in economic reconstruction."[12] To some degree, it mirrored the approach already taken by the Ministry of Northern Development and Mines. Riel Miller left the Treasury to join the senior management team of the new ministry so he could ramp up its community economic development work, alongside Sue Colley, who worked closely with Lankin. They were therefore instrumental in the hiring of Robin Murray, a founding member of the UK-based Conference of Socialist Economists, as the new Assistant Deputy Minister responsible for the CED Secretariat. Colley, who worked closely with Lankin, had known Murray's work in the early 1980s when she lived in London, England. This connection, like those with Miller and David Wolfe, proved important. For her part, Lankin had first met Murray at a 1991 conference on democratizing public administration held at York University. The Cabinet Office and Management Board (a committee of cabinet responsible for controlling spending), headed by Lankin at the time, co-sponsored the three-day conference that brought together leading lights in social democratic public administration, including Murray, who had once headed the economic policy unit of the Greater London Council, a left-wing bastion against Thatcherism in the early 1980s, as well as Hilary Wainwright, a well-known British socialist feminist who had headed the GLC's popular planning unit. Lankin, who offered the conference's opening remarks, recalled that she was "just blown away" by Murray's "dedication to community and the work that he had done in government."[13]

In his conference presentation in Toronto, Murray argued that the modern welfare state was undemocratic and organized on Fordist mass production principles of top-down central control. According to him, the "word 'bureaucracy' invokes much of what is wrong; red tape; tackling situations by the rule book rather than with common sense, leaving initiative to the user, engineering situations so that the user rather than the official appears in the wrong, diverting responsibility to other departments, avoiding mistakes instead of solving problems."[14] In his mind, post-Fordist communitarianism rejected big government in favour of the devolution of powers to local communities as well as wider communities of identification such as women's groups and those representing racialized or immigrant communities. Communitarianism in Ontario was complementary to neocorporatism, with Wolfe and Miller both speaking of their admiration for Murray and the ways that community economic development and corporatism were part of the same ideological impulse.[15] One of the few oppositional voices at the York University conference was that of American sociologist Frances Fox Piven, widely known for her work on poor people's movements, who suggested that the New Left's "distaste for the social welfare state was counterproductive." She reminded the conference that the social welfare state emerged out of the redistributive class politics of an earlier generation of progressives.[16] I would only add that community, while warm and fuzzy, is an ideologically ambiguous concept that actively submerges internal power structures and competing interests, not unlike "nation" itself.[17] It is also telling that the turn to local community in Ontario occurred alongside, and in response to, the globalization of capital.

ROBIN MURRAY AND THE GREATER LONDON COUNCIL

The Greater London Council in the UK was an important point of inspiration for Ontario New Democrats. The New Left controlled the GLC from 1981 to 1986, at which point Margaret Thatcher abolished the authority. When the Labour Party was first elected, it had promised a new industrial strategy for the deindustrializing metropolis. Manufacturing employment had fallen by 33 percent between 1961 and 1981, leaving only 150 surviving factories in Greater London employing more than 500 workers each in 1979.[18] By 1982, this number had plunged to just 75.[19] If London had almost a million factory workers in 1973, only 594,000 remained a decade later. Trade union resistance was fierce, with dozens of plant occupations, but failed to stop the destruction of workplaces and neighbourhoods, inflaming the inner-city crisis in the process.[20] In a sign of the times, nearly half of the Labour Party's mammoth 150-page election manifesto in 1981 was dedicated to industrial and employment policy:

> There are today three great issues facing the British economy: deindustrialisation, the economic collapse of Britain's major cities, and the conditions of life and labour of Britain's working people. They are not separate, but three alternative aspects—sectoral, spatial and social—of a common economic problem. In each case London has been at the eye of the storm.[21]

Like many Canadian left-nationalists of his generation, Robin Murray was influenced by underdevelopment studies and the dependency school in political economy. Before joining the GLC, Murray had worked at the Institute of Development Studies, where he'd focused on the Global South.[22] This global perspective gave him a unique take on the British metropolis, observing that "London's economy survived because of the empire" and its subsequent crisis was a manifestation of decolonization.[23] Under his leadership, the economic policy unit sought "social control over the process of restructuring" through popular planning, which culminated in the publication of the London Industrial Strategy in 1985.[24] It included twenty-three sectoral strategies "which highlight the restructuring process in each sector and their effects on workers."[25] Its stated goal was to restructure manufacturing *for* labour, emphasizing the development of a "consensus restructuring path" based on value-added, high-skill jobs as well as worker cooperatives. The GLC also focused on community development projects, the "archetypical model of the 'new urban left.'"[26] The London Labour Party's linkage of class, race, and gender was ahead of its time, as was its commitment to true participation.

If all this sounds familiar, it should. Murray, like David Wolfe later, was influenced by Piore and Sabel's research on Italy's

Emilia-Romagna region, which framed the economic transformation underway as one from Fordist mass production to flexible post-Fordist production.[27] Indeed, Michael Best, who published *The New Competition* in 1990, with its emphasis on the value of inter-firm linkages in Italy rather than the "bailout of sick firms in dying industries," worked closely with Murray at the Greater London Council.[28] Murray's industrial policy committed the GLC to make strategic investments in order to bolster London's manufacturing sector.[29] To that end, it created the Greater London Enterprise Board as "a new form of local state investment bank which would put public money into those higher-risk but employment-creating businesses the City and private banks— with their short-term profit horizons and preferences for overseas investments—ignored."[30] By requiring enterprise plans (for future production, investment, and job levels) for the troubled businesses that it invested in, Murray attempted, with mixed results, to involve the workforce in planning. His experience made him a convert to sector strategies rather than firm-level rescue efforts, a perspective that was shared by other members of the Ontario NDP brain trust.[31] Through these efforts, the GLC became a "genuine symbol of radical and effective government" that garnered considerable international attention and acclaim.[32] Yet researchers have since found that the concrete achievements of the GLC's industrial policy did not match the hype: "It is notable that much of what the GLC set out to do has not, in fact, happened. The grandiose claims of the [Greater London Enterprise Board] to be intervening in key sectors to 'restructure' them technologically and organisationally were not fulfilled."[33] This, as we will see, is a cautionary note that is just as applicable to Ontario's own experiment in community economic development.

After the demise of the GLC, Murray's influence continued to grow with the publication of a series of articles in *Marxism Today* on the need for the left to abandon its love affair with Fordism. His 1985 piece on "Benetton Britain" spoke of the decentralization of industrial production, using the example of the well-known Italian clothing company Benetton. Its colourful products were produced by a thick network of small contractors in the Italian region of Emilia-Romagna. Murray, like Wolfe and others, was therefore influenced by the "diffuse industrialisation" model that privileged small and medium sized firms rather than the largest ones.[34] As Murray wrote:

> The present economic crisis should be seen first and foremost as a crisis of restructuring. It is a restructuring which is taking place at great cost. The priority for the Left should be to intervene in this restructuring in order to change its course. This requires detailed popular planning, sector-by-sector and firm-by-firm, and the development of a material capacity for intervention at a national, as well as a local, level. This is what I mean by a strategy of alternative production.[35]

As we saw earlier, Murray then extended his post-Fordist thinking to the public sector itself, as it, too, was mostly Fordist in design, delivering standardized mass services.[36] To counter these "deep structures of Fordism" in the public sector, he called for a "new model of the public economy made up of a honeycomb of decentralised, yet synthetic institutions integrated by a common strategy."[37] Community economic development was therefore highly attractive to New Leftists outside the labour movement.

These two essays were foundational to the New Times project to rethink the British left for a new epoch, led by Stuart Hall and others at *Marxism Today*.[38] The influential 1989 book that resulted opened with the New Times manifesto and then Murray's two essays, before moving to twenty-nine newly written ones. The manifesto blamed the crisis of the left on its own "failure to find a role in the new times." Any future left-wing project must, the authors argued, "abandon any commitment to the centralising national state" and recognize social movements and post-materialist politics. This was especially urgent given organized labour's "gradual estrangement from society."[39] In effect, this approach was the marriage of communitarianism and socialism.

Some have since suggested that the New Times initiative provided the intellectual foundation for the progressive neoliberalism of Tony Blair's New Labour. After all, several writers in the group later became prominent Third Way thinkers. David Marquand, for example, was critical of the hold of Fordism on the imagination of the Labour Party, equating Fordism to an industrial prison.[40] Blair's New Labour government made communitarianism, and with it the idea of social citizenship, its intellectual foundation. After working with local economic development practitioners in South Africa for six months in 1992, Murray relocated to Ontario to lead the NDP government's own efforts, heading the Community Economic Development Secretariat from 1993 to 1995.[41] He was one of the smart "unusual people" brought into government that Rae expressed such pride in during our conversation. According to Stefano Harney, who worked with Murray, his "New Times orientation helped him interact with and activate myriad grassroots groups within the movement of the party. He quickly gathered others around him from inside and outside the government who shared his vision."[42]

ONTARIO'S NEW TIMES

The territorial approach to economic development in Ontario had hitherto been limited to historically disadvantaged or underdeveloped parts of the province, such as northern Ontario. With community economic development, a modified spatial approach was extended to the entire province and tethered to localities or communities of interest rather than region. No longer would the state be solely concerned with issues of "spatial redistribution," but rather with the "co-ordination of local and regional economies, the supply of inputs, the organisation of transport, and of land use planning."[43] To that end, the NDP cabinet approved a new policy on Regional and Rural Development in 1992 that laid the foundations for the new community-centred approach.[44] The Community Economic Development Act, passed the next year, enabled the creation of CED corporations, which were key to the government's overall strategy, as they were supposed to "set the stage for establishing stronger linkages and, ultimately, a more self-sufficient community."[45] In the new rhetoric of the times, there was, therefore, a move away from government being a "dispenser of financial aid" to government becoming a catalyst for "communities in planning and co-ordinating their own economies."[46] Like the setting up of corporatist bodies, the NDP sought to decentralize economic decision-making and devolve powers to stakeholders. At the same time, the government sought to extend economic democracy through the promotion of community enterprises, cooperatives, not-for-profits, and participatory economic planning more generally with the goal of the "decentralisation of economic decision-making at all levels of government."[47] This all sounds great, of course, but did it really engage substantially with the root causes and effects of the industrial crisis and create new jobs? Government promotional materials trumpeted job creation numbers whenever possible, but remained largely silent on the statistics in this instance—community economic development's ability to create permanent jobs was clearly limited. Ross McClellan, for one, doesn't think much of this approach, dismissively calling it "socialism light," and almost "meaningless."[48]

For better or worse, community economic development represented a signature initiative of the newly "transformed" Ministry of Economic Development and Trade under Frances Lankin's leadership, "with a broadened mandate to stimulate economic growth within our communities."[49] The ministry now sought to support communities as well as business and labour. According to Lankin, "most of all, it harnesses the creativity and energies of communities so that they can take control of their own destinies. Focusing these local energies helps to prepare communities for the rapid changes and challenges that define life in the nineties." In her mind, a strong network of communities provided the foundation of a strong provincial economy. "As we struggle with the recession, with its attendant job losses, plant closures and reduced financial stability," she explained, "we see a new opportunity to address our needs in innovative ways."[50] Lankin's aspirational communitarian language of economic self-sufficiency and grassroots democracy set the tone for the government's efforts in this area. The new approach, however, proved challenging for existing bureaucratic structures. Lankin told me:

> I had to spend a long time sitting and talking about what I was envisioning and why I thought it was important, and why the party over the years had supported the co-op movements—whether it's housing, food, or banking, or whatever—but that there was something about how you build community by empowering people to have a direct impact on their future, their families, and the people who live around them, and that strong communities have a resilience to them that is so ever helpful in difficult times, and there were certainly difficult economic times going on at that point.[51]

The government's emerging policy commitment to community economic development was bigger than any one ministry, even that of Lankin's new mega-ministry. Created in November 1993, the new CED Secretariat coordinated these efforts across a dozen ministries. Murray's brief was to develop a coherent strategy, support on-the-ground initiatives, set up pilot projects, and be the direct link between communities, front-line staff, and the government. His time in the secretariat was remembered for its wide-ranging—some might say scattered—CED projects from local bakery networks and francophone food cooperatives to food box schemes, Black music industry coalitions, First Nations cultural infrastructure, and community agriculture.[52] Emerging industrial districts were identified and efforts made to further "deepen" telecommunications in Ottawa, engineering in Kitchener-Waterloo, and cultural industries in Toronto. The secretariat's focus was on southern Ontario, as the funding in the North was simply channelled through the Ministry of Northern Development and Mines.

The cabinet's implementation strategy included new community financing tools. Fourteen community loan funds and eight community share corporations, involving provincial guarantees worth $9.2 million, were approved after legislation received assent in late 1993. Within a year, these community funds had provided more than fifty loans, mainly to business development corporations, of which only four defaulted. The Community Investment Share Program provided designated organizations the power to offer micro loans of up to $15,000 each for business start-ups or business expansion, backed by a 100 percent provincial guarantee. Nine community share corporations were approved by October 1995.[53]

The clear focus of community economic development in Ontario, as elsewhere, was on the ascendant new economy, rather than the declining old, to fill the void left by deindustrialization. There was also thought given to how these place-based efforts could be linked with the wider sectoral strategy. According to the strategic review of the government's community economic development efforts in 1994, authored by Murray himself:

> The policy of promoting small and medium firm innovation quickly raises the issue of local industrial policy. On the basis of the European and US experience, it requires the support of sectoral networks, of co-operation between the enterprises and public institutions, notably training providers, specialist colleges, research institutions, and the municipal and field offices of government.[54]

Here, again, we see the clear influence of the post-Fordist assumptions underpinning New Left thinking:

> In the past industrial policy has focussed on the promotion of mass production, notably through the attraction and support of branch plants, or through the overseas expansion of Ontarian mass producers. With increased globalisation and the reduction of provincial and national protection, there has been an exodus of plants, and the fear of a reduced supply of new investments. It was this which helps explain the Government's emphasis on endogenous

economic growth, and its interest in CED as a means to promote more integrated local economies. The idea of more rooted local economies, which also applies to economies based in strong communities of interest, provides a potential link between CED and sector strategies, and with the financial and labour market policies that formed part of the supply side approach.[55]

The complementarity of community economic development with the neocorporatist impulse, laid out in the previous chapter, is evident. Small business development was promoted and participatory economic planning undertaken in the name of the "democratisation" of the economy and the "empowerment of marginalised communities."[56] This shifting perspective is lionized throughout the archival record, though its tangible accomplishments are hard to discern.

JOBS ONTARIO COMMUNITY ACTION

The primary delivery system of community economic development was Jobs Ontario Community Action (JOCA), part of the suite of programs within the NDP's Ontario Jobs Strategy. JOCA directed $300 million over three years to communities with the idea that they would have more say in their own development.[57] To some degree, the program repackaged and reoriented twenty-two existing programs across six ministries, now delivered jointly by inter-ministerial teams and four hundred field staff.[58] It was an experiment in post-Fordist public administration, "empowering" civil servants in new ways of working. After the first year, 831 grants were approved for a total of $110 million. Most of the recipients represented rural areas or smaller towns, which reflected the profile of the previous programs that were merged into JOCA.

Robin Murray penned a relatively clear-eyed self-assessment of the CED program, noting that much of the funding was directed towards the building of recreational and tourist infrastructure, as it always had, things like marinas, arenas, community centres, and baseball diamonds. JOCA funds also encouraged the expansion of commercial spaces inside community centres and museums in the name of encouraging local entrepreneurship. Fully 11 percent of funding went to Indigenous communities, and Ontario's Afro-Caribbean community was also prioritized in the wake of the "disturbance" on Yonge Street in May 1992 that resulted in an inquiry led by Stephen Lewis into the challenges facing Black youth in the province. JOCA thus funded a new Black business resource centre, a Black credit union, the Caribana festival, and Black entrepreneurship more generally. Women's organizations were also prioritized with another twenty-one projects.[59] However, only 4 percent of the funds were classified, even by Murray, as "innovative" in the first six months. In looking back over the program's first year, Murray later wrote that the "one over-riding conclusion" was

> the difficulty of moving from a more inclusive process of economic planning to sustainable projects. It is the problem of how to connect CED to the mainstream economy, to production and trade, and to the macro issues of employment. In general, in the practice of CED, Ontario has been stronger on process and on creative micro projects, than on broader questions of economic development. The task for JOCA's second year is how to relate the micro projects to these broader issues in order to maximise the developmental impact of the funds available.[60]

In other words, these efforts had minimal economic impact and largely failed to respond to the wider structural challenges faced by the province. They were stronger at building community than developing the economy. Murray's subsequent January 1994 review of JOCA was similarly damning. Many of the community envisioning exercises undertaken as part of the program were said to have been dominated by the "local economic elite." Just because it was local did not necessarily mean it was more democratic. Murray's analysis of the concept of community is worth quoting at length:

They [communities], too, like all social organisations, have their power structures, based on gender, age, class and knowledge. The concept of community is in short ambiguous and problematic. Shifting power to communities does not in itself solve the problem of economic democracy but rather poses it at a different level. Nor does it solve the problem of inclusiveness. Communities by their very nature exclude as well as include, and within themselves they privilege some and marginalise others. This is not to say that the project to shift economic power to communities is a mistaken one, nor that the concept of community is not useful. Rather it is to recognise the difficulties, the tensions and the tasks in the making of communities. This is the key point. Communities are not a given. They are made and remade.[61]

Murray went on to speak of the US communitarian movement and the theoretical work of sociologist Amitai Etzioni. Given the fraying social structures that make community cohesion and belonging possible, community economic development "seeks to provide not only an economic underpinning of community, but a means for communities to 'make' themselves positively. That means recognising differences. . . . It also involves finding ways of developing shared perspectives, and even more important, common projects. For it is in doing things together that communities are made."

Administrative problems with the program were also identified. Murray had tried to tear down "departmental silos," empowering inter-ministerial area teams. This decentralized approach within the government's own civil service had decidedly mixed results, what Murray calls "the dark side of a post-modern administration." The lack of detailed assessment criteria didn't help. Yet Murray continued to wax eloquent about the flexibility of his "post-Fordist work teams" and the efforts to empower line workers. He contrasted his approach to the centralized "regulative" state, with its "distance between front line workers and the public.

A developmental approach depends on a closer interactive relationship." He saw government entering a "second transition," away from rules-based "regulatory bureaucracy" to a more "creative" and democratic "developmental bureaucracy."[62] This was no easy task in his mind:

> Up to now governments at all levels, and in all parts of the world, have found it difficult to make this transition, since the changes require a deconstruction of many of the central pillars of regulative bureaucracy, and their replacement by new forms of accountability, control, decision making and reward, by new types of professional skills, and new relations between public service and civil society. The changes taking place through JOCA involve nothing less than this. They are an attempt at inventing the transition. As the tasks at hand force old ways of doing things to be discarded, staff involved are having to develop new ones. The changes are not taking place according to a blue print mapped out by external management consultants and conveyed through disembodied training courses. They are taking place at every level of administration on a day to day basis, and . . . it is remarkable how much has been achieved within a year.[63]

Thus, for Murray, the "heart of JOCA's problems" was the fact that it was being introduced by a rules-based "regulative administrative structure" rather than any shortcoming in his own post-Fordist approach or community economic development itself.[64]

In Riel Miller and Isabella Bakker, Murray found kindred spirits. They championed the fact that new forms of public administration were starting to bud during the NDP years. They saw in the emergence of alternative state forms, such as community economic development, the beginning of the "disintegration of Fordism" in the public sector.[65] Indeed, "on the frontier where state workers meet citizens," they wrote, "important changes are taking place in what and how the state produces." According to Miller and Bakker, these "'grassroots' administrative reforms reflect a pragmatic response to both the reduction of public funding for many welfare state activities and the locally specific pressures created by economic, demographic and social need. In this period of disintegration of the old order, decentralization and flexibility are provoking the development of alternative methods for the provision of collective service as well as new types of public goods." They went so far as to claim that Jobs Ontario Community Action represented "a new way of government doing business with communities." Despite the high praise, however, they admitted that most of the funded JOCA projects were either developing tourism strategies, especially beautification projects, or undertaking "traditional forms of infrastructure" building that were "at best tangential to the challenge of economic transformation required to maintain existing economic activity and to introduce new ones."[66] In this regard, the program supported the decisive turn underway from manufacturing to bright new post-industrial futures.[67] Place rebranding efforts and culture-led redevelopment of former industrial and railway lands thus constituted much of the reality behind the lofty rhetoric, with its inevitable contributions to gentrification processes in some localities.

In our wide-ranging interview, Riel Miller conceded that his personal and class "bias" was "towards fluidity," though he appreciated "the fear that that induces or the pain and the loss that that can induce. But from a resilience perspective," he told me, "it seems more promising to me than defensive positions, than rearguard desperate actions, and less fear-based and more aspirational, positive aspirational."[68] Chuckling, he added that "resisting change always seemed to me to be a kind of stupid position to take." To ground his point, he recalled flying into small northern Ontario communities as part of his work with JOCA:

> The single-industry towns, places . . . where mines had been shut down or the paper plant had been shut down. And to go through the experience of saying, "Why are you accounting for your assets this way? Why are you buying

into some form of evaluation that has no bearing on the wellbeing and the value capacity of your community?"... To some extent it didn't sit that well because the mayor and the chamber of commerce and the trade union all wanted to figure out how Ontario could pay for Abitibi to come back. And what I was saying was, "Tell them to take a hike and think about how you can create your own community." These were pretty artificial communities to begin.

Community economic development, like skills training and post-Fordist thinking as a whole, was anchored in human capital theory, which treated human skills or knowledge as demonstrably valuable to the capitalist economy.[69] After he returned to the OECD, Miller authored the 1996 report *Territorial Development and Human Capital in the Knowledge Economy: Towards a Policy Framework*, where he used the example of Ontario's CED experiment to show how it sowed "new ways of thinking about local economic development." At the same time, he freely admitted that Ontario's "new territorial development policies" were a product of the fiscal crisis, as the NDP tried to find ways to "slice and dice" or reallocate, redeploy, and re-engineer existing programs. Miller concluded by saying that the Ontario NDP's CED experiment "worked because it helped make better use of human capital."[70]

CONCLUSION

Class analysis was on the wane inside the NDP long before the election of the Rae government in 1990, but once combined with the anti-state politics of the New Left, social democrats became very susceptible to neoliberal thinking.[71] Journalist Thomas Walkom, for one, came to this conclusion in 1994 when he wrote that the Rae government "no longer had a clear critique of either the economy or class."[72] Bryan Evans, a former civil servant in the Ministry of Labour, likewise points to Rae's lack of "any kind of political economy imagination" to explain why the government slid into austerity politics. It is not a big jump to suggest, as I do here, that the mirage of community self-reliance (in a world where capital is free to move across borders at will) provided ideological cover for this retreat.[73]

Another point of political contestation was over the effects of community economic development on grassroots organizations and the ways that they were transformed into a "dense network of contracting and subcontracting chains," undermining the public sector.[74] This new relationship with the state served to depoliticize community groups, who grew dependent on government funding. One of the first to raise critical questions was Roxana Ng, who published her study of a community-based employment agency in Toronto, entitled *The Politics of Community Services: Immigrant Women, Class and State*, back in 1981. Ng offered an early warning of the dangers of contracting out to community-based organizations in the name of grassroots autonomy or democracy.[75] Community groups risked becoming "an extension of the ruling apparatus through the funding arrangement" due to the practical need to maintain good relations with employers. These relationships led the organization (which was the subject of her case study) to turn its back on advocacy, focusing instead on individual worker placement. In her case, it also served to reinforce immigrant women's inferior position in the labour market hierarchy by matching their marketable skills and work experiences with the stated requirements of employers:

> A constant feature was that clients of the agency ended up in minimum wage, assembly-line jobs or as restaurant and domestic help. Unless a client had a high level of command of English and officially recognized educational credentials, it was almost impossible to enrol her in a skill-upgrading or job-training program.[76]

Much the same point could be made about the Rae government's resort to the "community broker" model to deliver its Jobs Ontario Training program. Ng argues this approach was a "compromise arrived at by two opposing forces: the need to cope with changing social and economic reality by the state on the one hand, and the increasing militancy of minority groups and their advocates demanding social programs to meet their needs on the other." However, in this accommodation, she found that worker adjustment became depoliticized, and displaced workers were themselves blamed for their own situation. If only they had been more flexible, had more education or a better can-do attitude, maybe then they would not have faced such difficulty adjusting to change. Geographer David Harvey, among others, has spoken in terms of the NGOization of the left during the 1980s and 1990s.[77] Communitarianism was central to the discourse of Third Way social democrats like Tony Blair, who identified community as one of the four core values.

National Rubber Company: Balbar Gill and Hang-Ji Hi uploading a sheet press, 1993. Photo by Peter MacCallum.

CONCLUSION

THE SEDUCTIVE MIST OF PRAGMATISM

> As Premier-elect Bob Rae ponders the shape of Ontario's first socialist government, he finds himself steering between two shoals. On the one hand lie the jagged rocks of too-much-too-quickly. On the other side, hidden behind the seductive mist of pragmatism, sits the reef of compromised principles.
> —THOMAS WALKOM, 8 September 1990[1]

If journalist Thomas Walkom offered a prescient warning to the incoming NDP government, just days after its unexpected election victory, even he could not have predicted that the high winds and stormy seas of the industrial crisis would lead the Rae government to quickly strike the jagged rocks of trying to do too much too quickly in the first year, damaging the ship of state, only to be wrecked in the mist of pragmatism after the government's too-sharp course correction. One can feel for the first-time captain and crew thrown into the thick of it without their old ideological compass—which was no longer trusted and quickly tossed overboard. There was a steep learning curve and mistakes were made. Chuck Rachlis and David Wolfe, two senior deckhands, looked back and concluded: "Constrained by its past, and deluged by the demands of trying to navigate a new course, even as it learned to manage the controls of an ill-equipped and slow-to-respond ship of state, the NDP did not transform itself quickly enough to avert the loss of much of its public support."[2] The party's five years in power nevertheless changed them. If the NDP entered government as a labour party, it left it five years later bitterly divided between those in Queen's Park whose thinking had evolved to something resembling the Third Way social democracy of Tony Blair or Bill Clinton, and the party's activist and labourist membership, who remained anchored in protest and the old redistributive politics. Their divergence was so great that the other side increasingly seemed unintelligible.

The defeat of the NDP government in June 1995 was no big surprise. One senior advisor likens it to the British reoccupation of the Falkland Islands in the South Atlantic after Argentina grabbed the disputed territory in the early 1980s. It took two weeks for the Royal Navy to sail south, as the world watched in anticipation. "We all kind of knew what was going to happen," they told me during our interview, laughing. The Ontario NDP went from seventy-four seats to just seventeen. The surviving caucus members came, with only a couple exceptions, from the old NDP bastions of Windsor, Hamilton, downtown Toronto, and northern Ontario. In fact, the NDP managed to hold onto eight of its ten seats in the North despite the fact that both opposition parties were led by northerners. Nearly half of the rump caucus was therefore from the region. The regionally divergent election results speak to the disproportionate number of legislative veterans in the Northern Caucus, but it was also a reflection of the government's bifurcated response to the industrial crisis. When Bob Rae toured northern ridings during the 1995 campaign, he could point to any number of "success stories." Thus, Rae told voters in Kapuskasing:

> Someone asked me recently how my government is different from the opposition. There's an easy answer. If the Liberals had been running things in 1991, Kapuskasing would be a very unhappy place today. The so-called experts on Bay Street and in Queen's Park said we shouldn't "bail out" companies. They told us if we got involved or provided any loans we'd lose our shirts. Some experts. Some shirts. Today Spruce Falls is one of northern Ontario's success stories, generating net earnings of $9 million in the quarter ending March 31, 1995.[3]

Naturally, Rae made it a point to stand in front of still functioning mills for the cameras—proof positive of the NDP's commitment to the North.[4] When his tour reached Sault Ste. Marie, he demanded to know where the other leaders were when Algoma Steel was in trouble. Answering his own question, he told the crowd that they were "sniping from the sidelines. They said government shouldn't be in the business of saving jobs and saving communities."[5] His economic message clearly resonated with traditional NDP voters in northern Ontario, who largely stuck with the party.

The NDP's pitch in southern Ontario was far less self-assured. The NDP leaned heavily on the relative popularity of Bob Rae himself and emphasized the "four cornerstones" of its economic renewal agenda: partnership, an industrial strategy, training, and public investment.[6] However, it was the last of these that did much of the heavy political lifting. There were new schools, daycares, co-op housing complexes, arenas, hospitals, and roads to point to in most communities, built with the massive public infrastructure investments made by the Rae government. But these examples proved to be far less persuasive to voters, especially in communities pummelled by plant closures. In Toronto, as elsewhere in southern Ontario, the NDP had done little to shore up the city's crumbling industrial base beyond De Havilland.[7] In automotive towns, the NDP also took credit for convincing the automakers to make major new investments in the province. But here, too, the message mostly failed to resonate. Early in the campaign, Rae spoke to the convention of the United Rubber Workers in Niagara Falls. He thanked them for their "loyal support," acknowledging that "maintaining this support has taken courage," given the union movement's hostility to the Social Contract. But, besides Bob Mackenzie's labour law reform, his speech dealt in generalities rather than the specific ways the NDP government delivered for Ontario's rubber workers. Rae certainly did not herald the NDP's hands-off response to the closure of the Kitchener tire plant.[8] How could he?

The Ontario NDP governed during a period of profound economic crisis and ideological transition. It initially ran on the class politics of redistribution, but governed mostly on the more consensual progressive competitive politics of neocorporatism and then communitarianism. Ambitiously, NDP policy makers tried to find their own alternative economic path to ascendant neoliberalism. However, the old labourist agenda lingered, interfering with the new, as labour law reform made it more difficult for the government to forge connection with business and the Social Contract ruptured its relationship with much of the labour movement. The Rae government's herculean efforts to build lasting European-style corporatist institutions were ruined as a result. Many would say that the government's quest for consensus was quixotic at best, or even delusional, especially during these polarizing times. In the wake of the Social Contract, the government turned to the warm embrace of community to fill the political void. Communitarianism offered an alternative consensual language to corporatism, but it failed, as far as I can tell, to make much of an economic difference. Nor did it cement, as intended, the support of the party's social movement supporters, who were among its chief beneficiaries.

At first, the Rae government's economic pragmatism took the form of a "firefighting" mindset, as the government did its best to douse the economic wildfires breaking out across the province. Worker ownership may not have lived up to its early promise, but it was enough to save several mill towns from oblivion. The government was at its most interventionist in northern Ontario, thanks to a strong regional caucus and a developmental mindset that viewed the region as exceptional. As a result, the North was largely shielded from the progressive competitive agenda during the NDP years. The government also worked to diversify hard-hit industrial towns throughout the province by continuing the Liberal government's relocation of public-sector jobs from Toronto or approving a casino, Ontario's first, for the automotive-manufacturing town of Windsor. Ignoring the opposition of much of the labour movement, the government approved the creation of labour-led venture capital funds, modelled on the Quebec Solidarity Fund, with the idea that they would financially support worker buyouts of troubled plants: a strategy that failed miserably. Meanwhile, a new Industrial Policy

Framework encouraged employers and unions to cooperate for mutual benefit in the development of sectoral strategies. But there was incremental progress at best. The feminist idea of social infrastructure proved more lasting, enabling the NDP government to substantially expand child care by tying it to worker retraining and new capital investments. There was also some effort to further soften the blow on displaced workers, extending the right to collectively bargain to the effects of plant closings and providing wage protection for workers in bankrupt firms. Taken together, this represents an energetic and fairly coherent approach to the industrial crisis.

There were clear limits, however, to how far the Rae government was willing to go. Not only did it refuse to interfere with corporate decision-making, failing to deliver on its promise to compel departing companies to justify their plant closing decisions, but it did not even see fit to expand the coverage of existing severance and advance notice legislation to cover smaller workplaces of ten to forty-nine workers. Finance Minister Floyd Laughren suggests that he doesn't know "how we could have done much more for our friends in the labour movement than we did."[9] Concern over the province's business climate increasingly put a political brake on its actions. Sam Gindin has therefore largely been proven right that progressive competitiveness was a political trap. As he told me, "I think one of the things that I was very conscious of, and tried to stress, was how powerful competitiveness was. Wasn't just them hammering you, it was actually something that was internalized."[10] The fear of becoming uncompetitive in the new global economy helps explain why the Rae government cut corporate and small business taxes but increased personal income taxes. Hugh Mackenzie later observed that "gains in individual real incomes since the early-1990s have gone entirely to Canadians in the top 10% of the income scale and that the resulting increase in the share of total income going to the richest 10% of Canadians has in fact gone predominantly to the richest 1% of Canadians."[11] The Ontario NDP did far too little to alter this trajectory.

Part of the problem was that there was no time during the economic storm to see the bigger political picture or reflect on the wider ramifications of the decisions being made. Cabinet ministers and senior advisors were run off their feet while learning on the job, and the unfolding economic and fiscal crises put enormous pressure on the government. Not surprisingly, many of the people I talked to spoke of being swept up in something beyond their control. "We were being buffeted on all sides," recalls Bud Wildman, "and things were not necessarily under our control."[12] They were simply swept along. "I think sometimes these things just ride along on a wave and you're along for the ride," recalls Frances Lankin, "and you dip the oar in now and then to adjust course; no big directional change in one term of government when you're in a recession is possible." Soon after the 1995 defeat, Lankin says she sat on the dock at her summer camp and tried to make sense of the past five years:

> Just thinking about it and thinking it through, and realizing—as a community organizer it was just something I knew—but where did our instincts go? I don't know—we didn't work with those communities and those stakeholders to include them in the planning of how we could go about this and how far we could go or not. And so, activists do what activists do—and what I would've done if I were on the outside instead of on the inside, which is to continue to push, push, push, and some people wanted to deliver, deliver, deliver on that—and others, you know, recognize that public opinion wasn't there yet. There's a job in leadership to explain yourself and to educate, to bring people along or realize they're not coming, they don't agree with you.[13]

Some things only became clearer with time. Ross McClellan, labour's man in the Premier's Office, now understands the disjuncture in terms of the neoliberal order. But in the early 1990s, "neoliberalism was a phenomenon without a kind of analysis."[14] He has spent the last three or four years reading as much as he can about its emergence in order to understand his own experience in government: "There's a whole library of information now that didn't exist; what we had then was firefighting, without putting it in a clear ideological context, that we could then counter with a counter-ideology. But we had a firefighting ideology, and I don't think it went far beyond that ... there wasn't a lot of time for that kind of reflection. And so, in a sense it didn't happen, and we were carried along." It is as good an explanation as I've come across.

But it would be a mistake to imagine the Ontario ship of state captained by Bob Rae as sailing alone on the turbulent political waters. In reality, the water was crowded with other social democratic and progressive vessels wildly zigzagging in search of an alternative route out of the economic storm, a route that wasn't guided by neoliberalism. Rae thus implored his critics inside the party to look around them, telling the Ontario NDP Provincial Council in November 1993:

> We are not in this alone. We are not the only party, we are not the only province, we are not the only group of women and men who are going through this difficult time. It is being experienced in every industrialized country that is comparable to ourselves. Every Social Democratic party that is either in government or in opposition is going through this period of change as well. Read the paper and see what Felipe Gonzalez is having to face in Spain; what the state governments in Germany are going through; what state governments in Australia are going through; what other progressive movements are having to wrestle with when they take office. And we have to recognize that what we are experiencing is understandable.[15]

He had a point. In one form or another, the progressive competitiveness model that we saw emerge in Ontario was adopted during the 1990s by social democratic and progressive parties across the OECD.[16] Human capital theory, and with it an emphasis on supply-side active labour market policies and public-private partnerships, was an integral part of the politics of Bill Clinton and

Tony Blair as well as Bob Rae.[17] All three men were affluent and well educated, about the same age, and thus shared a remarkably similar outlook. Third Way politicians emphasized personal moral obligations and responsibility as well as community.[18] Blair's New Labour, first elected in 1997 after eighteen years in opposition, thus downloaded state responsibilities onto community groups and other local stakeholders as part of its wider liberal market reforms.[19] Speaking in 2002, Third Way theorist Anthony Giddens explained:

> Labour today stands for a new progressivism, which aims to address the aspirations and needs of a wide constituency of the population. It is social democracy brought up to date and made relevant to a rapidly changing world. Social justice and economic competitiveness should not be treated as though they were distinct and separate from one another. A competitive economy is the necessary condition of job creation and the goal of sustaining full employment.[20]

These same words could have been said by Bob Rae a decade earlier.

If the era of Third Way social democratic politics is usually located in the second half of the 1990s and first half of the 2000s, finding its full expression under Blair's New Labour, this book suggests that the ideological pivot in social democracy was already well underway in the late 1980s and early 1990s. The social democratic parties of the Netherlands and Denmark regained power in 1989 and 1993, respectively, rolling back welfare in the name of national competitiveness.[21] Clinton, too, as Governor of Arkansas in the late 1980s, was influenced by Charles Sabel and Michael Piore's scholarship on flexible specialization in the Italian region of Emilia-Romagna, prompting him to undertake a pilgrimage to its famous small-scale factories.[22] As Governor, Clinton also visited Germany four times on trade missions to learn about its economic model. When he ran for US President, Clinton therefore promised a training agenda that was remarkably similar to that of

Ontario. A comparable story played out in western Canada, where NDP provincial governments in British Columbia, Saskatchewan, and Manitoba cracked down on illusory welfare cheats just as the Ontario NDP was doing the same. Saskatchewan's Roy Romanow went furthest in rationalizing social programs and cutting back on health and education spending, closing fifty-two rural hospitals and effectively killing the party's rural roots.[23] The Ontario NDP was thus very much part of the wider ideological transition, though we must remind ourselves that social democrats have almost always governed from the perceived centre.

Social democrats around the world had seen the French Socialists "forced to their knees" in the early 1980s "by the combined response of French and international capital."[24] The primary lesson that many took away from this defeat was that the old Keynesian prescriptions, so central to the postwar compromise and the emergence of the social welfare state, were no longer viable. There was, therefore, no point resisting economic globalization; the best social democrats could hope for was to make the post-industrial transition as equitable as possible.[25] But this stance had political consequences. Historian Xavier Vigna argues that the failure of the French left to slow industrial layoffs in the 1980s ruptured the alliance between workers and the social democratic left.[26] In 1981, 70 percent of working-class people voted for left-wing parties in France; 60 percent did so in 1988, and only 45 percent in 2002. The declining voting share had its corollary in the spectacular decline of French trade unionism.[27] We are living with the long-term political consequences today, as right-wing populism has taken root in the former bastions of the left in France and other countries.

Evolutionary thinking about post-industrial society and global competitiveness did manufacturing industries and working-class communities no favours in high-wage countries like Canada. Neoliberal globalization eviscerated "both economic and political forms of working-class power," leading social democrats to increasingly turn to other constituencies.[28] Once class analysis and the old redistributive politics became barriers to building a new cross-class coalition of "progressive" voters, unions and working-class voters were de-emphasized or abandoned altogether.[29]

The Rae government is, therefore, best understood as a transitional moment. When it was elected, the Ontario NDP was still a party very much grounded in the labour movement. Five years later, this relationship was in tatters and Rae's rhetoric was recognizably Third Way in its orientation. At one point during my interview with Rae, I shared my thoughts about the early 1990s being a transitional moment in social democracy, and the idea resonated with him:

> Well, not to flatter you, but I think that's very perceptive. I was very aware of the difference between my government and the Peterson government, but also the difference between my government and what later evolved in the debate around social democracy. And, I mean, I was very interested in these issues, these ways of thinking. . . . In some ways, when you look at the Labour Party in the 1970s and 1980s, and the debates that are going on inside SI [Socialist International], which was a real thing in those days. I mean, Michael Harrington, who was leader of the left in the United States, an intellectual leader, was a very close friend of mine. And he would come up to Canada. He came to caucus meetings and engaged with us on broader issues around social philosophy and what we were trying to do. And I think that's where our government was at the beginning, and I think at the end, we were trying to figure out, hell, where are we now? Now that we've gone through all this pain and anguish, what's the next stage? And I think that in many parts of the social democratic world, and in France and the Scandinavian countries, and Blair and Clinton, obviously, they cut through the umbilical cord and just said now this is where we're going now. . . . I think I'll just say your perception is right. That we were a transitional government. We were in the middle of this thing. But the thing you realize when you're in government

is: you have these institutional and in a sense ideological structures which we're coming up against, the changing global economy all the time. And I think we were trying to shift ground all the time and get people to think about the new values. And that's what a lot of my speeches were about, trying to say, this is the world as it's evolving.[30]

It was an unexpected moment of agreement. At the end of our conversation, Rae confessed to me that when he'd agreed to do the interview, he'd thought, "'I don't know whether this is going to be a trip to a dentist, or exactly what,' but it's actually been very enjoyable and very interesting." In truth, I had also been nervous about the interview, unsure how I would respond to being in conversation with the person whom I had long blamed for my own disillusionment with partisan politics. But I, too, found the conversation to be generative. This is not to say that I was in agreement with all of Rae's analysis, but I left with a better understanding of his point of view—which is one of the great values of oral history as a methodology. The encounter confirmed to me that the story was never about one person "giving away a miracle," as some would have it, but rather about the fundamental challenge that neoliberal globalization and capital flight have presented to social democratic parties everywhere. In my interview with Sam Gindin, he drew a similar conclusion, saying the problem wasn't "a Bob Rae thing, or an Ontario thing: it was a problem facing social democratic parties in general."

Soon after the Rae government's defeat, the Canadian Labour Congress initiated a review of its relationship to the New Democratic Party. In response, the "pink paper group" of private-sector unions wrote a strong brief in favour of continued affiliation with the NDP, insisting that the party must remain the labour movement's "central pivot point in the political arena."[31] These unions went on to say that the Ontario NDP's five years in power offer "useful lessons for the way we conduct ourselves as a labour movement and as a party in the future. It is enough to say that the consequences of our collective failure in Ontario is evident in the headlines of every major newspaper, virtually every day of the week. Let's be candid: labour's official voices, and some affiliate voices, helped to usher in the political equivalent of nuclear winter in Ontario" in the form of the shock treatment of the hard-right Mike Harris Tories. The pink paper unions went on to complain that those unions who participated in "pathbreaking worker-ownership projects" in Bob Rae's Ontario were "criticized by other unions for alleged capitulations of capital." Yet these worker buy-outs have shown "the possibility of long-term success" and saved thousands of jobs and entire communities. "This resistance within labour and other parts of the left to consider imaginative responses to the real needs of workers in crisis says a lot about the difficulties we must overcome to build real solidarity, and policy sophistication, within the ranks of the Canadian democratic left." It is an eloquent statement and a strong reminder of why trade unions need to remain central to left politics.

But progressive competitiveness quickly lost traction in the trade union movement after the defeat of the Rae government. Peter Warrian, an early proponent of social partnership, used the opportunity of the Sefton Lecture at the University of Toronto in 2001 to say that the "Empowering Workers" approach of the United Steelworkers was running out of steam, as it had largely failed to deliver the goods to union members.[32] Two years later, Tim Armstrong said he now "detected little appetite on either side for the revival of organizational change experimentation involving structured union/management collaboration."[33] Others regretted the missed opportunity. In our interview, John O'Grady called the early 1990s a one-time opportunity for organized labour to translate its economic power into political leverage: "There was the possibility of a kind of deal, as it were, in which unions agreed to a change in the work organization model." Ultimately, the union movement failed to fully exploit the moment. Since then, the rate of private-sector unionization has eroded substantially. Today, O'Grady sighs, "governments couldn't care less what the trade union movement thinks."[34] But there is reason to hope, as a younger generation breathes new life into the trade union movement in the US and Canada.

If labour solidarity in Ontario has been fractured by the bitter experience of being in power, so too has the provincial NDP. After the 1995 defeat, the open resistance of much of the party to the progressive competitive agenda pursued by the Rae government descended into recriminations. The leadership race that followed Rae's resignation as leader was a nasty one. Frances Lankin, one of the strongest ministers in the government, was clearly Rae's choice. She faced Rae's arch-nemesis Peter Kormos, the controversial MPP for Welland-Thorold who had been unceremoniously booted out of cabinet, supposedly for agreeing to be photographed fully clothed for the *Toronto Sun*'s "Sunshine" page, which usually featured young women wearing considerably less. While a provocation, the real reason for his ejection was because Kormos was a constant thorn in Rae's backside. Kormos was brash and arrogant, but was one of the few willing to defy the government's new direction from within caucus.[35] He opposed the abandonment of public auto insurance and the government's Social Contract. Kormos was therefore well placed to run his leadership campaign against the Rae government. The third candidate was Howard Hampton, from northwestern Ontario. A small-town lawyer who got his university degree from the US with the help of a hockey scholarship, Hampton served as Attorney General and then Minister of Natural Resources. Crucially, Hampton was not in Rae's inner circle and was an internal critic of some of the government's decisions, especially on auto insurance. He therefore had more political distance from Rae, making him well placed to be the unity candidate.[36]

Hampton's victory delivered a heavy blow to Rae, who took Lankin's defeat personally. One of Rae's closest advisors quoted the old saying, "I didn't leave my party, my party left me." For those in Rae's inner circle who "were in the [pause] fires of hell [laughs] we said, 'Well, haven't you learned anything?'" For them, the party went right back to the "single-minded opposition bullshit and that's not going to get us back into power." Rae said essentially the same thing, but more politely: the "party was actually not willing to change." As for Floyd Laughren, he told me that the party's inability to recognize the Rae government as "something unique" was hurtful, as they had done "their best in trying times." Of this, I have no doubt—it was a perfect economic storm. There was, and is, far too little recognition of the creativity and ambition of the Rae government. Laughren then shared how he was asked to say a few words on the occasion of Bob Rae's retirement as party leader at the Ontario NDP convention: "I got up to thank Bob, and I'd say a quarter or a third of the delegates walked out. And I thought, 'So that's where it's at.' And it was mainly public sector and CAW. And that is truly sad."[37]

Rae's decision to jump ship to the federal Liberals in 2006 had everything to do with his growing alienation from the NDP and his desire not to be defined by the political failure of his government. He told me that the process of leaving the party was not an easy one, but he felt he had no choice. He equates leaving the NDP to a divorce, "it's really, really difficult," not just for him but for others:

> I do realize how painful it was for some people. And it was painful for me. And I've said this to a number of people. I've said, "I haven't changed who I am. I haven't changed my thinking. I'm extremely proud of the government that I led. And the party that I led." I don't look back on it and say, "That was all, you know, a bad dream." Not at all. Quite the opposite.[38]

Ultimately, the federal Liberal Party was where he felt "more at ease, more at home" with himself. His leaving the NDP, however, meant that any lingering debate over the government he had led was well and truly over. Just as the NDP caucus took down Rae's portrait from the wall of their meeting room at Queen's Park, the party has done its best to pretend the Rae government never happened. I don't think this selective amnesia has served the NDP particularly well. We can learn much from what the Rae government did and did not do and why.

I always end my interviews with an open-ended question, asking if there is anything we haven't yet covered or that they would like to put on the record. Rae took this opportunity to return to our earlier conversation about the early 1990s being a period of ideological transition for the social democratic left:

> Listening to a couple of your comments were very helpful to me in trying to understand the moment. I think the main thing is the impact of events. And the extent to which in government, you're not really dealing with theoretical choices. You're dealing with options and possibilities—it's not like choosing a good thing or a bad thing. It's like choosing what's the least bad thing. Because that's sometimes the choices that life gives us. And I think that's really how I look at the experience.[39]

He went on to say that, once in power, "you make decisions in real time, and you don't make them because of some theoretical construct in your head." Ultimately, Rae thinks of himself as a pragmatist: "I say, 'How can you make things less bad for people than they would otherwise be?'" Accordingly, the NDP couldn't simply oppose economic change, "that doesn't work. It's not going to make life better for people. But we're going to have to figure out how do we actually make the economy, allow it to change." There is considerable truth to this statement. That said, there is little doubt that when "theoretical constructs" become hegemonic assumptions, they establish political horizons and determine what seems possible at any given time. This was certainly the case in the 1990s, which has frequently been described as the golden age of neoliberal globalization.[40] To be a pragmatist in neoliberal times is to bend to neoliberalism's will. Frances Lankin, who remains a good friend of Bob Rae, observes that his political instincts were "nearly neoliberal" as a result.[41]

Historians Nelson Lichtenstein and Judith Stein recently wrote a history of the Bill Clinton presidency entitled *A Fabulous Failure*, where they noted that the "ideological and generational coherence to the Clinton cadre" had "evoked a fresh set of hopes and aspirations" but demonstrated considerable ambivalence towards the state itself.[42] The same generational imprint could be seen in the

Rae government. In pursuing its progressive competitive agenda, the Rae government, like Clinton's presidency, stumbled towards neoliberalism. Calling it a "defining moment in modern Ontario politics," Bryan Evans and Charles Smith have suggested that Bob Rae's abrupt U-turn in 1991 and his government's slide into austerity politics opened the door to the neoliberalization of Ontario politics.[43] While I would argue that this door was already swinging open by the time the NDP came to power, there is little doubt in my mind that the NDP's years in power ultimately undermined the idea that a viable economic alternative to neoliberal globalization even existed. There is something to be said about an unapologetic left that generates new ideas and holds power to account.

Despite considerable effort and experimentation, political progressives across Europe and North America failed to figure out an effective response to the end of the postwar boom and the coming down of trade and investment barriers. Their eventual embrace of neoliberalism ruptured their long-standing relationship to the trade union movement and working-class voters in many countries.[44] As a result, the question posed by Michael Harrington in 1989 remains every bit as relevant today: How do you "control a wrenching economic transition and create a new and progressive social structure of accumulation"?[45] Having integrated our economies, what economic choices do we have left?

If the days of high tariff walls are gone, it took Donald Trump's renegotiation of the North American Free Trade Agreement in 2020 to remind us that we can insist on real labour protections in our international agreements. After all, the Auto Pact between Canada and the United States, eventually struck down by the World Trade Organization, once guaranteed that the same number of vehicles sold by the Big Three automakers in Canada would be built here. Trump's revisions to NAFTA were along the same lines, but smartly tied the guarantee to the proportion of the automobile made by higher-wage workers rather than US workers. This strikes me as the way to go. If done across the board, which would require political progressives and trade unionists to collaborate across borders, it has the potential to level up instead of levelling down. Only by working internationally can we cool the hyper-competitive global environment that has driven down wages, driven out trade unions, and undermined progressive tax systems, resulting in ever more extreme income inequality.

What, then, of closing factories? Let's be clear, the economy is dynamic and the idea of freezing the status quo is impossible. Plant closures, industrial restructuring, and even deindustrialization are "an essential element in the [normal] functioning of capitalism."[46] One 2005 Statistics Canada report showed that manufacturing plants have relatively short lives, with only 20 percent lasting more than fifteen years.[47] The question, therefore, becomes how economic change is managed and who pays the price. Rae understood this, which is one of the reasons why his landmark January 1990 "What We Owe Each Other" speech is so compelling. Though the NDP policy book was often the butt of jokes, I would also suggest that the party's 1990 election platform, *An Agenda for People*, got most things right.

Any just economic transition worthy of its name begins with strong unions. Workers need representation to ensure the redistribution of risk and the ultimate cost of economic change. Had the Rae government moved quickly to implement Bob Mackenzie's original labour law reforms, we would have seen a massive wave of unionization in the province. More than one interviewee told me that sectoral bargaining would have been a game changer. Yes, the Tories would have rolled this back too, but it would have proven much more difficult to put this particular genie back into the bottle. Likewise, had the NDP raised the minimum wage to 60 percent of the average wage, as promised (and eliminated the under-eighteen differential, I might add), it would have struck a serious blow against poverty that would have taken a decade or more to undo. The Rae government backed away from these promises.

It also begins with the expansion of the Ontario Employment Standards Act, the collective agreement of the unorganized, as Bryan Evans so eloquently put it. Severance pay and advance notice should be extended to all workers, and the notice period lengthened. Just as the introduction of workers' compensation laws created a strong financial incentive for employers to ensure safer workplaces, we need to financially encourage corporations to make layoffs and plant closures the last resort rather than the first. Increasing the advance notice period likewise offers workers more time to transition to new jobs and time for governments to deliver vital adjustment measures such as training. All research studies, going back to the 1960s, have shown that the time between the closure announcement and the last shift is critically important to a smooth transition for workers. Advance notice would also help surrounding communities adjust, an especially important factor in small or isolated places. Personally, I favour the worker-led model of Action Centres, which emerged out of the ruins of the Ontario Training and Adjustment Board during the 1990s. There, workers find peer support and solidarity as well as help finding work and retraining. Because they are run by the union, Action Centres also maintain the connection between the union and its members. But more research is needed into this model of adjustment; there is still a lot that we don't know.[48]

If advance notice is the foundation of worker adjustment, justification remains the basis for intervention. Ontario's trade union movement has long understood this truth. We regulate many parts of economic life, why not plant closing decisions, given their devastating socio-economic costs? Disclosure of the actual reasons for major mill and factory closures would provide unions and the state with a far better understanding of the underlying reasons for capital disinvestment and a starting point to assess possible alternatives. Worker ownership remains a viable option in some cases, but the fundamental problem of mill modernization remains. While public ownership is no panacea, there is a long history of successful government-run businesses in Canada, the memory of which has been actively suppressed in recent decades. There is also potential in temporary public stewardship of viable industries, giving them the chance to restructure before returning to the private sector. Canada stepped in to save the aeronautics industry in the 1970s, for example, after which Canada became a world leader with Bombardier.

Beyond the firm or factory, there is also something to be said about governments negotiating stronger job and investment guarantees in exchange for financial support, as Canada did in 1979 with Chrysler, a deal that heralded a period of reindustrialization at a time when the same automakers were closing plants in the US. This is still happening to some degree in the auto sector, where Unifor (previously the Canadian Auto Workers) has prioritized new investments and product mandates in its negotiations with the Big Three automakers, with the financial support of both levels of government. Recent government efforts to foster an electric vehicle industry in North America likewise demonstrate the continuing value of industrial planning and state intervention in the economy. If the 2020–21 global pandemic taught us anything economically, it is just how important it is for supply chains to be closer to home. Deindustrialization has made us far too vulnerable to global instability.

If this policy discussion sounds familiar, it should: it was essentially what the NDP promised Ontario voters in 1990. If anything, the intervening decades have confirmed the value of redistributive politics and the regulatory state. There is something to be said for membership-driven policy development. To be sure, Ontario's party of labour benefited enormously from the grounded economic knowledge of the trade union movement, giving it an expertise that other parties lacked. Indeed, the Ontario Federation of Labour's substantive policy statements adopted during these years have aged equally well.

As should be clear by now, I am skeptical of the technologically driven interpretations of economic change that dominated public policy making during the 1980s, 1990s, and early 2000s. Technological change is important, but it too often leads to evolutionary "stages of development" thinking that whitewashes history. The earlier focus on capital flight, by contrast, recognized the importance of corporate control over geography and the anti-union animus that so often determines where things are made. The world has not deindustrialized: everything around us is made somewhere. That somewhere, however, is usually where wages and environmental regulations are lowest. Sweeping technological changes may have facilitated the "new global economy," but the restructuring of the international division of labour has been driven by the desire for greater and greater returns on investment. It is this impulse, more than anything else, that is wrecking the planet.

As the world transitions away from fossil fuels for our collective survival, it is more important than ever that we learn from the failure of the post-industrial transition to equitably share the socio-economic costs and benefits of the transformative changes of the 1980s and 1990s. With trade liberalization and free trade, recalls Hugh Mackenzie, "the economy did grow, but the winners did not compensate the losers, and in fact, the winners became so much more powerful that they punished the losers."[49] Severance payments were clawed back, unemployment insurance eligibility restricted, and welfare rates slashed—all the while blaming those displaced for their inability to adjust. Some have optimistically suggested that the neoliberal order has now ended. While politically contested from both the populist right and the radical left, neoliberal globalization remains very much intact thanks to international trade and investment agreements that insulate capitalism from democratic interference. To achieve a different result, the political left needs to re-engage with issues of corporate control and investment, something that was largely abandoned along with economic nationalism in the 1980s, and rebuild its relationship to working-class voters and the trade union movement. The siren's call of right-wing populism in Ontario is now stronger than ever. It also needs to build new international institutions and agreements that serve people and not just corporations. Only then can we say that the neoliberal order has well and truly ended.

NOTES

PREFACE

1 Delegate Kit, May 1989 Joint Retreat of the Ontario NDP Caucus, Executive of the Ontario Federation of Labour, and the Executive of the Ontario NDP. In the possession of the author.
2 George Ehring and Wayne Roberts, *Giving Away a Miracle: Lost Dreams, Broken Promises & the Ontario NDP* (Oakville: Mosaic Press, 1993). This is a nasty book, but a revealing one. Supposedly on the party's left-wing, the authors sought to settle old scores and went so far as to denigrate how trade union leaders looked, repeatedly commenting on their lack of clothing style. Besides this everyday classism, Ehring and Roberts also critiqued the Rae government for its efforts to save mature industries and its capital works program, which was equated with the sewer socialism of the 1930s.
3 The Ontario New Democratic Youth (ONDY) had been officially disbanded in 1974 and replaced by a youth committee with two co-chairs elected by all delegates at convention. After young New Democrats convinced the federal party to recognize only autonomous youth section representatives as their delegates to Federal Council, the Ontario party agreed to reconstitute ONDY. Its first conference was at Carleton University in 1985. Andrew McNeill, "The Way We Were: A History of ONDY," Program, Fifth Annual Conference, ONDY (5–7 May 1989, University of Ottawa). In the possession of the author.
4 Maureen Hall, "Minimum Wage: The Two-Tier System," *ONDY Youth Viewpoints* (Winter 1989–90), 1; ONDY, Minutes of the Executive Meeting (Community Centre, Gravenhurst, Ontario, 17–18 June 1989). In the possession of the author.
5 "President's Report: What ONDY's Up To," *ONDY Youth Viewpoints* (Winter 1989–90), 9. In the possession of the author.
6 ONDY Fact Sheet, "Minimum Wage—Maximum Discrimination." In the possession of the author.
7 Steven High, ONDY Report, 22 September 1989. In the possession of the author.
8 Steven M. Barrett to Maureen Hall, 31 May 1990. Application—Declaration that Employment Standards Act "is inconsistent with

and infringes and denies rights and freedoms guaranteed by s.15 (1) of the Canadian Charter of Rights and Freedoms to the extent that it stipulates a minimum wage of $4.15 an hour for an employee who is a student under 18 years of age if the weekly hours of the student are not in excess of 28 hours, or if the student is employed during a school holiday." In the possession of the author.

INTRODUCTION

1. Bob Rae, "What We Owe Each Other." 10 January 1990. File: NDP Speaking Notes—Bob Rae, Mel Watkins (1990). B2019-0003/001/08. David Wolfe Fonds. University of Toronto Archives (UTA).
2. Benjamin Looker, "Visions of Autonomy: The New Left and the Neighborhood Government Movement of the 1970s," *Journal of Urban History* 38, no. 3 (2012): 577–98.
3. Herbert Marcuse, "The Failure of the New Left?," *New German Critique* 18 (1979): 3–4.
4. Conrad Black was later imprisoned for fraud in the United States, and eventually received a pardon from Donald Trump. Canada tends not to jail our white-collar criminals; we give them a regular op-ed in a national newspaper.
5. Sam Gindin, "Planned Trade and Greater Self-Sufficiency," in Michael Bradfield, John Dillon, Sam Gindin, and Alexander Lockhart, *Strategies for Canadian Economic Self-Reliance: Alternative Paths to Jobs, Development, Equality and Peace* (Ottawa: Canadian Centre for Policy Alternatives, 1985).
6. Of course, the fight against the Free Trade Agreement was about much more than trade.
7. Gerald P. Glyde, "Canadian Labour and the Free Trade Agreement," *Labor Studies Journal* 17, no. 4 (1993): 4.
8. Bob White to federal NDP Officers and Executive Members. 28 November 1988. In the possession of the author.
9. Neil Bradford and Jane Jenson, "Facing Economic Restructuring and Constitutional Renewal: Social Democracy Adrift in Canada," in Frances Fox Piven, ed., *Labor Parties in Postindustrial Societies* (New York: Oxford University Press, 1992), 206. James Laxer, *Rethinking the Economy: The Laxer Report on Canadian Economic Problems and Policies* (Toronto: Lorimer, 1984).
10. Ivor Crewe, "Labor Force Changes, Working Class Decline, and the Labour Vote: Social and Electoral Trends in Postwar Britain," in Piven, ed., *Labor Parties in Postindustrial Societies*, 30.

11 Frances Fox Piven, *The Breaking of the American Social Compact* (New York: New Press, 1998), 18.
12 Rob Manwaring and Josh Holloway, "A New Wave of Social Democracy?: Policy Change across the Social Democratic Party Family, 1970s–2010s," *Government & Opposition* 57 (2022): 174.
13 The term "Third Way" was apparently first used by policy consultants to Bill Clinton and then, later, adopted by Tony Blair. Thomas Meyer, "The Third Way at the Crossroads," *International Politics and Society* 3 (1999): 294.
14 The Swedish model was hailed for much of the postwar era, as it combined economic growth and full-employment through labour-management negotiation and partnership. See for example: Magnus Ryner, *Capitalist Restructuring, Globalisation and the Third Way: Lessons from the Swedish Model* (London: Routledge, 2002).
15 Paul Mason, "Overcoming the Fear of Freedom," in Heinrich Geiselberger, ed., *The Great Regression* (Cambridge: Polity, 2017), 94.
16 Steve Buckler and David P. Dolowitz, "Theorizing the Third Way: New Labour and Social Justice," *Journal of Political Ideologies* 5, no. 3 (2000): 314.
17 Alan Zuege, "The Chimera of the Third Way," *Socialist Register* (2000): 90.
18 Ben Clift, "Social Democracy and Globalization: The Cases of France and the UK," *Government and Opposition* 37, no. 4 (2002): 469.
19 David Osborne, *Laboratories of Democracy* (Boston: Harvard Business School Press, 1990), 332.
20 James Piazza, "De-linking Labor: Labor Unions and Social Democratic Parties under Globalization," *Party Politics* 7, no. 4 (2001): 413–35.
21 Judith Stein, *Pivotal Decade: How the United States Traded Factories for Finance in the Seventies* (New Haven: Yale University Press, 2010), 52.
22 Robert B. Reich, *The Work of Nations: Preparing Ourselves for 21st-Century Capitalism* (New York: Vintage Books, 1992 [1991]), 3.
23 Reich, *The Work of Nations*, 175.
24 Interview with Robert Reich by Patrick Sharma and Martin Meeker. 2010. Regional Oral History Office, Bancroft Library. University of California, Berkeley.
25 Christopher Lasch, *The Revolt of the Elites and the Betrayal of Democracy* (New York: W. W. Norton, 1995), 47, 28.
26 Thomas Frank, *Listen, Liberal: What Ever Happened to the Party of the People* (New York: Picador, 2016), 70–71.

27 Anthony Blair interviewed by Russell Riley and Robert Strong. 16 June 2010. William J. Clinton Presidential History Project. Miller Centre. University of Virginia.
28 Gary Gerstle, *The Rise and Fall of the Neoliberal Order: America and the World in the Free Market Era* (New York: Oxford University Press, 2022), 2, 5.
29 Milton Friedman, *Capitalism and Freedom* (Chicago: University of Chicago Press, 1962). See also: Quinn Slobodian, *Globalists: The End of Empire and the Birth of Neoliberalism* (Cambridge: Harvard University Press, 2018).
30 Ngaire Woods, *The Globalizers: The IMF, the World Bank and Their Borrowers* (Ithaca: Cornell University Press, 2006).
31 Gábor Scheiring, Darja Irdam, and Lawrence King, "The Wounds of Postsocialism: A Systematic Review of the Social Determinants of Mortality in Hungary," *Journal of Contemporary Central and Eastern Europe* 26, no. 1 (2018): 1–31.
32 Fredric R. Jameson, "On Habits of the Heart," in Charles H. Reynolds and Ralph V. Norman, eds., *Community in America: The Challenge of Habits of the Heart* (Berkeley: University of California Press, 1988), 98.
33 Lasch, *The Revolt of the Elites*, 106.
34 Christopher Lasch, "The Communitarian Critique of Liberalism," in Charles H. Reynolds and Ralph V. Norman, eds., *Community in America: The Challenge of Habits of the Heart* (Berkeley: University of California Press, 1988), 182.
35 Bob Rae interviewed by Steven High. 10 April 2023.
36 For more on the modernizers in the British Labour Party, see Leo Panitch and Colin Leys, *The End of Parliamentary Socialism: From New Left to New Labour* (London: Verso, 1997).
37 Crewe, "Labor Force Changes, Working Class Decline, and the Labour Vote," 42–43.
38 Bob Rae interviewed by Steven High. 10 April 2023.
39 David McGrane, John D. Whyte, Roy Romanow, and Russell Isinger, eds., *Back to Blakeney: Revitalizing the Democratic State* (Regina: University of Regina Press, 2019); Roberta Lexier, Stephanie Bangarth, and Jon Weier, eds., *Party of Conscience: The CCF, the NDP, and Social Democracy in Canada* (Toronto: Between the Lines, 2018); Dan Azoulay, *Keeping the Dream Alive: The Survival of the Ontario CCF/NDP, 1950–1963* (Kingston: Queen's School of Policy Studies, 1997); Alan Whitehorn, *Canadian Socialism: Essays on the CCF-NDP* (Toronto: Oxford University Press, 1992); and Dan Azoulay, "The CCF

and Post–Second World War Politics in Ontario," in Edgar-André Montigny and Lori Chambers, eds., *Ontario Since Confederation: A Reader* (Toronto: University of Toronto Press, 2000).
40 Craig Heron, "Labourism and the Canadian Working Class," *Labour / Le Travail* 13 (1984): 45.
41 James Naylor, "Whatever Happened to Labourism," *Left History* 21, no. 1 (2017): 56.
42 Heron, "Labourism and the Canadian Working Class," 72, 74.
43 Chuck Rachlis and David Wolfe, "An Insiders' View of the NDP Government in Ontario: The Politics of Permanent Opposition Meets the Economics of Permanent Recession," in Graham White, ed., *The Government and Politics of Ontario*, fifth ed. (Toronto: University of Toronto Press, 1997).
44 David Wolf, Interview Transcript, May 1995. File: Interview Transcript—NDP 1990 Transition, DW involvement, policy. 1995. B2019-0002/001 (07). David Wolfe Fonds. UTA.
45 That 40 percent of the caucus were trade unionists was something I heard several times in the interviews. Ross McClellan, for example, put it at 36 (of 74). At the time, journalist Kevin Ward suggested there were only 31. Kevin Ward, "Opposition Fears NDP's Labor, Union Sympathies," *Kitchener-Waterloo Record*, 15 October 1990.
46 "Rae Answers 'Hillbilly' Jibes against NDP," *Toronto Star*, 24 June 1991.
47 Bob Rae interviewed by Steven High. 10 April 2023.
48 Quoted in Douglas James Hall, "An Evaluation of Ontario's Industrial Policy Efforts: 1985–1995" (Political Science PhD: Queen's University, 1998), 239–40.
49 Membership Report. 30 April 1994. Accession 03-027, Box 32/56. Ontario New Democratic Party (ONDP) Fonds. Queen's University Archives (QUA).
50 Address by Julie Davis, Secretary-Treasurer, OFL to CUPE Annual Convention. Hamilton, Ontario. 28 May 1993. Accession 03-027, Box 7/8. ONDP Fonds. QUA.
51 Thomas Watson, "Ontario NDP Hammers Rae," *Hamilton Spectator*, 29 May 1993.
52 W. Rand Smith, *The Left's Dirty Job: The Politics of Industrial Restructuring in France and Spain* (Toronto: University of Toronto Press, 1998), 1.
53 Riel Miller to David Wolfe, 25 October 1990. File: Policy Notes and Memos from Riel Miller. B2019-0002/003. David Wolfe Fonds. UTA.
54 Gregory Albo, "'Competitive Austerity' and the Impasse of Capitalist Employment Policy," *Socialist Register* (1994): 149.

55   Stuart Hall, "The Toad in the Garden: Thatcherism among the Theorists," in Cary Nelson and Lawrence Grossberg, eds., *Marxism and the Interpretation of Culture* (Chicago: University of Illinois Press, 1988), 44.
56   Nancy Fraser and Linda Gordon, "A Genealogy of Dependency: Tracing a Keyword of the US Welfare State," *Signs* 19, no. 2 (1994): 310.
57   Briefing Notes for the National Economic Conference, 1985. B241052. F 4180-3. Ontario Federation of Labour (OFL). Archives of Ontario (AO).
58   Canadian Auto Workers, *Workplace Issues: Work Reorganization: Responding to Lean Production* (North York: CAW, 1993), 15.
59   United Steelworkers of America, Empowering Workers in the Global Economy: A Labour Agenda for the 1990s, Conference Proceedings (Toronto, Ontario, 22–23 October 1991), 3.
60   Bob Rae, "Towards a New Partnership for Ontario" in United Steelworkers of America, Empowering Workers in the Global Economy, 147.
61   Hall, "An Evaluation of Ontario's Industrial Policy Efforts," 254.
62   Bob Rae, *From Protest to Power: Personal Reflections on a Life in Politics* (Toronto: Viking, 1996), 214.
63   Mel Watkins, "The Book of Bob," *Journal of Canadian Studies* 31, no. 4 (1996–97), 176–78.
64   Peter Warrian, "The Long March: Politics, Spirituality and Resilience." Forthcoming essay. Shared with the author.
65   Confidential interview with X by Steven High. They were in Bob Rae's inner circle.
66   Bob Rae interviewed by Steven High. 10 April 2023.

CHAPTER 1: FIGHTING PLANT CLOSINGS

1   Canadian Federation of Independent Business. Brief to the Select Committee on Plant Shutdowns. File: Exhibit 79. Box C-295. RG 49-173. AO.
2   Statement of Robert White, Canadian Director UAW, Before the Select Committee on Plant Closures and Employee Adjustment. Exhibit 64. Files on 14 January 1981. Box C-295. RG 49-173. AO.
3   Canadian Federation of Independent Business. Brief to the Select Committee on Plant Shutdowns.
4   "List of Runaway Industry in Windsor." January 1962. File 7, Box 32. UAW Region 7. Walter Reuther Library, Wayne State University (WRL). Detroit, Michigan.

5   Peter S. McInnis, *Harnessing Labour Confrontation: Shaping the Postwar Settlement in Canada, 1943–1950* (Toronto: University of Toronto Press, 2002), 4.
6   Press Release, Canadian UAW. 20 September 1959. Folder 5, Box 32, UAW Region 7. WRL.
7   UAW. Brief Presented to the City Council of Windsor, Ontario on Industrial Location by Area Plant Movement Committee. Windsor, Ontario. 16 May 1962. Folder 7, Box 32, UAW Region 7. WRL.
8   David B. Archer, President, and Terry Meagher, Secretary-Treasurer, "Foreword," in John W. Eleen and Ashley Bernardine, *Shutdown: The Impact of Plant Shutdowns, Extensive Employment Terminations and Layoffs on the Workers and the Community* (Toronto: Ontario Federation of Labour, 1971), 14.
9   W. Darcy McKeough, Treasurer of Ontario to Terry Meagher, Secretary-Treasurer, OFL. 26 January 1972. File: Plant Closings, 1972. Box 83. RG 7-1-0-2124. AO.
10 Quoted in Abraham Rotstein, "Foreign Control of the Economy: A Screening and Ownership Policy," in Abraham Rotstein and Gary Lax for the Committee for an Independent Canada, *Getting It Back: A Program for Canadian Independence* (Toronto: Clarke, Irwin and Company, 1974).
11 Quoted in Abraham Rotstein and Gary Lax, eds., *Independence: The Canadian Challenge* (Canada: The Committee for an Independent Canada, 1972).
12 Harold Innis, *The Fur Trade in Canada: An Introduction to Canadian Economic History*, rev. ed. (Toronto: University of Toronto Press, 1956 [1930]); Innis, *The Cod Fisheries: The History of an International Economy* (Toronto: Ryerson Press, 1940).
13 Daniel Drache, "'Rowing and Steering' Our Way out of the Modern Staples Trap," in Jim Stanford, ed., *The Staple Theory @ 50: Reflections on the Lasting Significance of Mel Watkins' "A Staple Theory of Economic Growth"* (Ottawa: Canadian Centre for Policy Alternatives, 2014), np.
14 Mel Watkins, "A Staple Theory of Economic Development," *Canadian Journal of Economics and Political Science* 29, no. 2 (1963): 49–73.
15 Alberto Daniel Gago, "The Staples Trap in Developing Countries," in Stanford, ed., *Staple Theory @ 50*, np.
16 Jim Stanford, introduction to Stanford, ed., *Staple Theory @ 50*, np.
17 Karl Polanyi, *The Great Transformation* (New York: Farrar and Rinehart, 1944).

18 Sean Mills, "Without Surrender: An Interview with Kari Levitt," *Race and Class* 52, no. 1 (2010): 49–56.
19 Theotonio dos Santos (1970) quoted in Louis A. Perez Jr., "Dependency," *Journal of American History* 77, no. 1 (1990): 135. For English speakers, dependency theory was closely associated with André Gunter Frank, a radical economist trained at the University of Chicago, who published *Capitalism and Underdevelopment in Latin America* in 1967. Cristóbal Kay, "Andre Gunder Frank: 'Unity in Diversity' from the Development of Underdevelopment to the World System," *New Political Economy* 16, no. 4 (2011): 523–38. See also Fernando Henrique Cardoso and Enzo Faletto, *Dependency and Development in Latin America* (Berkeley: University of California Press, 1979).
20 Kari Levitt, "Canada: Economic Development and Political Disintegration," *New World Quarterly* 4 (1968): 57–139.
21 Mel Watkins, foreword to Kari Levitt, *Silent Surrender: The Multinational Corporation in Canada*, 1st ed. (Toronto: Macmillan, 1970).
22 Levitt, *Silent Surrender*, introduction.
23 Watkins, foreword to Levitt, *Silent Surrender*.
24 This story is recounted in an interview with Kari Levitt. Mills, "Without Surrender," 49–56.
25 R. T. Naylor, "The Rise and Fall of the Third Commercial Empire of the St. Lawrence," in Gary Teeple, ed., *Capitalism and the National Question in Canada* (Toronto: University of Toronto Press, 1972), 1–42. Many labour historians objected to the emphasis on external metropolitan-hinterland relationships rather than on internal class relations in industrializing Canada.
26 Mel Watkins, "Once Upon a Waffle," *Canadian Dimension*, 12 November 2009.
27 "May Day at Dunlop," *Toronto Star*, 1 May 1970.
28 City of Toronto, Department of the City Clerk to J.P. Robarts, Premier of Ontario. 17 April 1970. File: Trade and Industry Branch. Plant Closings Trade and Development. January–December 1970. Box 376. RG 3-26. AO.
29 Melville Watkins, "Dunlop's Demise Is Paid for by Taxpayers," *Toronto Star*, 2 April 1970.
30 "The Government Has a Duty," *Globe and Mail*, 1 April 1970.
31 "Democratic Gap," *Peterborough Examiner*, 4 May 1970.
32 Jim Renwick, "The Tory Answer to Dunlop Political Fallout," *New Democrat*, May–June 1970.

33 "End the Branch Plant Economy in Ontario." Volume 51. NDP Branch Plant Task Force—Correspondence and Papers, 1970–71. C-13139 Reel. MG 28 I268. United Steelworkers of America. Library and Archives Canada (LAC).
34 Don Taylor, "The Ontario Worker and the Branch-Plant Economy," volume 51. NDP Branch Plant Task Force—Correspondence and Papers, 1970–71. C-13139 Reel. MG 28 I268. United Steelworkers of America. LAC. For more on the nationalization of Sydney Steel, see Lachlan Mackinnon, *Closing Sysco: Industrial Decline in Atlantic Canada's Steel City* (Toronto: University of Toronto Press, 2020).
35 "Time of Grace," *Toronto Star*, 10 April 1970.
36 "Stephen Lewis Offers 10-Point 'Labor Charter,'" *Oakville Journal*, September 1970.
37 "Mr Lewis and Labor Law," *Globe and Mail*, 24 September 1970.
38 Judith Stein, *Pivotal Decade: How the United States Traded Factories for Finance in the Seventies* (New Haven: Yale University Press, 2010); Douglas A. Irwin, "The Nixon Shock after Forty Years: The Import Surcharge Revisited," working paper 17749, National Bureau of Economic Research, Cambridge, Massachusetts, 2012, nber.org.
39 V. J. Macklin, General Director, Office of Economics, Federal Industry and Trade Development to A. G. Kniewasser, Senior Assistant Deputy Minister. 10 September 1971. File 301-20 (volume 1), Box 43, RG 20. LAC.
40 The Nixon shock was an "epochal event in the history of Canada–United States relations." As quoted in Bruce Muirhead, "From Special Relationship to Third Option: Canada, the U.S., and the Nixon Shock," *American Review of Canadian Studies* 34, no. 3 (2004): 439–42.
41 David Wolfe interviewed by Steven High. 25 January 2023.
42 Robert Laxer, "Foreword," in Robert Laxer, ed., *(Canada) Ltd: The Political Economy of Dependency* (Toronto: McClelland and Stewart, 1973), 9, 23.
43 Jim Laxer, "Canadian Manufacturing and US Trade Policy," in Laxer, ed., *(Canada) Ltd*, 28, 146.
44 G. Brent Clowater, "Canadian Science Policy and the Retreat from Transformative Politics: The Final Years of the Science Council of Canada, 1985–1992," *Scientia Canadensis* 35, no. 1–2 (2012): 107–34. See also James Gilmour, "Industrialization and Technological Backwardness: The Canadian Dilemma," *Canadian Public Policy* 4, no. 1 (1978): 20–33.

45 See, for example, Kristian Palda, *The Science Council's Weakest Link: A Critique of the Science Council's Technocratic Industrial Strategy for Canada* (Vancouver: Fraser Institute, 1979).
46 Hugh Windsor, "Differences on Halting a Decline," *Globe and Mail*, 25 June 1980.
47 Economic Policy Statement. File: Canadian Labour Congress, 1976–1983. B2019-0003-002(03). David Wolfe Fonds. UTA.
48 L. H. Lorrain, CPU National President, Preliminary Report of the Investigative Mission by a Delegation from the Cdn Paperworkers Union to Study Industrial Relations Concepts, with Particular Reference to Industrial Democracy and Codetermination in Sweden and West Germany. 31 May 1977. Volume 47. File 5: Industrial Democracy. R16007. LAC.
49 Steven Langdon, "Labour's New Struggle: Industrial Democracy," *Canadian Forum*, September 1970, 203–5.
50 OFL. "An Industrial Development Strategy: Economic and Social Planning for Growth, Full Employment and an Improvement in the Quality of Life." 13–16 November 1978. Annual Convention. File: Lay Offs. Reports and Newspaper Clippings—1978–1981. B364900. F4180-24: OFL. AO.
51 OFL. Statement on Economic Nationalism and Foreign Ownership. 23rd Annual Convention. 27–30 November 1979. File: Lay Offs. Reports and Newspaper Clippings—1978–1981. B364900. F4180-24: OFL. AO.
52 "Problems of Ontario's Political Economy: A Working Paper Prepared by the Ontario NDP Task Force on Manufacturing." February 1979. File 2: Treasury: Industrial Strategy, Box 8, P006 Floyd Laughren Fonds. Laurentian University Archives (LUA).
53 Ontario NDP Task Force on Manufacturing. New Directions for Ontario's Political Economy. November 1979. File 2: Treasury: Industrial Strategy, Box 8, P006: Laughren Fonds. LUA.
54 Nickel Belt NDP, "Brief Comments on the resolution proposed by the ONDP Task Force on Manufacturing." File 2: Treasury: Industrial Strategy, Box 8, P006: Laughren Fonds. LUA.
55 Simon Rosenblum, "De-industrialization in one country?" nd (1979?) File 2: Treasury: Industrial Strategy, Box 8, P006 Floyd Laughren Fonds. LUA.
56 Provincial Council, April 1980, Resolution to Convention, "Manufacturing Strategy for the 80s." File 2: Treasury: Industrial Strategy, Box 8, P006: Laughren Fonds. LUA.

57 Yu-Jen Wu, "Comparative Policies of Legal Provisions for Plant Closure: Strike a Balance?," *Journal of Comparative Asian Development* 9, no. 1 (2010): 80–102; and Chris Jecchinis, *Public Policy and Institutional Arrangements Concerning Redundancies in Certain West European Countries and Their Relevance for Canada in General and Ontario in Particular* (Lakehead University: Department of Economics, 1978).
58 Frances Raday, "Individual and Collective Dismissal—A Job Security Dichotomy," *Comparative Labor Law Journal* 10, no. 2 (Winter 1989): 123, 132.
59 Tuesday 4 November 1980. Legislature of Ontario. Select Committee on Plant Shutdowns and Employee Adjustment. File: Transcripts PS-1, October 30, 1980. Box C294 4-32-5-10. RG 49-173. AO.
60 "Is Capitalism Working?," *Time*, 21 April 1980.
61 OFL. Statement on Shutdowns, Cutbacks and Layoffs. Annual Convention. 24–27 November 1980. File: Lay Offs—reports and statistics, 1980–1983. B364900. F4180-24: OFL. AO.
62 Hugh Mackenzie interviewed by Steven High. 7 November 2022.
63 The Labour Response to the Recession. Paper Prepared for York University Symposium, 8 June 1982. File 6 +5 The Political Economy of Wage Controls—Materials, 1982. David Wolfe Fonds. UTA.
64 The Labour Response to the Recession.
65 Robert White to All Ontario Local Unions, 11 August 1980, File 1, Volume 250, MG 29 I119 United Auto Workers. LAC; City Clerk, City of London to Secretary, Local 27, UAW. File: Plant Closures. Reference Material, Correspondence (1), 1979-80. Box 326. UAW. LAC.
66 "Ontario Says It Won't Ask Firms to Justify Plant Closings," *Toronto Star*, 23 July 1980.
67 Transcript. Legislature of Ontario. Select Committee on Plant Shutdowns and Employee Adjustment. Wednesday 26 November 1980. File: Transcripts PS-19-20. Box C294. RG 49-173. AO.
68 Transcript. Legislature of Ontario. Select Committee on Plant Shutdowns and Employee Adjustment. Thursday 13 November 1980. File: Transcripts PS-9. Box C294. RG 49-173. AO.
69 Transcript. Legislature of Ontario. Select Committee on Plant Shutdowns and Employee Adjustment. Tuesday 18 November 1980. File: Transcripts PS-11-1-2. Box C294. RG 49-173. AO.
70 Transcript. Legislature of Ontario. Select Committee on Plant Shutdowns and Employee Adjustment. Tuesday 2 December 1980. File: Transcripts PS-23-24. Box C294. RG 49-173. AO.

71 The company's terrible treatment of Dunnville workers is examined in Julie Guard, "Authenticity on the Line: Women Workers, Native 'Scabs,' and the Multi-ethnic Politics of Identity in a Left-Led Strike in Cold War Canada," *Journal of Women's History* 5, no. 4 (Winter 2004): 117–40; and Robert A. Ventresca, "'Cowering Women, Combative Men?': Femininity, Masculinity, and Ethnicity on Strike in Two Southern Ontario Towns, 1964–1966," *Labour / Le Travail* 39 (1997): 125–58.
72 Transcript. Legislature of Ontario. Select Committee on Plant Shutdowns and Employee Adjustment. Tuesday 9 December 1980. Box C294. RG 49-173. AO.
73 Ontario, Select Committee on Plant Shutdowns and Employee Adjustment, *Interim Report* (12 December 1980), 33.
74 Ontario Mining Association. Exhibit 98, 28 January 1981. See also, Toronto Board of Trade, 28 January 1981, Exhibit 90, CMA 29 January 1981, Exhibit 93. RG 7-11-0-54. AO.
75 New Democrats. *Job Security: The Unwritten Report of the Select Committee on Plant Shutdowns and Employee Adjustment*. 23 February 1981. Plant Shutdowns and Layoffs—briefs and submissions, 1977–1981. B364900. F4180-24. OFL. AO.
76 David Robertson and Chuck Rachlis, "The NDP Replying to Laxer," *Canadian Forum*, June–July 1984, 10–14.
77 Ross McClellan interviewed by Steven High. 18 August 2023.
78 Ontario, Legislative Assembly, Standing Committee on Resources Development, *Report on Plant Closures and Community and Employee Adjustment* (June 1987).
79 *Report on Plant Closures and Community and Employee Adjustment*.
80 Sam Gindin interviewed by Steven High. Session 2. 24 November 2022.
81 Sam Gindin interviewed by Steven High. Session 1. 15 November 2022.

CHAPTER 2: THE HAMILTON CHALLENGE

1 Richard Allen, "The Distant Thunder of Economic Policy: The Hamilton Challenge." For NDP Convention 1988. File 7, Box 17. Richard Allen. The William Ready Division of Archives and Research Collections. McMaster University Archives (MUA).
2 Stephen McBride, *The Political Economy of Training in Canada* (York University: Centre for Research on Work and Society, 1998).
3 Gary Gerstle, *The Rise and Fall of the Neoliberal Order: America and the World in the Free Market Era* (New York: Oxford University Press, 2022), 122.

4   Gregory J. Inwood, *Continentalizing Canada: The Politics and Legacy of the Macdonald Royal Commission* (Toronto: University of Toronto, 2005), 2.
5   Royal Commission on the Economic Union and Development Prospects for Canada, *Report, Volume 1* (Ottawa: Minister of Supply and Services Canada, 1985), xii, 233.
6   For a strong analysis of the opposition to Mike Harris's sweeping changes after 1995, see Douglas James Nesbitt, "Days of Action: Ontario's Extra-Parliamentary Opposition to the Common Sense Revolution, 1995–1998" (PhD History: Queen's University, 2018).
7   Nesbitt, "Days of Action."
8   Christoffer Green-Pedersen and Kees van Kersbergen, "The Politics of the 'Third Way': The Transformation of Social Democracy in Denmark and The Netherlands," *Party Politics* 8, no. 5 (2002): 512; Ian McKay, *Rebels, Reds and Radicals: Rethinking Canada's Left History* (Toronto: Between the Lines, 2005), 181; Michael Harrington, *Socialism: Past and Future* (New York: Arcade Publishing, 1989), 112.
9   Richard Allen, *The Social Passion: Religion and Social Reform in Canada 1914–28* (Toronto: University of Toronto Press, 1971).
10 James Naylor, *The Fate of Labour Socialism: The Co-operative Commonwealth Federation and the Dream of a Working-Class Future* (Toronto: University of Toronto Press, 2016), 22.
11 Peter Graham, "New Leftists, 'Party-Liners,' and Municipal Politics in Toronto," in Roberta Lexier, Stephanie Bangarth, and Jon Weier, eds., *Party of Conscience: The CCF, the NDP, and Social Democracy in Canada* (Toronto: Between the Lines, 2018), 83. See also, Peter Graham with Ian McKay, *Radical Ambition: The New Left in Toronto* (Toronto: Between the Lines Press, 2019); and Ian Milligan, *Rebel Youth: 1960s Labour Unrest, Young Workers, and New Leftists in English Canada* (Vancouver: University of British Columbia Press, 2014).
12 "Jobs, Justice and Recovery: The Challenge to Hamilton." A speech by Bob Rae, MPP, Leader Ontario NDP. Hamilton Convention Centre. 9 February 1983. File 22, Box 17. Richard Allen Fonds. MUA.
13 There is a sizable literature on the working-class and industrial history of Hamilton. A good place to start is Craig Heron, *Lunch-Bucket Lives: Remaking the Workers' City* (Toronto: Between the Lines, 2015).
14 Report of the Joint Manpower Planning Committee at Aerovox Canada Limited. 28 July 1972. File: Technological and Economic Change Adjustment Assistance. Aerovox Canada, Ltd (3837-1/A18). Volume 2. RG 118. LAC.

15   Val Bjarnason, Secretary-Treasurer, UE to John Eleen. 5 May 1980. File Plant Shutdowns and Layoffs. Reports and Statistics—1977–1980. B364900. F4180-24, OFL. AO.
16   Ontario Labour Relations Board, *Annual Reports*, 1980–81, 31–32.
17   Leaflet. Conference on the Layoffs & Their Effects. USWA Local 1005. Thursday 3–4 March 1983. Auditorium, Steelworkers Centre, Hamilton. File 6 +5 The Political Economy of Wage Controls—Materials, 1982. Wolfe Papers. UTA.
18   Media Reach Transcript TV 11 Newsroom CHCH-TV Hamilton. 6 January 1984. File: Stelco Inc—Canada Works—Hamilton. AO.
19   Social Planning and Research Council of Hamilton and District. Submission. October 31, 1983. File 0784. T-8403. Royal Commission on the Economic Union and Development Prospects for Canada. Canadiana Digitization Platform, heritage.canadiana.ca.
20   Hamilton and District Labour Council. Submission. November 1983. File 0946. T-8403. Royal Commission on the Economic Union and Development Prospects for Canada. Canadiana Digitization Platform.
21   Labour Council of Metropolitan Toronto. Submission. "A Time for Public Leadership: Industrial Strategies for Metropolitan Toronto." June 1983. File 0740. Reel T-8402. Royal Commission on the Economic Union and Development Prospects for Canada. Canadiana Digitization Platform.
22   Metro Toronto, *Industrial Development in Metropolitan Toronto: Issues, Prospects and Strategies* (June 1983).
23   Labour Council of Metropolitan Toronto, "A Time for Public Leadership."
24   Social Planning Council of Metropolitan Toronto. Democracy, Equality and Canada's Economic Future. Brief. November 1983. File 0857. T-8403. Royal Commission on the Economic Union and Development Prospects for Canada. Canadiana Digitization Platform.
25   The Hamilton Challenge. Report. June 1986. File 14: The Hamilton Challenge: Regional. Box 57. Richard Allen Fonds. MUA.
26   Hamilton and District Labour Council. The Full Employment Committee Report on the Hamilton Challenge. File 14: The Hamilton Challenge. Box 57. Richard Allen Fonds. MUA.
27   Gregory Baum, "Catholic Bishops on the Canadian Economy," *Ontario New Democrat* 22, no. 2 (March 1983).
28   Ted Jackson, "Worker Ownership and Economic Democracy: The Short and the Long of It." Prepared for the Alternative Paths to Jobs, Development, Equality and Peace Conference. Sponsored by

the Canadian Centre for Policy Alternatives. Toronto 22–24 March 1984. File 9: Funds for Workers Enterprise. Box 57. Richard Allen Fonds. MUA.

29 Baum, "Catholic Bishops on the Canadian Economy."
30 Allan Blakeney, "Discussion," John Richards and Don Kerr, eds., *Canada, What's Left? A New Social Contract: Pro and Con* (Edmonton: NeWest Publishers, 1986), 37.
31 Tri-State Conference on steel. File 7: Newspaper. Box 17. Richard Allen Fonds. MUA.
32 John Portz, *The Politics of Plant Closings* (Lawrence: University of Kansas, 1990), 95–96, 112.
33 Nat Weinberg to Leonard Woodcock, Meeting with Kelso, 9 January 1973. LR000262, UAW President's Office_ Leonard Woodcock Records—Part 1—Series I_ General Union Files (17-1)-001. WRL.
34 Louis O. Kelso to Woodcock. 3 October 1973. LR000262, UAW President's Office, Leonard Woodcock Records—Part 1—Series I_ General Union Files (17-4)-001. WRL.
35 Gregory D. Squires, *Capital and Communities in Black and White: The Intersections of Race, Class and Uneven Development* (Albany: State University of New York Press, 1994), 23.
36 Worker Ownership Development Foundation. Toronto. Partnership and Economic Democracy: A Response to the Employee Share Ownership Plan as Proposed in Ontario's May 13, 1986 Budget. 6 August 1986. ESOP (Employee Share Ownership Plan) Submission for Release. B309018. RG 6-67. OFL. AO.
37 Commonwealth of Pennsylvania. Pennsylvania Economic Development Partnership. Office of the Governor. *Task Force Report. Employee Ownership*. Harrisburg: Commonwealth of Pennsylvania, January 1988. File: Task Force Report Employee Ownership. Box 10. Robert P. Casey Papers, Penn State University, State College, Pennsylvania.
38 Jeremy Brecher, *Banded Together: Economic Democratization in the Brass Valley* (Chicago: University of Illinois Press, 2011), 81.
39 This was most clearly expressed in his 1992 book *Negotiating the Future*, co-authored with his father Irving Bluestone, a former UAW vice-president. On the book's front cover was an endorsement from Bill Clinton, which read: "The Bluestones offer a New Covenant for labor and management based on participation, co-operation, and teamwork." Barry Bluestone and Irving Bluestone, *Negotiating the Future: A Labor Perspective on American Business* (NY: Basic Books, 1992).

40 See, for example: J. Paul Grayson, *Corporate Strategy and Plant Closures: The SKF Experience* (Toronto: Our Times, 1985), introduction.
41 Canadian Centre for Policy Alternatives. Workshop: "Fighting De-industrialization—An Economists View." 18 February 1983. File: Miscellaneous—reports and newspaper clippings, 1982–83. B364900. F4180-24. OFL. AO.
42 William Johnson, "Reprieve—or Town Faces Death," *Globe and Mail*, 15 February 1972, 31.
43 Keven B. Kerr, "Employee Ownership." 14 February 1991. Research Branch. Library of Parliament. R11545 Volume 13 File Economy—Employee Ownership, 1991. LAC.
44 *Temiscaming, Québec* (Montreal: Office national du film du Canada, 1975), onf.ca.
45 Bob Schutte, "Pioneer Chainsaw Massacre: The Bitter Lesson Of," *Worker Co-Ops* 5, no. 3 (December 1985).
46 "Co-ops," *Ontario New Democrat* 20, no. 2 (1981).
47 Judith Forrestal, "Worker Co-ops," *Ontario New Democrat* 21, no. 6 (November 1982), 19.
48 John P. Hoerr, *And the Wolff Finally Came: The Decline of the American Steel Industry* (Pittsburgh: University of Pittsburgh Press, 1988), 413.
49 Appendix Four: Canadian Porcelain: An Historical Review. *Co-operative Work* (Toronto) Ltd. Canadian Porcelain Co-operative Ltd. Business Plan. April 1985. File 8: CPP Feasibility. Box 57. Richard Allen Fonds. MUA.
50 E. B. Priestner, Executive Vice-President Operations, Westinghouse Canada to Richard Allen, MLA, 4 March 1985. File 4: Canadian Porcelain Project Trustees. Box 57. Richard Allen Fonds. MUA.
51 Handwritten note dated 21 February 1985. File 5: Canadian Porcelain Project. Notes, Meetings and Discussions, 1985. Box 57. Richard Allen Fonds. MUA.
52 Richard Allen, MPP, Hamilton West, to Andrew Brandt, Minister of Industry and Trade. 18 February 1985. File 11: CPP Ministry of Industry and Trade. Box 57. Richard Allen Fonds. MUA.
53 Mike Pettapiece, "Brandt Approves Study of Porcelain Revival," *Hamilton Spectator*, 12 March 1985.
54 Philip Newell, Chairman, Christians for a Cooperative Society. 22 February 1985. Press Release. "Encouraging Week for Canadian Porcelain Project." File 5: Canadian Porcelain Project. Notes, Meetings and Discussions, 1985. Box 57. Richard Allen Fonds. MUA.

55 J. Monster, Chief Fundraiser, The Canadian Porcelain Project, The Canadian Porcelain Co-operative: Triumph or Tribulation? File 9: Funds for Workers Enterprise. Box 57. Richard Allen Fonds. MUA.
56 Handwritten note dated 21 February 1985. File 5: Canadian Porcelain Project. Notes, Meetings and Discussions, 1985. Box 57. Richard Allen Fonds. MUA.
57 Murray Campbell, "NDP Would Give Employees Buy-out Plan in Plant Closing," *Globe and Mail*, 4 April 1985.
58 The Ontario New Democrats. News Release. "Help Employees Protect Their Jobs." 3 April 1985. File 5: Canadian Porcelain Project. Notes, Meetings and Discussions, 1985. Box 57. Richard Allen Fonds. MUA.
59 John Flanders, "Minister to Be Lobbied by Porcelain Workers," *Hamilton Spectator*, 5 June 1985.
60 Martin Browning and Wayne Lewchuk, *Worker Preferences for Co-operatives versus Private Buy-outs* (Working Paper No 87-09. Department of Economics. McMaster University. April 1987). File 9: Funds for Workers Enterprise. Box 57. Richard Allen Fonds. MUA.
61 Editorial, "Canadian Porcelain: The Community's Case," *Hamilton Spectator*, 10 May 1985.
62 Editorial "Give Workers a Chance," *Toronto Star*, 27 May 1985.
63 Adam Mayers, "Pledges Part of Deal in Porcelain Buyout," *Hamilton Spectator*, 22 June 1985.
64 Mike Pettapiece, "Decision Tough Blow for Worker Group but Bid Worthwhile," *Hamilton Spectator*, 22 June 1985.
65 Steven Langdon, MP, Essex-Windsor, and Marion Dewar, MP, Hamilton Mountain, to Robert de Cotret, 8 March 1988. File 12: CPP Publicity. Box 57. Richard Allen Fonds. MUA.
66 Steven High, *Deindustrializing Montreal: Entangled Histories of Race, Residence and Class* (Montreal: McGill-Queen's University Press, 2022), 178–79.
67 Subcommittee on the Foreign Experience of the Task Force on Economic Adjustment and Worker Dislocation, "Evaluation of Programs to Assist Displaced Workers in Foreign Industrialized Countries," December 1986.
68 Subcommittee on the Foreign Experience, "Evaluation of Programs to Assist Displaced Workers," 21.
69 United States, Office of Technology Assessment, *Plant Closings: Advance Notice and Rapid Response*, Special Report (Washington, September 1986), 4.

70 Morley Gunderson and Andrew Sharpe, eds., *Forging Business-Labour Partnerships: The Emergence of Sector Councils in Canada* (Toronto: University of Toronto Press, 1998), 3.
71 Peter Warrian interviewed by Steven High. 21 July 2023.
72 David A. Wolfe and D'Arcy Martin, "Human Resources Think for Themselves: The Experience of Unions in the Sectoral Skills Council," in Gunderson and Sharpe, eds., *Forging Business-Labour Partnerships*, 101, 106.
73 Ontario, Premier's Council, *People and Skills in the New Global Economy* (Toronto: Queen's Printers, 1990), 177.
74 Ontario New Democrats. 19 December 1988. News Release. "It is time for a labour adjustment centre for Hamilton Workers." From Richard Allen, Brian Charlton, Bob Mackenzie. File 8 Box 22. Richard Allen. MUA.
75 Editorial, "To Cope with Crises: Keep the Job-Finders," *Hamilton Spectator*, 23 December 1988.
76 5 July 1990. The Report of the Regional Chairman's Working Committee on Employment Adjustment. File 2: Regional Chairman's Working Committee on Employment Adjustment. Box 58. Richard Allen Fonds. MUA.
77 30 January 1989. Saad Ghanem, Director, Scott Galbraith, Manager, Greater Hamilton Regional Municipality of Hamilton-Wentworth to Chairman and Members of Economic Development and Planning Committee. File 2: Regional Chairman's Working Committee on Employment Adjustment. Box 58. Richard Allen Fonds. MUA.
78 Seven Employment Adjustment Experiences: A Comparison. File 2: Regional Chairman's Working Committee on Employment Adjustment. Box 58. Richard Allen Fonds. MUA.
79 5 July 1990. The Report of the Regional Chairman's Working Committee on Employment Adjustment. File 2: Regional Chairman's Working Committee on Employment Adjustment. Box 58. Richard Allen Fonds. MUA.
80 Thomas Walkom, *Rae Days: The Rise and Follies of the NDP* (Toronto: Key Porter, 1994), 39.
81 Ontario NDP, *Policy Book: Last Revised after Convention 1988* (Toronto: Ontario NDP, 1988).
82 "NDP Caucus Increases Activity," *Ontario New Democrat* 21, no. 5 (November 1983), 5.

CHAPTER 3: COMPETING IN THE NEW GLOBAL ECONOMY

1 Ontario, Premier's Council, *Competing in the New Global Economy: Report of the Premier's Council*, Volume 1 (Toronto: Queen's Printer, 1998), 15.
2 Ontario Ministry of Industry, Trade and Technology. Statement by the Honourable David Peterson, Premier of Ontario, on the Release of the Premier's Council Report Competing in the New Global Economy. 11 April 1988. File 6: NDP Conference on Social Democratic Futures 1990. Richard Allen Fonds. MUA.
3 This is not to say that resistance ended altogether; it just took on new forms such as the anti-globalization movement of the late 1990s.
4 David A. Wolfe, "Networking Among Regions: Ontario and the Four Motors of Europe," *European Planning Studies* 8, no 3 (2000): 267–84.
5 Neil Bradford, "Ontario's Experiment with Sectoral Initiatives: Labour Market and Industrial Policy, 1985–1996," in Morley Gunderson and Andrew Sharpe, eds., *Forging Business-Labour Partnerships: The Emergence of Sector Councils in Canada* (Toronto: University of Toronto Press, 1998), 160.
6 Premier's Council, *Competing in the New Global Economy*, 35.
7 Premier's Council, *Competing in the New Global Economy*, 63.
8 Premier's Council, *Competing in the New Global Economy*, 19.
9 David Osborne, *Laboratories of Democracy* (Boston: Harvard Business School Press, 1990), 32.
10 Osborne, *Laboratories of Democracy*, 1
11 Osborne, *Laboratories of Democracy*.
12 Bill Clinton in Osborne, *Laboratories of Democracy*, xi.
13 Stephen K. Medvic, "Old Democrats in New Clothes," *Party Politics* 13, no. 5 (2007): 587.
14 Borrelli, "Finding the Third Way," 434.
15 Medvic, "Old Democrats in New Clothes," *Party Politics*, 591.
16 Osborne, *Laboratories of Democracy*, 13.
17 Osborne, *Laboratories of Democracy*, 152.
18 Osborne, *Laboratories of Democracy*, 177.
19 Osborne, *Laboratories of Democracy*, 195.
20 Osborne, *Laboratories of Democracy*, 208–9.
21 Evan Cleave, Godwin Arku, and Merlin Chatwin, "One Step Forward, Two Steps Back?: Consultant Influence on Local Economic Development Policy in Canada," *Canadian Public Administration* 62, no. 1 (2019): 103.

22 Christopher D. McKenna, *The World's Newest Profession: Management Consulting in the Twentieth Century* (Cambridge: Cambridge University Press, 2006), 24.
23 Ira Magaziner also chaired a high-profile commission whose report, *America's Choices: High Skills or Low Wages*, advocated European-style apprenticeships and job training programs. Nelson Lichtenstein and Judith Stein, *A Fabulous Failure: The Clinton Presidency and the Transformation of American Capitalism* (Princeton: Princeton University Press, 2023), 66.
24 Ira C. Magaziner and Robert B. Reich, *Minding America's Business: The Decline and Rise of the American Economy* (New York: Vintage Books, 1983), 6–7, 203.
25 Paul R. Krugman, "What Do Undergrads Need to Know About Trade?," *American Economic Review* 83, no. 2 (May 1993): 23.
26 Helen Burstyn, *Eleven Out of Ten: The Life and Work of David Pecaut* (Toronto: Dundurn, 2012), 69.
27 Bob Rae interviewed by Steven High. 10 April 2023.
28 John O'Grady interviewed by Steven High. 2 October 2022.
29 Fred Pomeroy to D'Arcy Martin, Leo Gerard and Gord Wilson. Re: Premier's Council Report of December 14th. File Premier's Council Report (1990). B2019-0002/002. David Wolfe Fonds. UTA. This document has since been withdrawn from the archives by Wolfe.
30 Sam Gindin, *The Canadian Auto Workers: The Birth and Transformation of a Union* (Toronto: Lorimer, 1995), 4.
31 David Robertson, CAW Technology Project, "Contrasting Agendas: Building a Training System." Presentation to Premier's Council Subcommittee on Training, 8 September 1989. Premier's Council—personal notes, memos (1990-1994). B2019-0002/002. David Wolfe Fonds. UTA.
32 United Steelworkers of America, Empowering Workers in the Global Economy: A Labour Agenda for the 1990s, Conference Proceedings (Toronto, 22–23 October 1991).
33 Ontario Federation of Labour Trade Union Project Proposals for the Technology Adjustment Research Programme. April 1989. Technology Adjustment Research Programme Trade Union Project Proposals, 1989. File: 4180-3, B847974. OFL. AO.
34 The Ontario Federation of Labour published a number of these studies in two volumes. Chris Schenk and John Anderson, *Re-shaping Work: Union Responses to Technological Change* (OFL: TARP, 1995) and *Re-shaping Work 2: Labour, the Workplace and Technological Change* (Canadian Centre for Policy Alternatives: Garamond Press, 1999).

35 Ontario Federation of Labour. *Statement on Education and Training*. 33rd Annual Convention. 20–24 November 1989. Box 3 B2019-002/003. David Wolfe Fonds. UTA.
36 John O'Grady interviewed by Steven High. 2 October 2022.
37 Hugh Mackenzie interviewed by Steven High. 7 November 2022.
38 David Wolfe interviewed by Steven High. 25 January 2023.
39 Fred Pomeroy to D'Arcy Martin, Leo Gerard and Gord Wilson. Re: Premier's Council Report of December 14th File Premier's Council Report (1990). B2019-0002/002. David Wolfe Fonds. UTA. This document has since been withdrawn from the archives by Wolfe.
40 D'Arcy Martin, *Thinking Union: Activism and Education in Canada's Labour Movement* (Toronto: Between the Lines, 1995), 97–98; see also: Rianne Mahon, *The Politics of Industrial Restructuring: Canadian Textiles* (Toronto: University of Toronto Press, 1984).
41 Leon Muszynski, *The Deindustrialization of Metropolitan Toronto: A Study of Plant Closures, Layoffs, and Unemployment* (Toronto: Social Planning Council of Metropolitan Toronto, June 1985); Pat Armstrong, *Labour Pains: Women's Work in Crisis* (Toronto: The Women's Press, 1984); Pat Armstrong and Hugh Armstrong, *The Double Ghetto: Canadian Women & Their Segregated Work*, third ed. (Toronto: McClelland & Stewart, 1994).
42 The Report of the Premier's Council on Education, Training and Adjustment. July 1990. Comment and Review. Ontario Federation of Labour. Premier's Council—personal notes, memos (1990-1994). B2019-0002/002. David Wolfe Fonds. UTA.
43 Chair Judith Maxwell to Henry Brehaut and Leo Gerard. 19 December 1989. Premier's Council—personal notes, memos (1990–1994). B2019-0002/002. David Wolfe Fonds. UTA.
44 Report of Premier's Council (12 April 1990 Draft). Comments and Recommended Changes. Gordon F. Wilson, Leo Gerard, Fred Pomeroy. 26 April 1990. Premier's Council—personal notes, memos (1990 1994). B2019-0002/002. David Wolfe Fonds. UTA. This document has since been withdrawn from the archives by Wolfe.
45 Ontario, Premier's Council, *People and Skills in the New Global Economy* (Toronto: Queen's Printers, 1990), 152.
46 Premier's Council, *People and Skills in the New Global Economy*, 3–4, 83–84.
47 Rianne Mahon, "Remise en cause des paramètres du post-fordisme au Canada et en Ontario," *Cahiers de recherche sociologique* 18–19 (1992): 207.

48 David A. Wolfe and D'Arcy Martin, "Human Resources Think for Themselves: The Experience of Unions in the Sectoral Skills Council," in Gunderson and Sharpe, eds., *Forging Business-Labour Partnerships*, 100.
49 *The Premier's Council on the Economy*. Final Report, 11 February 1991. R. I. G. McLean, Ernst & Young. File: Premier's Council—reports (1990–1994). B2019-0002/002. Box 2. David Wolfe Fonds. UTA.
50 Floyd Laughren interviewed by Steven High. 25 January 2024.
51 Riel Miller interviewed by Steven High. 3 January 2024.
52 Isabella Bakker, *Economic Policy Review: Issues for Discussion and Debate*. Prepared for the Ontario NDP Caucus Policy and Priorities Committee. August 1989. File Economic Policy, 1989-90. B353495. F4338-10: Bob Rae Papers. AO.
53 Mel Watkins. "An Economic Policy for the NDP." Notes for Discussion. January 1990. ONDP Fonds. QUA.
54 Roger Peters and Ted Jackson, "Full Employment and Economic Democracy," May 1989. Ontario NDP Caucus, Policy and Priorities Committee. Economic Policy Review. This paper was originally written for the Economic Policy Review of the Federal NDP. And published by the Canadian Centre for Policy Alternatives. March 1989. ONDP Fonds. QUA.
55 Ethan Phillips, "Encouraging Worker Ownership and Labour Investment in Ontario." June 1989. Ontario NDP Caucus. Policy and Priorities Committee. Economic Policy Review. ONDP Fonds. QUA.
56 Ontario Federation of Labour. Economic Restructuring and the Unequal Society. 32nd Annual Convention 28 November–1 December 1988. ONDP Fonds. QUA.
57 Preliminary First Draft. 9 March 1990. Prepared by Riel Miller for Economic Sub-Committee of the Planning and Priorities Committee of the ONDP Caucus, Floyd Laughren, Chair. File Economic Policy, 1989-90. B353495. F4338-10 Bob Rae Papers. AO.
58 Economic Policy Review Paper. Draft—15 May 1990. Chuck Rachlis and David Wolfe. File: Economic Policy Review Notes—Correspondence, 1989–1990. B2019-0003/001 (09). David Wolfe Fonds. UTA.
59 Riel Miller interviewed by Steven High. 3 January 2024.
60 Simon Rosenblum. 28 May 1990. Economic Policy Review Notes—Correspondence, 1989–1990. B2019-0003/001 (09). David Wolfe Fonds. UTA. This document has since been withdrawn from the archives by Wolfe.

61 Chuck Rachlis to Floyd Laughren and David Wolfe. "Reaction to Economy Policy Paper in London, May 26." 30 May 1990. Economic Policy Review Notes—Correspondence, 1989–1990. B2019-0003/001 (09). David Wolfe Fonds. UTA. This document has since been withdrawn from the archives by Wolfe.
62 Fred Glover. 28 May 1990. Economic Policy Review Notes—Correspondence, 1989–1990. B2019-0003/001 (09). David Wolfe Fonds. UTA.
63 *Greening the Party, Greening the Province: A Vision for the Ontario NDP*. A Policy Proposal Prepared for the Ontario NDP Caucus. March 1990. Accession 1999-047. Box 11/21. ONDP Fonds. QUA.
64 In the wake of *Our Common Future*, the final report of the World Commission on Environment and Development released in 1987, the OFL encouraged affiliates and local labour councils to form environment committees and established a province-wide committee that brought together trade unions and environmental groups.
65 Bob Rae Notes for a Speech delivered to OFL Convention. 21 November 1989. Sheraton Centre, Toronto. File Labour, 1983–1990. B353183. F4338-10. Bob Rae Fonds. AO.
66 Thomas Walkom, *Rae Days: The Rise and Follies of the NDP* (Toronto: Key Porter, 1994), 95–96.
67 Henry Milner, "What Canadian Social Democrats Need to Know about Sweden, and Why," in John Richards, Robert D. Cairns, and Larry Pratt, eds., *Social Democracy without Illusions: Renewal of the Canadian Left* (Toronto: McClelland and Stewart, 1991), 56.
68 John Richards, "Playing Two Games at Once," in Richards, Cairns, and Pratt, eds., *Social Democracy without Illusions*, 107.
69 Allan Blakeney, "The Social Democratic Challenge: To Manage Both Distribution and Production," in Richards, Cairns, and Pratt, eds., *Social Democracy without Illusions*, 51–52.
70 Simon Rosenblum and Peter Findlay, eds., *Debating Canada's Future: Views from the Left* (Toronto: James Lorimer and Company, 1991), iv.
71 Henry Milner and Arthur Milner, "Social Democracy versus Democratic Socialism: The Question of Public Ownership," in Rosenblum and Findlay, eds. *Debating Canada's Future*, 11.
72 John Richards, "Collective Bargaining Is Not Enough: The Case for a New Social Contract," in Rosenblum and Findlay, eds., *Debating Canada's Future*, 79.
73 Milner and Milner, "Social Democracy versus Democratic Socialism," in Rosenblum and Findlay, eds., *Debating Canada's Future*, 15.
74 Rosenblum and Findlay, eds., *Debating Canada's Future*, 88.

75 David A. Wolfe, "Technology and Trade," in Rosenblum and Findlay, eds., *Debating Canada's Future*, 106.
76 Wolfe, "Technology and Trade," 113.
77 Wolfe, "Technology and Trade," 123
78 David Wolfe interviewed by Steven High. 25 January 2023.
79 Leo Panitch and Donald Swartz, "The Case for Socialist Democracy," in Rosenblum and Findlay, eds., *Debating Canada's Future*, 29, 40.
80 Daniel Drache, ed., *Getting on Track: Social Democratic Strategies for Ontario* (Montreal: McGill-Queen's University Press, 1992), xiv.
81 Hugh Mackenzie, "Dealing with the New Global Economy: What the Premier's Council Overlooked," in Drache, ed., *Getting on Track*, 15, 224.
82 Sam Gindin and David Robertson, "Alternatives to Competitiveness," in Drache, ed., *Getting on Track*, 33.
83 Marcy Cohen, "The Feminization of the Labour Market: Prospects for the 1990s," in Drache, ed., *Getting on Track*, 110–11, 119.
84 Brief to the Ontario Government. A Community Based Response to the Premier's Council Report "People and Skills in the New Global Economy." From Advocates for Community Based Training and Education for Women. December 1990. Page 1. File OFL—Training Committee, 1986–1991. F 2190—1. D'Arcy Martin Fonds. AO.
85 John O'Grady interviewed by Steven High. 21 November 2022.
86 Nancy Fraser, *The Old Is Dying and the New Cannot Be Born* (London: Verso, 2019), 11.
87 Hugh Mackenzie interviewed by Steven High. 7 November 2022.
88 Sam Gindin interviewed by Steven High. Session 1. 15 November 2022.
89 Sam Gindin, "Putting the Con Back in the Economy," *This*, May 1992, 17.
90 Sam Gindin interviewed by Steven High. Session 2. 24 November 2022.
91 Gindin, "Putting the Con Back in the Economy," 17–18.
92 Gindin, "Putting the Con Back in the Economy," 20.
93 Paul Krugman, "Competitiveness: A Dangerous Obsession," *Foreign Affairs* 73, no. 2 (1994): 29, 32.
94 Krugman, "Competitiveness," 36–37.
95 Krugman, "Competitiveness," 39–40.

CHAPTER 4: AN AGENDA FOR PEOPLE

1 Gerald Caplan, "Ontario NDP Comes of Age at Convocation Hall," *Toronto Star*, 7 October 1990.
2 Bob Nixon quote in Kevin Ward, "Opposition Fears NDP's Labor, Union Sympathies," *Kitchener-Waterloo Record*, 15 October 1990.

3   An Agenda for People, 18 August 1990. File: Agenda for People. B368449. Box 24. F 4338: Bob Rae Fonds, AO.
4   "The NDP's 'Agenda for the People,'" *Kingston Whig-Standard*, 1 October 1990.
5   Frances Lankin interviewed by Steven High. 8 November 2023.
6   Michael Mendelson interviewed by Steven High. 18 July 2023.
7   Confidential interview with X by Steven High.
8   Howard Hampton interviewed by Cynthia Smith. 10 April 2002. Archive Code: C 81-4-0-99. Transcript: B437272. Osgood Society Oral History Project. AO.
9   Don Lajoie, "Labor Talks Tough: White Warns of Mass Sit-ins," *Windsor Star*, 31 May 1990.
10 Don Lajoie, "March on Queen's Park Ordered by Fed-Up CAW," *Windsor Star*, 2 June 1990.
11 Don Lajoie, "OFL Urges Protests over Plant Closings," *Windsor Star*, 13 August 1990.
12 Richard Mackie, "NDP's 'New Deal' Would Bring Deficits: Rae Predicts $1-Billion Shortfall to Finance Tax Reform, Help for Workers," *Globe and Mail*, 4 September 1990.
13 Jobs and Integrity in Liberal. 30 August 1990. Ontario Binder Election 90—Media Releases. Accession 1999-047. Box 20 of 21. ONDP Fonds. QUA.
14 Ross McClellan interviewed by Steven High. 18 August 2023.
15 "The Liberal record that David Peterson doesn't mention." 24 August 1990. Ontario Binder Election 90—Media Releases. Accession 1999-047. Box 20 of 21. ONDP Fonds. QUA.
16 James Rusk, "Business Nightmare Becomes Reality," *Globe and Mail*, 7 September 1990; Linda Leatherdale, business editor, "Oh-Oh!," *Toronto Sun*, 7 September 1990.
17 "Fighting the Recession," *Toronto Star*, 12 October 1990.
18 "Fighting the Recession."
19 Chris Hall, "NDP Will Work with You, Rae Tells Bay Street," *Ottawa Citizen*, 25 September 1990.
20 Bob Rae quoted in Richard Brennan, "NDP Will Do 'Right Thing' for Windsor, Rae Says," *Windsor Star*, 20 September 1990.
21 David Lewis, *The Corporate Welfare Bums* (Toronto: Lorimer, 1972)
22 Michael Mendelson interviewed by Steven High. 18 July 2023.
23 David Agnew quoted in Judy Steed, "Premier Bob: He's Not Just Another Little Rae of Sunshine," *Toronto Star*, 29 September 1990.
24 Ross McClellan interviewed by Steven High. 18 August 2023.
25 Michael Mendelson interviewed by Steven High. 18 July 2023.

26 The 1987 election results saw the NDP get 25.6 percent province-wide, with considerable strength in the three Windsor ridings (48%), the four Hamilton ridings (44.9%), and northern Ontario (37.3%). Tim Welch to Robin Sears. 22 October 1987. Accession 03-027, Box 7/8. ONDP Fonds. QUA.
27 Bob Rae interviewed by Steven High. 10 April 2023.
28 Peter Warrian interviewed by Steven High. 21 July 2023.
29 Caucus Organization—Internal Report. The report was prepared by David Agnew, David Reville, with input from Dave Christopherson, Dennis Drainville, Evelyn Gigantes, Floyd Laughren, and Tony Silipo. ONDP. QUA.
30 Confidential interview with X by Steven High.
31 Bob Rae interviewed by Steven High. 10 April 2023.
32 Jim Foulds interviewed by Steven High. 8 August 2023.
33 Bud Wildman interviewed by Steven High. 3 August 2023.
34 Confidential interview with X by Steven High.
35 D. Wolfe Interview Transcript. May 1995. File: Interview Transcript—NDP 1990 Transition, DW involvement, policy. 1995. B2019-0002/001. David Wolfe Fonds. UTA.
36 D. Wolfe Interview Transcript. May 1995.
37 D. Wolfe Interview Transcript. May 1995.
38 19 October 1990. D'Arcy to Fred. File: Discuss with Fred [Pomeroy, President of the Communications and Electrical Workers of Canada], 1990–91. F 2190—1: D'Arcy Martin Fonds. AO.
39 Ross McClellan interviewed by Steven High. 18 August 2023.
40 Ross McClellan interviewed by Steven High. 18 August 2023.
41 This reference to a Cold War era American science fiction horror film, remade in 1993, where people are cloned surfaced several times during the interview with Ross McClellan. 18 August 2023.
42 Opening of the 1st Session of the 35th Parliament on 20 November 1990. *Hansard*.
43 Thomas Walkom, "Suddenly Rae Looks Liberal," *Toronto Star*, 24 November 1990.
44 Robert Sheppard, "A Program with Less Than Meets the Ear," *Globe and Mail*, 21 November 1990.
45 Walkom, "Suddenly Rae Looks Liberal."
46 Haroon Siddiqui, "Words of Advice from NDP Premiers Past," *Toronto Star*, 1 October 1990.
47 Siddiqui, "Words of Advice from NDP Premiers Past."

48 Standing Committee on Finance and Economic Affairs, Pre-budget Hearings, Douglas Peters and Ruth Getter, Toronto-Dominion Bank, *Hansard*, 21 January 1991; 22 January 1991.
49 Standing Committee on Finance and Economic Affairs, Pre-budget Hearings, *Hansard*, 21 January 1991.
50 Laughren, *Hansard*, 10 December 1991.
51 Bob Rae interviewed by Steven High. 10 April 2023.
52 Greg Albo, "Divided Province: Democracy and the Politics of State Restructuring in Ontario," in Greg Albo and Bryan M. Evans, eds., *Divided Province: Ontario Politics in the Age of Neoliberalism* (Montreal: McGill-Queen's University Press, 2018), 19.
53 David A. Wolfe and Tijs Creutzberg, "Community Participation and Multilevel Governance in Economic Development Policy," Paper prepared for the Panel on the Role of Government (Toronto, August 2003), 74.
54 Frances Lankin quoted in Douglas James Hall, "An Evaluation of Ontario's Industrial Policy Efforts: 1985–1995" (Political Science PhD: Queen's University, 1998), 241.
55 Bob Rae 2001, Cynthia Smith. Osgood Society Oral History Project, 25 July 2001, for The Osgoode Society, for the Attorney General's project.
56 Floyd Laughren, Economic Outlook, *Hansard*, 4 December 1990.
57 Floyd Laughren, Updated Economic Outlook, *Hansard*, 18 March 1991.
58 Standing Committee on Finance and Economic Affairs, Pre-Budget Hearings, Douglas Peters and Ruth Getter, Toronto-Dominion Bank, *Hansard*, 21 January 1991; 22 January 1991.
59 Standing Committee on Finance and Economic Affairs, Pre-Budget Hearings, *Hansard*, 21 January 1991; 22 January 1991.
60 Bob Rae, *From Protest to Power: Personal Reflections on a Life in Politics* (Toronto: Viking, 1996), 196.
61 Thomas Walkom, *Rae Days: The Rise and Follies of the NDP* (Toronto: Key Porter, 1994), 98; and Nelson Wiseman and Benjamin Isitt, "Social Democracy in Twentieth Century Canada: An Interpretive Framework," *Canadian Journal of Political Science* 40, no. 3 (2007): 582.
62 Mel Watkins, Standing Committee on Finance and Economic Affairs, *Hansard*, 29 July 1991.
63 Budget Hearings, Standing Committee on Finance and Economic Affairs, *Hansard*, 1 August 1991.

64 Budget Hearings, Standing Committee on Finance and Economic Affairs, *Hansard*, 1 August 1991.
65 Budget Hearings in Cornwall, Standing Committee on Finance and Economic Affairs, *Hansard*, 27 August 1991.
66 Budget Hearings in Windsor, Standing Committee on Finance and Economic Affairs, *Hansard*, 19 August 1991.
67 Rae, *From Protest to Power*, 198.
68 Ross McClellan interviewed by Steven High. 18 August 2023.
69 John O'Grady interviewed by Steven High. 2 October 2022.
70 Michael Mendelson interviewed by Steven High. 18 July 2023.
71 Frances Lankin interviewed by Steven High. 8 November 2023.
72 Michael Mendelson interviewed by Steven High. 18 July 2023.
73 Monte Kwinter, *Hansard*, 11 June 1991.
74 *Hansard*, 16 May 1991.
75 Michael Decter, *Tales from the Back Room: Memories of a Political Insider* (Winnipeg: Great Plains Publications, 2010), 185–87.
76 Catherine Thompson, "An 'Unthinkable' Year: NDP Debut Not Easy as Recession Dominates," *Kitchener-Waterloo Record*, 31 August 1991.
77 Riel Miller interviewed by Steven High. 3 January 2023.
78 Party-Government Committee. 2 September 1991. Accession 2014-180. Box 53/56. ONDP Fonds. QUA.
79 I would have dearly loved to interview Julie Davis, but she died far too young.
80 Stephen McBride, "Ideological and Policy Failure in the Ontario NDP," in William K. Carroll and R.S. Ratner, eds., *Challenges and Perils: Social Democracy in Neo-liberal Times* (Halifax/Winnipeg: Fernwood Publishing: 2005).
81 David Wolfe interviewed by Steven High. 25 January 2023.
82 D. Wolfe Interview Transcript. May 1995. File: Interview Transcript—NDP 1990 Transition, DW involvement, policy. 1995. B2019-0002/001. David Wolfe Fonds. UTA.
83 Bryan Evans interviewed by Steven High. 4 August 2023.
84 Bud Wildman interviewed by Steven High. 3 August 2023.
85 Michael Mendelson interviewed by Steven High. 18 July 2023.
86 Bud Wildman interviewed by Steven High. 3 August 2023.
87 Rae, *From Protest to Power*, 5–6.
88 ONDP Provincial Council reaffirmed the policy on public auto insurance in October 1991. Accession 2014-180. Box 53/56. ONDP Fonds. QUA.
89 Discussion on Caucus-Party Relations. Background. 22 April 1992. Accession 2014-180. Box 53/56. ONDP. QUA.

90 Discussion on Caucus-Party Relations.
91 *The New Ontario Democrat* (June 1992). Accession 2003-027. Box 1/8. ONDP Fonds. QUA.
92 "Dancing with government." *The New Ontario Democrat* (June 1992). Accession 2003-027, Box 1/8. ONDP Fonds. QUA.
93 *The New Ontario Democrat* (September 1992). Accession 2003-027, Box 1/8. ONDP Fonds. QUA.
94 John Valleau and Jean Smith, "Party and Leader lock horns at November Council meeting." *The Ontario New Democrat* (February 1993). Box 2003-027 1/8. ONDP Fonds. QUA.
95 Valleau and Smith, "Party and Leader lock horns at November Council meeting."
96 Chuck Rachlis and David Wolfe, "An Insiders' View of the NDP Government in Ontario," in Graham White, ed., *The Government and Politics of Ontario*, fifth ed. (Toronto: University of Toronto Press, 1997).
97 Rae, *From Protest to Power*, 7.
98 Ross McClellan, "The Story of Ontario's First NDP Government," Draft #12, 30 March 1995, p. 2. McClellan shared a copy with the author.
99 Bob Rae interviewed by Steven High. 10 April 2023.
100 Bob Rae interviewed by Steven High. 10 April 2023.
101 Walkom, *Rae Days*, 120.
102 Thomas Walkom, "No Rae of Hope: Why a Year of Promise Has Gone Sour for Premier Bob," *Toronto Star*, 28 December 1991.
103 Sam Gindin interviewed by Steven High. Session 1. 15 November 2022.
104 John O'Grady interviewed by Steven High. 2 October 2022.
105 Floyd Laughren interviewed by Steven High. 25 January 2024.

CHAPTER 5: BOB MACKENZIE'S LABOURISM

1 Bob Callahan, *Hansard*, 19 June 1991.
2 Bryan Evans interviewed by Steven High. 4 August 2023.
3 Jim Foulds interviewed by Steven High. 8 August 2023.
4 Michael A. Brown, *Hansard*, 28 November 1990.
5 To learn more about Indigenous resurgence in the face of environmental injustice, see: Lianne C. Leddy, *Serpent River Resurgence: Confronting Uranium Mining at Elliot Lake* (Toronto: University of Toronto Press, 2022). For the socio-economic and health effects of the mine closures see: Anne-Marie Mawhinney and Jane Pitblado, eds., *Boom Town Blues: Elliot Lake Collapse and Revival in a Single-Industry Community* (Toronto: Dundurn, 1999).

6   Floyd Laughren interviewed by Steven High. 25 January 2024.
7   Shelley Martel, with her Deputy Minister, Brock Smith, The Standing Committee on Estimates met with the Ministry of Northern Development and Mines, *Hansard*, 6 November 1991.
8   Thomas Walkom, *Rae Days: The Rise and Follies of the NDP* (Toronto: Key Porter, 1994), 126.
9   Chuck Rachlis and David Wolfe, "An Insiders' View of the NDP Government of Ontario: The Politics of Permanent Opposition Meets the Economics of Permanent Recession," in Graham White, ed., *The Government and Politics of Ontario*, fifth ed. (Toronto: University of Toronto Press, 1997).
10 Bryan Evans interviewed by Steven High. 4 August 2023.
11 Bob Mackenzie, Standing Committee on Estimates, *Hansard*, 25 June 1991.
12 "An NDP Vision Forged by Reality," *Toronto Star*, 21 November 1990.
13 Robert Sheppard, "A Program with Less Than Meets the Ear," *Globe and Mail*, 21 November 1990.
14 George Dadamo, *Hansard*, 20 June 1991.
15 Randy Hope, *Hansard*, 20 June 1991.
16 Roxana Ng, "Worker Adjustment in the Garment Sector: Comparing Plant-Based and Sector-Based Committees," A Supplemental Report to The Great Sewing Exchange Research Project. 9 May 1994. File 6: Worker Adjustment in the Garment Sector comparing plant-based and sector-based committees. B2014-0005/028. Roxana Ng Fonds. UTA.
17 Chuck Rachlis to Bob Rae (cc Laughren, Mackenzie, Morin-Strom, Reville). "Layoffs, Premier's Council and Training." 7 December 1989. File: Layoff Protection, Ministry of Labour (1986-1990). Box 35. P006: Floyd Laughren Fonds. Laurentian University Archives (LUA).
18 J. Wilson, *Hansard*, 29 November 1990.
19 Remo Mancini, *Hansard*, 29 November 1990.
20 Bob Nixon, *Hansard*, 28 November 1990.
21 Offer, *Hansard*, 6 December 1990.
22 Bob Mackenzie, *Hansard*, 6 December 1990.
23 Mark Hallman, "NDP Sidesteps Issue of Jobs Protection Board," *Financial Post*, 7 December 1990.
24 Joan Fawcett, *Hansard*, 27 March 1991.
25 OFL. Not crying Wolf . . . Plant Closures and Ontario. 26 January 1991. File 8: Layoff and Closure Program 1990-91. R15805 Volume 22. United Food and Commercial Workers. LAC.
26 Monte Kwinter, *Hansard*, 4 June 1991.

27 David Ramsay, *Hansard*, 4 June 1991.
28 Ron DeRuyter, "Dreams Broken by Plant Closing, K-W Tire Worker Rolls to New Job," *Kitchener-Waterloo Record*, 20 June 1992.
29 Floyd Laughren, *Hansard*, 20 June 1991.
30 Floyd Laughren, *Hansard*, 17 June 1991.
31 Bob Mackenzie, *Hansard*, 27 June 1991.
32 Background. Ontario M of L. 27 June 1991. File Labour—Minimum Wage. Box 8. RG 3-9-0-169, B368638 Ross McClelland Materials. AO.
33 Paul Oliver, Director of Government Affairs, Ontario Restaurant Association to Richard Allen. 25 May 1992. File 8, Box 51. Richard Allen Fonds. MUA.
34 Ministry of Labour. Minimum Wage. Cabinet Submission. 22 April 1993. File Minimum Wage. B813639, Box 8. RG 3-9-0-169. AO.
35 Bob Mackenzie, Standing Committee on Estimates, *Hansard*, 26 June 1991.
36 Bob Mackenzie, Standing Committee on Estimates, *Hansard*, 26 June 1991.
37 Confidential interview with X by Steven High.
38 Bob Mackenzie, *Hansard*, 9 May 1991.
39 Bob Mackenzie, *Hansard*, 5 June 1991.
40 Carman McClelland, *Hansard*, 5 June 1991.
41 Bob Callahan, *Hansard*, 19 June 1991.
42 Bob Mackenzie, *Hansard*, 19 June 1991.
43 ILGWU and Canadian Textile and Chemical Union. 26 August 1991 to MITT. File: Industry, Trade and Technology. Box 8. RG 3-9-0-169, B368638. AO.
44 Standing Committee on Resources Development, *Hansard*, 31 July 1991.
45 D'Arcy Martin and Leo Dowhaluk of the Communications and Electrical Workers of Canada, Standing Committee on Resources Development, *Hansard*, 31 July 1991.
46 David Ramsay, Standing Committee on Resources Development, *Hansard*, 31 July 1991.
47 D'Arcy Martin, Standing Committee on Resources Development, *Hansard*, 31 July 1991.
48 *Employment Standards Amendment Act (Employee Wage Protection Program), 1991 / Loi de 1991 modifiant la Loi sur les normes d'emploi (Programme de protection des salaires des employés)*, SO 1991, c 16, digitalcommons.osgoode.yorku.ca.
49 "Provincial NDP, Grits Push through Wage-Protection Fund," *Ottawa Citizen*, 16 October 1991.

50 Ross McClellan, "The Story of Ontario's First NDP Government," Draft #12, 30 March 1995, p. 37. In the possession of the author.
51 Bryan Evans interviewed by Steven High. 4 August 2023.
52 McClellan, "The Story of Ontario's First NDP Government," 49.
53 Christina Gabriel and Laura Macdonald, "NAFTA and Economic Restructuring: Some Gender and Race Implications," in Isabella Bakker, ed., *Rethinking Restructuring: Gender and Change in Canada* (Toronto: University of Toronto Press, 1996), 173–74.
54 Ann Porter and Barbara Cameron, Impact of Free Trade on Women in Manufacturing (Ottawa: Canadian Advisory Council on the Status of Women, 1987), 1. File: Free Trade—Reports. Accession 2014-180, Box 44/56. ONDP. QUA.
55 Harry Shardlow, Ministry of Labour, Standing Committee on Estimates, *Hansard*, 26 June 1991.
56 Roxana Ng, "Worker Adjustment in the Garment Sector: Comparing Plant-Based and Sector-Based Committees," A Supplemental Report to The Great Sewing Exchange Research Project. 9 May 1994. File 6: Worker Adjustment in the Garment Sector comparing plant-based and sector-based committees. B2014-0005/028. Roxana Ng Fonds. UTA.
57 Ng, "Worker Adjustment in the Garment Sector."
58 Ng, "Worker Adjustment in the Garment Sector."
59 Roxana Ng, Chairperson, Apparel Textile Action Committee (ATAC). Final Report, 9 March 1992–8 March 1993. Submitted to Industrial Adjustment Services (IAS), Employment and Immigration Canada and Ontario Ministry of Labour. File 17: ATAC Final Report, 9 March 1992–8 March 1993, B2014-0005/028. Roxana Ng Fonds. UTA.
60 Jennifer Stephen, MLEC, "'What's Training Got to do with it?' Training and Unemployed Workers," CRWS Training and Education Working Group Workshop. 6 October 1993. File 6: ATAC: Resources on retraining, 1992–1993, B2014-0005/040. Roxana Ng Fonds. UTA.
61 Kim Moody, *An Injury to All: The Decline of American Unionism* (London: Verso, 1988), 4.
62 D'Arcy Martin, *Thinking Union: Activism and Education in Canada's Labour Movement* (Toronto: Between the Lines, 1995), 61.
63 Sam Gindin interviewed by Steven High. Session 2. 24 November 2022.
64 Bob Mackenzie, Standing Committee on Estimates, *Hansard*, 25 June 1991.
65 Bob Mackenzie, Standing Committee on Estimates, *Hansard*, 26 June 1991.
66 Bob Mackenzie, Standing Committee on Estimates, *Hansard*, 26 June 1991.

67 Rodney Haddow and Thomas R. Klassen, "Partisanship, Institutions and Public Policy: The Case of Labour Market Policy in Ontario, 1990–2000," *Canadian Journal of Political Science* 37, no. 1 (2004): 146.
68 Rachlis and Wolfe, "An Insiders' View of the NDP Government in Ontario."
69 Confidential interview with X by Steven High.
70 Kevin M. Burkett, "The Politicization of the Ontario Labour Relations Framework in the 1990s," *Canadian Labour & Employment Law Journal* 6 (1998): 170.
71 Burkett, "The Politicization of the Ontario Labour Relations Framework," 168.
72 Peter Warrian and John O'Grady, "Human Resource Development, Labour Adjustment, Work Organization and Labour Relations: An Integrated Strategy for Skill-Based Restructuring in the Traded Sector." July 1991. 17 July 1991. John O'Grady to Ross McClellan. File: Industry, Trade and Technology. File: Labour—Training and Adjustment. Box 8. B368638. RG 3-9-0-169, AO.
73 John O'Grady and Peter Warrian, "Work Organization, Labour Relations and Human Resource Management: The Negotiated Adjustment Option." Background Paper, July 1991. For Canadian Market and Productivity Centre's Project on Economic Restructuring. File: Layoff Protection, Ministry of Labour (1986-1990), Box 35. Laughren Fonds. LUA.
74 David Wolfe interviewed by Steven High. 25 January 2023.
75 Peter Warrian interviewed by Steven High. 21 July 2023.
76 Confidential interview with X by Steven High.
77 Haddow and Klassen, "Partisanship, Institutions and Public Policy," 147.
78 Proposed Reform of the Ontario Labour Relations Act. A Discussion Paper from the Ministry of Labour. November 1991. (p. 52–54) File ORLA. Box B353615. AO.
79 Conrad Black, "New Labor Relations Act: Bob Rae's Moment of Truth," *Financial Post*, 2 September 1991.
80 Daniel W. Crow, "From Protest to Powerlessness: A Marxist Analysis of the Ontario NDP" (Politics MA Thesis: Brock University, 1999), 112.
81 Alan Ernst interviewed by Steven High. 11 August 2023.
82 Ruth Wright, "The Alternative Agenda: An Interview with Bob White," *Canadian Business Review* 19, no. 4 (Winter 1992): 6–13.
83 Ross McClellan interviewed by Steven High. 18 August 2023.
84 Leo Gerard, *Hansard*, 6 August 1992.

85 Bud Wildman interviewed by Steven High. 3 August 2023.
86 John O'Grady interviewed by Steven High. 2 October 2022.
87 Peter Warrian interviewed by Steven High. 21 July 2023.
88 John O'Grady interviewed by Steven High. 2 October 2022.
89 "The Story of Ontario's First NDP Government," Draft #12, 30 March 1995, pp. 33–34. In the possession of the author.
90 Bryan Evans interviewed by Steven High. 4 August 2023.
91 "NDP Politician Bob Mackenzie Dead," *Hamilton Spectator*, 18 January 2011.

CHAPTER 6: WORKER OWNERSHIP
AND LABOUR-LED VENTURE CAPITAL

1 Fax to Ross McClellan from USWA Staffer. Algoma Steel. 30 January 1991. Notes on Future of Algoma Steel/Dofasco Operations in Sault Ste Marie and Wawa. Prepared by USWA Research. File: Labour—Algoma. B368638 Box 8. RG 3-9-0-169. AO.
2 Sean M. Di Giovanna, "Fighting for a Working Future: Emerging Models of Local Union Strategy in a New Era of Global Competition" (PhD Geography: Toronto, 1997), 7.
3 Linda Savory-Gordon, "Spillover Effects of Increased Workplace Democracy at Algoma Steel on Personal, Family, and Community Life" (PhD Policy Studies: Bristol, 2003), 70–71.
4 Correspondence between two staff members. Redacted. 24 January 1991. File: Industry, Trade and Technology. B368638 Box 8. RG 3-9-0-169. AO.
5 Hugh Mackenzie interviewed by Steven High. 7 November 2022.
6 Bob Rae, *From Protest to Power: Personal Reflections on a Life in Politics* (Toronto: Viking, 1996), 145.
7 Rae, *From Protest to Power*, 51, 53.
8 Rae, *From Protest to Power*, 146.
9 Duncan McDowall, *Steel at the Sault: Francis H. Clergue, Sir James Dunn, and the Algoma Steel Corporation, 1901–1956* (Toronto: University of Toronto Press, 1984), 6–7.
10 [redacted consultant], "The Algoma Steel Corporation: Recovery or Crisis. A Study Prepared by [consultant] and Associates for the United Steelworkers of America." January 1987. File 1: Worker Ownership Study, USWA. Box B368244. RG 3-97. AO.
11 Ross McClellan interviewed by Steven High. 18 August 2023.
12 Fax to Ross McClellan from [USWA Staffer]. Algoma Steel. 30 January 1991. Notes on Future of Algoma Steel/Dofasco Operations

in Sault Ste Marie and Wawa. Prepared by USWA Research. File: Labour—Algoma. B368638. G 3-97. AO.
13 Rae, *From Protest to Power*, 146.
14 Tim Armstrong, Standing Committee on Estimates continued, Hansard, 2 October 1991.
15 Bob Rae interviewed by Steven High. 10 April 2023.
16 Ken Delaney to Bob Rae. "Federal Government, Algoma Steel and the Steelworkers Union." 26 October 1991. File "Algoma Steel." B368449. G 3-97. AO.
17 Di Giovanna, "Fighting for a Working Future," 7–8; Janis Sarra, "Protecting Workers' Equitable Investments in the Firm: Viewing Corporate Governance Reform through the Lens of Dismantled Government Infrastructure" (LLM Thesis: University of Toronto, 1998), 105
18 Robert F. Nishman, *Worker Ownership and the Restructuring of Algoma Steel in the 1990s* (Queen's University: Industrial Relations Center, 1995), 16.
19 Ron Bloom quoted in Lynn Williams, *One Day Longer: A Memoir* (Toronto: University of Toronto Press, 2011), 250.
20 Noam Scheiber, "Manufacturing Bloom," *New Republic*, 7 December 2009.
21 Keven B. Kerr, "Employee Ownership." 14 February 1991. Research Branch. Library of Parliament. File Economy—Employee Ownership, 1991. R11545 Volume 13. LAC.
22 "A Worker Ownership Funding Mechanism for Ontario: A Review of the Experience of Other Jurisdictions and Its Relevance to Ontario." Study Prepared for the Industrial Restructuring Commissioner of Ontario. Research Study #18, May 1990. p29. File 1: Worker Ownership Study, USWA. Box B368244. RG 3-97. AO.
23 John P. Hoerr, *And the Wolff Finally Came: The Decline of the American Steel Industry* (Pittsburgh: University of Pittsburgh Press, 1988), 396–97, 413.
24 Philissa Cramer, "How Jewish Socialist Summer Camp Shaped Ron Bloom, One of the Men Responsible for the Postal Service's Future" *Jewish Telegraph Agency*, 1 June 2011.
25 Scheiber, "Manufacturing Bloom."
26 Ron Bloom interviewed by Mary Anne Chute Lynch. 18 May 2018. Yale Program on Financial Stability Lessons Learned Oral History Project. Transcript: ypfs.som.yale.edu.
27 Tony Martin, Hansard, 30 May 1991.

28 Nishman, *Worker Ownership and the Restructuring of Algoma Steel*, 16.
29 Rob Ferguson, "Hardrock Recruiting: Gutsy Steelworkers' Leader Wants More Union Workers," *Kitchener-Waterloo Record*, 20 August 1991.
30 Ken Delaney interviewed by Steven High. 10 January 2023.
31 Savory-Gordon, "Spillover Effects of Increased Workplace Democracy at Algoma Steel," 77–78.
32 Don Barill, *Algoma Steel and Sault Ste Marie: A History* (Sault Ste. Marie: USWA Local 2724, 2001), 215–16.
33 News Release. Office of Premier. 28 February 1992. File Labour/ITT—Algoma Steel. Box 19. B 397858. RG 3-97. AO.
34 Quoted in Sarra, "Protecting Workers' Equitable Investments in the Firm," 113.
35 Sarra, "Protecting Workers' Equitable Investments in the Firm," 117.
36 Algoma Steel Inc. *Annual Report 1994*. File 8, Box 51. Richard Allen Fonds. MUA.
37 Di Giovanna, "Fighting for a Working Future," 103–4.
38 Barill, *Algoma Steel and Sault Ste Marie*, 224.
39 Ken Delaney interviewed by Steven High. 10 January 2023.
40 Savory-Gordon, "Spillover Effects of Increased Workplace Democracy at Algoma Steel," 122.
41 Larry Sefton Memorial Lecture by Alexander (Sandy) Adam. 26 March 1997. Sefton Memorial Lecture Committee File. Laurel Sefton MacDowell Fonds. UTA.
42 Nishman, *Worker Ownership and the Restructuring of Algoma Steel*, 32.
43 Savory-Gordon, "Spillover Effects of Increased Workplace Democracy at Algoma Steel," 199–200.
44 Scheiber, "Manufacturing Bloom."
45 Peter Warrian interviewed by Steven High. 21 July 2023.
46 Hugh Mackenzie interviewed by Steven High. 7 November 2022.
47 Sarra, "Protecting Workers' Equitable Investments in the Firm," 121–22.
48 Algoma Steel Inc. *Annual Report 1994*. File 8, Box 51. Richard Allen Fonds. MU.
49 Ken Delaney interviewed by Steven High. 10 January 2023.
50 Scheiber, "Manufacturing Bloom."
51 Bill Saporito, "Ron Bloom," *Time—100 World Changers*, 29 April 2010.

52 Jim Foulds to Robert Nixon, Treasurer, 24 September 1986. ESOP (Employee Share Ownership Plan) Submission for Release. B309018. RG 6-67. OFL. AO.
53 John O'Grady interviewed by Steven High. 2 October 2022.
54 "A Worker Ownership Funding Mechanism for Ontario: A Review of the Experience of Other Jurisdictions and Its Relevance to Ontario." Study Prepared for the Industrial Restructuring Commissioner of Ontario. Research Study #18. May 1990. File: Worker Ownership Study, USWA, File-1. Box B368244. RG 3-97. AO.
55 Gord Wilson to Bob Rae, 3 March 1989. Accession 2014-180, Box 25/56. ONDP. QUA.
56 The Quebec Solidarity Fund: A model for Ontario? Developed by Gord Wilson, OFL Chair; Julie Davis, Vice-Chair, John Calvert, CUPE; Sam Gindin, CAW; Hugh Mackenzie, USWA; John O'Grady, OFL; Robin Sears, NDP. File: "Worker Investment". B179485. F 4180-24. OFL. AO.
57 John O'Grady. Labour Management of Development Funds: A Statement of Objectives and Principles. Draft #1. 4 May 1989. Accession 2014-180. Box 25/56. ONDP Fonds. QUA.
58 O'Grady, Labour Management of Development Funds.
59 Steven High, *Deindustrializing Montreal: Entangled Histories of Race, Residence and Class* (Montreal: McGill-Queen's University Press, 2022), 276.
60 Julie Davis to Robin Sears. 14 February 1989—share a paper. David Mackenzie, "The Quebec Solidarity Fund: A Model for Ontario?" 20 January 1989. Series 2014-180, Box 25/56. ONDP. QUA.
61 Sam Gindin to Robin Sears. 31 May 1989. File: Ontario Federation of Labour—Solidarity Fund. Box 2014-180 25/56. ONDP. QUA.
62 The public hearings of the Standing Committee on Finance and Economic Affairs on the Labour Sponsored Venture Capital Corporation Act (Bill 150) continued on 28 May 1992. *Hansard.*
63 "A Worker Ownership Funding Mechanism for Ontario." Study for the Industrial Restructuring Commissioner, 5.
64 Virginia Galt, "NDP Studying Ways to Bolster Investment: New Pension-Fund Rules, Investor Pools Being Considered," *Globe and Mail,* 30 April 1991.
65 Kevin Ward, "Ontario Hopes to Encourage Workers to Invest in Employers," *Kitchener-Waterloo Record,* 21 June 1991.
66 Ward, "Ontario Hopes to Encourage Workers to Invest in Employers."

67 Statement to the Legislature by Floyd Laughren, Treasurer of Ontario and Minister of Economics on Ontario Program for Worker Ownership. 20 June 1991. File: "Worker Investment". F 4180-24. B179485. OFL. AO.
68 Richard Mackie, "Worker Investing Proposed NDP Outlines Financing Idea," *Globe and Mail*, 16 August 1991.
69 Robert White, Director, CAW, to Bob Christie, Assistant Deputy Minister, Ministry of Treasury and Economics. 25 September 1991. File: "Worker Investment". F 4180-24. B179485. OFL. AO.
70 Ontario Federation of Labour. The public hearings of the Standing Committee on Finance and Economic Affairs on the Labour Sponsored Venture Capital Corporation Act (Bill 150). *Hansard*, 28 May 1992.
71 Sam Gindin, Canadian Auto Workers, The public hearings of the Standing Committee on Finance and Economic Affairs on the Labour Sponsored Venture Capital Corporation Act (Bill 150), *Hansard*, 28 May 1992.
72 Gindin, Hearings on Bill 150, *Hansard*, 28 May 1992.
73 Robin MacKnight, United Steelworkers of America, The public hearings of the Standing Committee on Finance and Economic Affairs on the Labour Sponsored Venture Capital Corporation Act (Bill 150), *Hansard*, 28 May 1992.
74 Gerry Phillips, Liberal MPP, The public hearings of the Standing Committee on Finance and Economic Affairs on the Labour Sponsored Venture Capital Corporation Act (Bill 150), *Hansard*, 28 May 1992.
75 Monte Kwinter, The Standing Committee on Finance and Economic Affairs continued to consider the Labour Sponsored Venture Capital Corporations Act (Bill 150), *Hansard*, 4 June 1992.
76 Paul Johnson, NDP MPP, The Standing Committee on Finance and Economic Affairs continued to consider the Labour Sponsored Venture Capital Corporations Act (Bill 150), *Hansard*, 4 June 1992.
77 Hearings on Bill 150, *Hansard*, 11 June 1992.
78 Shelley Wark-Martyn, Minister of Revenue, Hearings on Bill 150, *Hansard*, 11 June 1992.
79 Elinor Caplan, Hearings on Bill 150, *Hansard*, 11 June 1992.
80 Shelley Wark-Martyn, Third reading of the Labour Sponsored Venture Capital Corporation Act was moved in the legislature, *Hansard*, 16 July 1992.
81 Richard Mackie, "Ottawa Rejects Worker Plan: Ontario Fails to Get Backing for Industrial Investment," *Globe and Mail*, 7 October 1991.

82 Greg Sorbara, Liberal MPP, *Hansard*, 16 July 1992.
83 Savory-Gordon, "Spillover Effects of Increased Workplace Democracy at Algoma Steel," 117.
84 Tim Armstrong, "Contemporary Collective Bargaining: How Well Is It Working?," 21st Larry Sefton Memorial Lecture (Woodsworth College, University of Toronto, 2003), 27, 28–29.
85 Floyd Laughren, *Hansard*, 6 November 1991.
86 According to Hugh Mackenzie, the single most important legacy of the Rae government was the so-called Maple model of Ontario pension plans. Interviewed by Steven High. 7 November 2022. It was under Rae when the various public pension plans such as the Ontario Municipal Employees' Retirement System (OMERS) became jointly sponsored with union representation on their boards. Before that, public pension funds were largely run as a branch of the Ontario Treasury and concentrated on safe but low-return government bonds. The NDP thus opened the door to further financialization. Thomas Fraser, "Pension Fund City: Retirement, Real Estate, and Public Sector Labour" (MA History: Concordia University, 2022), 42–43. See also: Isla Carmichael, *Pension Power: Unions, Pension Funds, and Social Investment in Canada* (Toronto: University of Toronto Press, 2005); and Richard Lee Deaton, *The Political Economy of Pensions: Power, Politics, and Social Change in Canada, Britain, and the United States* (Vancouver: University of British Columbia Press, 1989).

CHAPTER 7: NORTHERN EXCEPTIONALISM

1 Floyd Laughren lecture notes for a class on regional development and regional disparity. David Robertson to Northern Members, "Resource Development and Regional Disparity." 21 November 1983. File 2135-2, B350151. F2135-2 Elie Martel Fonds. AO.
2 Ontario Liberal Party. *The Ontario Liberal Party and the North: A Fair Share in Ontario Prosperity*. March 1985. File NDP Research Information. B350151. F2135-2 Elie Martel Fonds. AO.
3 See, for example: Steven High, *One Job Town: Work, Belonging and Betrayal in Northern Ontario* (Toronto: University of Toronto Press, 2018); and Brittany Luby, *Dammed: The Politics of Loss and Survival in Anishinaabe Territory* (Winnipeg: University of Manitoba Press, 2020).
4 See, for example: Michel Beaulieu, *Labour at the Lakehead: Ethnicity, Socialism, and Politics, 1900-35* (Vancouver: University of British Columbia Press, 2012); and Ian Radforth, *Bushworkers and Bosses: Logging in Northern Ontario, 1900-1980* (Toronto: University of

Toronto Press, 1988), which was the first academic history book that I bought, at the 1988 Ontario NDP convention.
5   Half-jokingly, I made my partner read a book about working-class masculinity in my hometown before we married, "so she knew what she was getting into." Thomas Dunk, *It's a Working Man's Town: Male Working-Class Culture* (Montreal: McGill-Queen's University Press, 1991).
6   Jim Foulds interviewed by Steven High. 8 August 2023.
7   Bryan Evans interviewed by Steven High. 4 August 2023.
8   Floyd Laughren interviewed by Steven High. 25 January 2024.
9   Floyd Laughren interviewed by Steven High. 25 January 2024.
10 Heather Mary Hall, "Stuck Between a Rock and a Hard Place: The Politics of Regional Development Initiatives in Northern Ontario" (PhD Geography: Queen's University, 2012), 207.
11 Thomas Walkom, "North Waiting for Rae's Sunrise," *Toronto Star*, 20 May 1991.
12 Bud Wildman interviewed by Steven High. 3 August 2023.
13 Dioxin was first linked to the bleaching process in the pulp and paper industry by the US Environmental Protection Agency in 1985, but the study was only leaked to the public two years later by Greenpeace. David A. Sonnenfeld, "Social Movements and Ecological Modernization: The Transformation of Pulp and Paper Manufacturing," *Development and Change* 33 (2002): 4.
14 Ontario. Final Report and Recommendations of the Advisory Committee on Resource Dependent Communities in Northern Ontario. 26 May 1986. File: Report on Resource Dependent Communities in the North. B289130. F 2135-2: Elie Martel Fonds. AO.
15 Bud Wildman interviewed by Steven High. 3 August 2023.
16 November 4, 1992 Northern Caucus. Handwritten Notes. P006-31 Northern Caucus. Laughren Fonds. LUA.
17 Naomi Krogman and Tom Beckley, "Corporate 'Bail-Outs' and Local 'Buyouts': Pathways to Community Forestry," *Society and Natural Resources* 15 (2002): 120.
18 Bud Wildman interviewed by Steven High. 3 August 2023.
19 Bud Wildman interviewed by Steven High. 3 August 2023.
20 Bud Wildman interviewed by Steven High. 3 August 2023.
21 Ross McClellan. "The Story of Ontario's First NDP Government," Draft #12, 30 March 1995, p. 132. In the possession of the author.
22 Shelley Martel, Minister of Northern Development and Mines, legislative committee for Estimates, *Hansard*, 15 September 1994.

23 Shelley Martel, Minister of Northern Development and Mines, *Hansard*, 6 November 1991.
24 Shelley Martel, Minister of Northern Development and Mines. The Standing Committee on Estimates met with the Ministry of Northern Development and Mines. *Hansard*, 6 November 1991.
25 Shelley Martel, *Hansard*, 16 October 1991.
26 McClellan, "The Story of Ontario's First NDP Government," 23.
27 It ended up going to the courts, as the municipality didn't have the right to sign off on the partnership.
28 Kimberly-Clark Corporation. Press Release. "Kimberly-Clark and the New York Times Company Announce That Negotiations to Sell Spruce Falls Are Unsuccessful." 11 September 1990. Fonds Local 2995 du Syndicat des bûcherons et des employés de scieries. Centre d'archives de la Grande Zone argileuse (CAGZA), Hearst.
29 The Corporation of the Town of Kapuskasing. Press Release. Achat de la Spruce Falls par des employés. nd (est. December 1990). Fonds Local 2995 du Syndicat des bûcherons et des employés de scieries. CAGZA.
30 Wesley Cragg and Mark Schwartz, "Sustainability and Historical Injustice: Lessons from the Moose River Basin," *Journal of Canadian Studies* 31, no. 1 (1996): 62.
31 Jean Manore, "Nature's Power and Native Persistence: The Influence of First Nations and the Environment Is the Development of the Mattagami Hydro-Electric System during the Twentieth Century," *Journal of the Canadian Historical Association* 6, no. 1 (1995): 169.
32 Cragg and Schwartz, "Sustainability and Historical Injustice," 70.
33 Manore, "Nature's Power and Native Persistence," 176.
34 Jim Morris, "Oldman River's 'Death' Mourned," *Windspeaker*, 7 June 1991.
35 "Quebec Crees Warn of Violence," *Windspeaker*, 29 March 1991.
36 "Hydro Hearings Called Off," *Windspeaker*, 5 July 1991, 3.
37 Editorial, "Pulling the Plug," *Windspeaker*, 5 July 1991.
38 Sandy Nation First Nation, signed by Chief Jonas J. Fiddler and all the councillors, to Bob Rae. 6 August 1991. File: Spruce Falls Power, 1991–1992. B430045. RG 3-80-0-54. AO.
39 Richard Mackie, "Can't Afford Mill Bailout, Premier Says," *Globe and Mail*, 15 July 1991.
40 Bob Rae interviewed by Steven High. 10 April 2023.
41 Information Release to Employees—28 December 1990. Fonds Local 2995 du Syndicat des bûcherons et des employés de scieries. CAGZA.

42 Purchasing Employee Group Meeting with Darwin E. Smith—Monday, 21 January 1991. 12 noon. Fonds Local 2995 du Syndicat des bûcherons et des employés de scieries. CAGZA.
43 Bob Rae, *From Protest to Power: Personal Reflections on a Life in Politics* (Toronto: Viking, 1996), 141.
44 PEG to Mr. David Agnew. 25 January 1991. Fonds Local 2995 du Syndicat des bûcherons et des employés de scieries. CAGZA.
45 PEG's Presentation to Employees. 30 January 1990. Fonds Local 2995 du Syndicat des bûcherons et des employés de scieries. Centre d'archives de la Grande Zone argileuse, Hearst.
46 T. K. Jewell to David Agnew, Premier's Office. 1 April 1991. "Report—PEG Members Visit K-C Mill—Coosa Pines—Union Camp Mill—Savannah." B430045. RG 3-80-0-54. AO.
47 Canadian Paperworkers Union. 5 January 1991. Local 89 Membership Negotiations Update. Fonds Local 2995 du Syndicat des bûcherons et des employés de scieries. CAGZA.
48 T. K. Jewell, Mayor to Marcel Valliere, President, Local 89 CPU. 18 February 1991. File: Spruce Falls Power, 1991–1992. B430045. RG 3-80-0-54. AO.
49 27 March 1991. Ernst & Young, Management Consultants to James D. McClure, Assistant Deputy Minister, Ministry of Industry, Trade and Technology. File: Spruce Falls Power, 1991–1992. B430045. RG 3-80-0-54. AO.
50 Fred Campling, Spruce Falls Power and Paper Company Limited. To all Spruce Falls employees. Encloses a video tape by Darwin E. Smith on the future of the mill. File: Spruce Falls Power, 1991–1992. RG 3-80-0-54. B430045. AO.
51 Remarks by Darwin E. Smith about the future of Spruce Falls Power and Paper Company, Limited. 13 March 1991. Transcription of video. File: Spruce Falls Power, 1991-1992. RG 3-80-0-54. B430045. AO.
52 Pierre Albert, "Kapuskasing se mobilise pour sauver les emplois," *Le Régional*, 3 April 1991.
53 "Kapuskasing, April 4, 1991," *Northern Times*, 10 April 1991.
54 "A Symbol of Unity in Kap," *Northern Times*, 10 April 1991.
55 "A Symbol of Unity in Kap."
56 Darwin E. Smith, KC, to T. K. Jewell, Mayor, 28 March 1991. Fonds Local 2995 du Syndicat des bûcherons et des employés de scieries. CAGZA.
57 Spruce Falls Power and Paper Company, Limited. First Quarter Results and 1991 Forecast. Summary Comments. 17 April 1991.

Fonds Local 2995 du Syndicat des bûcherons et des employés de scieries. CAGZA.
58 T. K. Jewell to Premier Bob Rae. 8 April 1991. File: Spruce Falls Power, 1991–1992. B430045. RG 3-80-0-54. AO.
59 Darwin E. Smith to T. K. Jewell. 17 April 1991. Fonds Local 2995 du Syndicat des bûcherons et des employés de scieries. CAGZA.
60 Purchasing Employee Group. 19 April 1991. Kimberly Clark Accepts PEG Business Plan. Fonds Local 2995 du Syndicat des bûcherons et des employés de scieries. CAGZA.
61 Darwin E. Smith to T. J. Jewell. 2 May 1991. IWA. CAGZA.
62 Purchasing Employee Group. Information. 17 June 1991. Fonds Local 2995 du Syndicat des bûcherons et des employés de scieries. CAGZA.
63 Ontario. Ministry of Northern Development and Mines. News Release. "Martel says province ready to make Kapuskasing employee buy out work but challenges remain." 19 June 1991. IWA. CAGZA.
64 Thomas Walkom, "Kapuskasing Badly Hurt by NDP's Lack of Policy," *Toronto Star* [nd].
65 Ontario. Ministry of Northern Development and Mines. News Release. 28 June 1991. Fonds Local 2995 du Syndicat des bûcherons et des employés de scieries. CAGZA.
66 K.A.P. (Kill Amos Plan). Presented at the inaugural meeting of the K.A.P. Team by Rene Piche, Chair, 4 July, Civic Centre. Fonds Local 2995 du Syndicat des bûcherons et employés de scieries. CAGZA.
67 K.A.P. (Kill Amos Plan).
68 Dan Holder, CPU, National President, to Rae asking for immediate meeting to discuss Kap situation. 5 July 1991. Fonds Local 2995 du Syndicat des bûcherons et des employés de scieries. CAGZA.
69 Denis Turcotte, Chairperson, Employee Ownership Group, to Bob Rae, 16 July 1991. File: Spruce Falls Power, 1991–1992. RG 3-80-0-54. B430045. AO.
70 Kimberley Noble, "NDP Pulls Out of Kimberly-Clark Deal, 1,200 Jobs Lost," *Globe and Mail*, 17 August 1991.
71 "Tembec prend le contrôle de la Spruce Falls," *Le Nord*, 26 March 1997.
72 "Nos histoires, Notre histoire." Épisode 5. Il faut sauver Kapuskasing ! Video Transcript. TFO.org. Fonds Local 2995 du Syndicat des bûcherons et des employés de scieries. CAGZA.
73 Deputy's Briefing Note—Abitibi-Price Inc/Provincial Papers Division—Thunder Bay. Provincial Papers. File Provincial Papers (Minister of Natural Resources). Box B368703. AO; Jennifer Mitchell, "Provincial Papers Under Employee Ownership: A Case Study."

Jim Foulds Collection. Series A 98-2-1-2. Thunder Bay Historical Museum (TBHM).

74 Bud Wildman, *Hansard*, 35th Parliament, 1st Session, 26 November 1991.
75 Bob Rae interviewed by Steven High. 10 April 2023.
76 Sean O'Connor, "Final Plan for Mill from Management Going to Union," *Chronicle-Journal*, 27 January 1993.
77 Deputy's Briefing Note—Abitibi-Price Inc/Provincial Papers Division—Thunder Bay. Provincial Papers. File Provincial Papers (Minister of Natural Resources). Box B368703. AO.
78 Jennifer Mitchell, "Provincial Papers Under Employee Ownership: A Case Study." Jim Foulds Collection. Series A 98-2-1-2. TBHM.
79 Provincial Papers. Confidential Information Memorandum. Acquisition Opportunity. RBC Dominion Securities. October 1996. Jim Foulds Collection. TBHM.
80 Confidential Information Memorandum. Acquisition Opportunity. RBC Dominion Securities.
81 Editorial, "Best Luck: Mill Buyout a Triumph in the Making," *Chronicle Journal*, 29 January 1993.
82 Foulds CBC Commentary for Wed. Feb 16. Jim Foulds Collection. A 98-4-7-8. TBHM.
83 Jim Foulds interviewed by Steven High. 8 August 2023.
84 C. Ian Ross, Chief Executive Officer. Message to Shareholders Fiscal Year 1995. 12 March 1996. Jim Foulds Collection. Series A98-3-1. TBHM.
85 Provincial Papers. Confidential Information Memorandum. Acquisition Opportunity. RBC Dominion Securities. October 1996. Series A 98-2-1-2. TBHM.
86 Jim Foulds interviewed by Steven High. 8 August 2023.
87 Orenda. Corporate Financial Services. ND [1996] [report] Jim Foulds Collection. Series A 98-2-5-6. TBHM.
88 Provincial Papers. Strategic Options and Financing Implications. Volume 1. Orenda Corporate Finance Ltd. 22 May 1996. Jim Foulds Collection. Series A 98-2-9-11. TBHM.
89 Gowlings, Strathy and Henderson to the Members of the Working Group. Plan of Arrangement. Draft No 4 of the Provincial Papers Employee Shareholder Information Document. 10 April 1997. Jim Foulds Collection. Series A98-3-1. TBHM.
90 Conrad J. Fournier, 12 March 1996. Provincial Papers Union Coalition to Board of Directors. Jim Foulds Collection. Series A98-4-15-25. TBHM.

91 Board met with worker "petitioners" who had concerns about upper management. Jim Foulds Collection. Series A98-4-15-25. TBHM.
92 November 1996. Conrad Fournier, Chairman, Coalition to Jim Foulds. Fax—very faded (unreadable). Jim Foulds Collection. Series A98-4-30-32. TBHM.
93 Meeting Minutes. Senior Management Meeting. 14 November 1996. Jim Foulds Collection. Series A98-4-26-29. TBHM.
94 Operations Steering Committee. 18 November 1996. Jim Foulds Collection. Series A98-4-26-29. TBHM.
95 Jim Foulds handwritten notes after 18 November 1996 meeting. Jim Foulds Collection. Series A98-4-30-32. TBHM.
96 C. Ian Ross to Board of Directors. 16 May 1996. Orenda Report and Ernst & Young Report. Jim Foulds Collection. Series A98-4-26-29. TBHM.
97 Minutes of Meeting of the Board of Directors of Provincial Papers. 4 April 1997. 9am. Jim Foulds Collection. Series A98-4-33-39. TBHM.
98 David Akin, "Workers Like Mill Selloff," *Chronicle Journal*, 26 April 1997.
99 David Akin, "Mill Sale Looks Like Done Deal," *Chronicle Journal*, 25 April 1997.
100 Jim Foulds interviewed by Steven High. 8 August 2023.
101 Michael Brown, Standing Committee on Estimates with the Ministry of Northern Development and Mines, *Hansard*, 19 November 1991.
102 Hugh Mackenzie interviewed by Steven High. 7 November 2022.
103 Bud Wildman interviewed by Steven High. 3 August 2023.

CHAPTER 8: FROM DOWNSVIEW TO DAVOS

1 Bob Rae, *Hansard*, 22 October 1991.
2 Pre-Thatcherite Scotland offers the best example of the moral economy of the coalfields; see the work of historian Jim Phillips especially.
3 Press Background. The Future of de Havilland. 11 September 1990. CAW. File: De Havilland, 1985, 1990–1992. B430043. RG 3-89-0-25. AO.
4 The Future of De Havilland. A CAW Brief to Investment Canada on the Proposed Sale of Boeing—De Havilland to the Aerospatiale/Alenia Consortium. 6 May 1991. File: De Havilland, 1985, 1990–1992. B430043. RG 3-89-0-25. AO.
5 Memorandum Karen Gardiner to Glen Nichols, Briefing Note—De Havilland. 6 September 1991. File: De Havilland, 1991–1992. R-3391, Box 119. AO.
6 Liberal Monte Kwinter, *Hansard*, 11 June 1991.

7   The Future of De Havilland. A CAW Brief to Investment Canada on the Proposed Sale.
8   Richard Allen, Minister, to Bernard Valcourt, Minister of Employment and Immigration. 4 December 1991. File 1 Box 47. Richard Allen. MUA.
9   Throne Speech, *Hansard*, 6 April 1992.
10 Floyd Laughren to Donald Mazankowski, 11 December 1991. File 12: Ministry of Skills and Development—General Communications with Deputy Minister, 1991. Box 47. Richard Allen. MUA; and David A. Wolfe and Meric S. Gertler, "Globalization and Economic Restructuring in Ontario: From Industrial Heartland to Learning Region?," *European Planning Studies* 9, no. 5 (2001): 581.
11 Wolfe and Gertler, "Globalization and Economic Restructuring in Ontario," 582.
12 Linda Briskin and Patricia McDermott, eds., *Women Challenging Unions: Feminism, Democracy and Militancy* (Toronto: University of Toronto Press, 1993), 3.
13 Roxana Ng, "Work Restructuring and Recolonizing Third World Women: An Example from the Garment Industry in Toronto," *Canadian Woman Studies / les cahiers de la femme* 18, no. 1 (1998): 21–25.
14 [redacted], ILGWU and [redacted], Canadian Textile and Chemical Union. 26 August 1991. To Ed Philip, MITT. File: Industry, Trade and Technology. B368638. RG 3-9-0-169. AO.
15 There was a unit of the Ministry of Industry, Trade and Technology set up under the Liberals, headed by Peter Tanaka, who was active in efforts to stop closings. But these efforts were concentrated in the auto sector in the southern half of the province, as far as I am aware.
16 Murray Elston, *Hansard*, 9 May 1991.
17 Ed Philip, Minister of Industry, Trade and Technology, Estimates Committee, *Hansard*, 26 August 1992.
18 While Agnew's appointment raised the spectre of the politicization of the civil service, Armstrong's $300,000 consulting contract over two years also came under fire. "NDP Porkbarrel Manoeuvres Stink," *Kitchener-Waterloo Record*, 3 February 1993.
19 Defence Industry Productivity Program (DIPP). File: De Havilland 2, 1991–1992. B430043. RG 3-89-036. AO.
20 David Agnew to Tim Armstrong. 31 October 1991. De Havilland, 1985, 1990–1992. B430043. RG 3-89-0-25. AO.
21 Press Background. The Future of de Havilland. 11 September 1990. CAW. De Havilland, 1985, 1990–1992. B430043. RG 3-89-0-25. AO.

22 Press Background. The Future of De Havilland.
23 The Future of De Havilland. A CAW Brief to Investment Canada on the Proposed Sale of Boeing—DeHavilland to the Aerospatiale/Alenia Consortium. 6 May 1991. De Havilland, 1985, 1990–1992. B430043. RG 3-89-0-25. AO.
24 Bob Rae, *From Protest to Power: Personal Reflections on a Life in Politics* (Toronto: Viking, 1996), 151.
25 Bombardier to Bob Rae. 7 November 1991. B368449. File: De Havilland. AO.
26 Bombardier to Bob Rae. 7 November 1991.
27 Bob Nixon, *Hansard*, 20 June 1991.
28 Monte Kwinter, *Hansard*, 11 June 1991.
29 Tim Armstrong, De Havilland Status Report. 7 August 1991. File: De Havilland. B368449. AO.
30 Tim Armstrong to Rae, Philip and Peter Barnes. 14 August 1991. File: De Havilland. B368449. AO.
31 Tim Armstrong to Rae, Philip, Peter Barnes, Bryan Davies. 15 August 1991. File: De Havilland. B368449. AO.
32 Tim Armstrong, DM to File. 21 August 1991 File: De Havilland. B368449. AO.
33 Memorandum Karen Gardiner to Glen Nichols, re. Briefing Note—De Havilland. 6 September 1991. File: De Havilland, 1991–1992. Box 119. R-3391. LAC.
34 Memorandum Karen Gardiner to Glen Nichols, re. Briefing Note—De Havilland.
35 Ross McClellan interviewed by Steven High. 18 August 2023.
36 Arthur Andersen. Boeing Canada. De Havilland Division. Due Diligence Review. 4 October 1991. For Ministry of Industry, Trade and Technology. File: De Havilland 2, 1991–1992. B430043. RG 3-89-036. AO.
37 Jeff Finkelstein to David Agnew. 30 August 1991. De Havilland, 1985, 1990–1992. B430043. RG 3-89-0-25. AO.
38 Tim Armstrong to Rae, Philip. 18 October 1991. File: De Havilland. B368449. AO.
39 Tim Armstrong, *Hansard*, 2 October 1991.
40 Tim Armstrong to Rae, Philip. 18 October 1991. File: De Havilland. B368449. AO.
41 Tim Armstrong to Rae and Philip. 1 November 1991. File: De Havilland. B368449. AO.
42 T. E. Armstrong to Wilfrid G. Loeken, VP Finance, Boeing. 14 October 1991. File: De Havilland. B368449. AO.

43 Tim Armstrong to Rae, Philip. 18 October 1991. File: De Havilland. B368449. AO.
44 Bob Rae to David Agnew, Peter Barnes, Ed Philip, and Tim Armstrong. 2 December 1991 De Havilland, 1985, 1990–1992. B430043. RG 3-89-0-25. AO.
45 Laurent Beaudoin, Chairman and CEO, Bombardier to Bob Rae, 24 October 1991. De Havilland, 1985, 1990–1992. B430043. RG 3-89-0-25. AO.
46 De Havilland Preliminary Business Plan. 30 October 1991. De Havilland, 1985, 1990–1992. B430043. RG 3-89-0-25. AO.
47 Laurent Beaudoin, Bombardier, to Bob Rae. 7 November 1991. De Havilland, 1985, 1990–1992. B430043. RG 3-89-0-25. AO.
48 News Release. Michael Wilson, Minister of Industry, Science and Technology welcomes purchase. 22 January 1992. File 7: De Havilland Canada—Purchase by Bombardier, 1991–92. Box 9. R139555. LAC.
49 Tim Armstrong to Rae and Philip. 1 November 1991. File: De Havilland. B368449. AO.
50 Remarks made by Mr. Laurent Beaudoin, Chairman and Chief Executive Officer of Bombardier Inc at the ceremony marking the purchase of De Havilland on 22 January 1992. File: De Havilland 2, 1991–1992. B430043. RG 3-89-036. AO.
51 Phil Howell, MEDT. De Havilland Status Report 19 January 1994. File: De Havilland. B353188. AO.
52 T. E. Armstrong. Note to File—de Havilland Board of Directors' Meeting. 14 June 1993. File: De Havilland. B353188. AO.
53 Tim Armstrong to Premier Rae, Minister Lankin and Deputy Minister Barnes. "De Havilland." 17 June 1993. File: De Havilland. B353188. AO.
54 "De Havilland to Start Decommissioning Toronto Facility after Completing Dash Aircraft," *Toronto Star*, 8 November 2021.
55 Ross Marowits, "Production of De Havilland Turboprops Key to Negotiations as Strike Deadline Nears," *Globe and Mail*, 25 July 2021.
56 Frederick K. Larkin, "De Havilland Canada Says Goodbye to Downsview," *Skies Magazine*, 13 June 2022.
57 Michel Coté, "The Canadian Auto Industry, 1978–86," *Perspectives* 1, no. 2 (Autumn 1989).
58 Dimitry Anastakis, *Auto Pact: Creating a Borderless North American Auto Industry, 1960–1971* (Toronto: University of Toronto Press, 2005).
59 James H. Rubenstein, *The Changing US Auto Industry: A Geographical Analysis* (New York: Routledge, 1992), 98.

60 Dimitry Anastakis, "Industrial Sunrise?: The Chrysler Bailout, the State, and the Re-industrialization of the Canadian Automotive Sector, 1975–1986," *Urban History Review* 35, no. 2 (2007): 37.
61 Stanley Ing, Office of Aviation and Space, 21 January 1994. File: Davos—World Economic Forum. WEF 1993. B353188 AO.
62 Ross McClellan, "The Story of Ontario's First NDP Government," Draft #12, 30 March 1995. In the possession of the author.
63 Sean M. Di Giovanna, "Fighting for a Working Future: Emerging Models of Local Union Strategy in a New Era of Global Competition" (PhD Geography: Toronto, 1997), 8–9, 81.
64 Adopted Resolutions of the 1992 ONDP Convention. Hamilton Convention Centre. 19–21 June 1992. Accession 2014-180. Box 53/56. ONDP Fonds. QUA.
65 Adopted Resolutions of the 1992 ONDP Convention, 9.
66 Adopted Resolutions of the 1992 ONDP Convention, 156.
67 Sam Gindin interviewed by Steven High. Session 1. 15 November 2022.
68 Tim Armstrong to Peter Barnes. 2 November 1992. File General Motors. B368400 AO.
69 General Motors. News Release. 3 December 1992. File General Motors. B368400 AO.
70 Ed Philip, *Hansard*, 3 December 1992.
71 James Bradley, *Hansard*, 9 December 1992.
72 Buzz Hargrove to Bob Rae. 7 December 1992. File: Correspondence with MPPs. Accession 2014-180. 32/56. ONDP Fonds. QUA.
73 Tim Armstrong to Bob Rae. 18 January 1993. GM Foundry, St. Catharines. File: Tim Armstrong, B368296. AO.
74 Tim Armstrong to Bob Rae. 30 November 1992. Meeting with CAW on GM St. Catharines Foundry, 29 November 1992. File General Motors. B368400 AO.
75 Tim Armstrong to Bob Rae. 10 February 1993. Status of Automotive Projects. File: Tim Armstrong, B368296. AO.
76 Tim Armstrong to Bob Rae. 10 February 1993. Status of Automotive Projects.
77 Floyd Laughren, Treasurer and Minister of Economics, *1992 Budget: Meeting Ontario's Priorities*, 30 April 1992 (Toronto: Queen's Printer for Ontario, 1992).
78 Alissa Mazar, *Deindustrialization and Casinos: A Winning Hand?* (New York: Routledge, 2021), 1.
79 Bob Rae interviewed by Steven High. 10 April 2023.

80 Peter Barnes, Deputy Minister, Ministry of Economic Development and Trade. Ontario Competitiveness Report. September 1993. File 12, Box 48. Richard Allen. MUA.
81 "The Story of Ontario's First NDP Government," 23.
82 "The Story of Ontario's First NDP Government," 23.
83 See: Dimitry Anastakis and Steven High, "Negotiating Job Security and Capital Investments in Response to Deindustrialization: The Case of Canada's Auto Sector," *Labor History* (Advance Access).
84 David A. Wolfe and Tijs Creutzberg, "Community Participation and Multilevel Governance in Economic Development Policy," paper prepared for the Panel on the Role of Government (Toronto, August 2003), 74.
85 Bob Rae interviewed by Steven High. 10 April 2023.
86 World Economic Forum, 27 January–1 February 1994. File: Davos—World Economic Forum. WEF 1993. B353188. AO.
87 "Draft Q and A's Regarding Premier's Attendance at World Economic Forum." File: Davos—World Economic Forum. WEF 1993. B353188. AO.
88 Purpose of Visit / Key Themes. World Economic Forum. Davos, Switzerland. 27 January to 1 February 1994. Briefing Notes and Itinerary. 25 January to 1 February 1994. File: Davos—World Economic Forum. WEF 1993. B353188. AO.
89 Premier's Briefing Book. Prepared by Office of International Relations and Protocol, File Visit to Germany and Switzerland, World Economic Forum—Davos, 26 January–1 February 1993. B872374. RG 3-90-2. AO.
90 World Economic Forum. 1994 Annual Meeting in Davos. Press Release. 29 January 1994. File: Davos—World Economic Forum. WEF 1993. B353188. AO.
91 CAW Local 303 Heritage Committee, *You Can't Bring Back Yesterday: A History of CAW Local 303* (Toronto: Canadian Auto Workers, 1993).
92 CAW Local 303 Heritage Committee, *You Can't Bring Back Yesterday.*
93 Ken Clavette and Robert Hatfield, "Workers' Oral History: Recording, Preserving, and Promoting," *Oral History Forum* 35 (2015): 1–4.
94 Robert B. Kristofferson, "The Past Is at Our Feet: The Workers' City Project in Hamilton, Ontario," *Labour / Le Travail* 41 (Spring 1998): 181–97.
95 Workers' Heritage Committee of Ottawa-Carleton, Final Report: "Preserving Our Heritage: A Oral History Project." Workplace Heritage Grant OWH-010. In the possession of the author thanks to Ken Clavette. The Workers' Heritage Committee of Ottawa-Carleton

had the support of the Ottawa and District Labour Council and the Ottawa-Hull Construction and Building Trades Council.

96 Michael Mercier, review of "The People and the Bay: A Popular History of Hamilton Harbour Exhibition at The Ontario Workers Arts and Heritage Centre (OWAHC)," *Urban History Review* 27, no. 1 (1998): 54–56; Adrienne Shadd, review of the "Punching the Clock: Working in Canadian Factories, 1840s–1980s" and "Still I Rise: A History of African Canadian Workers in Ontario, 1900 to Present Exhibitions at OWAHC," *Canadian Historical Review* 84, no. 4 (2003): 639–42.

97 Leighton S. James, "Mining Memories: Big Pit and Industrial Heritage in South Wales," in Christian Wicke, Stefan Berger, and Jana Golombek, eds., *Industrial Heritage and Regional Identities* (London: Routledge, 2018), 13; Marion Fontaine, "Regional Identity and Industrial Heritage in the Mining Area of Nord-Pas-de-Calais," in Wicke, Berger, and Golombek, eds., *Industrial Heritage and Regional Identi*ties, 56.

98 Octave Debary, "Deindustrialization and Museumification: From Exhibited Memory to Forgotten History," *Annals AAPSS* 595 (2004): 125.

99 Mary Keczan-Ebos, "The Ontario Workers Arts and Heritage Centre: Art, Communities and Unions," *Cultural Geographies* 9 (2002): 349–53.

100 Craig Heron, "The Labour Historian and Public History," *Labour / Le Travail* 45 (2000), 174.

101 Kirk Savage, "Monuments of a Lost Cause: The Postindustrial Campaign to Commemorate Steel," in Jefferson Cowie and Joseph Heathcott, *Beyond the Ruins: The Meanings of Deindustrialization* (Ithaca: Cornell University Press, 2002), 237.

102 Jeffrey T. Manuel, *Taconite Dreams: The Struggle to Sustain Mining on Minnesota's Iron Range, 1915–2000* (Minneapolis: University of Minncsota Prcss, 2015), xxv.

CHAPTER 9: CORPORATISM'S MOMENT

1 Preliminary First Draft. Economic Policy Statement. Prepared by Riel Miller for the Economic Sub-Committee of the Policy and Priorities Committee of the ONDP Caucus, Floyd Laughren, Chair. (9 March 1990). ONDP Fonds. QUA.

2 David Wolfe, "Speaking Notes on The Government's Economic Renewal Agenda," January 1992. I want to thank him for sharing this document with me.

3 Michael Mendelson, Deputy Secretary of Cabinet to Bob Rae. Organization of the New Economic Secretariat. 11 October 1991. File: Cabinet Office. Box 38. Richard Allen Fonds. MUA.
4 Thomas Walkom, *Rae Days: The Rise and Follies of the NDP* (Toronto: Key Porter, 1994), 168.
5 Ontario, Minister of Finance, *Budget Paper E: Ontario in the 1990s*, 1991 Ontario Budget, 29 April 1991 (Toronto: Queen's Printer, 1991), 85.
6 Budget Paper E, 87.
7 Notes to a Speech by Premier Bob Rae for the Cunningham Visitorship Lecture at Queen's University. 10 March 1992. File 17: Ontario Training & Adjustment Board—General. Box 38. Richard Allen Fonds. MUA.
8 Bennett Harrison, *Lean and Mean: The Changing Landscape of Corporate Power in the Age of Flexibility* (New York: Basic Books, 1994), 32.
9 Chuck Robb quoted in David Osborne, *Laboratories of Democracy* (Boston: Harvard Business School Press, 1990), 331.
10 In 1989, Ira Magaziner and Hillary Clinton issued a report entitled *America's Choice: High Skills or Low Wages*, which provided the blueprint for the Clinton White House.
11 John Richards and Don Kerr, eds., *Canada, What's Left? A New Social Contract: Pro and Con* (Edmonton: NeWest Publishers, 1986).
12 John Richards, "Collective Bargaining Is Not Enough: The Case for a New Social Contract," in Simon Rosenblum and Peter Findlay, eds., *Debating Canada's Future: Views from the Left* (Toronto: James Lorimer and Company, 1991).
13 John Calvert, "Labour and the Social Contract: An Idea Whose Time Has Come and Gone," in Rosenblum and Findlay, eds., *Debating Canada's Future*, 53.
14 Bob Rae interviewed by Steven High. 10 April 2023.
15 Ross McClellan interviewed by Steven High. 18 August 2023.
16 Confidential interview with X by Steven High.
17 Premier's Council on Economic Renewal. Task Force to Review the Ontario Technology Fund. Minutes. 12 May 1992. File: Premier's Council—reports (1990–1994). B2019-0002/002. David Wolfe Fonds. UTA.
18 Mandate of the Premier's Council on Economic Renewal. File: MITT Re-organization, 1992. B2019-0002/003 (06). David Wolfe Fonds. UTA.
19 David West and Dennis Chand, "A Comparison of Work Force Skills and Wages Between Ontario, Canada and Selected States in the US."

Premier's Council on Economic Renewal. April 1993. File: Premier's Council on Economic Renewal. Box B399127. AO.
20 West and Chand, "A Comparison of Work Force Skills and Wages."
21 Meeting Materials. Prepared by the Task Force on the Organization of Work for the Meeting of the Premier's Council on Economic Renewal. 21 May 1993. Toronto. File: Premier's Council on Economic Renewal. Box B399127. AO.
22 Ross McClellan interviewed by Steven High. 18 August 2023.
23 Rianne Mahon, "Remise en cause des paramètres du post-fordisme au Canada et en Ontario," *Cahiers de recherche sociologique* 18–19 (1992): 212.
24 Advancing Our Labour Agenda or Managing Profound Change. 11 February 1991. File: Policy Notes and Memos from Riel Miller, 1990. B2019-0002/003. David Wolfe Fonds. UTA.
25 Alan Ernst, "Towards a Progressive Competitiveness?: Economic Policy and the Ontario New Democrats, 1988–1995," paper presented at the Annual Meeting of the Canadian Political Science Association, Montreal, 5 June 1995. I would like to thank Alan for sharing this excellent research paper with me.
26 Chuck Rachlis and David Wolfe, "An Insiders' View of the NDP Government in Ontario: The Politics of Permanent Opposition Meets the Economics of Permanent Recession," in Graham White, ed., *The Government and Politics of Ontario*, fifth ed. (Toronto: University of Toronto Press, 1997).
27 Riel Miller to David Wolfe, Wage and benefits policy in strategic perspective. 24 October 1990. File: Policy Notes and Memos from Riel Miller, 1990. B2019-0002/003. David Wolfe Fonds. UTA. This document has since been withdrawn from the archives by Wolfe.
28 Riel Miller to David Wolfe, 25 October 1990. File: Policy Notes and Memos from Riel Miller, 1990. B2019-0002/003. David Wolfe Fonds. UTA. This document has since been withdrawn from the archives by Wolfe.
29 Notes/rationales for a comprehensive social and economic framework/vision. File: Policy Notes and Memos from Riel Miller, 1990. B2019-0002/003. David Wolfe Fonds. UTA. This document has since been withdrawn from the archives by Wolfe.
30 Document. No title. File: Policy Notes and Memos from Riel Miller, 1990. B2019-0002/003. David Wolfe Fonds. UTA. This document has since been withdrawn from the archives by Wolfe.
31 Background Research Paper—Introduction/Draft. Competing Socialist Strategies for Economic Change. File: Policy Notes and

Memos from Riel Miller, 1990. B2019-0002/003. David Wolfe Fonds. UTA. This document has since been withdrawn from the archives by Wolfe.
32   Riel Miller to Floyd Laughren. Partnership discussion. nd. File: Policy Notes and Memos from Riel Miller, 1990. B2019-0002/003. David Wolfe Fonds. UTA. This document has since been withdrawn from the archives by Wolfe.
33   Bud Wildman interviewed by Steven High. 3 August 2023.
34   Research Agenda. Working Group on Financing Industrial Restructuring and Growth. 28 March 1991. File: Financing Industrial Restructuring and Growth, 1991. B2019-0002/003 (02). David Wolfe Fonds. UTA. This document has since been withdrawn from the archives by Wolfe.
35   Research Agenda. Working Group on Financing Industrial Restructuring and Growth. 28 March 1991.
36   Memo re. Meeting with folks at Bistro 990, April 18, 1991. File: Financing Industrial Restructuring and Growth, 1991. B2019-0002/003 (02). David Wolfe Fonds. UTA. This document has since been withdrawn from the archives by Wolfe.
37   Douglas James Hall, "An Evaluation of Ontario's Industrial Policy Efforts: 1985–1995" (Political Science PhD: Queen's University, 1998), 229.
38   Ms. Marion Boyd, Cynthia Smith. Osgood Society Oral History Project. 3 December 2001.
39   Kevin Skerrett, "Canada's Public Pension Funds: The 'New Masters of the (Neoliberal) Universe,'" in Kevin Skerrett, Johanna Weststar, Simon Archer, Chris Roberts, eds., *The Contradictions of Pension Fund Capitalism* (Champaign, IL: Labor and Employment Relations Association, 2017), 123–24.
40   Seminar on Economic Partnerships. 30 July 1991. Discussion Summary. File: Partnership Strategy, 1991. B2019-0002/003. David Wolfe Fonds. UTA. This document has since been withdrawn from the archives by Wolfe.
41   Seminar on Economic Partnerships. 30 July 1991. Discussion Summary.
42   Richard Allen, Minister of Skills Development, Standing Committee on Estimates, *Hansard*, 29 October 1991.
43   Chuck Rachlis and Ross McClellan to Zanana Akande, Marion Boyd, Elaine Ziemba. 24 May 1991. File: Premier's Council—reports (1990–1994). B2019-0002/002. David Wolfe Fonds. UTA.
44   James H. Turk, Director of Education, OFL. To Richard Allen and Bob Mackenzie. 8 May 1991. F 2190—1 D'Arcy Martin Fonds. AO.

45 *Ontario Training and Adjustment Board Act, 1993*, SO 1993, c 9 / *Loi de 1993 sur le Conseil ontarien de formation et d'adaptation de la main-d'oeuvre*, SO 1993, c 9, digitalcommons.osgoode.yorku.ca.
46 Local Training Boards: The Boundaries Issue for Brant/Haldimand-Norfolk. 2 April 1992. File 22 Ontario Training and Adjustment Board—Local Boards—Meetings. Box 17. Richard Allen Fonds. MUA.
47 Neil Bradford, "Prospects for Associative Governance: Lessons from Ontario, Canada," *Politics & Society* 26, no. 4 (December 1998): 540.
48 Minister's Briefing of the Opposition Critics. Ontario Training and Adjustment Board, Penny Lawler, 21 September 1992. File 16—O.T.A.B.—Briefing Notes from Meetings, 1992. Box 17. Richard Allen Fonds. MUA.
49 Neil Bradford, "Public-Private Partnership?: Shifting Paradigms of Economic Governance in Ontario," *Canadian Journal of Political Science* 36, no. 5 (2003): 1015.
50 Bradford, "Prospects for Associative Governance," 566.
51 Bradford, "Prospects for Associative Governance," 553.
52 Gordon Wilson, President, OFL to Richard Allen, Minister of Skills Development. 2 July 1992. File 23: Ontario Training & Adjustment Board—Labour, OFL. Box 17. Richard Allen Fonds. MUA.
53 Confidential Options Paper. What Options are Available to the Government if the OFL Declines to Participate Immediately in OTAB? File 23: Ontario Training & Adjustment Board—Labour, OFL. Box 17. Richard Allen Fonds. MUA.
54 Minister's Calls to Leo Gerard, Fred Pomeroy and Buzz Hargrove. 8 July 1992 File 23: Ontario Training & Adjustment Board—Labour, OFL. Box 17. Richard Allen Fonds. MUA.
55 Meeting with Labour Officials. Sunday 25 October 1992. 10am–1pm. Bristol Palace Hotel. With Leo Gerard, Jim O'Neil (representing Buzz Hargrove), Fred Pomeroy, Cid Ryan, Gord Wilson, Harry Hynd. Ministers Allen and Lankin. Ross McClellan, etc. File 23: Ontario Training & Adjustment Board—Labour, OFL. Box 17. Richard Allen Fonds. MUA.
56 13 March 1992. Naomi Alboim to Richard Allen. OTAB Project Consultation Update to March 13, 1992. Attaches summary consultation update. File 20 Ontario training & Adjustment Board—Consultation Briefings, 1992. Richard Allen Fonds. MUA.
57 Rodney Haddow and Thomas R. Klassen, "Partisanship, Institutions and Public Policy: The Case of Labour Market Policy in Ontario, 1990–2000," *Canadian Journal of Political Science* 37, no. 1 (2004): 149.
58 "Training Board Boycott," *Financial Post*, 14 July 1992.

59 J. G. Carnegie, Executive Director and P. A. Palmer, Ontario Chamber of Commerce, to Richard Allen. 2 November 1992. File 24: Ontario Training and Adjustment Board—Legislation. Box 17. Richard Allen Fonds. MUA.
60 Thomas G. Sosa, DM to Richard Allen, Minister of Skills Development. Personal and Confidential. nd. Addendum to OTAB Cabinet Submission / Response to your May 17th, 1991 letter regarding implications for colleges and workers. File 3: Ministry of Skills & Development—Memos, Confidential. Box 47. Richard Allen Fonds. MUA.
61 Barbara Cameron, "From Equal Opportunity to Symbolic Equity: Three Decades of Federal Training Policy for Women," in Isabella Bakker, ed., *Rethinking Restructuring: Gender and Change in Canada* (Toronto: University of Toronto Press, 1996), 70.
62 OTAB Consultation Meeting. Metro Toronto Board of Trade, Education Committee. 4 February 1992. File 20 Ontario Training & Adjustment Board—Consultation Briefings, 1992. Richard Allen. MUA.
63 24 February 1992. Council of Regents, Richard Johnston. File 20 Ontario Training & Adjustment Board—Consultation Briefings, 1992. Richard Allen Fonds. MUA.
64 Richard Johnston, Chair, Ontario Council of Regents for Colleges of Applied Arts and Technology. 24 February 1992. File 15—Ontario Training & Adjustment Board—Correspondence General, 1992. Box 17. Richard Allen Fonds. MUA.
65 Judy Steed, "Uneasy Partners: Management and Labor's Alliance on the Ontario Training and Adjustment Board Is in Trouble," *Ottawa Citizen*, 14 August 1993.
66 20 January 1992. Report of OFL Seminar on Training and Training Boards. File 20 Ontario Training & Adjustment Board—Consultation Briefings, 1992. Box 17. Richard Allen Fonds. MUA.
67 13 March 1992. Naomi Alboim to Richard Allen. OTAB Project Consultation Update to March 13, 1992. Attaches summary consultation update. File 20 Ontario Training & Adjustment Board—Consultation Briefings, 1992. Box 17. Richard Allen Fonds. MUA.
68 Thomas R. Klassen, *Precarious Values: Organizations, Politics and Labour Market Policy in Ontario* (Montreal: McGill-Queen's University Press, 2000), 113.
69 Bradford, "Prospects for Associative Governance," 540.
70 John O'Grady interviewed by Steven High. 21 November 2022.

71 Bill Thompson to Richard Allen. 20 April 1992. "Whither OTAB" File 17: Ontario Training & Adjustment Board—General. Richard Allen Fonds. MUA.
72 Steed, "Uneasy Partners."
73 Derek Ferguson, "NDP Job Training Bill Called 'Step Backwards' by Business," *Toronto Star*, 20 January 1993.
74 Ontario Federation of Labour. Labour Adjustment. 2nd Biennial Convention. 22–26 November 1993. File 12, Box 48. Richard Allen Fonds. MUA.
75 Thomas Dunk, Stephen McBride, and Randle W. Nelsen, eds., *The Training Trap: Ideology, Training and the Labour Market* (Society for Socialist Studies, 1996), 2–3, 6. Jamie Swift and David Peerla, "Attitude Adjustment: The Brave New World of Work and the Revolution of Falling Expectations," in Thomas Dunk, Stephen McBride, and Randle W. Nelsen, eds., *The Training Trap: Ideology, Training and the Labour Market*, Society for Socialist Studies #11 (1996), 7.
76 Martin Mittelstaedt, "NDP Industrial Policy Unveiled: Strategy Stressing Co-operation with Business, Labour, Wins Cautious Praise," *Globe and Mail*, 29 July 1992.
77 David Wolfe, "Harnessing the Region: Changing Perspectives on Innovation Policy in Ontario," in Trevor J. Barnes and Meric S. Gertler, eds. *The Industrial Geography: Regions, Regulation and Institutions* (NY: Routledge, 1999), 142.
78 Speaking Notes on the Government's Economic Renewal Agenda. David Wolfe, Cabinet Office, 16 February 1993. File Economic Renewal/Development, job link and jobsOntario, 1993–1994. B2019-0002/002 (06). David Wolfe Fonds. UTA.
79 Dinner Speech, David Wolfe, "Competitiveness," Executive Coordinator, Economic and Labour Policy, Cabinet Office, Government of Ontario. I would like to thank David Wolfe for sharing this document from 1991–92.
80 Michael E. Porter, *The Competitive Advantage of Nations* (New York: Free Press, 1990).
81 Michael J. Piore and Charles F. Sabel, *The Second Industrial Divide: Possibilities for Prosperity* (New York: Basic Books, 1984), 17.
82 Michael Best, *The New Competition: Institutions of Industrial Restructuring* (New York: Wiley, 1990).
83 Wolfe, "Harnessing the Region," 256.
84 Blanka Vavakova and David A. Wolfe, "Regional Innovation Policy: Rhone-Alpes and Ontario," *Regional & Federal Studies* 9, no. 3 (1999): 122.

85 David A. Wolfe and Meric S. Gertler, "Globalization and Economic Restructuring in Ontario: From Industrial Heartland to Learning Region?," *European Planning Studies* 9, no. 5 (2001): 585. See also: David A. Wolfe, "Networking among Regions: Ontario and the Four Motors of Europe," *European Planning Studies* 8, no. 3 (2000): 267–84.
86 Hall, "An Evaluation of Ontario's Industrial Policy Efforts," 99.
87 Hall, "An Evaluation of Ontario's Industrial Policy Efforts,", 109, 110.
88 Rae quoted in Hall, "An Evaluation of Ontario's Industrial Policy Efforts," 100.
89 Hall, "An Evaluation of Ontario's Industrial Policy Efforts," 106.
90 Wolfe, "Harnessing the Region," 253.
91 Wolfe, "Harnessing the Region," 150.
92 Bradford, "Prospects for Associative Governance," 560–62.
93 Frances Lankin, *Hansard*, 17 May 1994.
94 Floyd Laughren, Minister of Finance, *1993 Budget: Meeting Ontario's Priorities* (Toronto: Queen's Printer for Ontario, 1993).
95 Peter Warrian interviewed by Steven High. 21 July 2023.
96 Floyd Laughren interviewed by Steven High. 25 January 2024.
97 Walkom, *Rae Days*, 58.
98 Ron M. Sheldrick, "Welfare Reform under Ontario's NDP: Social Democracy and Social Group Representation," *Studies in Political Economy* 55, no. 1 (1998): 42–43.
99 Floyd Laughren interviewed by Steven High. 25 January 2024.
100 Ontario Job Strategy. Executive Summary. Priorities and Planning Committee, 24 February 1992. File 18—Ontario Job Strategy, 1991–2. Richard Allan Fonds. MUA.
101 Ontario Job Strategy. Executive Summary, 447.
102 Floyd Laughren and Peter Warrian, Standing Committee on Finance and Economic Affairs, *Hansard*, 24 June 1993.
103 Catherine Thompson, "Ontario NDP Feels Sting of Friends and Foes: Long-Time Allies Frustrated and Angry," *Kitchener-Waterloo Record*, 3 March 1993.
104 *Turning Point: New Support Programs For People with Low Incomes* (Toronto: Queen's Printer, July 1993).
105 Ross McClellan interviewed by Steven High. 18 August 2023.
106 Randall Ellsworth, Ian Morrison, Judith Keene, and Paul Rapsey, "Poverty Law in Ontario: The Year in Review," *Journal of Law and Social Policy* 10 (1994): 7.
107 Nancy Fraser and Linda Gordon, "A Genealogy of Dependency: Tracing a Keyword of the US Welfare State," *Signs* 19, no. 2 (1994): 311.

108 Report to Treasury Board. Draft. File 13 Box 47. Richard Allen Fonds. MUA.
109 Floyd Laughren to Donald Mazankowski. 11 December 1991. File 18—Ontario Job Strategy, 1991-2. Richard Allan Fonds. MUA.
110 Summary Notes on Job Strategy External Consultation. Ontario Coalition for Better Child Care. 21 January 1992. File 18—Ontario Job Strategy, 1991-2. Richard Allan Fonds. MUA.
111 Howard Hampton to Richard Allen. 17 June 1992. File 14 Ontario Training & Adjustment Board—Correspondence with MPPs, 1992. Box 38. Richard Allen Fonds. MUA.
112 Notes for Remarks by Honourable Richard Allen Minister Responsible for Jobs Ontario Training Fund. Announcing Transitions Corporate Strategies, a project of the Ontario Prevention Clearinghouse, as a Sectoral Broker for Jobs Ontario Training Fund. 10 December 1992. Toronto. File 17: Ontario Training & Adjustment Board—General. Box 17. Richard Allen Fonds. MUA.
113 Submission to Policy and Priorities Committee, File 18—Ontario Job Strategy, 1991-2. Richard Allan Fonds. MUA.
114 Summary Notes on Job Strategy External Consultation. Fair Tax Commission. 30 January 1992. File 18—Ontario Job Strategy, 1991-2. Richard Allan Fonds. MUA.
115 Summary Notes on Job Strategy External Consultations. Association of Municipalities of Ontario. 30 January 1992. Helen Cooper, Celia Fairclough, Joan Andrew, Elisabeth Wagner. File 18—Ontario Job Strategy, 1991-2. Richard Allan Fonds. MUA.
116 Summary Notes on Job Strategy External Consultations. Canadian Steel Trade and Employment Congress. 31 January 1992. Peter Warrian, Joan Andrew, Anna hertz, Ethan Phillips. File 18—Ontario Job Strategy, 1991-2. Richard Allan Fonds. MUA.
117 Meeting Attendance—Interministerial Committee—Links to Economic Development. 24 January 1992. Met in OTAB Project Boardroom. 595 Bay Street, 9th floor. File 18—Ontario Job Strategy, 1991-2. Richard Allan. MUA.
118 Basil "Buzz" Hargrove, National President, Canadian Auto Workers, to Richard Allen, Minister of Skills Development, 6 October 1992. File 2 Box 47. Richard Allen Fonds. MUA.
119 Lynn McLeod, Hansard, 27 April 1993.
120 Floyd Laughren, 1992 Budget: Meeting Ontario's Priorities, 30 April 1992 (Toronto: Queen's Printer for Ontario, 1992).
121 Rachlis and Wolfe, "An Insiders' View of the NDP Government in Ontario."

122 Hugh Mackenzie interviewed by Steven High. 7 November 2022.
123 Ross McClellan, "The Story of Ontario's First NDP Government," Draft #12, 30 March 1995. In the possession of the author.
124 Floyd Laughren interviewed by Steven High. 25 January 2024.
125 Bob Rae interviewed by Steven High. 10 April 2023. The dissenters included Karen Haslam, MPP for Perth and a former schoolteacher, who resigned her junior cabinet portfolio in protest.
126 Riel Miller interviewed by Steven High. 3 January 2024.
127 Ken Delaney interviewed by Steven High. 10 January 2023.
128 Peter Warrian interviewed by Steven High. 21 July 2023.
129 Bob Rae interviewed by Steven High. 10 April 2023.
130 Membership Report. 30 April 1994; New Democratic Party (ON). 1993 Membership Summary Report by Provincial Riding. 31 December 1993. Accession 2014-180. Box 32/56. ONDP Fonds. QUA.
131 OFL opposed to concession bargaining. Statement dated 21 May 1993. Accession 2014-180. 32/56. ONDP Fonds. QUA.
132 Gordon F. Wilson, President, OFL, to Julie Davis, 26 May 1993. Accession 2014-180. 32/56. ONDP Fonds. QUA.
133 "Council Clash!" *The New Ontario Democrat* (May 1993). Box 2003-027 1/8. ONDP Fonds. QUA.
134 Virginia Galt, "NDP Stalwarts Wants Answers: Rae Leadership Review Seen as a Remote Possibility," *Globe and Mail* (26 May 1993). 29 April 1993. W5 Steven Langdon Criticizes Ontario Government. Accession 03-027, Box 7/8. ONDP Fonds. QUA.
135 Arlene Rousseau, Windsor Sandwich, Provincial Council Delegate to Bob Rae. 5 April 1993. File 12—Social Contract and Labour Reaction, Box 96. 5th Accession. Richard Allen Fonds. MUA.
136 Provincial Executive Meeting. Agenda. 29 May 1993. Accession 03-027. Box 7/8. ONDP Fonds. QUA.
137 Paul D. Middleton to Jill Marzetti, Provincial Secretary, 3 November 1993. London and District Service Workers Union (Service Employees International Union). Accession 2003-027. Box 5/8. ONDP Fonds. QUA.
138 Emergency Resolution to the Ontario New Democratic Party Provincial Council, 19–20 June 1993. Submitted by the Ontario Federation of Labour. 14 June 1993. Accession 03-027. Box 7/8. ONDP Fonds. QUA.
139 "To the brink and back." *The New Ontario Democrat* (Summer 1993). Accession 2003-027, Box 1/8. ONDP Fonds. QUA.
140 W5 Ontario Provincial Council Meeting. 19–20 June 1993. 21 June 1993. Accession 03-027, Box 7/8. ONDP Fonds. QUA.

141 Transcript of Address by Premier Bob Rae at ONDP Provincial Council, Gananoque, Ontario, 19 June 1993. Accession 03-027 Box 7/8. ONDP Fonds. QUA.
142 Address by Premier Rae at ONDP Provincial Council, 19 June 1993.
143 Dave Killham, Political Action Coordinator, Locals 175 and 633, UFCW, to Mary Morrison, Assistant to the Principal Secretary of Premier. 14 September 1993. Wayne Samuelson. Draft #5 Labour and the New Democratic Party, Accession 03-027. Box 7/8. ONDP Fonds. QUA.
144 Jim Woodward, Legislative Assistant, CUPE Ontario, to Wayne Samuelson, Political Education Director, OFL. 27 August 1993. Accession 03-027. Box 7/8. ONDP Fonds. QUA.
145 Jim O'Neil, Secretary-Treasurer, to Gord Wilson, 7 September 1993. Accession 03-027. Box 7/8. ONDP Fonds. QUA.
146 Ontario Federation of Labour. Summary. [written notation "passed on the floor"]. nd (but clearly Fall 1993). File 12—Social Contract and Labour Reaction, Box 96. 5th Accession. Richard Allen Fonds. MUA.
147 The dissenting unions included ACTWU; Amalgamated Transit Union; Aluminum, Brick and Glass Workers of America; CEP; Communications Workers of America; Graphic Communications International Union; Glass, Moulders and Pottery Workers; Hotel Employees and Restaurant Employees; International Association of Machinists and Aerospace Workers; Labourers' International Union of North America; SEIU; Transportation Communications Union; United Food & Commercial Workers; United Resource Workers; United Steelworkers of America; United Transportation Union.
148 27 July 1993. Lucy, federal New Democrats to Marjory and Jill Marzetti. Locals Disaffiliating. Accession 2003-027, Box 5/8 ONDP Fonds. QUA.
149 Audrey to Karen. 3 November 1994. Ontario Locals Affiliated as at 31 October 1994. Accession 2003-027. Box 5/8. ONDP Fonds. QUA.
150 Local Affiliated to the New Democrats of Canada Association. Ontario—1 September 1995. Accession 2003-027. Box 5/8. ONDP Fonds. QUA.
151 Richard Allen annotation of motion to Hamilton West NDP Riding Association. 5 May 1993. File 12—Social Contract and Labour Reaction, Box 96. 5th Accession. Richard Allen Fonds. MUA.
152 Richard Allen to Mary Lou Tanner, 11 May 1993. Box 96, File 12—Social Contract and Labour Reaction. File 12—Social Contract and Labour Reaction, Box 96. 5th Accession. Richard Allen Fonds. MUA.

153 Barry Tooley, Chairperson, Political Action Committee, Local 6500, United Steelworkers of America. Letter to members. 17 June 1994. Accession 2003-027. Box 5/8. ONDP Fonds. QUA.

154 For more on this moment, see: Ian McLeod, *Under Siege: The Federal NDP in the Nineties* (Toronto: Lorimer, 1994).

155 Statement by Mel Swart at Queen's Park Press Conference, Friday, 29 October 1993. Press Release. Bob Rae's Leadership. Accession 2014-180. Box 53/56. ONDP Fonds. QUA.

156 Michael Davison, "NDP Becoming Different Party Than It Was Three Years Ago," *Hamilton Spectator*, 30 November 1993.

CHAPTER 10: NEW LEFT COMMUNITARIANISM

1 Frances Lankin, "Ontario Making Strides in Community Economic Development," *Economic Development Journal of Canada* (1994): 8–9.

2 Community Economic Development Secretariat, CED Strategic Review (Draft, December 1994), robinmurray.co.uk.

3 Peter Graham, "New Leftists, 'Party-Liners,' and Municipal Politics in Toronto," in Roberta Lexier, Stephanie Bangarth, and Jon Weier, eds., *Party of Conscience: The CCF, the NDP, and Social Democracy in Canada* (Toronto: Between the Lines, 2018), 83.

4 Hilary Wainwright, "A New Kind of Knowledge for A New Kind of State," in Gregory Albo, David Langille, and Leo Panitch, eds., *A Different Kind of State?: Popular Power and Democratic Administration* (Toronto: Oxford University Press, 1993), 116.

5 Riel Miller, *Territorial Development and Human Capital in the Knowledge Economy: Towards a Policy Framework* (Paris: OECD, 1996), 27.

6 Stefano Harney, *State Work: Public Administration and Mass Intellectuality* (Durham: Duke UP, 2002), 73.

7 Lesley Hyland Byrne, "Feminists in Power: Women Cabinet Ministers in the New Democratic Party (NDP) Government of Ontario, 1990–1995," *Policy Studies Journal* 25, no. 4 (December 1997): 608.

8 Frances Lankin interviewed by Steven High. 8 November 2023.

9 Frances Lankin interviewed by Steven High. 8 November 2023.

10 Ross McClellan, "The Story of Ontario's First NDP Government," Draft #12, 30 March 1995, p. 51. In the possession of the author.

11 Frances Lankin interviewed by Steven High. 8 November 2023.

12 Maureen Mackintosh, "Creating a Developmental State: Reflections on Policy as Process," in Albo, Langille and Panitch, eds., *A Different Kind of State?*, 38.

13   Frances Lankin interviewed by Steven High. 8 November 2023.
14   Robin Murray, "Transforming the 'Fordist' State," in Albo, Langille, and Panitch, eds., *A Different Kind of State?*, 58.
15   David Wolfe, "Harnessing the Region: Changing Perspectives on Innovation Policy in Ontario," in Trevor J. Barnes and Meric S. Gertler, eds., *The Industrial Geography: Regions, Regulation and Institutions* (NY: Routledge, 1999), 143.
16   Frances Fox Piven, "Reforming the Welfare State: The American Experience," in Albo, Langille and Panitch, eds., *A Different Kind of State?*, 66.
17   Greg Patmore, "Working Lives in Regional Australia: Labour History and Local History," *Labour History* 78 (2000): 1–6; Lucy Taksa, "Like a Bicycle, Forever Teetering Between Individualism and Collectivism: Considering Community in Relation to Labour History," *Labour History* 78 (2000): 7; James DeFilippis, *Unmaking Goliath: Community Control in the Face of Global Capital* (New York: Routledge, 2004), 54.
18   Aram Eisenschitz and David North, "The London Industrial Strategy: Socialist Transformation or Modernising Capitalism?," *Urban Praxis: International Journal of Urban and Regional Research* (1986): 419.
19   Robin Murray, "The Production of Industrial Strategy," SPRI Meeting of Economic Promotion Institutions of Industrial Regions in Bilbao (7–8 July 1988), p. 1, robinmurray.co.uk.
20   Robin Murray, "What Are the Lessons from London?," in Ken Coates, ed., *For Jobs: A New Internationalism* (London: Spokesman Press, 1985), 75, 57.
21   London Industrial Strategy (introductory chapter). Accession 03-027. Box 7/8. ONDP Fonds. QUA.
22   Frederic S. Lee, "Conference of Socialist Economists and the Emergence of Heterodox Economics in Post-war Britain," *Capital & Class* 75 (2001): 25.
23   Robin Murray, "London and the Greater London Council: Restructuring the Capital of Capital," *IDS Bulletin* 16, no. 1 (1985): 47.
24   Murray, "What Are the Lessons from London?," 74.
25   Eisenschitz and North, "The London Industrial Strategy," 423.
26   Eisenschitz and North, "The London Industrial Strategy," 420.
27   Jamie Gough, "Industrial Policy and Socialist Strategy: Restructuring and the Unity of the Working Class," *Capital & Class* 10, no. 2 (1986): 60.

28 Michael H. Best, *The New Competition: Institutions of Industrial Restructuring* (Cambridge: Harvard University Press, 1990), viii, 19.
29 Tim Joubert, "Bridging Bureaucracy and Activism: Challenges of Activist State-Work in the 1980s Greater London Council," *Urban Studies* 60, no. 11 (2023): 2251–70.
30 Michael Jacobs, "Farewell to Greater London Council," *Economic and Political Weekly* 21, no. 30 (26 July 1986): 1307.
31 Murray, "The Production of Industrial Strategy," 9.
32 Jacobs, "Farewell to Greater London Council," 1306. Other labour-controlled UK cities such as Sheffield, Cleveland, and the West Midlands were also undertaking such experiments during these years.
33 Jacobs, "Farewell to Greater London Council," 1307.
34 Robin Murray, *Local Space: Europe and the New Regionalism. Economic Practice and Policies for the 1990s* (February 1991), 6.
35 Robin Murray, "Benetton Britain: The New Economic Order," in Stuart Hall and M. Jacques, eds., *New Times: The Changing Face of Politics in the 1990s* (London: Verso, 1990), 63.
36 Robin Murray, *Breaking with Bureaucracy: Ownership, Control and Nationalisation* (Manchester: Centre for Local Economic Strategies (CLES) Report, 1987), 38.
37 Robin Murray, "Fordism and Post-Fordism," in Hall and Jacques, eds., *New Times*, 41, 52.
38 Jeremy Gilbert, "After Individualism: The Unfinished Business of New Times (Reflections on the Political Legacy of 'Marxism Today)," *Juncture*, special issue on *Marxism Today* (December 2011): 1.
39 "Manifesto for New Times: Realignment of Politics," in Hall and Jacques, eds., *New Times*, 448–49.
40 David Marquand, "Beyond Left and Right: The Need for a New Politics," in Hall and Jacques, eds., *New Times*, 375.
41 Robin Murray, "The Theory and Practice of Local Economic Development: A Guide" (Johannesburg, August 1992), robinmurray.co.uk.
42 Stefano Harney, *State Work: Public Administration and Mass Intellectuality* (Durham: Duke UP, 2002), 75.
43 Community Economic Development Secretariat, *CED Strategic Review* (Draft, December 1994), 1–3, robinmurray.co.uk.
44 *CED Strategic Review*, 5.
45 Lankin, "Ontario Making Strides in Community Economic Development," 8–9.
46 *CED Strategic Review*, 5.

47 CED Strategic Review, 6.
48 Ross McClellan interviewed by Steven High. 18 August 2023.
49 "A Message from Frances Lankin, Minister of Economic Development and Trade," *Economic Development Journal of Canada* (1994).
50 Lankin, "Ontario Making Strides in Community Economic Development," 8–9.
51 Frances Lankin interviewed by Steven High. 8 November 2023.
52 Canada: Community Economic Development (CED), 1993–1995, robinmurray.co.uk.
53 CED Strategic Review, 23.
54 CED Strategic Review, 4.
55 CED Strategic Review, 5.
56 CED Strategic Review, 7.
57 Floyd Laughren and Peter Warrian, Assistant Deputy Minister, Office of Economic Policy, 1993 Ontario Budget. 24 June 1993. Standing Committee on Finance and Economic Affairs; see also: McClellan, "The Story of Ontario's First NDP Government," 26.
58 CED Strategic Review, 18.
59 CED Strategic Review, 21.
60 CED Strategic Review, 27.
61 CED Strategic Review, 48.
62 CED Strategic Review, 53, 56, 59, 72.
63 CED Strategic Review, 72.
64 CED Strategic Review, 83.
65 Isabella Bakker and Riel Miller, "Escape from Fordism: The Emergence of Alternative Forms of state Administration and Output," in Robert Boyer and Daniel Drache, eds., *States against Markets: The Limits of Globalization* (London: Routledge, 1996), 266.
66 Bakker and Miller, "Escape from Fordism," 252, 254, 255.
67 M. Taabazuing, G. Arku, and P. Mkandawire, "Economic Development Approaches in a Changing Global Economy: What Do Practitioners Think?," *Urban Research & Practice* 8, no. 2 (2015): 145.
68 Riel Miller interviewed by Steven High. 3 January 2024.
69 The idea of human capital theory originated in the mid-1960s when it was promoted by Gary S. Becker, *Human Capital: A Theoretical and Empirical Analysis, with Special Reference to Education*, third ed. (Chicago: University of Chicago, 1994).
70 Riel Miller, *Territorial Development and Human Capital in the Knowledge Economy: Towards a Policy Framework* (Paris: OECD, 1996), 7, 27, 37.

71 Stephen McBride, "The Continuing Crisis of Social Democracy: Ontario's Social Contract Perspective," *Studies in Political Economy* 50 (1996): 69.
72 Thomas Walkom, *Rae Days: The Rise and Follies of the NDP* (Toronto: Key Porter, 1994), 167.
73 James Defilippis, Robert Fisher, and Eric Shragge, *Contesting Community: The Limits and Potential of Local Organizing* (New Brunswick, New Jersey: Rutgers, 2009), 7.
74 Defilippis, Fisher, and Shragge, *Contesting Community*, 86.
75 Roxana Ng, *The Politics of Community Services: Immigrant Women, Class and State*, 2nd ed. (Halifax: Fernwood, 1996), 11.
76 Ng, *The Politics of Community Services*, 15.
77 David Harvey quoted in Ng, *The Politics of Community Services*, 11.

CONCLUSION: THE SEDUCTIVE MIST OF PRAGMATISM

1 Thomas Walkom, "Captain Bob Must Steer between Rocks and Reefs," *Toronto Star*, 8 September 1990.
2 Chuck Rachlis and David Wolfe, "An Insiders' View of the NDP Government in Ontario: The Politics of Permanent Opposition Meets the Economics of Permanent Recession," in Graham White, ed., *The Government and Politics of Ontario*, fifth ed. (Toronto: University of Toronto Press, 1997).
3 Speaking Notes. 28 April 1995. Spruce Falls; Sheila Moore to Bob Rae, Confidential Briefing Note. Algoma and Spruce Falls. 28 April 1995. Accession 1999-047 Box 14/21. ONDP Fonds. QUA.
4 6 May 1995. Rae Says He's Never Stopped Fighting for Jobs. 6 May 1995. The Provincial Papers Turnaround in Thunder Bay. Backgrounder. Accession 1999-047, Box 14/21. ONDP Fonds. QUA.
5 Speaking Notes. 1 June 1995. Algoma Steel Restructuring/Algoma CHC. Accession 1999-047 Box 14/21. ONDP Fonds. QUA.
6 ONDP. The Right Choice for Ontario. Party platform document. Accession 1999-047, Box 14/21. ONDP Fonds. QUA.
7 Confidential Speaking Notes. Jobs in the GTA. 24 May 1995. Accession 1999-047 Box 14/21. ONDP. QUA.
8 29 April 1995. Speaking Notes. United Rubberworkers Convention. Confidential. Accession 1999-047, Box 14/21. ONDP Fonds. QUA.
9 Floyd Laughren interviewed by Steven High. 25 January 2024.
10 Sam Gindin interviewed by Steven High. Session 2. 24 November 2022.
11 Hugh Mackenzie, "Roots of the Crisis: How Growing Inequality Sowed the Seeds for an Economic Meltdown," 2009 Sefton Memorial Lecture (Toronto, 2009), 10.

12 Bud Wildman interviewed by Steven High. 3 August 2023.
13 Frances Lankin interviewed by Steven High. 8 November 2023.
14 Ross McClellan interviewed by Steven High. 18 August 2023.
15 Address by Premier Bob Rae to Provincial Council at the Ontario Institute for Studies in Education. 28 November 1993. File Speeches. Accession 03-027. Box 7/8. ONDP Fonds. QUA.
16 Gregory Albo, "'Competitive Austerity' and the Impasse of Capitalist Employment Policy," *Socialist Register* 30 (1994): 149.
17 Donley T. Studlar, "The Anglo-American Origins and International Diffusion of the 'Third Way,'" *Politics & Policy* 31, no. 1 (2003): 33.
18 Alan Zuege, "The Chimera of the Third Way," *Socialist Register* 36 (2000): 90.
19 Byron Sheldrick, "New Labour and the Third Way: Democracy, Accountability and Social Democratic Politics," *Studies in Political Economy* 67, no. 1 (2002): 137.
20 Anthony Giddens quoted in Shane Fudge and Stephen Williams, "Beyond Left and Right: Can the Third Way Deliver a Reinvigorated Social Democracy?," *Critical Sociology* 22, no. 4 (2006): 588.
21 C. Arndt and K. Kersbergen, "Social Democracy after the Third Way: Restoration or Renewal?," *Policy and Politics* 43, no. 2 (2015): 203–20; Christoffer Green-Pedersen, Kees Van Kersbergen, and Anton Hemerijck, "Neo-liberalism, the 'Third Way' or What?: Recent Social Democratic Welfare Policies in Denmark and the Netherlands," *Journal of European Public Policy* 8, no. 2 (2001): 307–25.
22 Nelson Lichtenstein and Judith Stein, *A Fabulous Failure: The Clinton Presidency and the Transformation of American Capitalism* (Princeton: Princeton University Press, 2023), 32–33.
23 Dale Eisler, *From Left to Right: Saskatchewan's Political and Economic Transformation* (Regina: University of Regina Press, 2022), see chapter 11 entitled "Pain and Suffering." Also see: Nelson Wiseman, "Social Democracy and the Canadian Welfare State," in David McGrane, John D. Whyte, Roy Romanow, and Russell Isinger, eds., *Back to Blakeney: Revitalizing the Democratic State* (Regina: University of Regina Press, 2019).
24 Frances Fox Piven, ed., *Labor Parties in Postindustrial Societies* (New York: Oxford University Press, 1992), 9.
25 Piven, ed., *Labor Parties in Postindustrial Societies*, 9.
26 Xavier Vigna, *Histoire des ouvriers en France au XXe siècle* (Paris: Perrin, 2012), 322.
27 The Confédération générale du travail (CGT) went from representing 1.3 million workers in 1979 to 540,000 in 2004; and the

Confédération française démocratique du travail (CFDT) went from a union of 800,000 in 1978 to representing just 450,000 in 2003. Vigna, *Histoire des ouvriers en France*, 327–28.

28   Frances Fox Piven and Richard A. Cloward, "Eras of Power," *Monthly Review* 49, no. 8 (January 1998): 16.
29   Zuege, "The Chimera of the Third Way," 88.
30   Bob Rae interviewed by Steven High. 10 April 2023.
31   Toward the Renewal of Social Democracy: A Submission to the CLC/NDP Review Committee. Toronto Ontario. 30 August 1995. Accession 2003-027, Box 5/8. ONDP. QUA.
32   Peter Warrian, "Can't Get There from Here: Old/New Unions in an New/Old Economy," 2001 Sefton Lecture (Woodsworth College, University of Toronto, 2001), 6–7.
33   Tim Armstrong, "Contemporary Collective Bargaining: How Well Is It Working?," 21st Larry Sefton Memorial Lecture (Woodsworth College, University of Toronto, 2003), 26.
34   John O'Grady interviewed by Steven High. 2 October 2022.
35   Larry Savage, *Socialist Cowboy: The Politics of Peter Kormos* (Halifax: Roseway Publishing, 2014).
36   Another former inner cabinet member, Tony Silipo, also ran, but was not a leading contender.
37   Floyd Laughren interviewed by Steven High. 25 January 2024.
38   Bob Rae interviewed by Steven High. 10 April 2023.
39   Bob Rae interviewed by Steven High. 10 April 2023.
40   Quinn Slobodian, *Globalists: The End of Empire and the Birth of Neoliberalism* (Cambridge: Harvard University Press, 2018), 283.
41   Frances Lankin interviewed by Steven High. 8 November 2023.
42   Lichtenstein and Stein, *A Fabulous Failure*, 1.
43   Bryan M. Evans and Charles W. Smith, "The Transformation of Ontario Politics: The Long Ascent of Neoliberalism," in Bryan M. Evans and Charles W. Smith, eds., *Transforming Provincial Politics: The Political Economy of Canada's Provinces and Territories in the Neoliberal Era* (Toronto: University of Toronto Press, 2015), 163, 170.
44   Andrew Jackson, *The Fire and the Ashes: Rekindling Democratic Socialism* (Toronto: Between the Lines, 2021), 10.
45   Michael Harrington, *Socialism: Past and Future* (New York: Arcade Publishing, 1989), 205.
46   Christopher H. Johnson, "Introduction: De-industrialization and Globalization," in Bert Altena and Marcel van der Linden, eds., *De-industrialization: Social, Cultural and Political Aspects International Review of Social History* 47 (2002): 29.

47 John R. Brown, *Death in the Industrial World: Plant Closures and Capital Retirement*, Economic Analysis Research Paper Series (Ottawa: Statistics Canada, 2005).
48 I am currently working with Dimitry Anastakis and Angelo DiCaro of Unifor on assessing their experience with Action Centres.
49 Hugh Mackenzie interviewed by Steven High. 7 November 2022.

INDEX

Page numbers in italics indicate photos and charts.

3 Rs, 96
1990 election: caucus of, 16–17; and northern Ontario, 230; platform, 4; swearing in, 113, *118*; winning, 113–14, *114*, 117–22; and women, 16, 337; worker adjustment promises, 115–16
1992 Budget: Meeting Ontario's Priorities (Laughren), 315

Abitibi, 248, 249, 250
Action Centres, 374
Adams, George, 203
Advisory Committee on Resource Dependent Communities in Northern Ontario, 229
Advocates for Community-based Training and Education for Women (ACTEW), 106
aeronautics industry, 259–61, 269. *See also* De Havilland
Aérospatiale and Alenia (A&A), 265–71
Aerovox, 54–5
Afro-Caribbean community, 349
An Agenda for People (1990 election manifesto), 114–15, 132, 136, 164, 326, 332, 373
Agnew, David, *115*, 124, *145*, 147, 153–4, 314, 422n18
Air Canada, 265
Airbus, 265
Akande, Zanana, 304

Algoma Steel, 193–200, *194*, 202–7, 213–14, 219, 221, 256–7, 267–8
Allegheny Conference on Community Development, 60
Allen, Richard, 51, 52–3, 59–60, 64–8, 71–2, *124*, 261, 304, 306, 307, 309, 319, 329–30
Allende, Salvador, 186
Alliston, ON, *281*
alternative economies, 59
Altobelli, Enzo, 246
Aluminum, Brick and Glass Workers International Union, 64
Amalgamated Clothing and Textile Workers Union (ACTWU), 45–6, 177–9
American Federation of Labor and Congress of Industrial Organizations (AFL-CIO), 9
Americanization, 29–30
Amos plan, 242
anti-intellectualism, 129–30
Apparel Textile Action Committee (ATAC), 177–9
Armstrong, Hugh, 91
Armstrong, Pat, 91
Armstrong, Tim, 198, 221, *263*, *268*, 270–1, 272, 273, 274, 276, 278, 280, 368, 422n18
Armstrong Cork, 45
"Atari Democrats, 9
Atikokan, ON, 234–6
audits, 232–3
austerity: overview, 19; and community economic development, 335–6; critiquing economy or class, 353;

and debt wall scare, 148; in France, 20, 146; and NDP government vs. party, 151–2; and social contract idea, 303
Australia, 292
auto insurance, 148–50, 152, 369
Auto Pact, 49, 372
automotive industry, 274–82, 275, 281, 375. *See also specific companies; specific unions*

bailouts, 170, 198, 241, 274, 342
Bakker, Isabella, 96, 351–2
bankruptcy court, 206
Barrett, Dave, 297
Barrett, Steven, xvi
Baum, Gregory, 59
Beach Foundry, 44
Beaudoin, Laurent, 266, 268, 272–3, 272
Bendix Automotive, 44, 46
"Benetton Britain" (Murray), 342–3
Best, Michael, 97, 311, 342
Best Outerwear, 173
Bill 40, 188
Bill 70, 171–2, 174–5
Bill 150, 213–20
Black, Conrad, 186
Black community, 349
Blair, Tony, 7, 10–11, 344, 355, 363–4, 379n13
Blakeney, Allan, 59, 102, 136–7
Blanchard, James, 82–3
Bloom, Ron, 194–5, 199–200, 201–2, 203, 206, 207–8
Bluestone, Barry, 62, 391n39
Bluestone, Irving, 391n39
Boeing, 265, 267
Bombardier, 266, 268, 270–3, 272
book overview, xvii–xx, 7
Boyd, Marion, 16, 302, 304
Bradford, Neil, 305, 309, 313
Bradley, James, 277
Bramalea, ON, 280, 281, 320
Branch Plant Task Force, 33–4

Brandt, Andy, 64–5
Brantford, ON, 171
Brecher, Jeremy, 62
Britain, 28, 51, 292
Broadbent, Ed, 5–6, 264
brokers, 354–5
Brown, Michael, 256
Budget Paper E, 98, 290
Burkett, Kevin, 182–3
business. *See* corporations/businesses
Business Council on National Issues, 282
buyouts. *See* cooperatives; worker ownership/buyouts

cabinet retreats, 131
Cairns, Robert D., 102
Caisse de dépôt et placement du Québec (the Caisse), 215, 299, 301–2
Callahan, Bob, 157
Calvert, John, 292
Cambridge, ON, 280, 281
Cameron, Barbara, 176–7
(Canada) Ltd (Laxer), 35
Canada Works, 55
Canada–United States Free Trade Agreement (1987). *See* Free Trade Agreement
Canada-US Auto Pact, 274
Canadian Advisory Council on the Status of Women, 176–7
Canadian Auto Workers (CAW): and Bill 150, 218; and competitiveness, 108; corporations/labour partnerships, 21–2, 87–8; and deindustrialization, 26; and Free Trade Agreement (1987), 4–6; and GM closures, 275–8, 283–4; and labour venture capital funds, 215; Rae on, 279; and recession, 142; and social contract critique, 328; and tax breaks, 214; and UAW, 87. *See also* Unifor; White, Bob
Canadian Charter of Rights and Freedoms, 169, 378n8

Canadian Conference of Catholic Bishops, 59
Canadian Development Fund, 57
Canadian Federation of Independent Business (CFIB), 26, 136, 307
Canadian Federation of Labour, 209, 220
Canadian Labour Congress (CLC), 6, 37, 44, 133, 367. *See also* White, Bob
Canadian Manufacturers' Association, 136
Canadian Paperworkers Union (CPU), 37, 237–8, 243, 245, 246, 247. *See also* Communications and Electrical Workers of Canada; Unifor
Canadian Porcelain, 64–6
Canadian Steel Trade and Employment Congress (CSTEC), 69–70
capitalism, 59, 100, 368, 373
Caplan, Elinor, 219
Caplan, Gerald, 113, 122–3
Carter, Jenny, 160
Cassidy, Michael, 73
caucus vs. cabinet, 128–9
centralized planning, 103
Century Brass, 62
Challenge to Hamilton, 53
change, 1, 3, 101
The Changing Workplace: A New Frontier conference, 205
Charlottetown agreement, 331
Charlton, Brian, 53
child care, 317, 337–8
Chinese Garment Workers' Association (CGWA), 178
Chow, Susi, *287*
Christian activism, 53, 59, 64
Christopherson, David, 16, 128
Chrysler, 41, 279, 280, *281*, 320
Clark, Charles, 45–6
class: overview of differences, 160; and B. Mackenzie, 158; and CED, 354; in *Giving Away a Miracle*, 377n2;

and high school streaming, 92; and liberals, 10; and NDP 1990 win, 17; and New Left, 353; vs. Third Way, 12
Clavette, Ken, 285
Clergue, Francis Hector, 196
Clinton, Bill, 8–9, 12, 69, 81–2, 294, 363–5, 371–2, 379n13, 391n39
closure of factories. *See* deindustrialization; layoffs
clothing industry. *See* garment sector
Co, Ling, *191*
coal industry, 260
Coalition for Fair Wages and Working Conditions for Homeworkers, 176
Cohen, Marjorie, 106
Cold War, 226
Colley, Sue, 339
Common Sense Revolution, 52
Communications, Energy and Paperworkers (CEP), 249, 254
Communications and Electrical Workers of Canada, 88–9, 174
communism, 225–6
communitarianism: overview, 11–12, 360; Allen's version of, 53; Fordist, 339–40; vs. left-nationalism, 53; and New Left, 11, 54; and Ontario policy book, 74; and Third Way, 355. *See also* community economic development
community, 82
community co-ownership, 236–7, 247. *See also* Purchasing Employees Group
Community Development Investment Fund, 58–9
community economic development (CED): overview, 335–7, 339–40, 346–7; and austerity, 353–4; Community Economic Development Act, 344–5; contracting and subcontracting chains, 354; and corporatism, 430; and decentralization, 343; JOCA, 348–53; and Ministry of Economic

Development and Trade, 345–6; and New Times initiative, 343–4; vs. redistribution, 6–7; small/medium firm innovation, 347–8
Community Investment Share Program, 347
Community-Based Economic Development, 74
Competing in the New Global Economy (report), 78, 79, 80–1, 84–5, 86, 105–6
"Competing Socialist Strategies for Economic Change" (Wolfe), 298
competition: and community economic development, 339–40; as constraint, 108; and corporate/labour partnership, 185, 302–3, 304; and economy, 140; and GATT, 55; Gindin's views, 105–6, 154; Krugman's views, 109–10; and NDP loss, 368; and neoliberalism, 146; and new economy, 81, 310; and recession, 295, 296; Robertson's views, 105–6; and skills training in 1991, 291; and social justice, 364; Stockwell and De Carlo interaction, 142; technology and cheap labour, 322; in throne speech, 136; and trade tribunals, 217; as trap, 361; and wage protection fund, 172
The Competitive Advantage of Nations (Porter), 310
Connolly, Kip, 173
consensus, 77, 291–2, 295, 296–7, 305–6
consultancy firms, 84
consultations, 40, 49, 66, 187
Cooke, Dave, 163–4, 278, 309
Co-operative Commonwealth Federation (CCF), 13, 14–15, 53
cooperatives, 60, 63–7, 346. *See also* worker ownership/buyouts
Coppen, Shirley, 120
corporate partnerships: and adjustment, 179–80; CAW's views, 21–2, 87–8; and CED, 354; and competition, 302–3, 304; and consensus, 305–6; and economic renewal 1991, 290–1; and globalization, 78; and investment, 375; and labour law reform, 182–3, 298, 303; *The New Competition*, 311; and non-Marxist economy, 103; OTAB, 304, 306–7; as performance pieces, 108; Sector Partnership Fund, 311–12, 313; *Social Democracy without Illusions*, 102; and USW, 89, 195
corporations/businesses: and Bill 70, 172; dependency theory, 31–3 (*see also* US economic domination; *specific companies*); and free trade, 4–5 (*see also individual trade agreements*); and investment, 37; and labour law reform, 186–7, 297; vs. labour venture capital funds, 211; left engaging with issues, 376; lowering taxes of, 320–2; and MITT, 158; and New Democrats (US), 8; Rae's ideas, 3; reactions to NDP in power, 145, 147; and responsibility for deindustrialization, 165; as skeptical of NDP win, 121; small business and adjustment, 70–1; as speculators, 174; and throne speech, 136. *See also* globalization; *specific companies*
corporations/businesses accountability: advanced notice of layoffs, 26, 69, 83, 161–2, 173, 374; Algoma Steel, 197; consultations, 40, 49, 66; disclosure, 33, 40, 44, 374; regulations for deindustrialization, 45–6; as root of deindustrialization, 56 (*see also* deindustrialization); and tech commodities, 57; tribunals for shutdowns, 49, 66; UE complaint, 55
COVID-19 pandemic, 375
creative class, 10
credit rating, 18, 141, 145, 148
Crown Forest Sustainability Act, 233
cultural changes, 204

culture of poverty theory, 8
CUPE, 329, *329*

Dadamo, George, 162
D'Aquino, Thomas, 282
Davis, Julie, 19–20, *115*, 151, 210
De Carlo, Nick, 142
De Havilland, 18, 259, 260–1, 264–74, *264, 269, 272*
Debating Canada's Future (ed. Rosenblum and Findlay), 102, 104
debt, 313–15, *315*
debt wall, 148, 154
decentralization of economy. *See* community economic development
decentralization of production, 342–3
decision-making process, 123–4
Declaration of Principles of the Socialist International, 98
Decter, Michael, 145–6
deficit, 140–1, 144–5, 152
deficit reduction: vs. economic disparity, 152; and Langdon, 324; members upset over, 324–5; NDP claiming deficit, 144, 152; OLF critique, 324, 325; politics of, 144; Rae on, 326; and social contract association, 293, 313–15; three-pronged approach, 322; vs. war on recession, 18–19
deindustrialization: overview, 7, 9, 25, 48; in 1980, 41–5; in 1990, 163–4; affecting unions, 180; automotive industry, 274–9; Branch Plant Task Force, 33–4; in Britain, 28; coal, 260; Community-Based Economic Development, 74; and free trade, 120, 137–8, 165; in Germany, 37–8; and globalization, 275; and government's role, 29, 40; in Hamilton, 54–9; history of, 27–30, 32–6; and left-nationalism, 165; and Liberal loss 1990, 119; as location change, 27, *27*, 46, 170, 375–6; as managed, 8; and Ministry of Industry, Technology and Trade, 422n15; Nixon shock, 34–5; in northern Ontario, 230–1, 238, 248, 249; OFL statements, 38–9; and Ontario Labour Relations Act, 162; as plant movements, 27, 170; preservation of memories, 283–6; and public ownership, 40; Rae on, 153; and recession, 162; as runaway shops, 27, *27*, 46; Science Council of Canada, 36; Select Committee on Plant Shutdowns and Employee Adjustment, 44–5; in southern Ontario, 263; in Sweden, 37–8; and throne speech, 136; in Toronto, 57–8; and unions, 41–2; and worker adjustment, 67–71. *See also* worker adjustment; *specific companies*
The Deindustrialization of America (Bluestone and Harrison), 62
Delaney, Ken, 42–3, 55, 195, 199, 203, 204–5, 206, 207, 222, 323
democracy, xx
Democratic Leadership Council (DLC), 8, 10, 82
democratic socialism, 98–9
dependency theory, 31–3
depoliticization, 354–5
Diamond, Billy, 240
dioxin, 416n13
direct action, 49–50. *See also* occupations
diversity and inclusion, 304–5, 336–7, 338
Dofasco, 55, 193, 196–7, 198–200, 203, 267–8. *See also* Algoma Steel
Dogru, Ahmet, *111*
Douglas, Tommy, 53
Dowhaluk, Leo, 174
Drache, Daniel, 105
Dukakis, Michael, 83
Dunk, Thomas, 416n5
Dunlop Tire, 32–3, 34
Dunnville, ON, 46

Eastern Europe, 11

Economic Restructuring, Trade and Technological Change (report), 96
economy: overview, 77–8; in 1980, 41; in 1980s/1990s, xiv; advisors and NDP, 129–30; alternatives, 59; Budget Paper E, 290–1; business and policy options, 146–7; competition and recession, 295, 296; and competitiveness agenda 1991, 289, 303–4; deficit, 140–1, 144–5; as devastated, 120; dilemma of, 51, 72, 103; in France, 146; and free trade impact, 376; and left-nationalism, 4; and local issues, 52–3; and NDP win, 137–9; percentage shrunk, 153; policy review, 94, 95–101; problems as structural, 109; restructuring, 96, 97–8, 106; risk diffusion, 300; saving jobs, 300; and skills, 77; skills training, 90–1; and social contracts, 292; and technology, 109; and trade, 77–8 (*see also* Free Trade Agreement; *specific trade agreements*); Working Group on Industrial Restructuring, 299–300. *See also* community economic development; competition; corporate partnerships; deficit reduction; deindustrialization; Premier's Council on the Economy; recession; restructuring
Ehring, George, 377n2
electrical/electronics industry, 261
Electrolux, 63
Elliot Lake, ON, 158–60
Elston, Murray, 262
Employee Ownership Group, 247
employee stock ownership plans (ESOPs), 60–1, 208–9
Employee Wage Protection Program, 169–70
employment. *See* full employment
Employment Standards Act, 165, 170, 184, 377–8n8

Employment Standards Act Review, 176
Empowering Workers in the Global Economy (United Steelworkers), 22
environmentalism, 100, 228, 375–6, 399n64, 416n13
Epp, Ernie, xv
Ernst, Alan, 186, 295
Essar Steel, 207
Essex Wire, 46–7
"Ethical Reflections on the Economic Crisis" (Canadian Conference of Catholic Bishops), 59
Etzioni, Amitai, 350
Europe, 40, 46. *See also individual companies; specific countries*
Evans, Bryan, 148, 161, 162, 176, 184, 189–90, 226, 227, 353, 372
exchange rate, 165

A Fabulous Failure (Lichtenstein and Stein), 371
factories' life spans, 373
Fair Tax Commission, 135
Fédération des travailleurs et travailleuses du Québec (FTQ), 208, 209, 210–12, 215–17
Fight for Jobs in Hamilton, 55
Findlay, Peter, 102
Firestone Adjustment Program, 70, 71
fish, 239
flexible manufacturing, 311
Ford Motor Company, 27, 279, 280–1, *281*
Fordism, 339–40, 342, 344. *See also* post-Fordism
foreign direct investment, 30–1, 38, 238
Foreign Investment Review Agency (FIRA), 63
foreign takeovers, 57, 73, 237
forest industry, 416n13. *See also* northern Ontario
forests, 232–4

Forging the Links (Science Council of Canada), 36
Forrestal, Judith, 63–4
Foucault, André, 247
Foulds, Jim, xv, xix, 73, 130, 158, 208, 226, 250–1, 252, 253, 254
Fournier, Conrad, 252–3
France, 20, 102, 146, 291, 365
Frank, Thomas, 10
Fraser, Nancy, 107, 317
Free Trade Agreement (1987), 5; overview, 4–7, 51; and competition, 55; and deindustrialization, 120, 165; as devastating economy, 120; and garment sector, 176–7; impact as exaggerated, 140; initial impact of, 137–8; and tax credits, 213
Freightliner, 280, *281*
Friends of Kapuskasing et ses ami-e-s, 244–5
From Protest to Power (Rae), 23
full employment, 7, 38, 57, 96, 144, 179

garment sector, 45–6, 173–4, 176–80, 261–2, *261*
General Agreement on Tariffs and Trade (GATT), 11, 37, 55, 138
General Motors (GM), 129, 275–8, *281*, 283–4
gentrification, 352
Gerard, Leo, 42, 78–9, 88, *88*, 90, 187, 198–200, 202–3, 206, 207, 213, 216, 217, 294
Germany, 37–8, 40, 80, 364
Gerstle, Gary, 11
Getter, Ruth, 139–40
Getting on Track (ed. Drache), 105
Giddens, Anthony, 364
Gigantes, Evelyn, 337
Gill, Balbar, *355*
Gindin, Sam, 49–50, 87, 105–6, 108–9, 154, 182, 210, 216, 218, 276, 361, 367
Giving Away a Miracle (Ehring and Roberts), 377n2

globalization: assumption about, 108–9; and corporate restructuring, 138; and corporate/labour partnership, 78; and deindustrialization, 275; as Feudal State, 57; heavy industry vs. high tech, 56–7; as inevitable, 7; and nations, 9–10; tech commodities, 57; and working-class power, 365–6
goods and services tax (GST), 138
Gordon, Linda, 317
Gore, Al, 9
grants. *See* community economic development
grassroots groups, 336–7. *See also* community economic development
Gray, Herb, 30
Great Depression, 296
Greater London Council (UK), 97, 340–2
Greater London Enterprise Board, 342
Greening the Party, Greening the Province (report), 100
Greenpeace, 230, 416n13
Grier, Ruth, 230
growth, 26, 30
guaranteed annual income, 56

Hall, Douglas James, 312
Hall, Stuart, 21, 343
Hamilton, ON, 54–9, 69–71, 285, 402n26. *See also* Allen, Richard; Mackenzie, Bob
Hamilton and District Labour Council, 56–7, 59
Hampton, Howard, 119, 230, 235, 318–19, 369
Hang-Ji Hi, *355*
Harding Carpets, 163
Hargrove, Buzz, 276, 277, 284, 320
Harney, Stefano, 336
Harrington, Michael, 366, 372
Harris, Mike, 52, 256
Harrison, Bennett, 62, 292
Hart, Gary, 8

Harvey, David, 355
Havaris, Nota, 173–4
Hayes, Patrick, 120–1
Heron, Craig, 14–15
High, Steven, xiv–xx, 225–6, 366–7, 416n5
high schools, 92
historical preservation, 283–6
Hoerr, John, 201
homeworkers, 176
Honda, *281*
Hoover, Herbert, 296
Hope, Randy, 121, 162
Houdaille Bumper, 44
Huget, Bob, 121
human capital theory, 353, 363–4
"Human Resource Development, Labour Adjustment . . ." (Warrian and O'Grady), 183–4

immigrants, 354
income disparity, 116
Indigenous Peoples: CED funding, 349; and environmentalism, 228; and high school streaming, 92; industrial colonialism, 225; and MNR, 232, 233; Smoky Falls hydro dam, 239–41, 245, 247; Statement of Political Relationship between First Nations and the Provincial Government, 233
Industrial Adjustment Services (IAS), 68–9, 71
Industrial Policy Framework for Ontario (report), 310–13
Industrial Sunset (High), 36
Industry, Trade and Technology Ministry, 185
inflation, 36–7, 117
Innis, Harold, 30
interest rates, 165
Interim Report, 47
International Association of Machinists (IAM), 46
international collaboration, 372–3

International Labour Organization (ILO), 40
International Ladies' Garment Workers' Union (ILGWU), 173, 177–9, 262
International Monetary Fund (IMF), 11
International Nickel Company (INCO), 73, 94, 226, 330
International Woodworkers Association (IWA), 237
Inwood, Gregory, 51
Italy, 341–3
It's a Working Man's Town (Dunk), 416n5

J. H. Warsh, 173–4
Jackson, Ted, 96–7
Jameson, Fredric, 12
Jewell, T. K., 237, 242–3, 245, 246
job security, 26, 40, 136, 161, 164, 165
Job Security (NDP report), 47
"Jobs, Justice and Recovery" (Rae), 54
Jobs Ontario Community Action (JOCA), 348–53
Jobs Ontario Training, 319–20, 337, 354–5
Johnson, Paul, 218
Johnston, Richard, 308
Jones, Alti, 223
Jones, Anne, 70
Jordin, J., 45
just transition, 3

Kanesatake resistance, 240
KAP (Kill Amos Plan), 246–7
Kapashesit, Randy, 240, 247
Kapuskasing, ON, 237–44
Kelsey-Hayes, 171
Kelso, Louis, 60–1
Keynesianism, 141
Kimberly-Clark, 238–9, 241–6
Kinnock, Neil, 13
Kitchener, ON, 166–7
Klassen, Thomas R., 308–9

INDEX 455

Kormos, Peter, 369
Kristofferson, Robert, 285
Krugman, Paul, 109–11
Kwinter, Monte, 166, 215, 216, 217–19, 260–1, 267–8

La Ping Fashions, *179*
Laberge, Louis, 209–10
Laboratories of Democracy (Osborne), 81
"Labour and the New Democratic Party" (discussion paper), 327
Labour Council of Metropolitan Toronto, 57–8
labour law reform: overview, 182–3; business backlash, 186–8, 189; and consensus, 297; and corporate/labour partnership, 298, 303; and OFL, 98; as rolled back, 189; and social contracts, 297; and strikebreakers, 185, 188; and union membership increase, 188; and unionization, 373; and Wagner Act, 102
Labour Party (UK), 13, 341
Labour Relations and Employment Statute Law Amendment, 188
labour security, 116
labour-management decision-making, 204, 205–6
labour/unions: overview, 373; 1980's as "stubborn period," 49–50; breaking from US base, 36; in caucus/cabinet of NDP, 128, 133–4; climbing numbers, 188; collective agreements in early 90s, xiv; concessions with 1992 social contract, 322–3; decline in France, 365; decline of, 7, 43; deindustrialization affecting, 180–1, 262; density chart, *181*; as docile, 28; and ESOPs, 61–2; and full employment, 144; and labour law reform backlash, 187; and Lankin, 338; and left-nationalism, 3, 4; membership decline, 180–1; merging, 43; and NDP affiliation decline, 328–30;

328–9; NDP history, 13–14, *14*; and NDP relationship, 133, 275, 367–8; and new progressivism, 364; Ontario in 1991, 166–7; and *People and Skills in the New Global Economy*, 90–1; plant occupations, 44, 120, 340–1; postwar compromise, 27–8; and Premier's Council, 86, 92–4; and race/ethnicity CED, 338; regulating layoffs, 374; and rural MPPs, 134; and skills training in private sector, 308; and social contracts, 292; staff layoff, 180–1; stand-alone locals, 41–2; student activists, 15; in Thunder Bay, 226–7; in UK, 340–1; union certification, 187; and unpaid days off, 322–3; venture capital funds, 208–9; and wage protection, 173; and women, 338–9. *See also* corporate partnerships; Ontario Federation of Labour; strikes; worker adjustment; worker ownership/buyouts; *individual unions*
Langdon, Steven, 324
Lankin, Frances, xix, 16, 117, *124*, 127–8, 129, 138–9, 144, *145*, 279, 282, 313, 335, *336*, 337–8, 345–6, 361, 369, 371
Lapp Industries, 64, 66–7
Lasch, Christopher, 10
Laughren, Floyd, xvi, xix, 18, 39, 94, 95–6, 98, 99, 101, *124*, 126–7, *127*, 139, *145*, 147, 154, 159, 167, 213, 221, 225, 226–7, 230, 278, 290, 298, 314, 315, 316, 322–3, 361, 369–70
lawyers, 188
Laxer, James, 6–7, 32
Laxer, Robert, 35
layoffs: automotive industry, 274–9, 283–5; and bankruptcy, 172; and capitalism, 373; compulsory advance notice, 26, 33, 374; in Hamilton, 55, 64, 67, 70–1; and nationalizing auto insurance,

148–9; negotiations in Sweden and Germany, 37–8; in northern Ontario, 231, 238, 248, 249; Ontario in 1970s, 32–4; Ontario in 1980s, 41, 173–4, 179; Ontario in 1990s, 163–4, 166, 173–4, 179, 207, 254, 255, 261; and union membership, 180–1; union staff layoffs, 180–1; and unions closing, 41–2. *See also* deindustrialization; unemployment; worker adjustment
leadership, 361
left-nationalism: overview, 3, 4, 72–3; in 1970s, 4, 29–33, 35–6; vs. communitarianism, 53; and deindustrialization, 35, 165; and dependency theory, 32–3; OFL statements, 38–9; public ownership, 40; and radicalizing NDP, 36
Levitt, Kari, 31
Lewis, David, 122
Lewis, Stephen, 34, *114*, 122–3
LGBTQ+ people, 134
Liberal Party: 1985 Ontario election, 48; attacking NDP, 163–5, 167; and deficit, 144; and deindustrialization, 36; and foreign direct investment, 30–1; losing election in 1990, 118; NDP-Liberal Accord, 48, 130; and Watkins Report, 32. *See also* Premier's Council on the Economy
liberals, 10
Lichtenstein, Nelson, 371
loan defaults, 314
loans, 234–6, 249
Local Economic Initiatives and Worker Ownership (report), 96
long term thinking, 139
Longview Aviation, 273–4
Lorée, Christine, 100
Lorrain, L. H., 37

MacCallum, Peter, xviii
Mackenzie, Bob, *124*; about, 16, 157; Bill 40, 188; and Carter, 160; communitarianism, 53; on corporate/labour partnership, 182, 183; on Essex Wire, 46–7; inquiry on woman and adjustment, 71; labour law reform, 182, 183, 184, 187, 373; minimum wage hike, 168; as Minister of Labour, 27; as outsider, 163; on plant closures, 164–5; Premier's Council on Economic Renewal, 294; as respected, 157; tributes to, 190; union membership, 157; on wage protection fund, 172
Mackenzie, Hugh, 42, 89–90, 105, 107–8, 181, 194–5, 207, 210, 222, 256, 320–1, 361, 376, 415n86
MacKnight, Robin, 217
Macmillan-Bloedel, 236–7
Magaziner, Ira, 12, 85, 110–11
Mahon, Rianne, 96, 295
Major, Wayne, 244–5
Mancini, Remo, 163–4
Manning, Preston, 331
Manore, Jean, 239
Manufacturing Recovery Program, 279
Marcuse, Herbert, 2
Marquand, David, 344
Martel, Shelley, 27, 47, *124*, 159, 230, 234–5, 246
Martin, D'Arcy, 69–70, 86, 90–1, 93, 133, 174, 180
Martin, Tony, 202, 230, 257
Marxism, 102, 225–6
Marzetti, Jill, *115*
Mason, Joe, 62–3
Massey Combine Corporation, 170–1, *170*
Mattagami River, 239
Mazar, Alissa, 278–9
McClellan, Ross, 48, 113, *115*, 120, 124–5, 133–4, 143–4, 150–1, 187, 193, 197, 208, 222, 269, *281*, 293, 294, 314, 315, 316, 321, 332, 345, 361–2
McDonnell Douglas, 142
McKeough, Darcy, 29

McLaughlin, Audrey, 324
meeting minutes, 123
Mendelson, Michael, 117, 122–4, 126, 144–5, 149, 154, 289
mercury poisoning, 228
Metro Toronto Labour Education Centre, 179
Miller, Riel, 12, 16, 20, 94–5, 98, 99, 129, 146–7, 289, 290, 295–9, 322–3, 332, 336, 339, 351–3
Milner, Arthur, 103
Milner, Henry, 102, 103
Minding America's Business (Reich and Magaziner), 84, 110–11
Mine Mill union, 226
minimum wage: 1990 election promises, 116; in 1991, 168–9; and age, xv–xviii, 116, 168–9, 377–8n8; homeworkers, 176; and poverty, 373; and skills training, 296
mining, 248
Minister of Industry, Trade and Technology (MITT), 158
Minister of Native Affairs, 232. *See also* Wildman, Bud
Minister of Natural Resources (MNR), 231–4. *See also* Wildman, Bud
Ministry of Economic Development and Trade, 335, 338, 339, 345
Ministry of Finance, 189–90, 293
Ministry of Industry, Trade and Technology, 262, 422n15
Ministry of Labour, 157, 161, 162–3, 165, 169, 171, 176, 182, 185–7, 189–90. *See also* Mackenzie, Bob
Ministry of Northern Development and Mines, 346
minutes in meetings, 123
Mitterrand, François, 20, 146, 291
modernization, 55, 67, 207, 221, 244, 245, 246, 251–2, 254
Mohawk Crisis, 240
Mr Suli Dress Factory, 261
Mulroney, Brian, 51, 66–7, 144, 265, 316, 331

Munk, Melanie, 282
Munk, Peter, 282
Murray, Robin, 97, 339–40, 341–4, 346, 347, 348, 349–51
Muszynski, Leon, 91

National Citizens' Coalition, 186
National Rubber Company, *50, 75, 111, 156, 191, 223, 258, 287, 333, 355*
National Union of Mineworkers, 51
nationalism. *See* left-nationalism
nationalization, 40, 73, 94, 103. *See also* auto insurance
nations, 9–10
Naylor, James, 15
Naylor, R. T., 31–2
NDP government vs. party: and austerity, 151–2; initially, 147–8; nationalizing auto insurance, 149–50, 152; party-government liaison committee, 147; Provincial Council resolution, 149–51; Sunday shopping, 151
NDP-Liberal Accord, 48, 130
Negotiating the Future (Bluestone and Bluestone), 391n39
neoliberalism: overview, 372; overview of politics, 11; and Harris government, 52; and Ministry of Finance, 293; and New Times initiative, 344; as over, 376; and pensions, 302; and pragmatism, 371; progressive neoliberalism, 107; Rae on, 3–4; in Sweden, 7; understanding, 361–2. *See also* policy U-turn
The New Competition (Best), 104, 311, 342
New Deal, 120
New Deal Order, 11
New Democratic Party (NDP): 1980s/ early 90s economy, xiv, 17; 1985 election, 48; 1987 election, 402n26; 1990 election (*see* 1990 election); 1993 election, 331; 1995 defeat, 24, 357–8, 367–70; overview, 359–62; *An*

Agenda for People, 114–15, 132, 136, 164; as anti-intellectual, 95; attacked by Liberals, 163–5, 167; backlash, 148, 151–2; cabinet composition, 124–6, *124*, 127–8, *145*; cabinet retreats, 131, 148; caucus vs. cabinet, 128–9; class difference overview, 160 (*see also* class); crisis overview, xiv, 17–19, 138–40, 153, 323–32 (*see also* recession); decision-making process, 123–4; and democracy, xx; economic policy dilemma, 51, 72, 103; economic policy review, 94, 95–101; election planning 1989, xiii; first budget, 141–5, 161; history of, 13; and labour history, 13–14, *14*, 19; and labour relationship, 133, 275; leadership race 1995, 369–70; and long term thinking, 139; as majority government, xiii–xiv; membership decline, 19, 323, 324, 328–30, 332; Ontario policy book, 72–4; as poor financial planners, 143; prepared for win, 16–17; press critiques, 186; Rae leaving, 24, 370; return to legislature, 130–1; and senior civil servants, 132–3; throne speech, 134–6; transitioning to power, 122–4. *See also* NDP government vs. party; Rae, Bob
New Democratic Youth, xvi–xvii, 377n2
New Democrats (US), 8–10, 82–3, 94
New Labour Party (UK), 364
New Left: overview of politics, 2–3; in 1980s, 53; and class analysis, 353; and communitarianism, 54; and community economic development, 335, 343, 347–8; GLC, 340–2; and Rae, 2; and social welfare state, 340
new mercantilism, 31
New Times initiative, 343–4
New York bond agencies, 18
New York Times (newspaper), 238, 245

Ng, Roxana, 177–8, 354–5
Nichols, Ken, 166
Nickel Belt, 39–40, 94, 225–6. *See also* northern Ontario
Nixon, Bob, 117–18, 130, 164, 266–7
Nixon, Richard, 30, 34
Nixon shock, 34–5
non-governmental organizations (NGOs), 355
North American Free Trade Agreement (NAFTA), 279, 372
Northern Caucus, 230
northern Ontario: overview, 225–6; 1987 election, 402n26; 1990 cabinet representation, 230; community co-ownership, 236–7 (*see also* Employee Ownership Group; Purchasing Employees Group); and community economic development, 344, 346, 352–3; employment in, 229; Hampton on, 318; loans for, 234–6, 249; Martel report, 234–6; and MNR, 231–4; NDP's treatment overview, 256; as one-industry towns, 202; populations in, 225, 229; Provincial Paper, 248–54; and Rae's success, 358–9, 360; Ramsay on, 166; and recession in 1990s, 227–8; re-election of politicians, 257; relocation of civil service branches, 229; Smoky Falls hydro dam, 239–44, 245–7; Thunder Bay as Red Finn, 225–7; and USW's NDP support, 330–1; worker buyouts overview, 230–1. *See also* Algoma Steel; Spruce Falls; *specific towns*
Northern Ontario Heritage Fund Corp, 234, 235–6
Novias, Maria, *333*
nuclear energy, 159–60

Oakville, ON, 279, 280, 281, *281*
Obama, Barak, 207–8, 323
occupations, 5, 44, 120, 340–1. *See also* strikes; worker ownership/buyouts

O'Grady, John, 85–6, 89, 90, 98, 105, 107, 133, 144, 155, 183–4, 188, 209, 210–11, 303, 309, 368
Oka standoff, 240
One Job Town (High), 236
O'Neil, Jim, 272, 327
Ontario Coalition for Better Child Care, 317
Ontario Development Corporation, 73, 279–80, 301–2
Ontario Employment Standards Act, 373–4
Ontario Fair Tax Commission, 320–1
Ontario Federation of Labour (OFL): and Bill 150, 218; and deficit, 314, 325; deindustrialization statements, 29, 38, 41; and economic policy review, 97–8; and economic reality, 21; election planning 1989, xiii; emergency motions in 1993, 325–6; free trade protest, 5; *Getting on Track*, 105; and high schools, 92; "Labour and the New Democratic Party," 327; labour law reform, 98; and labour venture capital funds, 208, 209–10, 215; NDP crisis in early 90s, xiv; and OTAB, 307; *Our Common Future*, 399n64; policies as current, 275; protest 1980, 44; on recession, 140; and *Skills to Meet the Challenge*, 306; social contract critique, 328; and training, 89, 309; worker adjustment, 91; on worker buyouts, 214; workers vs. deficit, 324. *See also* Wilson, Gord
Ontario Heritage Foundation, 285
Ontario Hydro, 239–40, 247. *See also* Smoky Falls hydro dam
Ontario in the 1990s: Promoting Equitable Structural Change (report), 290–1
Ontario Jobs Strategy, 317–20. *See also* Jobs Ontario Community Action
Ontario Labour Relations Act, 116, 162, 180

Ontario Labour Relations Board (OLRB), 184
Ontario Lead Investment Fund, 301–2
Ontario Mining Association, 47
Ontario Municipal Employees' Retirement System (OMERS), 415n86
Ontario New Democratic Youth (ONDY), xvi–xvii, 377n2
Ontario Public Service Employees Union (OPSEU), 329
Ontario Restaurant Association, 168
Ontario Royal Commission on Northern Environment (1985), 229
Ontario Select Committee on Plant Shutdowns and Employee Adjustment, 25–6
Ontario Teachers' Pension Plan, 302
Ontario Training and Adjustment Board (OTAB), 18, 71–2, 106, 163, 304–9, 337, 374
Ontario Workplace Heritage Program, 284–5
Organisation for Economic Co-operation and Development (OECD), 99
Osborne, David, 81
Oshawa, ON, 280
Osman, Prudence, 258
Ottawa, ON, 285
Our Common Future (World Commission on Environment and Development), 399n64
Outboard Marine, 45, 63

Panitch, Leo, 104–5
paper industry. *See* forest industry; northern Ontario
Parizeau, Jacques, 209
Parti Québécois, 209
patents, 264
The Path to Prosperity (report), 82–3
Pawley, Howard, 136–7
pay equity, 116
Pecaut, David, 84–5, 89–90

pensions: Algoma Steel, 206; the Caisse, 299, 301–2; and Dofasco, 199; and ESOPs, 61; legacy of Rae, 415n86; and neoliberalism, 302; Ontario Lead Investment Fund, 301–2; vs. venture capital funds, 215
People and Skills in the New Global Economy (report), 78, 79, 89–91, 93
Peterborough, ON, 63
Peters, Roger, 96–7
Peterson, David, 48, 77, 78, 90, 117, 120, 209, 266
Philip, Ed, *124*, 166, 262, 272, 277, 294, 310
Phillips, Carol, 133
Phillips, Ethan, 96, 97
Phillips, Gerry, 217
Piché, René, 246
Pilkey, Allan, *124*, 158, 165–6
pink paper group union support, 328, 367–8
Pioneer Chainsaw, 63
Pittsburgh Paint, 86
Piven, Frances Fox, 340
plant closures. *See* deindustrialization; layoffs
plant movements, 27, 28, 170
Policy and Priorities, 123–4, 185
policy U-turn, 146, 152, 153–5, 168, 372
The Politics of Community Services (Ng), 354
pollution, 228
Pomeroy, Fred, 79, 86, 88, 90, 133
Porter, Ann, 176–7
Porter, Michael, 310
post-Fordism, 347–8, 350, 351–3. *See also* Fordism
post-Keynesianism, 51–2
Pouliot, Gilles, 230
poverty, 8, 317, 373
power, 23
pragmatism, 20–1, 81–2, 155, 357, 360, 371
Pratt, Larry, 102

Premier's Council on Economic Renewal, 294
Premier's Council on the Economy: overview, 78–82, 83–5; and *An Agenda for People*, 114; *Competing in the New Global Economy*, 78, 79, 80–1, 84–5, 86, 105–6; and consensus, 77; corporations/labour partnerships, 86, 87, 89–90; *Getting on Track*, 105; and labour's counter-report, 92–3; and NDP policy review, 96, 100–1; *People and Skills in the New Global Economy*, 78, 79, 89–91, 93; purpose of, 94; Technology Adjustment Research Programme, 89
Premier's Councils (general), 293
press critiques, 121, 145
privatization, 11
profits, 37, 46
Progressive Conservative Party: 1985 Ontario election, 48; and advance notice of layoffs, 33; and Algoma Steel, 199; and Canadian Porcelain, 65–6; deficit reduction, 144; and deindustrialization, 48–9; and labour reforms in 1995, 188–9; and wage protection, 175
progressive neoliberalism, 107
prosperity, 1–2
protectionism, 4–5, 34–5. *See also* left-nationalism
protest, 5, 23, 44, *175*, 228, 228, 283
Provincial Council, 149–51, 152
Provincial Paper, 231, 248–54
public ownership, 40, 374
Purchasing Employees Group (PEG), 237, 241, 242–5, 247. *See also* Employee Ownership Group

Quebec, 62–3, 183, 331

race/ethnicity, 92, 337, 338, 349
Rachlis, Chuck, 16, 98–9, 100, 124, 182–3, 189, 295, 320–1, 332, 357

Rae, Bob, 115, 118, 124, 127, 145, 264, 301; overview of politics, 2–3, 12–13; about, 15–16, 126–7; and Agnew, 124; on aircraft industry, 259; and Algoma Steel, 195, 197, 198–9, 206, 221; appointment of women to cabinet, 337; and Armstrong, 263; arrested, 228; and B. Mackenzie's union membership, 157; on Bill 150, 220; on binaries, 291; Black on, 186; and Canadian Porcelain, 66; on CAW, 279; on change, 1, 3, 101; Charlottetown agreement, 331; and class analysis, 353; on class condescension, 17; on creating wealth, 155; on crisis management, 17; and De Havilland, 265–6, 268, 270–3, *272*; and debt wall video, 148; on deindustrialization, 153; as discouraged in 1995, 257; donation to public archives, xviii; on early days, 131; and economic renewal 1991, 291; Ehring and Robert critique, 377n2; election planning 1989, xiii; and federal interest, 331; and first budget, 157; focus of, 289; on Ford CEO, 280–1; *From Protest to Power*, 23; on free trade, 137–8; and Gerard, 198–9; and GM closures, 276–8; government as transitional, 366–7, 371; on government limits, 22; and human capital theory, 363–4; as internationalist, 54; invoking Roosevelt, 120; on job security, 165; "Jobs, Justice and Recovery" speech, 54; and Lankin, 338; and Laughren, 126–7; as leader, 119; leadership race 1995, 369–70; leaving NDP, 24, 48, 370; on nationalizing auto insurance, 149; on NDP crisis, 326; on NDP in power, 363; on NDP success, 358–9; on NDP-Liberal Accord, 130; as neoliberal, 371–2; on neoliberalism, 3–4; northern vs. southern Ontario labor, 279; and OMERS, 415n86; and Pecaut, 85; personality and tensions, 152; pink paper group union support, 328; and Pittsburgh Paint, *86*; policy U-turn, 153–4, 155, 372; on postwar prosperity, 1–2; in power, xiv; as pragmatist, 20–1, 357, 360, 371; and Premier's Council, 101; press on recession, 121; on recession, 139; senior civil servants, 132–3; as under siege, 23; on Smith, 242; and Smoke Falls dam project, 241; and social contract, 54, 322–3; and Swart, 331–2; and Temagami protest, 228, *228*; throne speech, 134–6; as UN ambassador, xix; and Uniroyal-Goodrich layoffs, 166–7; and United Steelworkers, 22, 195; on Valley, 248; and venture capital funds, 222; Warrian on, 185; WEF (1993/4), 281–2; on welfare recipients, 316; "What We Owe Each Other," 1–2, 3, 136, 373; and White, 134, 186; Williams influence, 292; worker buyouts, 66, 214. *See also* New Democratic Party

Rae Days, 293, 323

Rae Days (Walkom), 72, 314

Ramsay, David, 166, 174–5

Raposo, Natalia, *156*

Reagan, Ronald, 51

recession (early 80s), 43–4

recession (early 90s), xiv, 121, 137–46, 153, 162, 174, 295, 296

Red Scare, 226

redistribution of wealth, 136, 146

Reform Party, 331

Reich, Robert, 9–10, 83–4, 110–11

Renwick, Jim, 33

Report on Plant Closures and Community Adjustment (report), 48–9

research, 89

resignations, 19, 323, 324, 328–30, 332

restructuring, 22, 96, 97–8, 106, 198–200, 202–3, 204–5, 210, 213, 289–90, 299–300, 343
retention bonuses, 204–5
retirement, 199, 202
Reville, David, 115
Richards, John, 102, 103
right-wing populism, 376
risk diffusion, 300
Robb, Chuck, 292
Roberts, Wayne, 377n2
Robertson, David, 86, 105–6
Rogerio, Fernando, 111
Rolland, 254, 255
Romanow, Roy, 365
Rosehart, Robert, 229
Rosehart Committee, 229
Rosenblum, Simon, 102, 292
Ross, C. Ian, 251
Rousseau, Arlene, 324
Royal Bank, 197
Royal Commission on the Economic Union and Development Prospects for Canada, 51, 56
Royal Dressed Meats, 173
runaway shops, 27, 27, 46
Rust Belt, 60, 82–3, 140, 143, 208, 292

Sabel, Charles, 311
Sadlowski, Ed, 195
Sainte-Thérèse, QC, 283
same-sex couples, 134
Samuelson, Wayne, 327
Sarah Brophy and Jason Baines, Plaintiffs v. Attorney General of Ontario, xvi
Sarakiya, Ismael, 111
Sault Ste. Marie, 193, *194*, 195, 196, 204
Savory-Gordon, Linda, 205–6
Sawmill Adjustment Initiative, 234–5
scabs, 116, 183, 185, 188, 190
Scarborough, ON, 283–4
Schenk, Chris, 215
Schwab, Klaus, 281
Science Council of Canada, 36

Sears, Robin, 12, 95, 210
The Second Industrial Divide (Porter and Sabel), 311
Sector Partnership Fund, 311–12, 313
sectoral bargaining, 188
Select Committee on Plant Shutdowns and Employee Adjustment, 44–5, 46–7
senior civil servants, 132–3
Service Employees International Union (SEIU), 329
severance pay, 26
Silent Surrender (Levitt), 31
Simao, Nivia, *156*
Skills to Meet the Challenge (report), 306
skills training: brokers, 317–18, 337, 354–5; and CAW, 88; as common ground, 83; and competition in 1991, 291; Gindin's views, 109; *Industrial Policy Framework for Ontario*, 310–13; Jobs Ontario Training, 319–20, 354–5; in *Minding America's Business*, 84; Ontario Jobs Strategy, 317–20; payroll tax, 93; *People and Skills in the New Global Economy*, 78, 79, 89–91, 93; private trainers, 308; for-profit training, 308; and women, 106, 178–9, 308. *See also* Ontario Training and Adjustment Board
small businesses, 348, 356. *See also* cooperatives
small towns, 119, 120–1, 134, 202, 262
Smith, Charles, 372
Smith, Darwin, 238–9, 241–6
Smoky Falls hydro dam, 239–44, 245–7
social assistance. *See* welfare
social contract: overview, 291–3, 300–1, 360; and deficit, 314; in Europe, 298–9; and labour, 292; and labour concessions, 322–3; and labour law reform, 297; Miller on, 289, 290; OLF

critique, 328; Rae overview, 54, 326; and wage increases, 295–6; Wolfe on, 298
Social Democracy without Illusions (ed. Richards, Cairns and Pratt), 102
social justice, 364
Social Planning and Research Council of Hamilton and District, 56
Social Planning Council of Metropolitan Toronto, 58
socialism, 32, 225–7, 289, 343
Socialist Party (France), 102
solidarity, 368–9
Solidarity Fund, 208, 209, 210–12, 215
Sorbara, Greg, 220
southern Ontario, 259–60, 359. *See also* De Havilland
specialization, 251
Spirits Rising monument, 204
Spruce Falls, 237–9, 241, 244–5, 247, 358
"S.S. Provincial [Paper]" (drawing), 255
St. Catharines, ON, 275–7
St. Thomas, ON, 280, *281*
standard of living, 92, 96
Standing Committee on Finance and Economic Affairs, 141, 214, 217
Standing Committee on Resource Development, 48–9, 172–3
Stanford, Jim, 30
"A Staple Theory of Economic Development" (Watkins), 30
staples production, 30
Statement of Political Relationship between First Nations and the Provincial Government, 233
Steed, Judy, 309
Steel Company of Canada (Stelco), 42, 55
Steel Congress, 69–70
steel industry, 60, 207. *See also specific companies*
Steel Valley Authority, 60

Stein, Judith, 371
Stephen, Jennifer, 179–80
Stockwell, Chris, 142
Stokes, Jack, xv
"The Story of Ontario's First NDP Government" (McClellan), *281*
strikes, 27–8, 67, 197, 204, 226. *See also* occupations
student activists, 15
Student Minimum Wage Consultation Group, 169
Sturgeon Falls, ON, 236–7, *237*
subsidization, 259
Sunday shopping, 151
supply chains, 375
surcharges, 34–5
Sutherland, Kimble, 219
Swart, Mel, 331–2
Swartz, Donald, 104–5
Sweden, 7, 37–8, 80, 104–5, 379n14
Sydney Steel, 268

takeovers. *See* foreign takeovers; occupations; worker ownership/buyouts
Tanaka, Peter, 422n15
tariffs, 38, 138. *See also* trade
Task Force on Foreign Ownership and the Structure of Canadian Industry, 30
Task Force on Manufacturing, 39
Task Force on People and Technological Change, 73
tax credits, 208, 212–13, 214, 217, 222
taxes, 116, 135, 171, 320–2
technology: overview, 77, 290; at Algoma Steel, 207; and economic policy, 103–4; and economy, 109; Gindin's views, 109; and globalization, 57; and low-wage countries, 322; and NDP policy, 73; whitewashing history, 375
Technology Adjustment Research Programme (TARP), 89
Temagami, 228, *228*
Tembec, 62–3, 231, 245–6, 247

Territorial Development and Human Capital in the Knowledge Economy (Miller), 353
Thatcher, Margaret, 51, 340
Third Way: overview, 364; vs. class analysis, 12; and communitarianism, 355; in *Debating Canada's Future*, 102–3; as dividing NDP, 357–8; history of word, 379n13; and New Times initiative, 344; and Premier's Council on the Economy, 79; Rae and, 22–3; as reimaging social democracy, 7–8
Thompson, Bill, 64, 309
throne speech, 134–6
Thunder Bay, ON, 225–7, 248–54
A Time for Public Leadership (Labour Council of Metropolitan Toronto), 64
Tome, Eugenia, 50
Tooley, Barry, 330
Toronto, ON, 80
Toronto Board of Trade, 172
Tough, George, 233
tourism, 352
Toyota, 280
Trachsel, Bill, 46–7
trade, 5–7, 11, 77–8, 376. *See also* globalization; *individual trade agreements*
transfer payments, 140–1, 316
Trump, Donald, 372
Truscon Steel, 211
Tung-Sol, 44
two-tier minimum wage, xv–xviii, 116, 168–9, 377–8n8

unemployment: in 90s recession, 143, 153, 163–4; costs of, 137; and deficit reduction, 144; in Elliot Lake, 158; in Hamilton, 56; vs. inflation, 36–7; insurance, 141; in manufacturing, *138*; in northern Ontario, 229; rate in Canada 1982, 58; rate in Ontario 1990, 137, *138*; and workfare, 83; of youth, 168. *See also* layoffs; welfare
unemployment insurance, 316
Unifor, 375. *See also* Canadian Auto Workers; Canadian Paperworkers Union
Uniroyal-Goodrich, 166–7
United Association of Plumbers and Steamfitter, 324–5
United Auto Workers (UAW), 28, 42, 87, 180. *See also* White, Bob
United Electrical (UE) workers, 55
United Farmers of Ontario, 14
United Food and Commercial Workers, 173
United Rubber Workers, 180, 359
United States, 68–9, 81–3
United Steelworkers of America (USW), *88*; overview, 41–2; Algoma Steel (*see* Algoma Steel); and Bill 150, 216–17; and business, 22; and concession bargaining, 43; and corporate partnerships, 89, 195; deindustrialization affecting, 180–1; and Elliot Lake, 159; Empowering Workers in the Global Economy, 108–9; layoffs, 55; and NDP support 1993, 328; and Rae, 330; in Thunder Bay, 226; and worker buyouts, 194–6, 198, 200–1, 202–7, 213–14. *See also* Gerard, Leo
United Technologies, 46
unpaid days off, 293, 322–3
uranium mining, 158–9
Urban Transit Development Corporation, 266
US economic domination, 31–2, 34–5. *See also* Americanization
USSR, 103

Valley, John, 248–9
value-added idea, 110–11
Varity Corporation, 170–1

venture capital funds, 208, 209–10, 221–2. *See also* Bill 150
Vigna, Xavier, 365
voting rights, 200

Waffle movement, xv, 32, 35
wage protection, 169–74
wages: and corporate taxes, 321–2; and deindustrialization, 375–6; and ESOPs, 61; freezes, 322; gains in, 361; vs. job security, 161; vs. profits, 37; and social contracts, 295–6, 297
Wagner Act (US), 102
Wainwright, Hilary, 335, 339
Walkom, Thomas, 72, 101, 136, 154, 314, 353, 357
Ward, Brad, 121
Wark-Martyn, Shelley, 219–20, 230
Warrian, Peter, 15, 24, 69, 128, 183–4, 185, 188, 206–7, 313–14, 323, 368
water, 239
Watkins, Mel, 23, 30–1, 32–3, 55, 96, 141
The Weakest Link (Science Council of Canada), 36
Weirton Steel, 203
welfare, 141, 143, 315–20, 376
welfare state, 82, 339–40
West Nipissing Economic Development Committee, 236
Westinghouse, 55, 64
Weyerhaeuser, 237, 248
"What We Owe Each Other" (Rae), 1–2, 3, 23, 136, 373
White, Bob, 5–6, 26, 108, 114, 134, 142–3, 186, 187, 214, 264
Wildman, Bud, xix–xx, 124, 126, 130, 149, 158, 188, 227–8, 229, 230, 231–4, 248, 256, 298–9, 361
Williams, Lynn, 64, 200–1, 292
Wilson, Gord, 79, 90, 142, 157, 210, 283, 294, 307, 324. *See also* Ontario Federation of Labour
Wilson, Michael, 272

Windsor, ON, 27, 46, 171, 278–9, 280, 281, 402n26
Witmer, Elizabeth, 174
Wolfe, David, xviii, 16, 35, 43, 58, 69–70, 79, 91, 93, 96, 97, 98–9, 103–4, 105, 124, 129, 131–2, 148, 171, 182–3, 185, 189, 290, 295, 298, 301–2, 310–11, 320–1, 332, 357
women: and 1990 election, 337; in auto insurance industry, 148–9; CED funding, 349; child care and employment, 317; deindustrialization in Hamilton, 54–5, 71; diversity and inclusion politics, 337; garment sector, 261–2; immigrants, 354; and labour, 338–9; and OTAB, 304–5; skills training, 106, 178–9, 308; as vulnerable to restructuring, 106. *See also* garment sector
Women Working with Immigrant Women (WWIW), 178
Wood, Len, 246
Woodcock, Leonard, 60
Woodsworth, J. S., 53
Woodward, Jim, 327
The Work of Nations (Reich), 9–10
Work Organization and Adjustment Service, 185
worker adjustment: overview, 67–71; 1990 election promises, 115–16; ATAC, 178–9; and corporate/labour partnership, 179–80; in Elliot Lake, 159–60; "Human Resource Development, Labour Adjustment . . .," 183–4; Metro Toronto Labour Education Centre, 179; and OFL, 91; and Premier's Council, 92. *See also* skills training
Worker Co-ops (periodical), 64
worker ownership/buyouts: Canadian Porcelain, 64–7; and capital, 207, 208, 215; and cultural changes, 204; ESOPs, 60–1; labour critique of, 368; and New Left, 72; OFL's

views, 214–15; Pioneer Chainsaw, 63; Provincial Paper, 249–50, 252–4; Rae on, 214; in southern Ontario, 264; Tembec, 61–2; in *A Time for Public Leadership*, 64; Toronto vs. Hamilton, 57; and USW, 194–6, 198, 200–1, 202. *See also* Algoma Steel; cooperatives; Spruce Falls
Workers Arts and Heritage Centre (WAHC), 285–6
Workers' City Project, 285
workers' compensation, 205
workfare, 83, 319
Working Group on Industrial Restructuring, 299–300

Workplace Health and Safety Agency (WHSA), 307–8
workplace injuries, 205
World Bank, 11
World Commission on Environment and Development, 399n64
World Economic Forum (WEF), 281–2

You Can't Bring Back Yesterday, 284

Ziemba, Elaine, 304

STEVEN HIGH is a professor of history at Concordia University in Montreal, where he co-founded the Centre for Oral History and Digital Storytelling. He has authored a number of books and articles on structural and mass violence as well as deindustrialization as a political, socio-economic, and cultural process. He is currently the head of the transnational "Deindustrialization and the Politics of Our Time" (DEPOT) research project, which brings together researchers, museum professionals, archivists, and trade unionists across Europe and North America.